ROUTLEDGE LIBRARY EDITIONS:
THE ECONOMICS AND BUSINESS OF
TECHNOLOGY

Volume 5

TECHNOLOGICAL INNOVATION AND ECONOMIC CHANGE IN THE IRON INDUSTRY, 1850–1920

TECHNOLOGICAL INNOVATION AND ECONOMIC CHANGE IN THE IRON INDUSTRY, 1850–1920

ROBERT A. BATTIS

LONDON AND NEW YORK

First published in 1989 by Garland Publishing, Inc.

This edition first published in 2018
by Routledge
2 Park Square, Milton Park, Abingdon, Oxon OX14 4RN

and by Routledge
711 Third Avenue, New York, NY 10017

Routledge is an imprint of the Taylor & Francis Group, an informa business

British Library Cataloguing in Publication Data
A catalogue record for this book is available from the British Library

ISBN: 978-1-138-50336-6 (Set)
ISBN: 978-1-351-06690-7 (Set) (ebk)
ISBN: 978-1-138-55968-4 (Volume 5) (hbk)
ISBN: 978-0-203-71104-0 (Volume 5) (ebk)

Publisher's Note
The publisher has gone to great lengths to ensure the quality of this reprint but points out that some imperfections in the original copies may be apparent.

Disclaimer
The publisher has made every effort to trace copyright holders and would welcome correspondence from those they have been unable to trace.

Technological Innovation and Economic Change in the Iron Industry, 1850–1920

Robert A. Battis

Garland Publishing, Inc.
New York & London
1989

Library of Congress Cataloging-in-Publication Data

Battis, Robert A.
Technological innovation and economic change in the iron industry, 1850–1920 / Robert A. Battis.
p. cm. — (Garland studies in entrepreneurship)
Includes bibliographical references.
ISBN 0-8240-3394-9 (alk. paper)
1. Thomas Iron Company—History. 2. Iron industry and trade—Pennsylvania—Lehigh River Valley—History.
I. Title. II. Series.
HD9519.T47B38 1989
338.4'56691'097482209034—dc20 89-37795

Printed on acid-free, 250-year-life paper

Manufactured in the United States of America

To Ruth, David, and Jim
for their continuing support
and inexhaustable patience

Acknowledgments

This book was undertaken and brought to completion with the encouragement and guidance of Professor Ralph W. Hidy, the assistance of Jim Fitzpatrick who prepared the illustrations, and Marjorie Kohlmeyer who typed the manuscript with meticulous care.

TABLE OF CONTENTS

LIST OF TABLES

Table		Page

LIST OF ILLUSTRATIONS

LIST OF CHARTS

CHAPTER I

INTRODUCTION

In July, 1922, the president of The Thomas Iron Company announced that the required amount of the firm's stock had been deposited with Drexel and Company, investment bankers of Philadelphia, and that with that transaction the bankers' agreement to purchase the iron company would become effective.[1] With this announcement the sixty-six year life span of what was at one time the leading merchant furnace company in the nation came to an end. Earlier, in 1914, when this same iron company produced the last few thousand tons of anthracite pig iron in one of its old stone stacks, the anthracite iron age had also ended. These two events marked the victory of open-hearth steel and the integrated steel works over the once widespread and picturesque merchant pig iron industry, and it represented the eventual disappearance of all merchant furnaces in the Lehigh Valley.

In this present day of the large integrated steel plants it is difficult to realize that the first great impulse to the production of crude iron on a large scale in the United States came with the successful use of anthracite coal as fuel in stone stacks. During the twenty years preceding the Civil War, and for approximately ten years after the war years, the site of the iron industry was governed by the location of this

---

[1] *Iron Age*, Vol. 110 (July 6, 1922), 171

coal. Eastern Pennsylvania became the main iron producing sector of the nation, and the most rapid advance in the production of iron occurred in the Lehigh Valley, the location of the Thomas Iron Company. Little, however, has ever been written on the development and decline of these anthracite furnaces which had held the leadership in pig iron production until 1875. Whatever justification there is for this present effort to tell the story of The Thomas Iron Company, as a by-product it may provide a partial story of the development of the anthracite pig iron industry.

While the history of an individual business firm cannot be the history of an industry, it is entirely possible to examine some new facets in the development of an industry through the study of an individual firm. Just as the history of a country or mankind is the end product of the history of individuals, the development of an industry is the outcome of the forces which lead individual or groups of entrepreneurs to expand or contract their production. Thus, the following study of the Thomas Iron Company has been written in an attempt to provide some further knowledge pertaining to the economic development of the iron industry in the United States between 1839 and 1921.

Further, this case history, unlike many histories of business firms, provides an opportunity to study how and why a group of managers failed to meet the problems peculiar to the iron industry during the last half of the ninteenth century as the industry assumed the characteristics of the modern steel industry. Throughout the study of this merchant furnace company an attempt has been made to discover the central problems of a group of business managers faced with the appearance of industrial innovations which continually tended to undermine their firm's very existence and to provide a whole new set of optimal conditions necessary for the survival of the firm. This history provides an excellent example of the destructive nature of industrial innovation and also points up the full meaning of Schumpeter's discussion of the inability of most businessmen "to act with confidence beyond the range of familiar beacons . . . ."[2]

It is known that the science of economics utilizes tools of analysis which permit predictions of the effects of change in various factors impinging upon the operation of the economic system. Also, economists analyze the economic effects of these factors upon the conditions of the firm, and from these deduced changes predict what the characteristics of the new firms in the environment may be. Economics, however, does not predict that all firms will have changed toward the new optimal conditions.[3]

Generally economic theory says very little about the failure of business firms or the failure of entrepreneurs to innovate or adopt innovations when all about these entrepreneurs other firms are striving to meet the new conditions of the trade. While economists continually write

---

[2]Joseph A. Schumpeter, _Capitalism, Socialism, and Democracy_ (New York, 1950), p. 132. Fritz Redlich, "The 'Daimonic' Entrepreneur," as found in Richard Wohl, ed., _Change and the Entrepreneur_ (Cambridge, 1949), pp. 30-32.

[3]Armen A. Alchian, "Uncertainty, Evolution, and Economic Theory," _Journal of Political Economy_, LVII (June, 1950), 211-21; Edith Tilton Penrose, "Biological Analogies in the Theory of the Firm," _American Economic Review_, XLII (December, 1952), 804-19; Armen A. Alchian, Stephen Enke, and Edith Tilton Penrose, "Biological Analogies in the Theory of the Firm: Comment and Rejoinder," _American Economic Review_, XLII (September, 1953), 600-609.

about the withdrawal of business firms, they seldom provide any analysis of business failures, nor do they define or generally employ the word "failure". It is quite true that the broader problems of economics are the problems of adjustment, but the problem of firms which do not adjust or "fail" is also quite important.

Alfred Marshall, in his Principles of Economics, simply explains the demise of business firms as a consequence of the guidance of the business falling "into the hands of people with less energy and less creative genius, if not with less active interest in its prosperity.[4] But these are not the only causes of business failure; there are a multitude of situations which tend to bring about failure; some are remote while some are more immediate. Any discussion of these causes must recognize these distinctions.

For purposes of analysis in this study several causes of business failure have been singled out: economic change and development, the trade cycle, and incompetence. Though these causes are not completely separable, they are logically separable for purposes of analysis. For example, it will be observed in this study that the immediate cause of "failure" of the Thomas Iron Company was an alleged shortage of working capital. The shortage of working capital, however, was the resultant of economic change, the pressures of the trade cycle, and managerial incompetence. But the firm could not continue operations because it lacked working capital. Over the years the iron industry had seen the introduction of a

---

[4]Alfred Marshall, Principles of Economics (New York, 1949), pp. 314-16. See also p. 287.

new product - steel, new methods of production had been introduced, new sources of supply were being developed, and a change in the organization of the industry had occurred to which the managment had not adapted the firm.[5] But further, the business conditions arising from the business depression, and the incompetence of the firm's management in making financial decisions also created conditions which helped finally to bring about the reduction in working capital and the "failure" of the firm. And the failure occurred despite the firm's sixty-six years of trade experience.

Because the study of this firm's history encompasses both a period of growth as well as a period of decline and "failure," it offers an opportunity to compare policies associated with success to those associated with decline. As the vast majority of business enterprises that are created generally fail for some reason or other, this firm's history, unlike most business histories of firms that have survived, may be more representative of the life cycle of the majority of business enterprises. The study, however, is primarily presented as a small contribution toward a clearer understanding of the destructive forces of industrial innovation and the place of creative entrepreneurship in the survival of the firm.

---

[5]The classification of developmental changes has been adapted from Joseph A. Schumpeter, *The Theory of Economic Development* (Cambridge, 1934, especially Chaps. ii and iv.

CHAPTER II

ORIGINS OF THE ANTHRACITE PIG IRON INDUSTRY

Introduction of the Hot-Blast and Use of "Stone" Coal In the British Iron Industry

Sixteen years after the Welsh practice of using anthracite coal as blast furnace fuel had been introduced into the United States, eighteen men met at a small tavern in Centre Square, Easton, to discuss plans for the organization of The Thomas Iron Company. These men were not "innovators" in the Schumpeterian sense; they were not attempting to develop "something outside of the range of existing practice,"[1] but rather they were businessmen adapting themselves to a field which had already seen a successful and rapid growth commencing in the late 1830's. They had no new good to introduce, no new method of production, no new market or new sources of raw material to exploit, nor were they attempting to create a monopoly position.[2] They had seen only a growing market for pig iron and had decided to obtain some gain from this growth. Their success depended, in a large part, upon the successful application of old techniques of iron manufacture and the continued growth of the economy.

Of course, any innovation that these men might have had would probably have offered them greater opportunity for success. However, it was

---

[1]Joseph A. Schumpeter, "The Creative Response in Economic History," _Journal of Economic History_, VII (1947), 149-50

[2]Schumpeter, _The Theory of Economic Development_, p. 66.

to be their fate that others were later to introduce innovations which would lead to their firm's demise. To understand better their momentary success as the leading merchange pig iron producers of the eastern coastal area and subsequent decline, it is essential to commence this part of the study with a brief recapitulation of the technological development which contributed to the creation of this corporation.

Any historical study of the development of the production of iron might be carried back to the early ages of antiquity, but for this paper we are concerned only with the most important antecedents of the production of pig iron with anthracite coal. To fix upon these, we must turn to the history of the British iron industry of the eighteenth and early nineteenth centuries. The whole world is indebted to the British iron industry for providing the necessary impetus for the growth of this key industry of the modern industrial world. Abraham Darby was the first man of record to use coke as a blast furnace fuel; Smeaton is supposed to have invented the cast-iron blowing cylinders, while Neilson discovered the greater efficiency of the hot-blast. There are others, such as Payne and Hanbury, who first developed rolled sheet iron; Huntsman, the making of steel in crucibles; and Cort, the innovator of the grooved rolls and the puddling furnace. These last and others, however, are not the immediate antecedents to Crane's successful application of "stone" coal as a blast furnace fuel. For these we must go back to the first three mentioned innovations; the use of coke, the cast-iron blowing cylinders, and the hot-blast.

For the first, the use of coke as a smelting fuel, it is necessary to drop back to the sixteenth and seventeenth centuries when Great Britain was faced with a problem of rapidly decreasing supply of timber for both its iron and shipbuilding industries. This short supply of timber threatened the national security and brought forth restrictive statutes aimed at preserving certain of these natural resources for shipbuilding. As a consequence, ironmasters were forced to turn to more distant sources for fuel to operate their furnaces or search for possible alternatives for charcoal.[3] Blacksmiths, in some areas of Great Britain, had already been making use of coal for the processing of bar iron into finished products; it was quite a natural development, therefore, for the ironmasters to turn to coal as a possible substitute for charcoal. It is reported that patents for the use of coal for smelting iron ores were granted as early as 1589;[4] however, the first technically and economically successful method of applying coal to blast furnace practice was not developed until sometime in the first half of the eighteenth

---

[3]Thomas S. Ashton, Iron and Steel in the Industrial Revolution (New York, 1924, pp. 9-10. Abbott P. Usher, Industrial History of England (Boston, 1920), p. 120. John Percy, Metallurgy: Iron and Steel (London, 1864), pp. 883089.

[4]Ibid. pp. 10-11. Usher, Industrial History of England, p. 320. Commissioner of Patents, Specifications Relating to the Manufacture of Iron and Steel (London, 1858), p. 1. This work will hereafter be cited as Comm. of Patents, Manufacture of Iron and Steel. Patents of record were granted in 1612 to Simon Sturtevant and in 1613 to John Stevenson, but both were surrendered shortly therafter, an indication that their methods were unsuccessful. In 1621 Lord Dudley was granted a patent and Dud Dudley reported in 1665 that he had been able to produce about 3 tons of iron in a week when he used coal as fuel. However, it is doubted that a good quality pig iron could have been produced with the blowing apparatus in use at that time.

century.[5] This development is credited to Abraham Darby. He sought no patent for this indirect method of producing malleable iron,[6] and at first the iron produced in this manner was thought to be of inferior quality to that produced with charcoal, because it lacked the tensility and ductility of charcoal iron. Because of this, it was not used by the leading forgemasters until 1750.

This application of coal to smelting arrested a decline in the number of smelting furnaces in Great Britain and provided an impulse for further development in the more efficient technique of application of coal. This first success proved to be only a first stage in the transformation of the iron industry - the beginning rather than the end - for though it provided the ironmaster with a commercially practicable process, it was still an imperfect one.

---

[5] *Ibid*., pp. 31-35. Usher, *Industrial History of England*, p. 321. Percy, *Metallurgy: Iron and Steel*, pp. 883-89.

It is generally agreed that the successful application of coal (in the form of coke) as a smelting fuel was introduced at the Coalbrookdale furnaces; however, it is a point of question as to which Abraham Darby, the first or second, should receive credit for this important innovation. Both Percy and Usher have given credit for the process to Abraham Darby the second, whose experiments were presumably made sometime between 1730 and 1735. Professor Ashton, on the other hand, has discovered evidence which he believed showed that Abraham Darby the first was responsible for the successful adaption of mineral fuel to blast furnace use. His solution to the problem was supposed to have been achieved as early as 1709. Scrivenor placed the date at 1713 and credited the first Darby with the innovation. See Harry Scrivenor, *A Comprehensive History of the Iron Trade* (London, 1854), p. 56.

[6] Usher, *Industrial History of England*, p. 315. Percy, *Metallurgy: Iron and Steel*, pp. 349-50. This smelting method is called "indirect" because the product produced is not a malleable iron but a cast iron. It is a necessity that the pig iron produced be subjected to further processing to eliminate carbon and silica and convert the pig iron into wrought iron or steel.

The use of coke in the blast furnace was found to require an improved bellows with a stronger blast, as has been pointed out, but once the fuel was adapted new methods of blowing the furnaces were sought. John Smeaton shortly developed a successful blowing cylinder at the Carron Iron Works in Scotland.[7] The Carron works had been the first in Scotland to use coke but had met with many failures, because of the particular coal they were using. Eventually Smeaton, who had been working on some cast-iron blowing cylinders, was invited to carry out tests with his new air-pump on one of their furnaces. By 1760 he was able to provide, with his cast-iron blowing cylinders, a stronger and almost continuous blast for the furnace. This permitted the Carron Iron Works to smelt iron ore with the coal at hand, and in time the furnace which had been yielding 10 to 12 tons of pig iron a week could produce 40 tons. In order to obtain greater uniformity in the blast, further improvements were made by blowing the air into chambers or regulators, as they were called, from which the air was transferred to the blast furnace. In time this new and much more efficient blowing machine was adopted throughout the industry, while the old-fashioned bellows were cast aside, just as the charcoal furnace had been a few years earlier.[8]

While the development of the steam engine provided ironmasters with a new market for their product, they soon found they had even more than a market. The application of the steam engine to the blowing machinery for

---

[7] Scrivenor, _A Comprehensive History of the Iron Trade_, p. 82.

[8] Percy, _Metallurgy: Iron and Steel_, p. 889.

the blast furnaces was found possible by 1780 and was adopted by a number of works. An advantage was realized in the ability of the engine to operate blowing machinery whether it was winter or spring, dry or wet. The ironmaster's production was no longer regulated by the seasons. However, the cheapness of water power, relative to the high initial cost for the steam engine, deterred many of the ironmasters from adopting this new innovation. Thus the importance of the steam engine in the iron industry was not realized until later; instead, there was a more important development that stands as the third major antecedent to the production of anthracite pig iron, the discovery and use of the hot or heated blast.

Previous to 1828 the furnaces of all iron producers were blown with a cold-blast, and it was universally believed the colder the blast the better the quality and the larger the quantity of the iron produced. This opinion was strengthened by the often observed fact that the furnaces oft times functioned better in winter than in summer. Some ironmasters, in order to obtain better production, artificially cooled the air-blast before it entered the furnace by passing it over cold water.[9]

However, in 1828, James Beaumont Neilson was granted a patent for an improved method of applying air "to produce heat in fires, forges, and furnaces, where bellows or other blowing apparatus are required."[10] Neilson, who was manager of the Glasgow gas-works, began his experiments

---

[9] Ibid., p. 397. William Fairbairn, Iron: Its History, Properties and Processes of Manufacture (Edinburgh, 1861), pp. 55-56. John H. Clapham, An Economic History of Modern Britain, I (Cambridge, England, 1932), 426-27.

[10] Comm. of Patents, Manufacture of Iron and Steel, p. 33.

with the hot-blast technique in 1825, and his discovery was finally and successfully applied at the Clyde Iron Works in 1828.[11] His work proved to be the technical foundation upon which the Scottish iron industry was to build, and it enabled these Scot ironmasters to compete with the English and Welsh furnaces. In time it was to be the key which opened the secrets to the successful use of anthracite coal as a smelting fuel.

The immediate economic advantage derived from this innovation was the economy in fuel consumption. Before the hot-blast had been used at the Clyde works, the furnaces had required coke from 8 tons 1¼ cwts. of coal to produce 1 ton of pig iron, but when the blast temperature was raised to 300° Fahrenheit, they required only 5 tons 3¼ cwts. of coal to make the necessary coke for the production of 1 ton of pig iron. Later, in 1833, the consumption of coal at these works was reduced to 2 tons 13¼ cwts. for 1 ton of pig iron.[12] In 1831 the substitution of raw coal for coke at the Calder Iron Works provided an additional saving of fuel.[13] After this success raw coal was adapted in most of the Scottish iron works.

---

[11] Clapham, _An Economic History of Modern Britain_, I, 426-27. Percy, _Metallurgy: Iron and Steel_, pp. 394-95.

[12] Fairbairn, _Iron: Its History, Properties and Processes of Manufacture_, pp. 72-73. Percy, _Metallurgy: Iron and Steel_, p. 398.

[13] Clapham, _An Economic History of Modern Britain_, I, 148. Fairbairn, _Iron: Its History, Properties and Processes of Manufacture_, pp. 72-77. Fairbairn, in his discussion on this technique of smelting, pointed out that at a later date higher temperatures were used (800° and 900° Fahr.) in the blast which continually provided more savings in fuel consumption. These higher temperatures were only reached through a step by step process of experimentation over a long period of time.

As has been pointed out, the hot-blast had enabled the ironmasters of Scotland to save fuel by heating the blast and using raw bituminous coal in the furnace, even though sulphur and other deleterious materials were not so easily done away with as when coal was used in the form of coke. Any success in the use of raw coal as a blast furnace fuel depended upon the quality or type of coal being used; some coals contain more moisture, sulphur, and other ingredients, while others range close to pure carbon and contain very little of this extraneous matter. Peat and anthracite are the extreme types, while between these two are a whole range of various type bituminous coals. Most of the British furnaces were using bituminous coals, and they were either coked prior to their use in the blast furnace or were used raw and in effect coked as the great heat of the furnace currents passed through the load as it descended to the furnace hearth. But nothing had been done with anthracite coal up to that time.

In 1820 the first experiments in smelting iron ore with anthracite coal were commenced, but they met with little success or approval, though this coal contained fewer deleterious ingredients than any other type fuel. Nevertheless, the coal, ready to be exploited, was there in Wales extending in a great vein from the upper part of the Vale Neath, in Glamorganshire, on the east, to Saundersfoot in Pembrokeshire, on the west. Finally the Yniscedwin Iron Works, in the Swansea Valley, which had been hauling its coking coals for a distance of fourteen miles, but was located on a four-foot seam of anthracite, carried out the first successful use of raw anthracite coal as a blast furnace fuel after sixteen years of experimentation. The first attempts had been made by mixing anthracite and coke and using a cold-blast but with no success.

Later the bosh, the lower sector of the furnace, was raised to 11 feet in order to permit a slower descent of the iron ore, coal, and flux in the furnace while the stack was raised to 45 feet, a tall stack for that period. This change in design resulted in an improved iron, but it was still an unprofitable technique.

On February 5, 1837, the blast was heated to a temperature of about 600° Fahrenheit before it entered the furnace, and a good grade of pig iron was produced with anthracite coal. The operators of the Yniscedwin works had shown it was technically and economically feasible to produce iron with "stone" coal. The consequence was a revolutionary change in the growth and structure of the iron industry of the United States.[14]

There, separate research and experimenting was being carried on along the same lines that Crane had been working, but it was only when David Thomas, the superintendent of the Yniscedwin works, moved to

---

[14] Comm. of Patents, *Manufacture of Iron and Steel*, p. 41.
The patent was granted to George Crane, owner of the Yniscedwin works, in 1836. By Feburary, 1837, his furnace was prepared with heating ovens attached to it and the first blast was made February 5, 1837.

There is some question of just which individual thought of using the heated blast, whether it was Crane or David Thomas, the superintendent of the works. For a discussion on this matter see Samuel Thomas, "Reminiscences of the Early Anthracite-Iron Industry," *Transactions of the American Institute of Mining Engineers*, XXIX (1900), 902-3. Abram Hewitt "On the Statistics and Geography of the Production of Iron," *Engineering pamphlets* (New York, 1856), pp. 22-23. J. Russell Smith, *The Story of Iron and Steel* (New York, 1908), pp. 48-49. Smith reported the use of the hot-blast in a primitive form was employed by the natives of Peru centuries before the discovery in Great Britain.

Pennsylvania and provided the technological "know-how" that the great new iron area and era were to be opened up. But before that development is considered, it will be profitable to consider the organization of the iron industry of the United States as it was prior to 1839.

The Iron Industry of the United States, 1800-1840

While technological innovations and changes in demand were moving the British ironmasters into new areas of production and the establishment of larger works, the demand for iron in the United States, in the early nineteenth century, remained pretty much as it had been in the colonial period. A rural market for iron and iron products called for the production of cast ironware and malleable bar iron which could be worked very easily at the smith's or farmer's forge. Generally the product consisted of cast hollow-ware, domestic utensils such as skillets, pots, andirons, and heavy boiling pans. Bar iron of assorted sizes was the leading product of the forges, which was many times stocked by the local country store for the farmer or blacksmith, the iron fabricator of the period. The bar iron was generally worked into various forms, such as horseshoes and nails, or implements like shovels, axes, saws, and other edge tools, as well as bits and stirrups. At the outset of this period iron plates were of secondary importance; as yet the engineering firms which would later demand this product were not an important part of the market.

The process of iron production itself consisted of two stages, smelting and refining, though a quantity of pig iron was made directly in the bloomery furnaces for purposes of forging. The bloomery forges, however, were limited to a few areas of the country. Generally the iron was first smelted in a small charcoal blast furnace, and its final product was a crude cast iron, the so-called pig iron. Some of this was remelted in air furnaces or cupola furnaces at foundries and then cast in different forms.[15] A major part of the blast furnace product, however, was refined a second time in order to remove the remaining impurities. In the early period this required a process of alternative heatings and beatings from a water-driven trip hammer, all of which aided in removing the impurities and changing the internal structure of the iron, giving it the malleable qualities so necessary for working it at the farmer's forge.

The unit of production was invariably a small scale operation. The ironmaster drew his ores from small local surface mines, while his fuel consisted of charcoal produced from timber found in nearby woodlands. The materials were generally located on the ironmaster's property, and the works were under his personal guidance. In addition to supplying capital and raw material, the ironmaster very often maintained a store where all the necessities and a few luxuries could be obtained, a blacksmith's shop, the gristmill, the sawmill, and the homes for the workers, sometimes even a school and a church. Nearby were fields for farming and the woodlands for timber. Remote from other areas, the iron works and other buildings made up an almost self-sufficing community over which the

---

[15] H. M. Boylston, _An Introduction to the Metallurgy of Iron and Steel_ (2d ed.; New York, 1936), pp. 138-49. The cupola furnace was used in foundries for melting pig iron for castings. The iron came in direct contact with the coal in this furnace. The air furnace was a reverberatory furnace in which the iron could be melted or heated with hot gases which kept the carbon content of the iron down to a minimum.

ironmaster sometimes assumed an almost feudal control. A typical iron works of this period was capable of turning out several tons of pig iron a day in a season of twenty or thirty weeks.[16]

Beset with the problem of inadequate transportation facilities, the iron master was compelled to rely upon local sources of raw materials and thus his scale of operation was generally limited in size. Often, as near-at-hand supplies of raw materials were depleted, he was forced to abandon his furnace or forge. A further consequence of this transport problem was the establishment of many local iron works throughout the states, iron being made in almost every state prior to 1840. Blast furnaces were forced to locate near the abundant but widespread ore and timber supplies, though foundries and forges more often were found located closer to their market. At first they produced only hollow wares for domestic use, but with the advent of the machine age such works began preparing castings to order for the various parts of the machinery.[17]

At the close of the Revolutionary War period many cold-blast charcoal furnaces and foundries had been built in scattered areas throughout

---

[16] Alfred Gemmell, "Manuscripts Shed New Light on Lehigh County's First Furnace," _Proceedings Lehigh County Historical Society_ (Allentown, 1949), pp. 48-68. James Swank, _Iron in All Ages_ (Philadelphia, 1892), p. 535. Swank reported that in 1831 "the American blast furnace which could make four tons of pig iron a day, or 28 tons in a week, was doing good work."

[17] Louis C. Hunter, "Heavy Industries Before 1860," as found in Harc Williamson, ed., _Growth of the American Economy_ (2d ed.; New York, 1951), pp. 173-75. This short essay on the iron industry is probably the best brief description of the iron industry of the period. The story is also told in Victor S. Clark, _History of Manufactures in the United States,_ I (New York, 1929), as well as in Swank, _Iron in All Ages._

the thirteen former colonies, extending from New England to Georgia and from the seacoast to the Appalachian valleys. Iron was made wherever the blacksmith's and farmer's needs were made evident, and rich ores were found in outcroppings in many places, along with abundant timber and water supplies as well as beds of limestone (in some cases, sea shells) so essential for fluxing purposes.

Nothwithstanding this wide geographical dispersion, the important primary manufactures were located in fairly well-defined areas. The smeltingof bog ores was carried out in the furnaces of eastern Massachusetts, Rhode Island, and eastern Connecticut, though later these furnaces were forced to import ores from New Jersey and Pennsylvania in order to continue their operations. Between 1825 and 1840 these furnaces gradually withdrew from the production of pig iron, though various rolling mills and forges which began to use coal were able to maintain their operations.[18] This was the case also with the bog-iron works of Delaware and New Jersey as the increased production along the belt of iron ores from Rutland, Vermont, through the western part of Massachusetts and on into New York state and Morris County, New Jersey, entered the market. In New York production was increased in the Lake Champlain area, where rich magnetic ores were found and adapted to the production of low-grade steel for agricultural implements and cutlery.[19]

In Pennsylvania production of iron had been extended well into the

---

[18]Clark, <u>History of Manufactures in the United States</u>, I, 496.

[19]<u>Ibid</u>., p. 497.

Juniata Valley by the end of the eighteenth century, and a few furnaces had been built in the vicinity of Pittsburgh. The major areas of production in this state were in the Schuylkill and Susquehanna valleys, but little production had been developed in the Lehigh Valley until after 1810. By 1820 there had been thirty iron works, fourteen charcoal blast furnaces, and sixteen bloomeries established in Pennsylvania, though there had been a continual decline in prices. Bar iron prices dropped from a high of $140 a ton to $90 and $100 in 1818, and pig iron was sold at $30 a ton.[20] Pittsburgh, faced with little competition from the East because of the high cost of transportation, had seven rolling mills in active operation in addition to eight foundries and a cupola furnace. All were producing either bar iron or agricultural implements for the rural markets.[21] There were no blast furnaces in Pittsburgh, its pig iron being obtained from the furnaces in the Juniata Valley and the area immediately outside of Pittsburgh.

Between 1783 and 1815 numerous forges and a few charcoal furnaces had been constructed on the slopes of the Blue Ridge and Allegheny Mountains in southwestern Virginia and western Carolina as well as in Tennessee and Kentucky. However, it was only after 1810 or later that forges or furnaces were in operation in Georgia or Alabama, and only

---

[20]Leander J. Bishop, *History of American Manufactures* (Philadelphia, 1868), p. 259. Swank, *Iron in All Ages*, p. 514. Swank reported Philadelphia prices for charcoal pig iron in 1818 to be $42.25 a ton and hammered bar iron at $110. These prices had dropped from $53.75 and $144.50 a ton in 1815.

[21]*Ibid.*, p. 301.

between 1825 and 1840 were furnaces built west of the Mississippi in the area of Pilot Knob and Iron Mountain, Missouri. In the Ohio Valley, around the Hanging Rock district of Kentucky, development was carried out between 1818 and 1840, and shortly after 1818 furnaces were blown in from Portsmouth to the Hocking Valley in Ohio.[22]

The census of 1810 listed 153 charcoal blast furnaces in operation in the United States that produced 53,908 tons of pig iron.[23] This figure contains some duplication, for it includes the product of furnaces which were used merely to reduce pigs for casting. Also there were 153 bloomeries which were reducing the iron ore directly for casting purposes. Pennsylvania led all of the states for value of production, manufacturing nearly 50 percent of the total output. New York followed Pennsylvania, while New Jersey and Maryland held third and fourth positions.

By 1840 the census reported 804 furnaces in blast, turning out 283,000 tons of pig iron and castings.[24] Nearly one-half of these furnaces were in New York state and Pennsylvania, the latter having 213 furnaces which had reported a product of 98,395 tons of cast iron. Pennsylvania also contained 169 bloomeries, forges, and mills. There had been 123 iron works built in Pennsylvania between 1830 and 1840. Of this

---

[22]Clark, History of Manufactures in the United States, I, 498.

[23]Ibid., pp. 449-50. Bishop, History of American Manufactures, pp. 423-24. Swank, Iron in All Ages, p. 532. See also Tench Coxe, Tabular Statements of the Several Branches of American Manufactures: 1810 (Philadelphia, 1813), Tables 9 and 10.

[24]Ibid., p. 500. The statistics provided by Clark are substantially the same as those provided by Bishop and Swank. Bishop, History of American Manufactures, pp. 423-34. Swank, Iron in All Ages, p. 536.

number there were 72 charcoal blast furnaces, 46 bloomeries, rolling mills, and forges in addition to 5 blast furnaces designed for the use of mineral fuel, of which more will be said later.[25]

While iron production was expanding with the growth of the number of furnaces and mills, there were very few new technical innovations made in the production of pig iron. The changes in iron production that were taking place in Great Britain did not have an immediate influence upon the production in this country. Cold-blast charcoal iron was the furnace product, and about the only improvement in the blast furnace methods from the time of the first Puritan iron furnace to the late 1830's was the introduction of the cast-iron blowing cylinders which gradually replaced the bellows. The refining forges, pressed by labor shortages and a growing demand for bar iron, began to substitute capital equipment for labor after 1817 when Henry Cort's innovation of the grooved rollers was adopted by operators in Fayette County, Pennsylvania.[26] In this mill the blooms or slabs from the heating furnaces were rolled, instead of being hammered, to expel the impurities and then formed into bars or plates of various sizes and shapes without coming in contact with the fuel. This method of refining saved time and reduced the necessary man power required by the established practice of refining and shaping by hammering.

At about the same time that Cort's rolling mill technique was

---

[25]Bishop, History of American Manufactures, p. 424.

[26]Arthur C. Bining, "The rise of Iron Manufacture in Western Pennsylvania," Western Pennsylvania Historical Magazines, XVI (1933), 245-46. This work will hereafter be cited as Bining, "The Rise of Iron Manufacture in Western Pennsylvania."

adopted, his puddling process was also introduced. In this process a reverberatory furnace was used to heat the iron without bringing it into contact with the fuel, a method which permitted the substitution of coal for charcoal. Coal could not be used with the timeworn process of direct heating with the charcoal because of the impurities it would have imparted to the iron. Coal, in the form of coke or anthracite, was also being used in the rolling mills by 1820, and as the rolling mills increased the consumption of coal increased. Further, the increasing use of coal had a centripetal effect, for it provided a great impetus for the centralization of the iron industry which was to be accentuated even more after coal was introduced as a blast furnace fuel.

Competition from the British Iron Industry

Preceding the Revolution many ironmasters of these British colonies had been exporters of pig iron, but the restriction on trade arising out of the war provided an opportunity for growth of the iron industry for domestic consumption. It has been estimated that the total works in operation by 1783 were capable of producing about 30,000 tons of charcoal pig iron per annum.[27] Following the war the trade of the new nation was opened to the world once again, and the British began to export rolled iron as well as other manufactures into this market. Because of this influx of trade, some of the furnaces which had been initiated during the war suffered a severe setback as the cheaper bar iron was

---

[27]B. F. French, *History of the Rise and Progresss of the Iron Trade of the United States: 1621-1857* (New York, 1858), p. 12. This work will hereafter be cited as French, *Iron Trade*.

imported from Great Britain. But Great Britain was not the only iron exporter causing concern for the American ironmaster. There were about 4,500 tons of hammered bar iron annually imported from both Russia and Sweden at this time. This iron, unlike the British product, was a charcoal iron refined by hammering.[28] However, the greatest threat to the domestic furnace owners came from Great Britain.

By 1788 British coke furnaces were producing about 68,000 tons of pig iron a year, while their production of refined iron was being increased continuously with the easier and cheaper puddling and rolling processes. Though this rolled bar iron was considered of inferior make, its low price compensated for its quality. The new British processes were also promoting a growth of large scale production with their economies of scale, which consequently permitted the ironmasters to sell their iron at prices lower than any other country.

Domestically the use of charcoal in the blast furnace limited the size of the furnace because of the friability of the fuel. The older charcoal furnaces were from 12 to 18 feet high and the output was but 20 to 30 tons of pig iron a week. In Great Britain, on the other hand, where coke was being used, the furnaces had been increased in height from 40 to 60 feet, for the more dense fuel could carry a heavier load of ore and flux. The increase in furnace size permitted a single coke furnace of that day to turn out 1,546 tons in a single year, while the average output of the best constructed furnace was 2,615 tons a year, an amount

---

[28]Bishop, History of American Manufactures, p. 153

nine times as great as the output of most charcoal furnaces; the last named were considered efficient if production reached 294 or 300 tons of pig iron per annum.[29]

With the passing of time further improvements were made in British coke furnaces and the average blast furnace yield was raised to 2,400 tons a year. The introduction of Neilson's hot-blast provided for furthur gains, while coal consumption was reduced for each ton of iron produced. For example, in 1829 the average output of pig iron for the furnaces of the Clyde Iron Works was 37 tons a week. These particular furnaces were operated with a cold-blast and coke. With the application of the hot-blast in 1830, the weekly output of these furnaces was raised to 54 tons of pig iron a week and later, with the use of raw coal and the hot-blast, the same furnaces were able to run out 61 tons a week. In each instance the consumption of coal was reduced for each ton of iron produced.[30]

Partially as a result of these more efficient production methods the total product of the British iron industry was continually increased. In 1796 output had been 125,029 tons, but by 1825 it had been increased to 581,367 tons. One year after the introduction of Neilson's hot-blast technique, production was raised to 678,417 tons a year and by 1836 it

---

[29] Scrivenor, A Comprehensive History of the Iron Trade, p. 282. Hewitt, "On the Statistics and Geography of the Production of Pig-Iron," Engineering pamphlets, p. 8.

[30] Scrivenor, A Comprehensive History of the Iron Trade, pp. 296-297.

had reached 1,000,000 tons.[31] With the use of anthracite coal, which supplemented the potential fuel supply, and site locations for iron production, British output was further increased; by 1839 the ironmasters of that country could produce as much as 1,248,781 tons of iron a year. One year later this output had been increased to 1,396,400 tons.[32]

While rapid increases in iron production were taking place in Great Britain, iron manufacturers in the United States continued to operate with their now technically outmoded charcoal furnaces. Not until 1806 had any number of ironmasters used blowing cylinders in place of the "tubs" or bellows. But none had reverted to the use of coke or coal of any type. Their blowing equipment was generally motivated by water power; consequently, their blast was often irregular and weak while in dry seasons or winter freezes they were incapable of providing the necessary power to operate the mechanism. The resulting production of such methods was an output for a single furnace of about 352 to 400 tons of pig iron a year or 20 to 30 tons per week. In 1810 the total production of 153 furnaces of record was placed at 54,000 tons.[33] Thus, only as the number of furnaces was increased did the total production of the American iron

---

[31] Ibid., pp. 282-300. Hewitt, "On the Statistics and Geography of the Production of Pig-Iron," Engineering Pamphlets, pp. 10-11.

[32] Scrivenor, A Comprehensive History of The Iron Trade, p. 292.

[33] French, Iron Trade, p. 18. Hunter, "Heavy Industries Before 1860," p. 178.

Industry expand. But throughout that period of hostilities, between 1807 and 1815, there was a gradual growth in the number of such furnaces.

After hostilities had ceased, British ironmasteres discovered that the increase in British capacity created to meet the demands of war had outgrown ordinary peace-time requirements of their domestic market, and they were prepared, therefore, to sell their iron at lower prices. Moreover, they were quite anxious to recapture their share of the American market. As British prices of iron declined, some British ironmasters were forced to blow out their furnaces as necessary economic readjustments were made.[34]

Similarly, readjustments took place in the United States as ironmasters faced this peace-time market with the increasing competition from additional domestic furnaces, and the lower priced British iron. Shortly thereafter production in the United States dropped to 20,000 tons (1818-19), but it slowly recovered and by 1828 production had reached 130,000 tons per year. This was an expansion which had been contrived with great hesitation because of the continued influx of rolled iron from Great Britain and the continuous flow of hammered bar iron from Sweden and Russia. In this plight the only salvation for the American ironmaster seemed to be protective tariffs.

Tariff Policy

In 1789 the Federal government had adopted a general 5 percent duty on all imported goods, a tariff originally introduced by the Congress of

---

[34]Ashton, _Iron and Steel in the Industrial Revolution_, pp. 150-54.

the Confederation. A few specific duties had been levied on cordage, hemp, nails, manufactures of iron, and glass, while *ad valorem* duties were placed on certain luxury items. Though the duties were not high and served as a source of revenue, the intent to protect was still there.[35] This tariff policy remained unchanged for a number of years, though duties were raised from time to time to obtain more revenue. Even Hamilton's "Report on Manufactures" in 1792, which advocated protective tariffs, did not change the policy. Meanwhile, imports of iron from Norway, Russia, and Sweden continued while England alone exported to the United States an average of 6,170 tons per annum between 1796 and 1805. By 1807 these imports had risen to 8,229 tons.[36]

The situation was changed drastically in 1808 when the international problems with England and France led to the Embargo Act in 1807 and later the Non-Intercourse Act of 1809. Finally the war with England served to exclude British iron momentarily, but with the Treaty of Ghent trade was opened once again.

Ironmasters throughout the country after the War of 1812, accustomed to the absence of British competition, now saw their only hope for the preservation of their investment through increased duties on imported iron. Supported by other industrialists, the ironmasters of the western as well as the eastern regions supported the tariff of 1816, an act which

---

[35]Clark, *History of Manufactures in the United States*, I, 270. Frank W. Taussig, *Tariff History of the United States* (6th ed.; New York, 1931), p. 15.

[36]Scrivenor, *A Comprehensive History of the Iron Trade*, p. 419.

was fully intended to protect the industry of the nation. The protection offered the iron industry in this act was $30 a ton ($1.50 cvt.) for rolled bar iron, $9.00 a ton (45 cents cwt.) for hammered bar, and a 20 percent ad valorem tariff on pig iron. The heavier duty was maintained on rolled iron in an attempt to ward off the threat of the cheaper productive process used by the British.[37] Ironmasters declared at that time that the higher duty on rolled bar iron was to protect the consumer from an "inferior quality" product.[38]

But this was not enough, and the ironmasters demanded increased rates once again. Congress responded with lower rates in 1818, despite the decline in domestic iron prices.

Prices for bar iron at Atlantic seaports, which had moved from $90 to $95 a ton in 1793 to $110 and $120 a ton in 1816, now began to drop with the influx of imported iron and the decline in economic activity which occurred in 1818-20. By 1818 the price was listed as $90 and $100 a ton, and, regardless of the tariff, it continued dropping to reach $85

---

[37] Taussig, Tariff History of the United States, pp. 50-51. French, Iron Trade, p. 21.

[38] Louis C. Hunter, "Influence of the Market upon Technique in the Iron Industry in Western Pennsylvania Up to 1860," Journal of Economic and Business History, I (1928-29), 241-81.

For some time the claim that iron manufactured with coke was inferior was sustained in part because charcoal iron was more suited to the chief needs of the domestic market. The malleability and welding properties of that iron provided it with greater utility of the manufacture of domestic hardware and agriculture equipment at the blacksmith's forge. The iron made with coke, on the other hand, was much more suitable for railroad construction and other modern industrial purposes. As the industrial sector of the economy expanded, there was an expanded demand for the rolled iron.

and $95 a ton in 1822.[39]

This drop in prices meant that the specific duties became proportionately heavier but, regardless of the subsequent burden this placed upon the consumer, rates were raised again in 1824 and later. The duty on hammered iron was moved to 90 cents cwt. in order to keep out Russian and Swedish hammered iron while the duty on rolled iron remained at $1.50 cwt. Again, in 1828, still further increases were made, and the duty on pig iron was raised to 62½ cents cwt. ($12.50 a ton), hammered bar was one cent a pound ($22.40 a ton), and rolled bar was raised to $37 a ton.[40] The effect of this last increase was further additions to government revenues, enough so as to permit the payment of its war debt. Further, it united an aroused opposition that soon became strong enough to persuade the Congress to reduce duties to the 1824 level.

A Compromise Act was written in 1833 under which the duties of 1824 were to be maintained for two years, then gradually reduced until 1842 when they would reach a level of 20 percent. By June, 1842, the tariff on English bar iron had dropped from $30 a ton, the 1832 rate, to $7.50; the pig iron duty fell from $9.50 per ton in 1834 to $4.50 in 1842, while railroad iron was to be imported duty free.[41] With the change in tariffs there was an increase in imports of rolled bar and pig iron while hammered iron became a proportionately smaller part of the total. The

---

[39]French, Iron Trade, p. 15.

[40]Ibid., p. 26. Taussig, Tariff History of the United States, p. 51.

[41]Ibid.

latter was probably indicative of the change in the character of the economy as it slowly proceeded to move from an essentially agricultural society to an industrial economy. (See Table 1.)

During this period of protection, no evidence appears of progress in the techniques of production enabling consumers to obtain iron more cheaply than by importation. The tariff served as a burden upon the consumer rather than as a stimulus to domestic producers to discover new and cheaper methods of production.[42]

With the advent of lower duties some protectionists thought that the country was on the verge of ruin while others hoped for a revival of their program at a later date. Most important was the ability of the iron industry to make readjustments later during a period of economic prosperity. Fianlly, as tariffs were gradually reduced, extensive efforts were made to find the solution to the use of coal in the blast furnace.

Dr. Geisenheimer's Patent

During 1820 the first regular commercial shipments of anthracite coal were made over the Lehigh Canal to Philadelphia. Throughout that year a total of 365 tons of such coal were shipped from Mauch Chunk and

---

[42] Taussig, Tariff History of the United States, p. 59.

Taussig concluded that "the duties simply taxed the community; they did not serve to stimulate the industry, though they probably did not appreciably retard its growth. We may therefore conclude that the duties on iron during the generation after 1815 formed a heavy tax on consumers; That they impeded, so far as they went, the industrial development of the country; and that no compensatory benefits were obtained to offset these disadvantages."

See Clark, History of Manufactures in the United States, I, 300.

TABLE 1

IMPORTS OF IRON, 1830-40
(Figures indicate gross tons, 000 omitted)

Year	Pig Iron	Rolled Iron	Hammered Iron	Total Imports
1890	1	7	31	48
1831	7	15	23	55
1832	10	21	38	84
1833	9	28	36	89
1834	11	29	32	87
1835	12	28	31	87
1836	8	47	33	108
1837	14	48	31	113
1838	12	36	21	84
1839	12	60	36	131
1840	6	33	29	83

Source: _The Quarterly Journal of Economics_, II (1888), 379. B. F. French, _History of the Rise and Progress of the Iron Trade of the United States: 1621-1857_, pp. 27-30.

sold to consumers for $8.50 a ton.[43] When the first load of this coal had been shipped to Philadelphia, prior to the building of the Canal, in 1814, the price had been $14 a ton.[44] Though the coal shipped in 1820 was not the first of such to be shipped to market, that shipment marks the beginning of a regular commercial traffic. That same year George Crane of Wales began his experiments with anthracite coal in his blast furnaces.

Josiah White and Erskine Hazard, the two entrepreneurs that had

[43]Bishop, _History of American Manufactures_, p. 260. Chester L. Jones, _The Economic History of the Anthracite-Tidewater Canals_ (Philadelphia, 1908, p. 12.

[44]_Ibid._, p. 203.

developed this new and cheaper means of navigation to Philadelphia and had thereby opened up the Lehigh coal fields to exploitation, had earlier used this hard coal in the production of iron wire. It is probably safe to imagine that they had also speculated on other possible uses of this fuel in iron manufacture as they prepared their route to the coal fields in order to open them up for commerce. Actually it was but a short time after they had commenced their shipments of the fuel to Philadelphia that they built a small charcoal-type furnace at Mauch Chunk to experiment with this coal in smelting iron ores. They first began their experiment by introducing some anthracite coal mixed with charcoal, and step by step they tried to increase the coal content of the furnace fuel. At that time (1826) their coal was selling for half the price of imported coal and less than charcoal.[45] Certainly a rich prize would have been theirs had they succeeded in the venture, but their experiments were failures, and the furnace was turned back to the production of charcoal iron.[46] Meanwhile, similar experiments were made with anthracite in Kingston Furnace, Plymouth County, Massachusetts, but with little success.[47]

In other areas of iron manufacture, anthracite coal was found an acceptable substitute for charcoal and was utilized by a number of iron

---

[45]French, Iron Trade, p. 22.

[46]Mathew S. Henry, History of the Lehigh Valley (Easton, 1860), p. 346. Swank, Iron in All Ages, p. 353.

[47]Swank, Iron in All ages, p. 353. Swank reported that a Peter Ritner of Perry County, Pennsylvania, had attempted to use anthracite coal with charcoal at about the same time. As no other record is available, it must be assumed that the application of coal in this instance was not made successfully.

works. The Phoenixville rolling mill at Philadelphia used it in 1825 for generating steam power. Later, at the same iron works, it was used for puddling, while at the same time the Boston Iron Works purchased and used Lehigh coal for heating iron for the rolls in the mill as well as for smith work.[48] However, no one as yet had uncovered the secrets which would permit its use in smelting iron ore.

Shortly after a patent for the use of the hot-blast technique in smelting was issued by the British government (1828), that innovation was applied quite successfully with coke or bituminous coal in the British furnaces. While this technique was being assimilated in the British iron industry, a little known Lutheran clergyman of New York City commenced investigations into the use of anthracite coal as a smelting fuel.

This investigator was Dr. Frederick Geisenheimer (Geissenhainer), clergyman, bituminous and anthracite coal mine operator, owner of a charcoal iron furnace in the Schuylkill Valley, projector of the Schuylkill Valley Railroad, and probably the first man in the United States to discover methods which would enable ironmasters to use anthracite coal in smelting. He began his tests in a small experimental furnace in New York City prior to 1831, and he had advanced far enough by that year to file an account of his invention with the United States Patent Office in Washington. His patent was finally granted in 1833.[49]

---

[48] James M. Swank, Iron Making and Coal Mining in Pennsylvania (Philadelphia, 1878), p. 22.

[49] Swank, Iron in All Ages, pp. 354-55. Walter R. Johnson, Notes on the Use of Anthracite in the Manufacture of Iron (Boston, 1841), pp. 12-13. This work will hereafter be cited as Johnson, Notes on the Use of

Upon reading the statement of what the patent covered, it appears that he had relied largely upon the effect of a strong blast of air rather than the use of heated air. He asserted that the anthracite coal could be used by applying "a blast or column, or a stream, or a current of air in or of such quantity, velocity, and density or compression as the compactness or density and the continuity of the anthracite coal requires." Then he added, in what seems to have been a not too important afterthought, "The blast may be of common atmospheric or of heated air. Heated air I should prefer in an economical point of view."[50]

With the patent in hand, Dr. Geisenheimer set out to construct a furnace at Silver Creek in Schuylkill County, and by 1836 he succeeded in making a small amount of pig iron with the exclusive use of anthracite coal. He used a heated blast. Smelting in this furnace was halted in order to permit improvements in the blasting machinery, but before the Reverend Geisenheimer could commence operations again he died.[51]

While Geisenheimer's experiments were taking place, record is also made of the production of anthracite pig iron at Cressona in Schuylkill County in a furnace built by a John Pott. Mr. Pott, however, does not seem to have continued production of this type of pig iron, for no further record of such is available after his experiment. Later his furnace

---

Anthracite. See also William Firmstone, "Sketches of Early Anthracite Furnaces" Transactions of the American Institute of Mining Engineers, III (1874-75), 152-53.

[50]Johnson, Notes on the Use of Anthracite, pp. 12-13. Swank, Iron in All ages, p. 354.

[51]Swank, Iron in All Ages, p. 355.

was destroyed by a freshet in 1841.[52] These early efforts to smelt iron ores with anthracite coal were abortive, a result of the failure of those experimenting to use a heated blast, i.e., a blast heated to a high enough temperature to enable the coal to function properly.

In the western part of Pennsylvania were other men quite as inquisitive as those in the anthracite regions, and while the anthracite experiments were being carried on, efforts were also made in western Pennsylvania to adopt an already successful technique; a few western ironmasters tried to use coke in their blast furnaces. This fuel had already been used in the rolling mills of western Pennsylvania, but it had never before been used in smelting. Finally, in 1836, F. H. Oliphant of Fayette County made a quantity of pig iron with coke.[53] He did not continue his production of iron with coke, probably because, as W. R. Johnson reported in 1841, of "the higher value put upon charcoal iron" in that sector of the country.[54] That area was still in a stage of agricultural development, and the farmers required a more workable iron for their forges than that which a coke furnace could turn out.[55]

Ibid. p. 357.

[53]Ibid., p. 368. The earliest attempt to use coke was probably at Bear Creek furnace in Armstrong County, Pennsylvania (1819). The blast was cold and probably too weak to work effectively. After the production of several tons of iron, the furnace chilled which led the operator to revert to charcoal.

[54]Johnson, Notes on the Use of Anthracite, pp. 408.

[55]Hunter, "Influence of the Market upon Technique in the Iron Industry in Western Pennsylvania up to 1860," Journal of Economic and Business History, I (19289), 244-46. Bining, "The Rise of Iron Manufacture in Western Pennsylvania," pp. 247-48.

Similar endeavors were made at Karthaus and Farrandsville, on the west branch of the Susquehanna River, but in these instances the poor qualities of the ores and coal, the lack of adequate transport facilities, as well as the quality of iron, forced the furnaces to discontinue such production.[56]

Pushed by British success and its cheaper iron, persuaded by the growth of the American economy, with the advent of the steam engine, steamboat, the railroad, all of which were potential users of iron, a few enterprising ironmasters continued the rather perplexing struggle to unlock the secret of the use of anthracite coal in smelting iron ores. Success had been "reported," a patent had been granted for a process of producing pig iron with anthracite coal, but up to 1836 (the British had been using coke in their furnaces for about one hundred years) no one had established a going concern to produce anthracite iron. Even though tariff schedules were changed, with the rates moving downward, and in spite of the panic of 1837-38 followed by the depressed conditions of 1840, those who saw the tremendous gains to be made continued their quest for the solution. Eventually the most important event in the history of the American iron industry up to that time, the possibility of substituting anthracite coal for charcoal, was made accessible with the importation of foreign (Welsh) practice. For this revolutionary development we now turn to certain favorable developments which occurred between 1837 and 1840

---

[56]Johnson, Notes on the Use of Anthracite, pp. 4-8.

Establishment of the Lehigh Crane Iron Works

Earlier and to the east, the Lehigh Coal and Navigation Company, impressed with the importance of its profit account of a further increase in their sales of anthracite coal and navigation tolls, had offered inducements to individuals or companies to develop on their lands the smelting of iron ore with anthracite coal. In 1834 it had offered grants of water power, coal at reduced rates, and passage of coal on its waterway toll free to that individual or company that could bring to fruition such a process and would establish this business on the canal. The economic gains for the Coal and Navigation Company would be an increase in tolls and revenue from the shipment of raw materials and pig iron as well as the sale of coal to this company and other enterprises that would probably follow.[57]

But not only the Lehigh Coal and Navigation Company was interested in the discovery of this process, for in 1835 the Franklin Institute of Philadelphia offered a gold medal to anyone who could produce 20 tons of pig iron with anthracite coal.[58] (A similar offer was made for the person who would produce pig iron with coke.) A year later the Legislature of Pennsylvania passed "An Act - To encourage the manufacture of iron

---

[57]Samuel Hazard, ed., United States Commercial and Statistical Register, II (Philadelphia, 1840), 157-60. This work will hereafter be cited as Hazard, United States Register, II. See also Richard Richardson, Memoir of Josiah White (Philadelphia, 1873), pp. 100-101.

[58]Swank, Iron in All Ages, p. 362.

with coke or mineral fuel, and for other purposes"[59] Under this act the governor was given the power to charter companies with corporate privileges, the corporation to have a capital of not less than $100,000 nor more than $500,000 in $50 shares. The corporations were to be organized to manufacture, transport, or sell iron made with coke or mineral fuel.

That very same year George Crane and David Thomas, at the Yniscedwin works in Wales, capped their long endeavors with the discovery that pig iron could be produced with anthracite coal when a hot-blast was used to raise the temperature of the furnace fire. Crane received the patent for the process in 1836, and by 1837 he had constructed and commenced operations of a single furnace on a commercial basis. This furnace was capable of producing 36 tons of pig iron a week.

The Yniscedwin discovery was not immediately reported in the United States, and individual research was continued into the possible use of Pennsylvania anthracite for the same purpose. Eventually, and in that same year, 1837, Joseph Baughman, Julius Guiteau, and Henry High succeeded in producing pig iron with a mixture of charcoal and anthracite (80 percent coal). Oddly enough, their experiment was accomplished in the old Lehigh Coal and Navigation Company furnace at Mauch Chunk, built twelve years previously for similar research purposes.

Later these three men, now joined by F. C. Lowthrop, built nearby a more adaptable furnace for the use of anthracite coal. This time their

---

[59] Pennsylvania Laws, 1835-1836, p. 497. Johnson, Notes on the Use of Anthracite, pp. 4-8. Bishop, History of American Manufactures, p. 409.

first attempt to produce iron in the new furnace was halted to improve the heating apparatus for the blast which had only been able to develop a heat of 200° Fahrenheit. The new blowing machine, which was powered by water, and the new heating equipment, which consisted of 200 feet of cast-iron pipes placed in a brick chamber located at the tunnel-head and heated by the tunnel flamed, proved to be much more effective. Using only anthracite coal, they were able to produce pig iron for about five weeks, but then they ran out of ore (January, 1839). In the spring of that year, with an enlarged hearth for the furnace, they put the furnace in blast once again, and with a blast of air heated to 400° to 600° Fahrenheit they succeeded in producing about 100 tons of pig iron.[60] The furnace however was but 21½ feet high and only large enough to produce 1½ tons of iron in one day or about 8 tons a week.

They had discovered the process accidentally, but the productivity of their furnace was quite disappointing and the cost was prohibitive.[61] It must be remembered a charcoal furnace could produce about 30 tons of pig iron in a week, and even though charcoal was becoming more and more expensive as accessible supplies of woodland became more scarce, this small output of anthracite iron was produced at too high a cost. But it

---

[60] Swank, *Iron in All Ages*, pp. 358-59. Alfred Mathews and Austin N. Hungerford, *History of the Counties of Lehigh and Carbon, in the Commonwealth of Pennsylvania* (Philadelphia, 1884), p. 800. This work will hereafter be cited as Mathews and Hungerford, *Lehigh and Carbon Counties*.

[61] Johnson, *Notes on the Use of Anthracite*, pp. 28-31.

must not be forgotten that it was built as an experimental furnace.[62]

In the interim Crane's success had been recognized by the iron industry, and shortly after he had begun production on a commercial scale a young American engineer, Solomon Roberts, nephew of Josiah White, made a visit to these works. Upon careful observation of the furnace and its operations, he wrote to his uncle in 1837 and advised him of the quality of the project inquiring whether such a furnace would interest them, viz., the Lehigh Coal and Navigation Company. His correspondence was enough to set these men into a hurried and quite informal organization of the Lehigh Crane Iron Company, which shortly thereafter sent Erskine Hazard to Wales to acquaint himself with the work of the Yniscedwin furnaces.[63] These two men, White and Hazard, were the same two that had begun experiments with anthracite coal twelve years earlier. Now at last they were going to be able to reap the harvest which had waited so long to be

---

[62]Mathews and Hungerford, _Lehigh and Carbon Counties_, p. 802. In a letter published in the _Mauch Chunk Democrat_ (1872), F. C. Lowthrop wrote the following note in reply to contemptuous statements about their use of a small furnace.

"In a matter, which at that time was looked upon, even by iron-masters, with much uncertainty as to its ultimate success, it would have been very unwise to go to the expense of building a large furnace at a cost of many thousands of dollars, when it was known that if the thing could be accomplished _with a small furnace, it could be done much more easily, and far more profitably, with a large one._

"We did not enlarge our furnace, as one writer has stated, but simply the hearth, and we blew it out because it was too small to work at a profit; and, not having funds with which to construct large works, we returned the property on which the furnace was built to the Lehigh Coal and Navigation Company, from whom it was leased, which was the last we had to do with it."

[63]Richardson, _Memoir of Josiah White_, pp. 100-101. Mathews and Hungerford, _Lehigh and Carbon Counties_, p. 238.

exploited. The erection of the works at Craneville (now Catasauqua) commenced in 1839, the same year in which the Lehigh Crane Iron Company was formally organized under the Pennsylvania Act of 1836.

Before the Craneville furnace was completed another anthracite furnace was completed and blown in at Pottsville, Pennsvylania. This furnace, later known as the Pioneer Furnace, was built by William Lyman of Boston for Marshall, Kellog & Company with the aid and guidance of David Thomas. Also, with the assistance of a Mr. Perry, an English iron founder, the furnace was successfully blown by steam power with a blast raised to 600°. Later Mr. Lyman was awarded $5,000 and the honor of being cited as the first to establish a commercially successful anthracite blast furnace in the United States.[64] The furnace was 35 feet high and capable of producing 28 tons of pit iron a week.[65]

---

[64]Hazard, United States Register, I (Philadelphia, 1839), 336. Solomon Roberts reported to a Joseph Chandler: "When passing through Pottsville on Saturday evening last, I visited the furnace of Mr. Wm. Lyman, now in blast with Anthracite Coal, under the direction of Benjamin Perry, an experienced English furnace manager, familiar with Mr. Crane's process. The furnace had been in blast eight days, and had made about thirty tons of good pigs, from a mixture of the argillaceous iron of the coal region with other ores from the valley of the Schuylkill. . . .no coal but anthracite was used, the cinder was flowing freely, the make of iron was increasing, and the whole process was going on in a businesslike manner. It reminded me of what I saw at Mr. Crane's works in Wales two years ago; and if no unforeseen accident accours [sic], I believe that the furnace will continue to work well."

[65]Mathews and Hungerford, Lehigh and Carbon Counties, p. 801. These authors cited the Pottsville Miners' Journal on the problems of the furnace.

"The iron trade was at that time so much depressed under the compromise tariff of 1833, reducing the duties down to twenty percent in

Then in quick succession four more furnaces were blown in during 1840. They were all located in different sectors of Pennsylvania; one, the Danville Furnace in Montour County, a second at Phoenixville, a third at Roaring Creek, and a fourth at Danville, the so-called Columbia Furnace.[66] Then on July 3, 1840, the Lehigh Crane Iron Company's first furnace was blown in. The product of the furnace was 50 tons of good foundryiron a week, all made from local brown hematite ores.[67] This was the first economically operative anthracite furnace in the Lehigh Valley. Its success was to accelerate the growth of the iron industry of the nation and lead the Lehigh Valley into a predominant position among the merchant pig iron producers.

1840, and the opposition to the use of anthracite iron by the charcoal interests, that Mr. Lyman failed a short time after . . . . The furnace was afterwards run by other parties who had but little capital, and they too failed."

See also Johnson, <u>Notes on the Use of Anthracite</u>, pp. 28-31.

[66]The Danville Furnace was built for Biddle, Chambers & Company and was placed in operation in April, 1840. This furnace was equipped with steam-powered blowing apparatus. It was 30 feet high and capable of turning out 30 tons of pig iron in a single week.

The Phoenixville Furnace, built for Reeves, Buck & Company by William Firmstone, was in production by June 17, 1840. This furnace was 33 feet high and its blowing machinery was powered by water. The furnace could produce about 28 tons of pig iron in one week.

Roaring Creek Furnace was built by Burd Patterson and was blown in on May 18, 1840. It was 30 feet high with a water-powered blast. The furnace could turn out about 40 tons of pig iron in a week.

The last of this group of furnaces was the Columbia Furnace. This work was placed in operation in July 2, 1840. The furnace was 33 feet high with blowing machinery motivated by steam power. It had a weekly capacity of 31.5 tons of pig iron.

See Johnson, <u>Notes on the Use of Anthracite</u>, pp. 128-31. Firmstone, "Sketches of Early Anthracite Furnaces," <u>Trans</u>. <u>AIME</u>);874-75), pp. 153-55.

[67]<u>Ibid</u>.

Not long after this furnace was blown in, four others were built and commenced operations in other parts of Pennsylvania and New Jersey.

Conclusion

The economic implications of these developments in Pennsylvania were recognized by many interested parties, and they soon led in a race to increase the production of iron. (Often this increase in production has been attributed exclusively to the tariff of 1842.) The change provided the first great impetus to the production of pig iron on a much larger scale than ever carried on before, and in the next few years. Furthermore, the location of the iron industry was now being governed by the site of anthracite coal deposits, just as coke had influenced the British industry. Eastern Pennsylvania, despite its nearness to the seaboard and foreign competition, was to become the main producing area, while for a time Philadelphia was to be the central market. However, it was some time after the close of the Civil War that the product of the anthracite ironmasters was to be the largest share of the total ouput of the iron industry.

Certainly a debt of gratitude was owed to the British ironmasters, if one wished to assign technical changes to particular persons as their separate discoveries, though it is hardly possible for one to do this after reviewing the development of the iron industry up to 1840. Instead, it appears that each innovation seems to have been a product of accumulative knowledge, which makes it impossible to assign the development of the techniques described herein to any particular individuals, though mention has been made of those who supposedly were the inventors or discoverers. But upon considering the British iron industry in general, it provided the most valuable production techniques and, one might say, the competition which led to the utilization of these improvements by the American iron industry. The British had developed and brought to fruition those innovations which were to permit the American iron industry to expand, especially the cast-iron blowing cylinders, the hot-blast, and, though valiant efforts had been made in the United States, the use of anthracite coal as a fuel.[68]

The successful attempts at smelting iron ore with anthracite coal having now been made known, the subject began to excite considerable attention. The Miners' Journal of Pottsville boastfully announced: "The most remote fears of success - the voice of the thousand croakers, and the sage speculations of those who could have done 'so much better themselves,' are all stilled in reference to the Anthracite Furnace in our Borough. Its success is triumphant beyond the most sanguine hopes of the most ardent well wishers."[69]

For the country this successful innovation was hailed as the

---

[68]Swank, Iron in All Ages, pp. 357-58. Swank reported that Crane tried unsuccessfully to obtain a patent in this country, but because of Geisenheimer's prior claim he was unable to register his technique. Later, in 1838, he purchased the patent right from Geisenheimer's estate and in 1839 Crane's agents made it known that they were prepared to issue licenses for the patent for a fee of 25 cents on each ton of pig iron produced.

In Wales, Crane was successful in extricating royalties from the Welsh ironmasters but had little success in doing the same in this country. Presumably Lyman, at Pottsville, was reported to have obtained such a license for the construction of that first successful anthracite furnace.

[69]Hazard, United States Register, I, 335.

opportunity which would enable the American economy to break away from British dominance. Nicholas Biddle delivered a speech at Pottsville in praise of Mr. Lyman's success, remarking on the changes that this discovery would make and speculating on the independence it would establish. He concluded his speech in part with these words:

> My hope, therefore, is, that when the country shall see what marvelous results will repay its industry in their new career, it will enter upon it with characteristic energy. If coal and iron have made Great Britain what she is; if this has given her the power of four hundred millions of men, and impelled the manufactories which made us, like the rest of the world, her debtors, why should not we, with at least equal advantages, make them the instruments of our own independence?[70]

Thus the country looked forward eagerly to the vast improvements that could be rendered by William Lyman's "discovery," for the time had come when iron rails, iron ships, and possibly even "footways of iron" would replace the old facilities. Governor Porter in his message to the Pennsylvania Legislature recognized the great boon to Pennsylvania industry which this process would affect. Like Biddle, he also visualized the independence it offered the country in its process of economic development.

> The coal and iron of Pennsylvania are more valuable as sources of wealth and employment, than mines of the precious metals are in countries where they are found. They furnish investments for large amounts of capital - give constant employment to numerous operatives; and under ordinary circumstances with prudent management, yield a certain and regular profit to all engaged in the business. They pay a large proportion of the tolls upon our public improvements, and constitute the most important share of freight for those engaged in transportation upon our canals and railroads, as well as

---

[70] Ibid., II, 230-31.

> for numerous vessels engaged in the coasting trade . . . . Should the experiment become generally successful, of which little doubt is entertained, it will save us the necessity of importing large amounts of iron for railroads, as well as other purposes, which Pennsylvania in that event would be able to furnish in abundance, not only for her own use, and that of her citizens, but for a large portion of her sister states . . . .[71]

The Lehigh Coal and Navigation Company directors calculated the success in revenue for their company which would be based upon the tolls from the transport of coal, ore, and limestone, as well as the hauling of pig iron. As they saw it, the sale of water power would net further revenue as would the sale of coal from their own coal lands. Other anticipated effects would be the attraction of new business firms along their waterway, of which they believed once settled they could never be withdrawn from the Lehigh.[72] The interested businessmen envisioned the long-run advantages in these terms. However, while the iron industry was to grow and prosper in the Lehigh Valley, technological change, just as it had opened up the area to development, was in time to bring about a decline in its output and a concentration of the iron industry on the coking-coal fields of western Pennsylvania.

Another observer noted that the blast furnaces had "continued to meet the most sanguine expectations of their owners, improving both in the quality and quantity of the metal . . . . Several puddling furnaces are in operation, giving great satisfaction to the proprietors." He commented further on the state of economic affairs being such that it would

---

[71]*Ibid.*, II, 47.

[72]*Ibid.*, II, 157-60.

take a return to normal in order to release all the capitalists who "are really unable or unwilling to look at any project, however brilliant or clear, . . ." and further advance the growth of the industry. He concluded his note with an indication of the optimism that prevailed for the industry.

> The subject of iron already occupies the attention of a very large portion of our citizens, and every day some new object to which it can be applied beneficially, or some new development is presented to their notice.[73]

By 1841 W. R. Johnson reported that in little more than three years the anthracite furnaces had "commanded the attention of many enterprising parties," and already eleven or twelve such furnaces had been constructed in Pennsylvania. Three or four more were already contemplated while four were in construction in New Jersey on the line of the Morris Canal.[74] With these developments a new iron era had commenced as the new technological methods were imitated by other entrepreneurs in the area of the anthracite coal deposits. Though the rate of adaptation was slow at first, more and more anthracite furnaces were to be built and by 1855 the output of the anthracite iron furnaces of the country exceeded the product of the charcoal iron furnaces. That was the same year in which The Thomas Iron Company was organized.

---

[73] Ibid., IV (Philadelphia, 1841), 207.

[74] Johnson, Notes on the Use of Anthracite, pp. 9-11.

CHAPTER III

EARLY MANUFACTURE OF IRON IN THE LEHIGH VALLEY, 1800-1840

Industrial Location and Technological Change

The selection of a manufacturing site generally requires the combining and balancing of various economic and geographic factors in order to obtain the least-cost combination of the factors of production. The manufacturer must have access to markets, raw materials, and sources of power, all of which may require the transport of commodities. Further, the manufacturer must obtain a supply of capital and labor to sustain and operate his plant, though these latter elements are generally more mobile than markets, raw materials, and power. Seldom does the entrepreneur find all the necessary components for production in close proximity in any region; therefore he seeks that site which permits the minimization of unit costs. In every instance the optimum economic location of the manufactory will depend upon the efficient combination of these factors, though the importance of each will vary among different industries, and one, rather than the others, may play the dominant role. Occasionally there are other physical or institutional elements which may be interposed that will determine the selection of the site, and then again some have ofttimes asserted that the location of a particular industrial undertaking is the result of historical accident. Because of this, it must be recognized that industries frequently have not been located in the optimum economic situation.

Down through the history of the iron industry new furnace sites have generally been selected with the intent to minimize costs of production; furnaces have not been located haphazardly, but their sites have been selected as "optimum" points of production. Historically, however, technological change has resulted in the establishment of new optimum industrial sites while the older sector of the industry continued operations in marginal or submarginal locations.

Early in the development of the United States iron industry the inadequate transport facilities precluded the location of iron furnaces in a particular area of concentration and, as a result, iron furnaces were scattered throughout the states. The sites selected within the various states were chosen because of their proximity to charcoal sources, iron ore, the necessary limestone flux, and markets.

Early in the nineteenth century the location pattern of iron production was not as readily identifiable as it is today. The business firms within the industry were small and were continuously faced with strong currents of change which tended to bring about adjustments in location. The charcoal iron industry continually faced the problem of the depletion of resources, especially the destruction of the oak and hickory wood so necessary for the production of charcoal. Changes in refining and smelting techniques necessitated further reorganization of the industry's locational pattern in order to adapt to new production techniques to meet the demands of a rapidly expanding economy and a continuously shifting population.

With the substitution of coal for charcoal in the smelting process and improvements in transport facilities, the dominant locational factor was to be, for many years, the location of coal resources. Though charcoal furnaces continued to operate in the marginal areas, every business depression eliminated more of the poorly located enterprises.[1] When further innovations in smelting and refining processes were made and changes in demand led to an increase in the consumption of steel, there were still further structural changes and the output of the industry was concentrated into a smaller area though production was greater than that previously obtained. Today, as further improvements in organization and technique have been developed, the locational pull of coal resources has lost its dominance and the industry is once again developing a new structural pattern.[2]

This process of innovation is both creative and destructive in nature. The very act of adapting new fuels in iron smelting, a creative act, resulted in a form of destruction, for the adoption of new processes destroyed the value of already existing real capital in the form of marginal charcoal furnaces that might have been used for many more years. Further, the creative response has resulted in a shift in location and, in some instances, this has spelled almost total extinction to some communities. The economic development of the Lehigh Valley was created

---

[1] Clark, _History of Manufactures in the United States_, I, 373 and 500. Taussig, _Tariff History of the United States_, p. 132. Convention of Iron Masters, _Documents Relating to the Manufacture of Iron in Pennsylvania_ (Philadelphia, 1850).

[2] Walter Isard, "Some Locational Factors in the Iron and Steel Industry Since the Early Nineteenth Century," _Journal of Political Economy_, Vol. 56 (1948), 203-17.

largely through the growth of the anthracite industry within the valley, but further technological advances, while not destroying the total economy of the valley, have had a decided deterring effect upon its rate of growth in the recent past. Many of the communities in the valley, former iron furnace towns, have languished with the disappearance of the anthracite blast furnace and the shift of the industry to new centers of concentration.

To explain this change, a change which includes the growth and decline of the Thomas Iron Company, it is necessary to study closely the region's physical resources and its economic development prior to the introduction of the anthracite iron furnace. An outgrowth of that investigation will be an attempt to indicate the most influential locational factors which were to recommend the Lehigh Valley as an advantageous furnace site to those eighteen businessmen that met in Easton in 1854 to organize that company. Further, an effort will be made to shed some light on the process of growth of that part of the iron industry concentrated in the Lehigh Valley.

The Lehigh Valley in 1800

West and northwest of the Piedmont, extending from the Hudson River to beyond the Potomac, lies a zone of parallel narrow ridges and valleys which are a distinctive physical feature of the landscape of Pennsylvania and Maryland. Among these ridges and valleys is the so-called Kittatiny Valley, bounded on the south by a chain of hills that reach from the Delaware to the Schuylkill. This chain of mountains, the South Mountains, presents a rather broken boundary throughout the entire length of the valley. At the north, however, the 165-mile valley is circumscribed by a very regular mountain wall called the Kittatiny or Blue Mountains. The breadth of the valley is about 15 or 20 miles, and throughout its whole distance it presents surface features of a generally undulating character approximating a somewhat level plain with an occasional series of low hills. The greatest extremes of a mountainous nature are found at its northern boundary near the foot of the Kittatiny Mountains.[3]

The northern half of this valley is made up of argillaceous slate or shale while the southern portion is underlain with a limestone formation. In the northeast-southwest ridges of the northern boundary are found the great anthracite coal beds of Pennsylvania created by the geologic folding that has created the peculiar physical features of that part of the state. Running transverse to the ridges are several rivers that have cut narrow gaps through the mountains. One of the rivers is the Lehigh, on which this study is concentrated.

The Lehigh River starts as a mountain stream near Wilkes-Barre and rushes in a southerly direction toward the ocean. In its upper reaches it passes down between high wooded or sometimes barren mountain walls on either side and is quite often met are various junctures by creeks or streams which serve to increase its volume of water. As it breaks out of this rugged terrain and flows into the southern portion of the Kittatiny Valley, it meanders and glides past rolling hills where beautiful farms

---

[3]Henry D. Rogers, Geology of Pennsylvania (Philadelphia, 1858), p. 237. The southern boundary, the South Mountain range, extends beyond the Schuylkill River to the wouthwest in a broken pattern from York, Pennsylvania, to Dills, Maryland.

have been built upon the rich limestone soil of the region. At Allentown, faced by the South Mountain range, the river abruptly changes its course and thrusts out in a northeasterly direction for 18 of its 83 miles until if flows past Easton and empties into the Delaware.

The extreme upper limit to the region is that point or settlement which was to be called Mauch Chunk (now Jim Thorpe), the area in which the first Lehigh Valley anthracite coal was discovered. The lower end of the valley lies at Easton and Phillipsburg, New Jersey, which is directly opposite the mouth of the Lehigh. The boundaries on either side of the valley are much less substantial or definite but generally consist of that area lying within the boundaries of Lehigh, Carbon, and Northampton counties, or what was, until 1812, a major portion of "old" Northampton County. Here, within this area, nature had stored minerals which were to provide the basic raw materials so necessary for iron production. Immediately beyong Mauch Chunk there was to be practically no iron production in the vicinity of the Lehigh, due, in the main, to inadequate supplies of iron ores, a burdensome transportation problem, and the lack of a neighboring market of any proportion. Even those iron manufacturers who had built their works next to the coal mines at Mauch Chunk discovered that more than a deposit of coal was essential for the profitable production of iron.

To the south, in the lower portion of the Lehigh Valley, great deposits of limestone had been formed and exposed by natural phenomena and were easily exploitable for local consumption. In close juxtaposition to this valuable fluxing material were deposits of iron ore located along the northern slopes of South Mountain and in a number of the smaller valleys among the rolling hills of the larger Lehigh Valley. These deposits were to be found in a belt running from a point north of Allentown, in a crescent formation of either side of the river, almost to Easton.[4]

The ore deposits were of two types; one was a brown limonite which was called brown hematite by the local miners, and the other a magnetite ore, similar to that found along the same mountain range in northwestern New Jersey. The brown hematite was found in several different forms, and the characteristics of these deposits led to distinct masses of the ores from the different deposits, such as "bombshell" or "pot" ore and "wash" or "Pipe" ore. All of these deposits were irregular in extent; some occupied pockets of 100 feet or more in diameter while others followed certain veins of rock strata. The mountain ores were generally covered with a float rock from the higher ground and often required shaft mining while others were close enough to the surface to permit open-cut mining. In some areas the valley ores were concealed by heavy glacial deposits, but many other deposits of such ore were found within a few feet of the surface. The magnetite ores of the valley were of little economic consequence because of their sparsity, though they were mined intermittently throughout the nineteenth century. The more abundant supply of such ore in New Jersey served as the major source of such raw material for the

---

[4]*Ibid*., pp. 263-66. See also Benjamin L. Miller, *Topographic and Geologic Atlas of Pennsylvania*; *Allentown Quadrangle* (Harrisburg, 1924), pp. 33-35. This work will hereafter be cites as Miller, *Allentown Quadrangle*.

iron furnaces of the Lehigh Valley.[5]

Thus, in that part of the Lehigh Valley between Mauch Chunk and Easton, a distance of 83 miles, and reaching out on either side of the river for 15 or 20 miles, were to be found a diffuse and diversified group of resources. At the north was an almost inexhaustible supply of coal for industrial purposes while brown hematite deposits were scattered over a wide area in conjunction with valuable supplies of limestone for fluxing purposes or the manufacture of hydraulic cement. Also there were slate and zinc deposits, in addition to rich farm lands, as well as timber that could be turned into charcoal or lumber. Admidst it all ran the Lehigh River which, if properly controlled, could provide a means of transportation. At the turn of the century, however, the Lehigh Valley was nurturing only a small number of backwoods agricultural communities while little had been done to exploit the valuable mineral deposits.

Though anthracite coal had been discovered at Mauch Chunk as early as 1791, little was known about its use; thus, a market did not exist for it. In 1803, when the first load of such coal was shipped to Philadelphia, it could not be made to burn properly and was thrown away as useless for any purpose except "gravel footwalks."[6]

As for the other minerals that were present in the valley, they were still hidden from man and their economic value unrecognized. Not until 1836 was any systematic study of the mineral resources of

---

[5]Miller, Allentown Quadrangle, pp. 68-69.

[6]Swank, Iron Making and Coal Mining in Pennsylvania, pp. 118-19.

Pennsylvania undertaken and then it was not public information until 1858, when Rogers" Geology of Pennsylvania was published. However, before that time uses had been found for these minerals and a quest for their location was made throughout the valley.

In 1800 the Lehigh Valley was a sparsely settled country, and, though the area was rich in farm lands and potential timber supplies, little emphasis had been placed on any expansion of production of exportable surpluses. The roads were few and difficult to travel; the trip from Easton to Philadelphia required the better part of two days. The Delaware River was used in flood seasons or periods of high water for the shipment of a few locally produced commodities and sometimes a few hardy and adventurous passengers. Such a trip down the river required the services and skills of a vigorous group of riverboat men to wield the long oars and iron-shod poles which guided the loaded vessels through the dangerous rapids along the way to the commercial metropolis of Philadelphia.[7] Because of these obstacles, little economic specialization occurred, and most of the communities in the area were of a self-sufficing nature.

The Lehigh River seems to have been of much less use as a means of transport than the Delaware, although movements to improve it as a channel of communication commenced very early. The river was declared a public highway in 1771, and attempts were made, through private means, to improve it. When the legislature appropriated funds for such improvements

---

[7]Henry, History of the Lehigh Valley, p. 153.

in 1791, the funds were found inadequate and provided little in the way of success. Shortly after the discovery of coal, certain interested groups commenced to make further improvements, but with as little cuscess as in the previous attempts. It was only after 1800 that such effort was finally to attain fruition.[8] Until success prevailed in this venture, travel throughout the interior of the valley continued over the Indian trails or rough roads by means of foot, horse, wagon, or stage. At that time the trip from Bethlehem, like the trip from Easton to Philadelphia, consumed two days, although a mail stage commenced operations from that community with a proposal to "run the stage through in a day." [9]

The most important and heavily populated community in the valley at this time was Easton, which consisted of fourteen hundred souls, two hundred dwelling houses of stone or frame construction, and a few log cabins.[10] Because of its advantageous location at the confluence of the Delaware and Lehigh rivers, it served as a general market area, drawing produce of every kind from the interior. Further, it served as the county seat where the public offices were located and local justice dispensed.

Within the confines of the borough were located four gristmills, four sawmills, one oil mill, two bark mills, three tanneries, and one

---

[8]Jones, The Economic History of the Anthracite-Tidewater Canals, p. 4.

[9]Henry, History of the Lehigh Valley, p. 240.

[10]Ibid., p. 117.

iron forge, but not a single iron furnace.[11] Out of these mills and workshops moved produce for local consumption, or raw materials to be made into consumable commodities by local craftsmen.

Traveling a distance of 12 miles west on the Lehigh, one came upon the settlement of Bethlehem, originally a communal settlement, which was by its political nature and location a more isolated community than Easton. But like Easton, the six hundred residents of the community had built within the confines of their village a variety of manufactories. In this borough were to be found a flour mill, a sawmill, an oil mill, a tannery, a fulling mill, and a dyeing manufactory as well as a pottery, all of which had originally been organized by the Moravian Brethren.[12]

Northamptontown (Allentown), a few miles further up the Lehigh, was in 1800 a community of very little importance containing but ninety dwellings with little in the way of manufactories. Though located at the juncture of the Lehigh River and Jordan Creek, amidst a rich agricultural area, it still had not developed a business community or market center of importance. This community had a single gristmill and a few skilled craftsmen who performed their production in their household or at their

---

[11] _Ibid._, p. 118 A few miles below Easton, on the Delaware River, were located two iron furnaces and two forges at Durham. These works, which were originally commenced in 1727, probably provided much of the necessary iron for the area, though most of the product from these furnaces was shipped to Philadelphia. See Swank, _Iron Making and Coal Mining in Pennsylvania_, p. 16.

[12] _Ibid._, p. 223.

customer's home.[13]

Northamptontown marked the extent of development of the Lehigh Valley up to 1800, for beyond this point were little more than isolated farms and forest regions. Prior to the Revolution several settlements had been established in the upper reaches of the Lehigh; these outposts of civilization were attacked by Indians and completely destroyed. After the Revolution more communities were established in the upper reaches of the river, but these, like the earlier attempts, failed. Not until 1803 or 1804 were communities of any durability built in those more inaccessible regions, although the discovery of coal at Summit Hill did entice a few speculative Philadelphia and Easton citizens to take up large tracts of land in the area.[14] However, even with the commencement of land speculation in the area, it was to remain for some years "a perfect wilderness covered with forest trees and underbrush."[15] Nowhere is there record of a single charcoal blast furnace being built in the area prior to 1800, though all of the necessary raw materials for the prosecution of such works existed in abundance.

---

[13]Mathews and Hungerford, Lehigh and Carbon Counties, pp. 124-26. Henry, History of the Lehigh Valley, pp. 270-77.

[14]Ibid., p. 593. It is recorded that a hunter, Philip Ginter by name, accidently discovered anthracite coal at Summit Hill in 1791. He advised a Jacob Weiss of his discovery and Weiss, with other Easton and Philadelphia citizens, formed the Lehigh Coal Mine Company which mined and shipped some of this hard coal to Philadelphia. Coal shipped into that city from Richmond and Liverpool was much less expensive and rendered their venture unprofitable. Because of this condition, the Lehigh discovery failed to arouse much interest. See Jones, The Economic History of the Anthracite-Tidewater Canals, p. 2.

[15]Henry, History of the Lehigh Valley, p. 335.

The First Blast Furnace in the Lehigh Valley

In 1793 the Lehigh Coal Mine Company, armed with warrants from the Commonwealth for rights to 10,000 acres of land and a claim to Ginter's coal discovery recently purchased from Jacob Weiss, proceeded to open up mines in the Summit Hill area and build a road from the mine to the river. Stockholders of the company had appropriated 10 pounds ($26.67) for this venture, hardly enough, even in that day, to succeed at such a heavy undertaking. After several unsuccessful attempts to move the coal to market over an inadequate roadway and down the Lehigh, which was unnavigable in its unimproved state because of rapids and an insufficient flow of water during the dry season, the company permitted its property to remain idle for a number of years when further contributions for improvements were not forthcoming from the shareholders.[16]

Then, in 1807 the mining company leased a portion of its land to the firm of Rowland and Butland for twenty-one years. This company was given the privilege of mining iron ore and coal for the production of iron. No charge was made for three prerogatives, the grant being made with the hope that any success achieved would bring to notice the potential of these coal fields. The project was an abortive venture and was soon abandoned.[17]

From that date to 1813 nothing more was done to exploit these coal lands or the potential transport value of the Lehigh River. Such

---

[16] Hazard, United States Register, III, 81.

[17] *Ibid*.

ventures were not carried out successfully until more daring and resourceful speculators were to come upon the scene. Meanwhile, the restrictions on the free flow of trade, brought about by the Embargo and Non-Intercourse acts, and the consequential drop in iron imports from England provided a propitious opportunity for a few enterprising souls to commence the production of iron in the Lehigh Valley. In 1808 a William Henry built a forge in Northampton County from which he drew his first bar of refined iron in 1809.[18] During that same year David Heimbach and four partners, three other ironmasters and a local physician, built Hampton furnace near Shimersville, in what was then Northampton County.[19] But the number of furnaces and forges in the valley did not increase with great rapidity, for further growth is only recorded in 1820 when the same David Heimbach, with his son who had been trained at Hampton furnace, built Clarissa forge on Aquashicola Creek, a tributary of the Lehigh. The proximity of the Lehigh Valley to Philadelphia and the rising competition from foreign imports of iron that moved through that port in increasing quantities probably served, in part, to obstruct further ventures into the field.

How important was this competition as a factor of constraint is difficult to ascertain, for other forces hindered the growth of the industry at this time. Among the other limitations was a shortage of labor, especially skilled furnace men and experienced ironmasters, as

---

[18] Henry, History of the Lehigh Valley, p. 165.

[19] Gemmell, "Manuscripts Shed New Light on Lehigh County's First Furnace," pp. 49-50.

well as a limited supply of capital and a burdensome transportation problem which still had to be solved. In addition to these restraints, the financial crisis of 1818-20, with a resulting drop in iron prices, probably deterred any venturing into the field by the uninitiated.

Then, between 1824 and 1828, the increasing duties on iron imports, improved financial conditions, and the development of a more efficient transportation facility all seemed to nurture the growth of iron production in the Lehigh Valley, for in that time period four additional charcoal furnaces and two more forges were constructed. All of these works were built on tributaries of the Lehigh River, where cheap water power was available for the operation of the blowing equipment, while iron ore and wood for charcoal were near at hand.[20] Also nearby were a number of common blacksmith's works turning out the indispensable iron work for the local farmers and mills in the area. By 1818 some of these blacksmith's fires were being fueled with anthracite coal, and in 1826 an abortive

---

[20]Swank, Iron in All Ages, pp. 191-92. The additional charcoal furnaces were called Catherine Furnace, New Hampton, Lehigh, and Clarissa furnaces. All of the furnaces were located in rather isolated areas, none being built in the larger communities of the valley. But, unlike the earlier works, they were located closer to the Lehigh River in order to use the newly constructed canal for shipping purposes.

The reason for locating on the smaller tributary creeks rather than on the Lehigh River itself was probably due to the following circumstances. First, the construction of a larger dam on the Lehigh may have been financially prohibitive because of the relatively heavy capital requirements for the furnace itself. Secondly, Josiah White and Erskine Hazard had obtained, in 1818, privileges to all water rights of the river. Thus the construction of any dam on the river would have required some agreement with the Lehigh Coal and Navigation Company and probably the payment of a rental for the use of water power.

attempt was made to use anthracite coal in smelting iron.[21]

For the purpose of later comparison and evaluation of the technological and economic advance made when the anthracite blast furnace was introduced, it may be helpful to pause here and survey the organization and production of David Heimbach's Hampton furnace.

This furnace, the first charcoal furnace built in the Lehigh Valley, was constructed some distance from the banks of the Lehigh River on Perkiomen Creek. There, Heimbach and his four partners built or had constructed two dams and a raceway which served to provide the necessary water power for the operation of the cold-blast. The massive stone furnace, built in the shape of a truncated pyramid around a hollow sandstone-lined chamber, was situated against a hillside to facilitate the charging of raw materials. The furnace was about 32 feet high, with a 9-foot bosh and one tuyere for the blast.[22] Using the local brown hematite ore, this furnace turned out two qualities of iron, a "close gray" iron and a "white" iron which was sold to a nearby forge or shipped to market in Philadelphia.[23]

---

[21]Henry, History of the Lehigh Valley, p. 346.

[22]The tuyeres are the pipes through which the blast entered the furnace. In the early furnaces there was generally only one tuyere but as furnace techniques and design were modified the number of tuyeres was increased. See Boylston, An Introduction to the Metallurgy of Iron and Steel, p. 81.

[23]Gemmell, "Manuscripts Shed New Light on Lehigh County's First Furnace," p. 53.

ILLUSTRATION 1

SECTIONAL VIEW OF COLD BLAST CHARCOAL FURNACE, 1800's

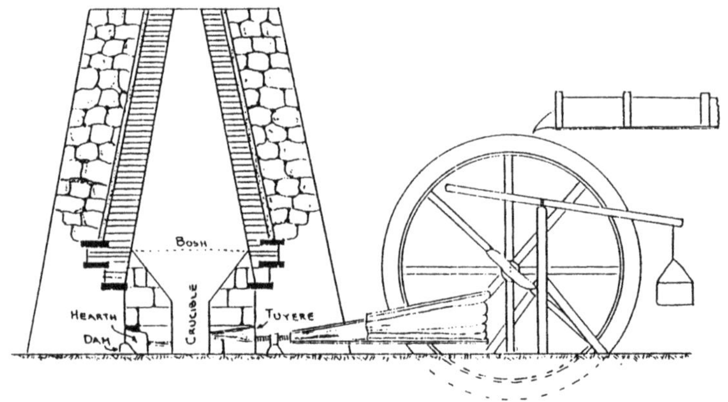

Typical sectional view of a cold blast charcoal furnace in early part of the nineteenth century [Hampton Furnace]

Source: R. Peters, Jr., _Two Centuries of Iron Smelting in Pennsylvania_ (Philadelphia, 1921), p. 70.

In 1810 the output of this furnace was reported to be 300 tons.[24] The season for such production was generally eight to twelve weeks in length with the blasts commencing late in the spring or early summer and continuing into the fall, if freezing conditions did not interfere with the water power or the mining and transportation of ores and other necessary materials.

The operation of the furnace required the services of a number of skilled workers in addition to the ironmaster or manager. Sometimes it called for the aid of various part-time employees. The regular work force generally consisted of the manager and general clerk for administrative work, a skilled founder or furnace keeper, a gutterman, and blacksmith, all with helpers or apprentices. At the top of the furnace was the furnace filler, who distributed the alternating charges of ore, charcoal, and limestone. In addition, there were ore raisers (miners), woodcutters, coalers (charcoal burners), and teamsters.

The more highly skilled work of founding required the hiring of more than one such specialist, for the furnace was operated on a twenty-four-hour basis with a tap made several times a day. In addition to this regular work force, there were part-time or day laborers employed, generally itinerants, neighboring repairmen, or farmers from nearby who wished to earn a few dollars. These workers carried out the tasks that

---

[24]Tench Coxe, _A Statement of the Arts and Manufactures of the United States of America; for the Year 1810_ (Philadelphia, 1814),Tabular Statements, Table 48, pertaining to "State of Pennsylvania Manufactures." This work will hereafter be cited as Coxe, _Arts and Manufactures of the United States_.

required less skill, such as carpentry work, quarrying limestone, mason work or general hauling as well as coaling or charcoal burning.[25]

The coaling or charcoal burning required twenty-four-hour vigilance, for if the hearth broke out in flame the end product would be ashes, not charcoal. The burning was done in circular clearings or "hearths" in the surrounding hills. Sometimes land was leased to obtain the wood, but quite often the wood was purchased by the cord. The price for oak and hickory, while it lasted, was low; the real cost of the charcoal was the labor time required for cutting, burning, and hauling. The inability to provide a continuous supply of this valuable fuel ofttimes required shutting down the furnace to permit the furnace hands to help the cutters and burners stock more charcoal before the furnace was put in blast once again. Each ton of iron produced required about 2 loads of charcoal, or around 300 bushels, to smelt 2 tons of iron ore.[26]

The iron ore for the furnace was obtained within a few miles of the works, the mining of which required the services of a number of ore raisers who were paid on a piece-work basis if day labor, or monthly if a regular employee. The hauling of ore to the furnace was an arduous task becasuse of the poor roads, and called for almost full-time use of the furnace teams and provided part-time occupation for many of the local farm teams.

In addition to the furnace land, the purchase or lease of ore and

---

[25]Gemmell, "Manuscripts Shed New Light On Lehigh County's First Furnace," pp. 54-55.

[26]*Ibid*., p. 59

woodlands became a necessity. This particular ironmaster, David Heimbach, who had purchased his partners' shares by 1811, held 224 acres of land to which he added additional parcels to obtain new sources of raw materials. With the furnace and buildings, which included a sturdy charcoal storage house, tenement houses, a store, and the ironmaster's home, the property was valued at $10,500 in 1810[27] The original capital requirements and the nature of the risk involved in the venture had originally necessitated the use of a partnership organization, but within two years Heimbach had accumulated enough capital to buy out the other interests for a price of 2,293 pounds, 18 shillings, and 3 pence, or about $6,079.10.[28]

The product of the furnace in 1820 was valued at $20,000 and had required 1,500 tons of ore and 1,000 loads of charcoal at a cost of $16,125. At that time there were only five full-time employees working at the furnace owing to a decline in cash sales and a drop in prices for pig iron.[29]

However, despite the price decline, the ironmaster found resources enough to complete the building of a forge on Aquashicola Creek, construction of which had commenced in the more prosperous year of 1817. (This accumulation of capital equipment would all seem to indicate that Hampton furnace had been a profitable venture.) Later, when more prosperous

---

[27]Coxe, Arts and Manufactures of the United States, Table 48.

[28]Gemmell, "Manuscripts Shed New Light on Lehigh County's First Furnace," p. 50. The price was based upon an exchange rate of $2.65 for the pound sterling.

[29]Tench Coxe, Digest of the Accounts of Manufacturing Establishments in the United States (Washington, 1823), n.p.

conditions set in once again, he built, with a younger son, another furnace and forge in the same vicinity as the one mentioned above.

In ten years this ironmaster, having achieved a measure of success, had trained his two sons to manage similar works and had built, with his own capital, two more charcoal furnaces and forges. His success, for that day, was probably very great, and his ability to adapt the old and proven techniques of production served him well.

David Heimbach did not try to experiment with the anthracite coal which was so abundant in the area and was already being used in rolling mills and blacksmiths' shops. He and others like him who operated charcoal furnaces were interested only in maintaining the value of their existing capital and the tariff seemed to have provided adequate economic security. It was to be businessmen outside the field of charcoal iron smelting who were to develop and finance the successful innovations which would destroy the value of the local charcoal ironmasters' furnaces and spell the extinction of the isolated communities built up around their furnaces. Though Hampton Furnace was to continue to operate for several years after 1832, it was never as prosperous as it had been when in the hands of David Heimbach. Shortly, the introduction of the hot-blast in this country was to result in the disappearance of charcoal furnaces from the Lehigh Valley scene.

Pennsylvania's Economic Development and Government Policy

Prior to 1860 the national government intervened but little in the economic affairs of the nation though there were indirect effects on economic development through the government's fiscal policies. Doubtless the tariff policy had some influence upon economic growth; its influence has already been noted in the growth of the number of charcoal furnaces in the Lehigh Valley between 1824 and 1833. At best this influence was of a circuitous nature, there being no effort made to provide direct aid to industry. Also, as has been pointed out by Taussig, the tariff policy fostered by the iron interests probably delayed the introduction of innovations in iron smelting.[30]

While the federal government maintained a minimum of responsibility in this field, a policy which seems to have hinged upon the nature of our early American federalism, the state governments did not hesitate to promote commercial and industrial development within their sphere of influeence.

Pennsylvania's legislature, one of the more agressive participants in the struggle to attain economic expansion, undertook this task through a rather indulgent charter policy, a public works program, the joint ownership of mixed corporations, and the regulation of economic activity.[31] However, aid to manufacturing industries, the iron industry included, unlike aid to other ventures having more of a public utility nature, was indirect rather than direct.[32] The policy of developing

---

[30]Taussig, Tariff History of the United States, p. 59

[31]Louis Hartz, Economic Policy and Democratic Thought: Pennsylvania, 1776-1860 (Cambridge, Massachusetts, 1948). This work will hereafter be cited as Hartz, Economic Policy.

[32]Ibid., p. 56. The author records several instances of direct aid to firms processing iron. These grants were made on the grounds that "works of public importance deserve public encouragement." That type of aid was not a general part of the government's program.

turnpikes, canals, and railroads with government assistance or public works projects provided, in a way, a stimulus to iron production by facilitating the reduction of transportation costs and consequently domestic iron prices. The charter policy, in many individual instances, was most liberal and, as shall be pointed out, had some influence on the establishment of anthracite iron works in the Lehigh Valley.

Though the relationship may seem rather tenuous, the influence of state policy in the realm of iron production in the Lehigh Valley commenced with a legislative act of 1818 which gave Josiah White, Erskine Hazard, and George F. A. Hauto power to establish navigation on the Lehigh River.[33] When the act was passed, many of the members of the legislature disparaged the schemes for development by characterizing them as "impracticable" and "chimerical." These enterprisers were optimistic men, however, and they continued to nurture the notion that their "plan for the cheap improvement of river navigation . . . would serve as a model for many other streams in the State."[34]

The act chartering the company provided these men and other

---

[33]Two of these men, White and Hazard, were most influential in attracting other entrepreneurs into the Lehigh Valley. Any history of the region would be remiss if no mention of their efforts was included.

[34]Hazard, <u>United States Register</u>, III, 81. Previous attempts had been made to take Lehigh coal to market. In 1814, 24 tons were conveyed from Mauch Chunk to Philadelphia at a cost of $14 a ton, and nothwithstanding this cost there was a continuing demand for it through 1815. When peace was restored, coal from Liverpool and Richmond came into the port in greater abundance and the hard kindling anthracite fell to a price far below the cost of the shipment. At this juncture the Lehigh coal trade was abandoned until 1820. See William O. Niles, ed., <u>National Register</u>, Vol 56 (1839), 131; Henry, <u>History of the Lehigh Valley</u>, pp. 375-82.

investors in the company the sole jurisdiction of the Lehigh River for a distance of 83 miles, with mining privileges as well as navigation rights.[35] White and the others had already obtained a twenty-year lease from the old Lehigh Coal Mining Company on all its coal lands, the annual rental fee for the land to be one ear of corn. In both instances the passage of a charter which unified both mining and navigation privileges and the low value placed on the coal lands seem to indicate that many people were convinced that the scheme was fated for eventual failure. Moreover, little thought could have been given to any evaluation of the potential economic power that would accrue to that company if the plans were carried out successfully; the mining and navigation privileges granted in the charter permitted the unification of potentially strong mining interests with a major transportation facility.[36] But that was for the future.

After surveying the mine road and the river route, White, Hazard, and Hauto organized the Lehigh Navigation Company and the Lehigh Coal Company. The former company was to develop the navigation on the river while the latter was to open the mine and build a road to the river. Plans were also made to build flat-bottomed arks, for use on the waterway,

---

[35]Hartz, Economic Policy, p. 59. Pennsylvania Laws (1817-18), pp. 197-205.

[36]Ibid., p. 58. According to Hartz, mining privileges were never granted when the sole objective was mining. The legislature preferred to offer mining rights as an inducement to companies in order to have them undertake what were considered objects of greater public interest.

from timber cut on lands already purchased for that purpose.[37]

Two separate and unincorporated companies were formed because of the diversity of opinion on the value of the two projects. Some investors sensed sucess in the navigation project but felt that there was little real value to the scheme of exploiting the coal lands. Many thought, at that time, that a market would never "be found for it [coal] among a population accustomed wholly to the use of wood."[38]

The first attempt by White and Hazard to develop the navigation on the Lehigh was upset by a severe summer drought which lowered the water level to an ineffective depth. With little hesitation they plunged ahead and constructed a system of artificial freshets which would carry the arks downstream in their flow. The next spring ice floes demolished some of the sluice freshets. These misfortunes called for more funds to rebuild the damaged facilities and also led to the merger of the two companies into the unincorporated Lehigh Coal and Navigation Company.[39] Up to that time the venture had resulted in the shipping of but 365 tons of coal to market.

Further improvements on the canal were required in 1821, and new funds for this purpose were sought but were found difficult to acquire. Reasons for the timidity prevailing among the stockholders and potential investors probably proceeded from the poor business conditions that

---

[37]Hazard, _United States Register_, III, 81-82.

[38]_Ibid._, p. 82.

[39]_Ibid._, pp. 82-83.

existed. It was reported that many people doubted that a large market for coal would ever be attained while others showed an evident lack of interest because of an uneasiness about the personal liability of the shareholder in such a large and expanding organization.

In order to reduce this hesitation and skepticism, White and Hazard made application to the legislature of the state for a charter of incorporation. When the charter was granted, the company was able to increase its capital stock. That same year the company's annual sale of coal had increased to 2,240 tons or 1,167 tons more than had been shipped to Philadelphia during the previous year.[40]

By 1825 the demand for coal had increased to a point where 38,393 tons were shipped to Philadelphia via the Lehigh. But that same year a new source of competition appeared with the shipment of coal to market via the Schuylkill slack-water canal.

Shortly thereafter plans were made to build a slack-water system on the Lehigh and to extend similar improvements down the Delaware. This program called for legislative authorization, but the legislature had other plans for the Delaware. The state had decided to build its own canal down the Delaware, in part, an effort to bring to a halt the expansion of the Lehigh Coal and navigation Company. Though not permitted to build on the Delaware, the Navigation Company was permitted to continue its improvements on the Lehigh.

Disappointed but not discouraged by the state policy, the board of

---

[40] Ibid., p. 83. The authorized capital stock of the corporation was $1,000,000.

managers proceeded to make their own improvements while commencing new ventures in other fields of engineering and economic development. In 1826, under the advice of Josiah White, the board passed a resolution to build a blast furnace in which anthracite coal would be used as fuel. Realizing the immense opportunity for the company in increased sales of coal if they succeeded, the furnace was constructed and experiments carried out. The venture proved unsuccessful; the project was dropped and later the furnace was leased to a local ironmaster who immediately reverted to the use of charcoal.

Meanwhile, faced with a burdensome operating expense arising from road repairs on the mine road, the board of managers looked about for a solution to their problem. The same year that they experimented with the use of anthracite coal in iron smelting they decided to build a gravity railroad between the mine and the river. By 1827 the company completed and was operating what is supposed to have been the first "railroad" in Pennsylvania which connected its Summit Hill mines with the canal at Mauch Chunk. Four years later it constructed a second such railroad in the same area.

While experimenting with iron and building railroads, the managers of the company were also busy carrying out the development of new communities on the banks of the canal and improving the canal itself. The Town of Mauch Chunk was built as the first company town, and upon completion of the canal the development of South Easton as an industrial community was commenced. The annual report of 1831 also indicated a further interest in the possibility of reviving the iron industry along the route of the Morris Canal with the use of Lehigh coal in the furnaces and forges.[41]

Earlier, and not without financial and political difficulties, the slack-water system between Easton and Mauch Chunk had been completed. However, the state program on the Delaware, delayed by engineering problems, was not completed and fully navigable until nearly three years later, a circumstance that reduced the potential traffic that could have been handled by the rebuilt Lehigh system.[42]

The successful completion of the Navigation Company's improvements had required the sale of the remainder of the company's authorized capital stock and also necessitated a further request to the legislature for authorization to increase the shares of stock of the corporation. The public and the legislature were, by that time, fully cognizant of the economic implications of the economic power that had been placed in the hands of the company in 1818 and they hesitated before granting further powers. Josiah White's toll and land policy had deterred individual miners from entering the Lehigh Valley region and had stirred up a great antipathy to the corporate form of business venture.[43]

---

[41] _Report of the Board of Managers of the Lehigh Coal and Navigation Company_, 1831, p. 8. These reports will hereafter be cited as _Rep. Bd. Mgrs. LCNC_.

[42] Hazard, _United States Register_, III, 85.

[43] Hartz, _Economic Policy_, p. 59. See also Jules I. Goben, _The Anthracite Railroads; A Study in American Railroad Enterprise_ (New York, 1927), pp. 20 ff.; Eliot Jones, _The Anthracite Coal Combination in the United States_ (Cambridge, Massachusetts, 1914), pp. 10-21; Jones, _The Economic History of the Anthracite-Tidewater Canals_, pp. 19-20.

The following debate over the Lehigh Company's request led to a heated argument about the corporate type of business organization, the belief being that the corporate enterprise "led inevitably to monoply and high prices," fears expressed much earlier by Adam Smith. The newspapers, meanwhile, showed no hesitation in developing the theme and, with the advantage of hindsight, picked up the attack, not only on the Lehigh Coal and Navigation Company but also on the corporate form of business venture in general emphasizing the dangers of absentee ownership. Meanwhile, local committees were formed to protest the evils of corporations and at the same time warmly applauded the virtues of the individual proprietors.

A Pennsylvania Senate committee which investigated the local situation reported that only individual enterprise could attain the most economical division of mining operations for "there were four distinct functions involved, land ownership, mining, transportation, and sales"; a single company, the committee reported, could not combine the four functions effectively. From this report there were similar arguments developed against forges, blast furnaces, and rolling mills being organized under a corporate charter.[44]

The Lehigh Company did not hesitate to counterattack. First, its spokesmen pointed out that the high prices were not the result of any monopoly power on its part. Instead, the board of managers declared, the failure of the state to carry out the rapid completion of the Delaware

---

[44]<u>Ibid</u>., pp. 58-60.

Canal had maintained a burdensome operating cost on anyone interested in mining in the Lehigh region; this situation "turned the attention of persons desirous of entering into the coal business to the Schuylkill coal region . . . ."[45] Further, they argued, the expansion of the coal trade was going to require even more corporations, for it would be increasingly difficult for individual producers to survive in mining and any restriction on corporate growth would consequently retard expansion of the coal trade.[46]

The temper of the times was such that, unless certain of the original privileges were given up by the company, the legislature would be forced to hold back any further grants of privileges. Though the legislature conceded that the company was within its rights, a recommendation was made that the state purchase the canal. The board of managers of the canal company refused to surrender the company's privileges in order to attain the right to issue more capital stock and, consequently, was forced to resort to borrowing the necessary funds it had hoped to obtain through further stock sales.[47]

The increase in the public revulsion to the corporate form of enterprise soon led to a reduction in the number of individual charters issued by the Pennsylvania Legislature, but with the development of the speculative period of the 1830's the stigma was overlooked and the number

---

[45] Hazard, United States Rgister, III, 85.

[46] Hartz, Economic Policy, p. 61.

[47] Jones, The Economic History of the Anthracite-Tidewater Canals, p. 21.

of special charters granted was gradually increased. Only in the 1850's, however, did the business world of Pennsylvania make a much more extensive use of the corporate form of business.[48]

Now more aware of the economic implications involved in granting corporate charters, but anxious to further the economic development of the state, the legislature passed, in 1836, "An Act - To encourage the manufacture of Iron with Coke or Mineral Coal . . . ."[49] This act permitted the incorporation of companies organized for the purpose of making iron with mineral fuel without special legislative action. Upon meeting the proper requirements, the governor could issue the charter. The requirements included the necessity of an investment of $100,000, a stipulation which must have deterred some enterprising souls. Further, no more than $500,000 in $50 shares of stock could be issued, and the life of the corporation was limited to twenty-five years. During that time the corporation's sole purpose was to be the manufacture and sale of iron. The company could not own mines or transportation facilities, nor could it hold more than 2,000 acres of land.[50] The law was certainly not lenient and because charters of a more indulgent and flexible nature might be obtained through direct negotiation with the legislature, few

---

[48]William Miller, "Note on the History of Business Corporations in Pennsylvania, 1800-1860," _Quarterly Journal of Economics_, LV (1940-41), 155.

[49]_Pennsylvania Laws_ (1835-36), pp. 799-807.

[50]_Ibid._, p. 801.

charters were issued under it.[51]

Thus it is apparent that state aid to industrial development was rather liberal in the field of public utilities, but played little part in the establishment of iron manufacturing. The greatest influence in this direction came from businessmen who were more directly attracted by the successful development of any such ventures.

For example, while maintaining a monopoly over the major route of transportation in the valley, mainly as a result of the lack of interest on the part of others that might have constructed a railroad,[52] the managers of the Lehigh Coal and Navigation Company continually sought to improve their economic position. Anxiously they made efforts to develop new industrial opportunities which would supplement the assets controlled by the firm, coal mines, water power, and transportation facilities. Certainly in the case of the establishment of iron manufactures in the region, the members of the board of managers were prime movers.

---

[51]Hartz, Economic Policy, p. 40. The author writes, "There is ample evidence to indicate that industrial capitalists themselves preferred a policy of special legislative grants."

[52]Bogen, The Anthracite Railroads; A Study in American Railroad Enterprise, p. 108. Anthony Brzyski, "The Lehigh Canal and its Effect on the Development of the Region Through Which It Passed, 1815-1879," unpublished doctoral dissertation, New York University, 1957, pp. 594 ff.

Bogen emphasized that the canal company, through its monopolistic control over the coal trade of the valley, served to hold up railroad building between Mauch Chunk and Easton for twenty years. Brzyski, on the other hand, indicates that very little interest in building a railroad in the valley existed until 1846. At that time there was still some hesitancy because adequate funds for construction did not come forth very quickly. Not until Asa Packer took over the stock of the Delaware, Lehigh, Schuylkill, and Susquehanna Railroad in 1852 was an effective construction program evolved.

TABLE 2

COAL, IRON ORE, AND IRON SHIPMENTS
ON THE LEHIGH CANAL, 1833-40
(In tons)

Year	Coal	Iron Ore	Iron
1833	122,928	1,047	-
1834	106,518	1,378	-
1835	131,250	1,490	-
1836	148,211	2,134	1,197
1837	223,902	4,487	1,237
1838	214,211	6,258	2,203
1839	221,850	8,657	6,638
1840	225,318	7,075	4,395

Source: Report(s) of the Board of Managers of the Lehigh Coal and Navigation Company, 1833-40.

Despite efforts to secure a more diversified economic development, the appearance of new industries in the valley was relatively slow and most of the shipments over the firm's canal consisted of coal for tide-water ports. But, in improving the facilities for the carriage of coal, the firm continually reduced transport costs and increased the opportunities for the entry of new industries. In 1832 the toll rates on the canal were reported to be $1.04 per ton for 46 miles or .0212 cents per ton mile.[53] By 1838-39 the rate had fallen to .0166 cents per ton mile and in the difficult year of 1837 they had been as low as .0065 cents per ton mile.[54] Gradually commodities other than coal were moved in larger

[53] Jones, The Economic History of the Anthracite-Tidewater Canals, p. 19.

[54] Ibid., p. 30.

quantities and by 1833 iron ore appeared for the first time on the shipping lists. By 1836 iron was also moved in quantity. These changes were indicative of the future direction of development in the Lehigh Valley.

CHAPTER IV

ANTHRACITE IRON PRODUCTION IN THE LEHIGH VALLEY, 1840-1854

Innovation in the Lehigh Valley

Though plagued by political entanglements, public relations problems, and financial limitations, and burdened with the prosecution of its land development schemes, the board of managers of the Lehigh Coal and Navigation Company continued to maintain its interest in the quest for a feasible method of smelting iron ore with anthracite coal. Quite conscious of the expansive effect of such a discovery upon its business, but now anxious to shift its activities to the collection of rents and tolls, it decided to hold out inducement to others to try their efforts in that field of endeavor.

In 1834 the company made a policy statement which was designed to encourage the inquisitive and acquisitive ironmaster to take up the task that they, the managers, had dropped. The company now offered economic aid for experimentation with anthracite coal in the blast furnace, and upon the successful completion of such tests further assistance would be forthcoming to carry the technique over into commercial practice. Whether or not the policy statement was an original idea of some member of the board of managers, it was certainly issued only after application for such aid had been requested by Howard Nott and Company.[1]

---

[1] Minutes of the Managers Meeting of the Lehigh Coal and Navigation Company (November 25, 1834). All references to these minutes are cited

The terms of agreement to provide aid show that the Navigation Company had offered 1,000 tons of coal for experimental purposes if the tests were carried out within a two-year period. Successful completion of the experiments required the production of 20 tons of No. 1 pig iron per week, with such efforts to be continued for three consecutive months. If these requirements were satisfied, a bonus of 1,000 tons of Lehigh coal per year at $1.00 less than the regular price would be provided to the iron producer for a twenty-year period. Furthermore, the Lehigh Company would permit the shipment of 1,000 tons of coal per annum on its canal, or the equivalent weight of iron, toll free.

Anxious to attract interested parties, the company made public its offer with the further promise of the use of any "unoccupied water-power, mill or furnace, now belonging to the Company . . . and Sufficient room on the ground for making experiments in Smelting iron ore with Anthracite coal & also as much coal as may be necessary to make a fair and full experiment, together with So much of any iron ore or limestone now belong to the Company as may be necessary for the purpose."[2] To this original bonus the managers added a gratuitous grant of a water power site for the development and operation of any such permanent works. However, any who might take the offer and gain the bonus had to complete the

---

from Anthony Brzyski, "The Lehigh Canal and its Effect on the Development of the Region Through Which It Passed, 1818-1873," unpublished doctoral dissertation, New York University, 1957. The minutes will hereafter be cited as Min. Mgrs. Meeting LCNC.

[2] Ibid., (December 12, 1834).

test successfully within a two-year period commencing August 15, 1835.[3]

At approximately the same time The Franklin Institute of Philadelphia offered a gold medal to the person who would successfully manufacture 20 tons of anthracite pig iron.[4] Later that same year it was announced that a Pottsville, Pennsylvania, citizen had "made a successful experiment of puddling or refining iron with Anthracite coal," though the achievement was belittled by "A Pennsylvania Ironmaster" who reported that a number of Pennsylvanians had been acquainted with this "trifling knowledge."[5]

But no statement of success or accomplishment was reported on Howard Nott and Company's efforts to smelt iron ore with anthracite coal. The Lehigh Coal and Navigation Company records carry no progress report on the experiment. The efforts probably were unsuccessful, for in 1836 the Lehigh Company once again announced its previously proffered proposal.

The second offer was investigated by a local ironmaster, Stephen Balliet, and a small group of partners. For a decade Balliet had successfully operated a nearby charcoal blast furnace (Lehigh Furnace) but now sought the opportunity offered by the Coal and Navigation Company to experiment and possibly improve on the method of production he had been using. The Lehigh Company's offer of assistance in this instance was not

---

[3] *Ibid.*

[4] Samuel Hazard, ed., *Hazard's Register of Pennsylvania, Jan.-July, 1835* (Philadelphia, 1835), p. 342.

[5] *Ibid.*, pp. 383 and 415.

as liberal as that offered to Howard Mott and Company. The proffered assistance evidently was never accepted by the second group, for nothing more was reported on the matter in the Company's minutes.[6]

By that date Dr. Frederick Geisenheimer had already filed a patent for a process of smelting iron ore with anthracite coal, and that very year he had completed his furnace in Schuylkill County where, it is reported, he had produced a small amount of pig iron with the exclusive use of anthracite coal. The Lehigh Coal and Navigation Company, however, seems to have been oblivious of this development. One might also add that the local newspapers of the period offered no information on the success which had supposedly been achieved in the neighboring valley.

During the spring of 1837 an endeavor was made at South Easton by a John Van Buren to smelt iron ore with local Lehigh coal. His experiments were financed by Easton parties with interests in the Lehigh Valley coal trade, though they were in no way connected with the Lehigh Coal and Navigation Company. Van Buren, it is reported, was momentarily successful in his efforts toward that end, but when further financial aid was not forthcoming he was forced to discontinue his efforts.[7] As to why further financial aid was not provided, one can only speculate. Probably the financial conditions of the time created a feeling of timidity among the interested parties that resulted in their unwillingness to continue the project. Then again, it is quite possible that they had

---

[6]Min. Mgrs. Meeting LCNC (October 10, 1836).

[7]Henry, History of the Lehigh Valley, p. 165.

already heard of Crane's success in Wales and preferred to wait for someone else to adapt that technique while they continued to sell coal.

That same year Baughman, Guiteau, and High, attracted by the Lehigh Coal and Navigation Company's proposition, began experimenting in the old Mauch Chunk furnace built in 1825 by White and Hazard. (For a more complete discussion of the early efforts, see Chapter II.) Attaining their first success in that furnace when they combined charcoal and anthracite coal, Baughman, Guiteau, and High proceeded, in July of 1838, to build a new and more adequate furnace to continue their experiments.

Shortly thereafter Josiah White received a letter from his nephew, Solomon Roberts, concerning the success of Crane and Thomas at the Yniscedwin works which he had observed. Word was quickly passed on to the stockholders of the Lehigh Coal and Navigation Company: "The grand discovery of the mode of using anthracite coal in the smelting of iron ore had at last been made by Mr. Crane, an extensive iron master near Swansea, in Wales."[8]

That same year the Lehigh Company prepared still another proposal for those interested in experimenting with the process. This time it offered to furnish, "in fee simple, all the water power of any one of the dams between Allentown and Parryville (except So much thereof as may be necessary for the Navigation and one hundred inches of water under a three feet head for other purposes)." To be eligible for this offer the company required the successful venture to have a capitalization of

---

[8] Rpt. Bd. Mgrs. LCNC, 1838, p. 19.

$50,000 and to expend $30,000 or more on the iron works it was to build. The furnace itself would have to be so constructed that it could produce at least 27 tons of pig iron a week and to have done so for a period of three consecutive months.[9]

At this juncture it became the conviction of the company's board of managers that a long time would elapse before an experiment, on the scale deemed suitable, would be carried out unless some group having an interest in the Lehigh Coal and Navigation Company were to carry out the undertaking. Under these circumstances, three of the managers persuaded others to join them in an association to carry out a construction program. That fall the Lehigh Crane Iron Company was organized by eight men, six being members of the board of managers of the Lehigh Coal and Navigation Company.[10] Then, shortly after the organization of this company, Erskine Hazard was selected to visit Wales to observe Crane's iron works and, if possible, obtain the services of a capable furnace operator; this man would have to be one who could build and operate an anthracite blast furnace.

Thus, as the ability to use anthracite coal in iron smelting moved closer to realization, the managers of the Lehigh Coal and Navigation Company acted in such a way as to gain the first opportunity possible to exploit further the vast resources under their control. Now, as the time grew shorter, more value was placed on the profit opportunity to be

---

[9]Min. Mgrs. Meeting LCNC (October 2, 1838).

[10]Hazard, United States REgistery, II, 157.

gained by being first in the production of anthracite iron. Time was essential.

In January the board of managers announced:

> The long agitated question of Pennsylvania anthracite coal being adapted, as a substitute for charcoal, or coke coal, to the purpose of smelting iron ore, appears not to be fully established by our enterprising citizens Messrs. Guiteau, Baughman, High, and Lowthrop, who have a furnace in Mauch Chunk, which is now, and has been for thirty-two days continuously free from all interruption, in full blast exclusively with anthracite coal from our mines, and although a very small furnace, yields, on an average, one and a half tons per day.[11]

Four days previous to this announcement a more formal organization of the Lehigh Crane Iron Company had been completed. Already that company, through the efforts of Erskine Hazard, had obtained the services of Crane's furnace superintendent, David Thomas, who was to construct and operate the new furnace. A few days after the report on Messrs. Guiteau, Baughman, High and Lowthrop's furnace at Mauch Chunk had been published that very same furnace was taken out of blast due to a lack of iron ore.

Spring of 1839 found the Mauch Chunk furnace, with improved hot-blast equipment, back in operation, while the Lehigh Crane Iron Company was still deep in the planning stage of its construction program. Shortly thereafter the Mauch Chunk furnace produced about 100 tons of pig iron with the exclusive use of anthracite coal. However, because of the partners' inability to raise further financial assistance and the inefficiency of their furnace, production was halted and the furnace

---

[11] _Rpt_. _Bd_. _Mgrs_. _LCNC_, 1839, p. 30.

property returned to the Lehigh Coal and Navigation Company from whom it had been leased.[12]

Without a doubt this was the first furnace in the Lehigh Valley to produce anthracite pig iron, but the operators did not receive the benefits of the bonus offered by the Lehigh Coal and Navigation Company in the previous October. Though no information is available to substantiate the following, quite possibly the failure of Guiteau, Baughman, High, and Lowthrop to obtain the proferred bonus was partially the result of the Lehigh Coal and Navigation Company's eagerness to retain the benefits for members of its own board. After all, they could point out, the partnership had failed to meet a number of the necessary stipulations, among them being the financial requirements, the size of the furnace works, and, most important, the furnace's productive capacity. As one looks back on the performance of their furnace, it is recognized that relative to charcoal furnaces of the period this coal-burning furnace was most inefficient. Nevertheless, these men had solved a problem which had been perplexing the curious few in the iron industry for a number of years.

April of 1839 found the Lehigh Crane Iron Company finally incorporated under the legislative act of 1836 which had been written to encourage the construction of just such iron works. The corporation had an authorized capitalization of $100,000 with 2,000 shares of stock, all of which were subscribed for by the original organizers. The first paid-in funds of $25,000 were used to finance the construction of the furnace,

---

[12]Mathews and Hungerford, Lehigh and Carbon Counties, p. 802.

initiated the following August shortly after David Thomas arrived in this country.[13]

Prior to leaving Wales, Thomas had ordered all of the necessary parts for the construction of blowing machinery and hot-blast stoves which were later shipped to Philadelphia. The blowing cylinders for the furnace had to be constructed in this country, but because of their extraordinary size it was found difficult to locate a firm equipped to fabricate them. Finally, however, the Southwark Foundry of Philadelphia was persuaded to enlarge its boring equipment and prepare the cylinders. Thomas also had to import firebrick for the furnace lining from Wales, none being made in this country at that time.

The building program underway, the Lehigh Coal and Navigation Company, with a steadfast desire to exploit the resources it controlled, offered inducements to any interested parties willing to search out still undiscovered ore deposits on the company's lands. In the fall of 1839 the board of managers announced the adoption of a resolution to open the company's unused lands to any prospectors willing to search out the elusive iron ore that might be buried there. The successful prospector would be granted the right to mine the land for five years, the only cost to be 10 cents for each ton of ore extracted from the mine.[14] Whether any hopeful prospectors succeeded in discovering new ore deposits on the

---

[13] _Ibid_., p. 239. See also Thomas, "Reminiscences of the Early Anthracite-Iron Industry," _Trans_. _AIME_, XXIX, 906.

[14] Hazard, _United States Register_, I, 336.

company's land is not known, but the Navigation Company was to transport a good many tons of local ore to furnaces constructed all along the river in a very few years.

David Thomas, who had been struggling with technical problems of a most difficult nature, was finally able to bring his furnace into blast on July 3, 1840, with the first run of anthracite iron made the following day. In spite of a lack of skilled and experienced labor for the project, and a variance in the constituents of the ore and fuel brought to him to work with, the superintendent created the first technically and commercially successful anthracite iron furnace in the Lehigh Valley. With that first run of iron made on July 4, in large part the product of David Thomas's energy and tenacity, there commenced a flow of technical changes in the iron industry of this country which were to provide a whole new era in the economic development of the Lehigh Valley and the United States.

The first cargo of the furnace's iron was shipped, via the Lehigh Canal, to Philadelphia that August at which time the Philadelphia _North American_ announced:

> It is the opinion of those best qualified to judge in relation to such matter, that this application of the anthracite with which our mountains abound forms an era in the history of Pennsylvania of which it would be difficult to overestimate the importance. We may add that this conviction is gaining strength with every new trial of this mode of smelting iron ore.[15]

The following January the Lehigh Coal and Navigation Company's

---

[15] _Ibid_., III, 141.

ILLUSTRATION 2

SECTIONAL VIEW OF ANTHRACITE BLAST FURNACE, 1840

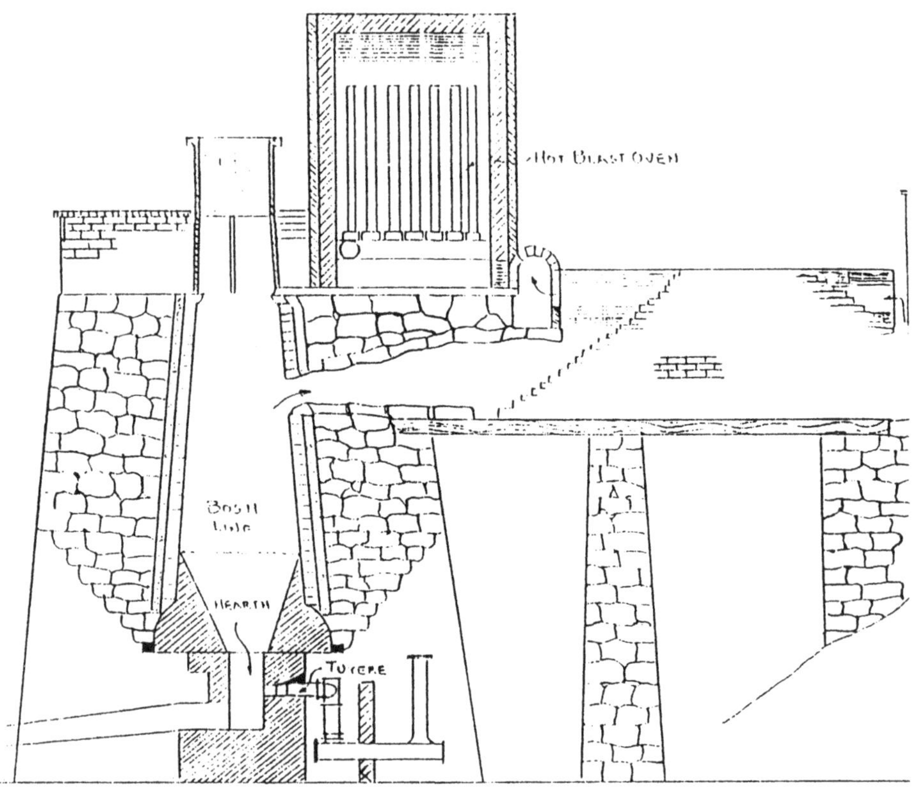

Source: Richard Peters, Jr., Two Centuries of Iron Smelting in Pennsylvania, p. 70.

board of managers reported the furnace a "complete success." The company had already sold 6,000 tons of coal to the furnace company and expected to sell double that quantity in the ensuing year.[16]

Though engineering or scientific schools had already been developed in this country, the acceptance of this type of technical training had grown very slowly. Thus it is that this furnace can be considered an outstanding engineering work and a notable example of the great reliance the United States placed on the technical achievements of pragmatic men such as David Thomas. The furnace was of heavy masonry construction, having an interior stack 42 feet high and a bosh of 12 feet. The weekly output of the furnace was 50 tons of good foundry iron, which was soon to find a favorable market in many local and New England machine shops.

The blast for the furnace was blown through three tuyeres and was heated to 600° Fahrenheit by four hot-blast ovens. The blowing machinery for the blast was motivated by a breast wheel 12 feet in diameter and 24 feet long that was turned by a head of water built up by a dam owned by the Lehigh Coal and Navigation Company.[17]

The pig metal was produced from local brown hematites, some New Jersey magnetite, limestone, and anthracite coal from the Lehigh Coal and Navigation Company's mines near Mauch Chunk. The only means of transportation for the coal and magnetite ore was the canal, but the hematite ore and limestone were transported to the furnace by team and wagon. The

---

[16] _Rep. Bd. Mgrs. LCNC_, 1841, p. 11.

[17] Mathews and Hungerford, _Lehigh and Carbon Counties_, p. 239.

price paid for the transporta tion of these ores sometimes ranged as high as $2.00 and $3.00 a ton. A tremendous amount of labor was required to pile the coal necessary to run the furnaces during the winter months. The unloading and piling of this coal was all done with wheelbarrows; the accumulation of materials commenced in the spring when navigation opened and continued until the canal was closed.[18]

There being no hill steep enough and high enough near the furnace site to permit the construction of a bridge for the delivery of these raw materials to the furnace top, as was the practice at the smaller charcoal furnaces, Thomas was forced to substitute a power hoist for this purpose. In this case it was a vertical hoist called a water-balance, which consisted of two square boxes, one at each end of a chain that was passed over a large wheel with a brake attached. When a sufficient amount of water was admitted into the box at the top of the hoist, it permitted the raising of a load of material in barrows to men at the top, known as top fillers, who took the barrows off the car, distributed them around the furnace top, and dumped them. The other box, upon reaching the bottom of the hoist, was automatically emptied and more loaded barrows were rolled on the platform to be hauled to the furnace top by the weight of the descending box.[19] Already the size of the furnace was creating technical problems which were going to have to be answered; this hoist, for example, was the first phase of the development of the present skip hoist.

---

[18]Thomas, "Reminiscences of the Early Anthracite-Iron Industry," <u>Trans</u>. <u>AIME</u>, XXIX, 925.

[19]<u>Ibid</u>., p. 927.

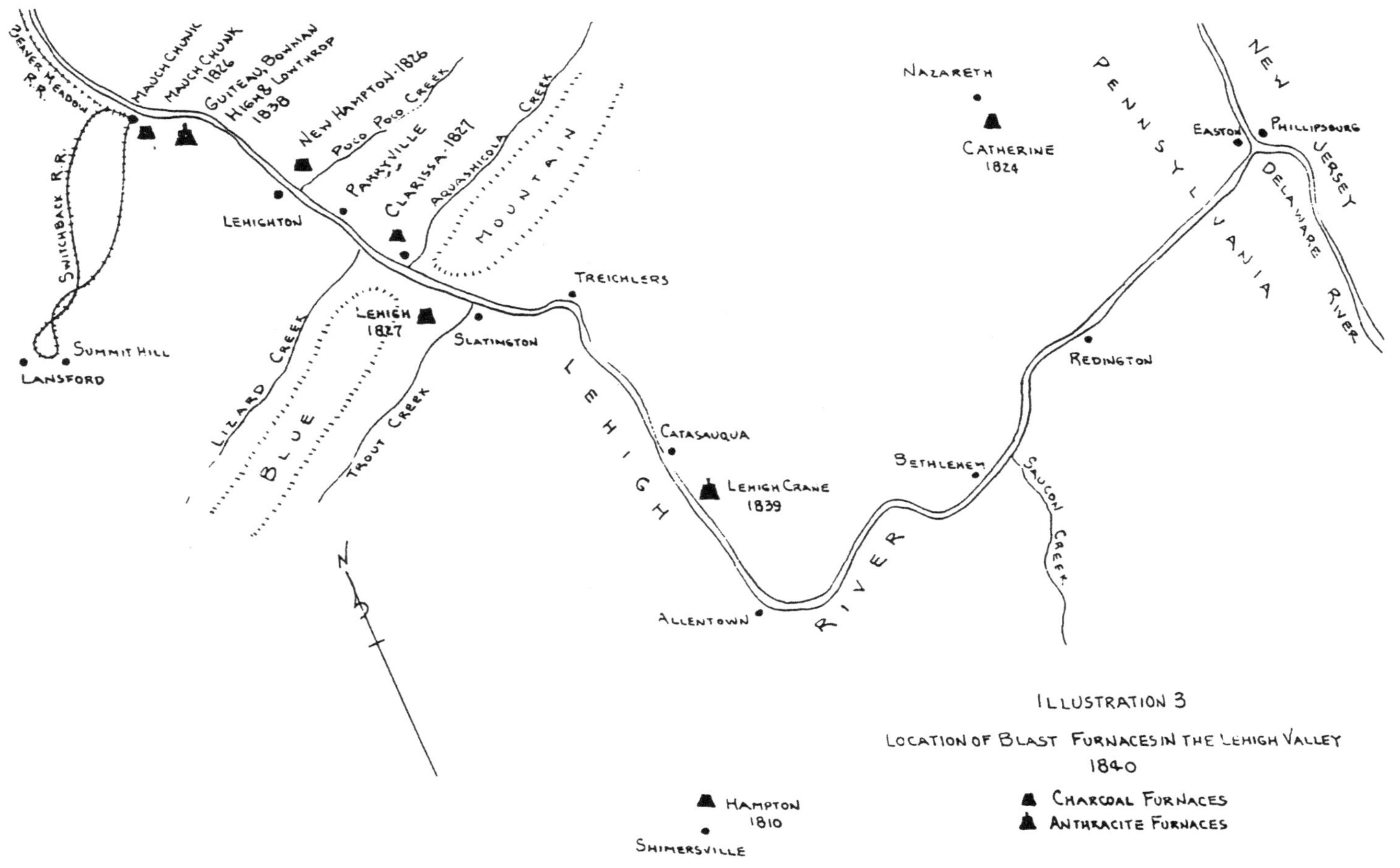

Illustration 3

Location of Blast Furnaces in the Lehigh Valley 1840

On the east side of the Lehigh River, and very near the iron works, ran the canal which was used to transport much of the raw materials to the furnace and ship the pig iron to market in Philadelphia or New York. The only problem the river presented was the danger of flood and in January, 1841, the furnace fires were extinguished by a sudden and unprecedented freshet. Relighted the following May, the furnace continued in blast until August, 1842. In that time the company had produced 3,316 tons of pig iron.[20] Also the foundation of a second furnace had been thrown up, the furnace itself being completed that same year.

Expansion of Anthracite Iron Production: 1840-54

During the same year that the Lehigh Crane Iron Company completed its second anthracite furnace there developed a change in business conditions. The financial crisis which had commenced in 1837 drew to a close. It is not the purpose of this paper to explain the cause of this business revival, but note will be taken of some of the forces which influenced the expansion of business activity at this time. Throughout this period the country was growing, both in numbers and in territorial expanse. Immigrants poured into the country to provide additional hands for the rising industrial sectors of the country while settlers extended the line of western settlement. At the same time there occurred a rapid growth of urbanization in the East. In conjunction with these developments there were continuous and extensive improvements in transportation facilities, especially railroads which were already providing the

---

[20]Mathews and Hungerford, Lehigh and Carbon Counties, pp. 239-40.

domestic iron industry with a cheaper means of access to market and a new market for its product.

The availabaility of capital was made somewhat easier through better banking facilities, the influx of capital from England once again, and new gold discoveries in the West.[21] However, the country was still largely agricultural, and general business conditions were still responsive to the changing economic conditions of Europe, particularly those of English origin.[22]

During the early years of this period of economic revival imports of iron were impeded by high duties while domestic iron production increased as additional numbers of new charcoal and anthracite furnaces were constructed. The actual increase in production is in dispute, but it seems to have risen from around 300,000 gross tons in 1841 to about 563,000 gross tons in 1850.[23] Certainly some part of this growth resulted through the protection offered by the tariff of 1842, but the use of anthracite coal also provided stimulus to the expansion of the iron trade.

Though there were but six anthracite furnaces in operation in 1840, that number had been increased to about twenty-two in 1844. Then as the price of pig iron increased from $25.75 a ton in 1844 to $30.25 a ton in

---

[21] W. B. Smith and A. H. Cole, Fluctuations in American Business: 1790-1860 (Cambridge, Massachusetts, 1935), pp. 81-84.

[22] Ibid., p. 92.

[23] American Iron and Steel Institute, "Pig Iron Statistics." This data has been provided in a photstatic reproduction issued by the Library of the American Iron and Steel Institute.

1847, there was a sudden increase in the number of such furnaces, fourteen being built in 1845, ten in 1846, and nine the following year. By 1848 there were approximately fifty-nine anthracite blast furnaces in operation, all located east of the Allegheny Mountains.[24]

Though iron duties were reduced to 30 percent in 1846, there was little immediate effect of that change upon the iron industry, for prices continued to rise. Then in 1849 anthracite and charcoal pig iron prices dropped, production decreased, but iron imports continued to rise.[25]

Ironmasters throughout the country began to grumble about their position and loudly demanded relief as the price of pig iron dropped to about $20 a ton and imports increased from 179,000 gross tons to 402,000 tons between 1848 and 1850. Memorials to Congress went unheeded, and a number of the industry's less efficient charcoal furnaces succumbed to the competition of the period while some of the recently constructed anthracite furnaces were forced to halt operations momentarily.[26]

After a year or two of these business conditions the price of pig

---

[24] S. R. Daddow and B. Bannan, _Coal, Iron, and Oil; or the Practical Miner_ (Pottsville, Pennsylvania, 1866), pp. 684-93. This work will hereafter be cited as Daddow and Bannan, _Coal, Iron and Oil_.

Pig iron prices are provided by Swank, _Iron in All Ages,_ p. 514.

Grosvenor, "Does Protection Protect?" p. 215, reported the construction of twenty-three charcoal furnaces in 1844, thirty-five in 1845, forty-four in 1846, thirty-four in 1847, and twenty-eight in 1848. Cited by Taussig, _Tariff History of the United States_, p. 132, n. 3.

[25] F. W. Taussig, "Statistics of Iron; 1830-1860," _Quarterly Journal of Economics_, II (1888), 379.

[26] Convention of Iron Masters, _Documents Relating to the Manufacture of Iron in Pennsylvania_. See Tables appended to the report of the convention.

iron once again commenced to move upward despite the continued increase in imports. By 1853 the price of anthracite pig iron had risen to its highest level of $36.12 a ton and continued to rise in the next year.[27]

That same year, 1854, the estimated average cost for a ton of pig iron at the furnace was approximately $16.10. This included the cost of labor, materials, and interest charges.[28]

The difference between the price and the cost plus transport charges evidently provided enough return to warrant a sudden flurry in the building of anthracite furnaces. That year 12 additional anthracite furnaces were built, the following year 19 more were completed, and by 1854 an estimated 109 such blast furnaces had been constructed, approximately 80 of these being located in Pennsylvania.[29]

Estimated total output of pig iron in the United States in 1850 was 657,337 gross tons, an increase over the previous year of approximately 83,582 tons. At the same time imports of pig iron reached a peak of 160,000 tons, though this was to drop rapidly and continuously until 1860.[30]

Probably the most significant feature of the change being wrought in the iron industry at this time was the relative shift in importance of anthracite pig iron. While anthracite iron production progressed quite

---

[27] Swank, *Iron in All Ages*, p. 514.

[28] J. M. Swank, *The American Iron Trade in 1876* (Philadelphia, 1876), p. 185.

[29] Daddow and Bannan, *Coal, Iron, and Oil*, pp. 684 ff.

[30] American Iron and Steel Institute, "Pig Iron Statistics."

steadily, the relative production of charcoal iron fell just as steadily. In 1844 the twenty anthracite furnaces had produced only 65,000 gross tons of pig iron, but with an increase in the number of furnaces total anthracite pig iron production reached 115,000 tons in 1849. Then, after the momentary drop in prices between 1851 and 1852 which eliminated a number of the antiquated charcoal furnaces, the output of anthracite pig iron almost equaled the production from the charcoal furnaces in 1854.[31] The total anthracite iron production reached 303,087 tons in 1854, while the total charcoal pig iron product moved to 305,623 tons. The following year more anthracite iron was produced than charcoal iron. Thus one era of the history of the iron industry was drawing to a close as another commenced.[32]

New Anthracite Furnaces in the Lehigh Valley

At the time the Lehigh Crane Iron Company's first furnace was

---

[31]T. Dunlap, *Statistical Report of the National Association of Iron Manufactureres for 1872* (Philadelphia, 1873), p. 56 Dunlap reported a reduction in the total number of furnaces of 163, between 1845 and 1850. In 1845 there had been 540 furnaces of record but in 1850 only 377 furnaces were listed. The total number of charcoal furnaces of record in 1840 was 804; thus in the ten-year period there had been a reduction of 427 furnaces.

Despite the decline in the furnace numbers, total production had risen because the ironmasters had improved the productivity of each furnace.

[32]The production figure for 1849 is found in J. Peter Lesley, *The Iron Manufacturer's Guide to Furnaces, Forges and Rolling Mills* (New York, 1859), p. 752. This work will hereafter be cited as Lesley, *The Iron Manufacturer's Guide.*

The production figures for 1854 are reported in American Iron and Steel Institute, *Annual Statistical Report for 1922* (New York, 1923), p. 9.

placed in operation, there were other furnaces in other parts of Pennsylvania that had already been completed or were nearing completion. There were no other such ventures in the Lehigh Valley. Then, after 1840, the growth of the number of iron furnaces in the Lehigh Valley was expanded as local and out-of-state businessmen seized the new opportunity.

The remarkable success of David Thomas's furnace offered the Lehigh Coal and Navigation Company a propitious opportunity to advertise the desirability of a valley location for other such works. Thus it announced to those who would read the annual report:

> Probably no location more favorable for it [iron manufacture] can be found in the country, the great supply of the various materials, their superior quality, the abundance of power, and facility of access to market, being all taken into view.[33]

The next year the managers notified their stockholders that, despite the unfortunate business conditions, they had "recently let a gentleman from Boston, a water power of 900 inches, near South Easton, for a furnace for smelting iron, preparations for the erection of which have been commenced."[34]

For the Coal and Navigation Company this meant an increase in the consumption of its water power, transport services, and coal. Also it offered the hope that other such establishments would be attracted by any success attained by a new iron company. The following year there were three anthracite-using furnaces in operation in the valley. Also the old

---

[33] Rpt. Bd. Mgrs. LCNC, 1843, p. 15

[34] Ibid., p. 9

furnace built by Baughman, Guiteau, and High in 1838 had been leased to J. Richards & Sons for operation with coal. Though unfortunately located, being distant from the better ores and remote from the major market, Philadelphia, the improvement and operation of this furnace seemed, at that time, to offer a likely economic opportunity. That same year another anthracite furnace was constructed at Glendon only a short distance west of Easton.

With expectations kindled by the rise in the price of pig iron to $30 a ton, there was a more rapid influx of capital into the Lehigh Valley. Four more furnaces were built. One of these new furnaces was a further addition to the Lehigh Crane Company's works. Two other furnaces were built in Allentown in 1846 and 1847, and a fourth was constructed at Glendon.[35]

Then in 1850, though the price of pig iron had declined somewhat, three more furnaces were blown in in the Lehigh Valley. Two of these were additions to the Lehigh Crane Iron Company facilities and one was an addition to the works already in operation at Glendon. Meanwhile, across the Delaware and opposite the mouth of the Lehigh River, in Phillipsburg two furnaces had been built in 1847.

In 1849 nine of the ten furnaces in the Lehigh Valley, excluding the Phillipsburg works, produced a total of 35,759 tons of pig iron.

---

[35]David Thomas's contract provided that he should receive a salary of £200 a year until the first furnace was completed. With the completion of the first furnace his salary was raised to £250 and then for each additional furnace he was to have an additional £50 increase in his annual salary. By 1846 Thomas had constructed three furnaces. See Mathews and Hungerford, Lehigh and Carbon Cpounties,p. 238.

This output was approximately 32 percent of the total anthracite iron produced in Pennsylvania that year. All Pennsylvania furnaces (anthracite) in blast that year produced 109,168 tons, while the total for the nation was 115,000 tons.[36]

Interestingly enough, the capital of the Lehigh Valley iron works, which was a sizable amount by 1850, generally came from sources foreign to the valley. For example, the three furnaces at Glendon and the single one at South Easton were owned by Charles Jackson, Jr., a Boston capitalist. (His furnace superintendent, William Firmstone, like David Thomas, came from England and brought with him all the necessary technical abilities.) Likewise the furnaces constructed by the Lehigh Crane Iron Company were financed by Philadelphia interests.[37] In Allentown local parties had entered upon the organization of an anthracite iron company in 1844, though it came to naught. Shortly thereafter Bevan and Humphries, a very successful shipping firm of Philadelphia, financed and built the first of such works in Allentown.[38] The works in Phillipsburg, New Jersey, were built by Peter Cooper and Abram Hewitt, owners of the Trenton Iron Company's rolling mills and wire works. These works represented New York Capital.[39]

When, in 1852, the price of anthracite iron began to rise again,

---

[36] Daddow and Bannan, _Coal, Iron, and Oil_, p. 684.

[37] Henry, _History of the Lehigh Valley_, pp. 166 and 295.

[38] Mathews and Hungerford, _Lehigh and Carbon Counties_, p. 156.

[39] Henry, _History of the Lehigh Valley_, p. 7.

reaching a peak of $36.88 a ton in 1854, three additional furnaces were built in the Lehigh Valley. The first was an expansion of the Cooper works at Phillipsburg and the second was a further addition to the Allentown furnaces which had passed into the hands of the D. E. Wilson Company in 1851. The last-mentioned furnace provides the first indication of any large financial investment in such works by local citizens. The D. E. Wilson Company had been organized by an active group of Allentown businessmen in conjunction with and the assistance of a small group of Philadelphia capitalists.

The third furnace built in 1854 represented the first completely local investment project. The construction of these works had originally been planned in 1853 by Stephen Balliet & Company, a partnership made up of four local residents. When Balliet died that same year, the association was dissolved but shortly reorganized as a corporation by the same local people, plus two additional valley citizens. In 1854 they constructed their first anthracite furnace at Coplay and commenced operations as the Lehigh Valley Iron Company.[40]

With these additions the Lehigh Valley contained sixteen anthracite blast furnaces. The total works were estimated to have represented approximately $2,5000,000 of invested capital.[41]

But the anthracite furnaces were not the only iron facilities in the Lehigh Valley at that time, for there were still in operation three

---

[40] Mathews and Hungerford, Lehigh and Carbon Counties, pp. 156 and 504.

[41] Daddow and Bannan, Coal, Iron, and Oil, p. 685.

hot-blast charcoal furnaces and one cold-blast charcoal works, Hampton furnace. Though all but one of these works were out of blast in 1850, they commenced operations once again as the price of pig iron moved upward. In addition to the blast furnaces there were also four bloomery forges which had been built between 1820 and 1848, as well as two charcoal forges, and a single rolling mill at South Easton. These works represented in 1850 a total investment of $269,500.[42]

The iron works employed a growing number of people, as well as oxen, horses, and mules. The anthracite furnaces alone were reported to have 1,003 men and boys at work in 1850, while they were using about 578 animals to haul raw materials from the nearby mines and quarries. The other works, the forges, charcoal furnaces, and rolling mill employed an additional 450 men and boys and 236 animals.[43] Furthermore, there were more men, boys, and animals employed by independent mining and quarrying companies.

Thus, during the years that had elapsed between 1800 and 1854, and with the opportunity opened up by the Lehigh Coal and Navigation Company through its assistance to the Lehigh Crane Iron Company and the services and raw materials it offered for sale, a number of new business firms had entered the Lehigh Valley to exploit the comparative advantage the valley had over other areas. Moreover, the next two decades were to see a continuous expansion in this number of merchant iron furnaces as more and

---

[42]Convention of Iron Masters, _Documents Relating to the Manufacture of Iron in Pennsylvania_. See Tables 1-7.

[43]_Ibid_.

more companies entered into the economic rivalry in what was, for a time, a most competitive industry. Though the history of the anthracite iron industry after 1876 was quite different from this early period of growth, there was in 1854 no early indication that the life of the industry was to be so short. At that time there were only economic indicators providing an air of optimism which had been stimulated by the great achievements of the anthracite ironmasters. Charcoal ironmasters, on the other hand, faced a bleak future as more and more of their fellow furnace owners were forced out of production.

After ten years the early technological advance that had been initiated by the anthracite furnace men had reached fruition. The first Lehigh Crane furnace with its 42-foot stack and 12-foot bosh had provided, along with the hot-blast and anthracite coal, an annual estimated output of 4,000 tons of pig iron, though its actual make in 1849 was but 3,639 tons. Simultaneously this type furnace was slowly being forced to retreat before the advance of the larger and more productive furnaces. The fourth and fifth furnaces constructed by David Thomas were built 45 feet high and with 18-foot boshes. Each furnace was also equipped with seven tuyeres. By that date Thomas had finally persuaded Josiah White, much against White's ideas on the matter, to substitute steam power for water power to motivate the blowing machines for all five of the furnaces. The use of steam power enabled Thomas to increase the pressure of the blast and increase the output of his furnaces.[44] The estimated

---

[44]Swank, _Iron in All Ages_, p. 455. See also Thomas, "Reminiscences of the EarlyAnthracite-Iron Industry," _Trans. AIME_, XXIX, 916 ff.

capacity of each new furnace was 8,000 tons and in 1850 this had been raised to 8,960 tons of pig iron per annum after 10 additional feet had been added to the stacks.[45] These furnaces had an output of approximately 150-200 tons of pig iron per week. A short ten years earlier the Lehigh Crane Company had announced quite proudly that its new furnace had a weekly capacity of 50 tons of pig iron.

At that time, 1850, local hot-blast charcoal furnaces had estimated capacities which ranged between 1,000 tons and 2,000 tons per annum, while Hampton furnace, a cold-blast furnace, had raised its annual capacity from 300 to 800 tons per annum.[46]

While similar changes in furnace specifications were made by other Lehigh Valley furnace operators, none had achieved such continuously rewarding results as David Thomas. Probably the next most successful operator in the Lehigh Valley was William Firmstone, manager of the Glendon furnaces operated by Charles Jackson. At Phillipsburg the Cooper works had been able to produce, on one occasion, 257 tons of pig iron in one week, though this level of output does not seem to have been maintained on a continuous basis.[47]

Not all of David Thomas's experiments were as successful as those mentioned above. In 1843, when he tried to utilize the waste gases from

---

[45] Convention of Iron Masters, Documents Relating to the Manufacture of Iron in Pennsylvania, Table 2. Thomas, "Reminiscences of the Early Anthracite-Iron Industry," Trans. AIME, XXIX, 924.

[46] Ibid., Tables 2-4

[47] Swank, Iron in All Ages, p. 455.

the furnace head for refining iron, he met with little success. In this experiment he attempted to conduct waste gases by way of a conduit built of brick which ran against one side of the furnace into one end of the refinery. These hot gases were then mixed with a hot-blast which was blown into a refinery very similar to a puddling furnace. Just as long as the material going into the blast furnace was dry, the gases came down to the refinery at a temperature which was intense enough to help melt the iron for further refining purposes. When it rained, however, the wet material that entered the furnace so reduced the temperature of the gases conducted to the refinery that it was impossible to melt the iron. Owing to the irregularity of the temperature of the gas, the experiment was abandoned at the end of six weeks.[48]

In 1847, with a view to expediting the loading of coal, a water-balance for elevating the coal from the canal barge to the coal pile was built, but freezing weather made the process difficult. This labor-saving device was abandoned after two years and wheelbarrows resorted to once again.[49]

That same year David Thomas tried to use electricity in the refining process in order to dispel some of the phosphorous present in the ores. First, it was introduced at the casting bed, where a current of electricity was run through the iron when the iron was still flowing and for twenty minutes after the iron was set. The technique was abandoned

---

[48]Thomas, "Reminiscences of the Early Anthracite-Iron Industry," Trans. AIME, XXIX, 918.

[49]Ibid., p. 926

when one of the furnace men was "knocked almost senseless" in an attempt to use an iron bar to remove one of the wires from the casting bed.

Not one to yield after the first failure, Thomas tried still another technique to rid his iron of its phosphorous content. In his second attempt a bar of iron was suspended from the top of the furnace down into the furnace material to a depth of about 10 feet, and a wire was attached to this bar and to one of the tuyere pipes. A current of electricity was conducted through the furnace for two weeks, but the results produced in the experiment showed no change in the iron. The project, as a result, was abandoned as unworkable.[50] Thus we find in David Thomas the same inquisitive spirit that was so typical of Josiah White and many of the other "practical" engineers of the period.

While Thomas was building and experimenting with his iron furnaces, there was a continual growth in the consumption of the raw materials necessary for iron production. As the number of furnaces increased, more iron ore mines were opened up by independent mining companies. These mining companies required little in the way of capital investment because of the chara[illegible] of the ore deposits; thus many of the local people entered into the business of trying to satisfy the almost insatiable appetites of the furnaces. Some of the furnace companies, in order to assure themselves supplies of these raw materials, proceeded to lease ore properties and establish their own mining companies.

The yield of each mine varied with the size of the deposit and the

---

[50] *Ibid.*, p. 924.

ease of extraction. Some of the local mines had 2,000 to 3,000 tons of ore extracted each year, while at other sites the yield ran as high as 10,000 tons a year. Most of the deposits provided opportunity for open cut operations, but in time it often became necessary to revert to shaft mining. Whereas open cut mining required little in the way of elaborate mining equipment, shaft mining necessitated more capital. Problems of support, elevation, and water seepage all added to the cost and reduced daily output. Furthermore, much of the ore was found mixed with clay, a circumstance which required ore washing equipment to prepare the ore for shipment. All of these conditions limited the output of the mines, with a number of them yielding but 15 tons per day, while some of these mines, those using the simpler mining techniques and equipment, were able to attain an output of approximately 35 tons of ore a day.[51]

Records are available which show the increase in trade in iron ore, iron, and coal between 1830 and 1854. Though these records do not provide certain very desirable data, such as destination and type of ore or iron product, they do offer some indication of the growing importance of the Lehigh Valley's iron industry between 1840 and 1855.

The data in Table 3 shows only the movement of iron ore via the canal, but many of the sixteen furnaces in the area drew their supplies of ore from nearby mines located on the west side of the Lehigh River. The ore from those neighboring mines was generally hauled by team and wagon to the iron furnaces, as previously mentioned. The richer

---

[51] Miller, Allentown Quadrange, pp. 48-50.

TABLE 3

COAL, IRON ORE, AND IRON SHIPMENTS
ON THE LEHIGH CANAL FOR SELECTED YEARS
(Net tons)

Year	Coal	Iron Ore		Iron	
		Ascending	Descending	Ascending	Descending
1837	223,902	3,413	1,073	756	481
1840	225,318	6,189	885	1,705	2,690
1841	143,037	2,204	489	480	2,710
1845	429,453	11,593	10,106	971	15,793
1846	517,116	17,001	10,393	2,342	18,888
1850	690,456	26,878	2,537	4,920	36,478
1851	964,224	34,292	2,515	2,935	38,261
1854	1,246,592	87,814	7,875	6,775	51,750
1855	1,276,367	63,489	7,249	7,464	64,542

Source: Report(s) of the Board of Managers of the Lehigh Coal and Navigation Company, 1837-55.

magnetite ore from New Jersey was moved to the furnaces by means of canal barges; it is that ore which is probably represented in Table 3. Between 1840 and 1854 the tonnage of such ore ascending the canal was increased over 1300 percent, an indication of the very rapid expansion taking place in the region's iron production.

The canal also provided the most efficient means then available for the transportation of the increasing quantities of pig iron to iron mills located closer to the major markets. The expansion of such sales by the Lehigh ironmasters is represented in the tonnage figures of iron descending the canal. Thus, between 1840 and 1854, as the number of furnaces was increased from one to sixteen, iron shipments to outside mills had increased approximately 1400 percent. By 1854 the Lehigh Valley was reputed to be one of the most important iron producing centers in the United States.[52]

Western Pennsylvania Iron Production

The advances in smelting technology so effectively adapted and developed by the Lehigh Valley and other eastern furnace operators were not accompanied by equivalent achievements in that part of the iron industry located west of the Allegheny Mountains. Though provided with abundant bituminous coal supplies which had been used in smelting local iron ores as early as 1836, the western Pennsylvania ironmasters continued to use charcoal in preference to coal or coke. Inquiries into the cause of delay in the adaption of this technique which had been used by British ironmasters for one hundred years have been pursued by other writers; therefore, this paper will merely summarize the explanations already proffered.

James Swank, presumably one of the most authoritative writers on the American iron industry, found the cause for the delay to be: an inadequate transport service, the abundance of timber for charcoal, and a prejudice against coke-produced iron held by the forges, foundries, and smiths. Furthermore, he believed that much of the bituminous coal being

---

[52] In 1855 the Lehigh Valley, including Phillipsburg, New Jersey, contained 20 iron furnaces capable of producing 168,224 net tons of anthracite pig iron per annum or approximately 31.2 percent of the total capacity of Pennsylvania. See Daddow and Bannan, _Coal, Iron, and Oil_, pp. 684-93.

used was not suitable for coking purposes.[53] V. S. Clark, in his extensive History of Manufactures in the United States, generally accepted Swank's explanation. He stated that the use of coke and raw bituminous coal, "common in Great Britain for many years, was deferred in America by the abundance of charcoal, the conservatism of iron-masters, a prejudice in favor of charcoal iron, and a lack of good coking coal, and by the fact that suitable soft coal did not, like anthracite, lie immediately tributary to developed iron mines and established furnace districts."[54]

Louis Hunter, in his "Influence of the Market upon Technique in the Iron Industry in Western Pennsylvania Up to 1860," declares that the new technique was not introduced at an earlier date because of the absence of a demand for the iron. While the coke furnace iron was cheaper, it was not a satisfactory substitute for the wrought iron used by the farmers in that agricultural area. Furthermore, Hunter has pointed out that the financial difficulties faced by western ironmasters tended to restrain the business of iron manufacture. There was a continuous lack of capital, and much of what there was available for the iron trade in that region was often tied up by the long credit terms used in the trade. These conditions, with the poor banking facilities of the area, all served to make the iron trade uncertain and difficult and retarded its growth.[55]

---

[53] Swank, Iron in All Ages, p. 81.

[54] Clark, History of Manufactures in the United States, I, 419.

[55] Louis C. Hunter, "Financial Problems of the Early Pittsburgh Iron Manufactures," Journal of Economic and Business History, II (1930), 543 f. Bining, "The Rise of Iron Manufacture in Western Pennsylvania," pp. 253-55.

As late as 1854 Hunt's Merchant Magazine remarked on this situation as follows: "It is a matter of much astonishment that attention of Eastern capitalists has not been directed more to Pittsburgh, and that investments which promise such rich, such speedy, and such certain returns have not long ago been made." However, the writer acceded to the fact that the development of the railroads had demanded the use of most of the available capital at that time. "Thus only can we account for the neglect, that would otherwise be unpardonable, in not establishing certain manufactories which would pay most largely and munificently."[56]

Whatever the causes of delay, competition for eastern furnaces from the West was precluded by the absence of more productive facilities. Actually eastern anthracite iron often found a market in the West.[57] When iron prices dropped in 1849 and 1850, the western iron works suffered an economic catastrophe probably more difficult than that faced by eastern iron manufacturers.

At that time there were seven raw bituminous coal furnaces already constructed, four were out of blast, three of them having failed, while only three were able to sustain production. There were also four coke furnaces at Brady's Bend that were owned by M. P. Sawyers and others of Boston. All four of these furnaces were out of blast in 1850. In the eastern region only twenty-eight of the fifty-seven anthracite blast

---

56Hunt's Merchant Magazine and Commercial Revue, Vol. 34 (1854), 438 f.

57Ibid., p. 439.

furnaces then constructed were out of blast.[58]

Production of the western bituminous coal and coke furnaces in 1849 was estimated to be 25,600 gross tons of pig iron while the production of the anthracite furnaces was 221,400 tons. To this must be added the output of the charcoal furnaces of both areas. The West had 113 charcoal furnaces as compared with 127 charcoal furnaces in the East. The eastern furnaces were capable of producing 170,999 gross tons of pig iron while the western furnaces could produce 133,360 tons. This gave the eastern Pennsylvania furnaces a preponderance of production (392,399 gross tons over the western furnaces' 158,960 tons).[59]

Upon the recovery in pig iron prices after 1850, the western coke furnaces were blown in again and the Cambria Iron Company, at Johnstown, completed the construction of four more coke furnaces. These furnaces, with the others already constructed, turned out a total production of bituminous iron of 54,485 net tons in 1854. This was a rather impressive expansion in output, but when compared with the 339,298 net tons poured out by the anthracite furnaces and the 342,298 tons produced in the charcoal furnaces, it was still a very small part of the total domestic production.

Though bituminous pig iron was not a large part of the nation's total pig iron product, it is interesting to note the change in the organization of production that was taking place in western Pennsylvania

---

[58]Convention of Iron Masters, <u>Documents Relating to the Manufacture of Iron in Pennsylvania</u>, Tables 2 and 8.

[59]<u>Ibid</u>., Tables, 2, 8 and 9.

at that time. The two works, Brady's Bend iron works and the Cambria iron works, represented a new method of organization, one the iron industry was to develop more extensively in the future; both were integrated mills. The works at Brady's Bend originally consisted of four blast furnaces which were to provide pig iron for the Pittsburgh market. As the iron refiners of Pittsburgh refused to adopt the coke pig iron, the blast furnace company built an extensive rolling mill near its blast furnaces to work up the product of the furnaces. Later, when the Cambria works were built, a similar system of furnaces and rolling mills was placed in operation to turn out rails for that important new market, the railroad industry.[60]

While anthracite pig iron production was forging ahead to a position of leadership, experiments were being carried on in a Mercer County furnace with Lake Superior iron ores. Smelting alone and sometimes with local ores, the lake ores were found to be of a superior quality and were used regularly, after that first experiment in 1854, by a number of the western Pennsylvania furnaces.[61] The opening of the Sault Ste Marie Canal in 1855 provided direct communications with the Lake Superior deposits, resulting in reduced costs for the lake ores which provided further inducement for the expansion of the western iron industry.[62]

Though seemingly unimportant to the eastern furnace operators at

---

[60]Bining, "The Rise of Iron Manufacture in Western Pennsylvania," p. 251.

[61]Swank, *Iron in All Ages*, pp. 324-25.

[62]Clark, *History of Manufactures in the United States*. I. 348.

that time, these developments - the construction of the integrated works, the use of Lake Superior ores in western Pennsylvania furnaces, and the construction of the canal - were to facilitate the growth of the bituminous iron furnaces and eventually to lead to the decline and demise of the merchant iron furnaces in the East. For the moment, however, the western bituminous coal and furnaces offered practically no competition to the eastern anthracite pig iron furnaces. The situation brought forth the following commentary from a contemporary writer:

> That coke furnaces cannot prosper on the eastern side of the Allegheny Mountains is not strange, for against the anthracite furnaces they cannot successfully compete; but how it happens that coke furnaces cannot prosper in the Eastern States, is more than we are able to comprehend.[63]

Conclusion

Through the study of the development of the early anthracite furnaces in the Lehigh Valley and the somewhat more gradual adoption of the coke furnaces to the west, it is possible to discern a wider pattern of technological and organizational developments which were to provide the mainspring for the gradual reorganization of the iron industry. With David Thomas's first furnace, a product of 50 tons of pig iron had been produced in a single week. His fourth and fifth furnaces were even more productive, for they were able to turn out between 150 and 200 tons of pig iron in a week. His first furnace provided a 250 percent increase in output over the charcoal furnaces of the period, but the furnaces built

---

[63]F. Overman, The Manufacture of Iron in All Its Various Branches (3d ed.; Philadelphia, 1854), p. 174.

in the late 1840's permitted for a phenomenal increase of output of 750 to 1000 percent over the older charcoal furnace.

The dramatic increase in output by the anthracite furnaces was the product of inquiring minds prodded by an acquisitive zeal admidst a rapidly growing economy. Anxious to reduce the cost of producing iron, and cognizant of the limitations of the charcoal furnaces, these enterprising men delved into the possibility of using the cheaper fuel, anthracite coal, to smelt iron ores. Having once succeeded in their efforts, they proceeded to the task of reducing the costs of production even more by devising new techniques of production which would save on fuel costs and increase the producitivity of their furnace laborers by providing them with ever more efficient equipment to work. To that end they began to manipulate the variables in furnace construction and operation, the pressure and heat of the blast, the height of the furnace, width of boshes, number of tuyeres, the use of waste gases, and the handling of raw materials.

David Thomas was one of the more successful in such endeavors. Though he did not develop any new principles of furnace operation, he was successful in turning older techniques into higher and higher levels of output. By using a larger blowing cylinder than had been built previously, building taller furnaces (the first one being 40 feet high and the fourth and fifth being 55 feet), with wider and higher boshes and additional tuyeres, he was able to raise the output of his works to new levels. Other furnace operators were to continue the work commenced by Thomas and eventually would provide the practical engineering skills and knowledge necessary to build the behemoth furnaces of today.[64] Their efforts, however, required further assistance from foreign ironmasters, but more on that in later chapters.

The further consequences of these innovations in the anthracite iron industry and that part of the industry using bituminous coke and coal were a gradual change in the type of business organization utilized by the furnace operators, an expansion in market areas, and a concentration of iron production in fewer geographic locations. Originally most iron furnaces were owned and operated by single proprietors or partners and were generally only large enough to provide for the local market. Gradually it was recognized that the larger, more productive iron works required an extraordinary amount of capital to cover construction and operation costs, and the product of these larger works was more than that required by the local market. Solutions to these problems were to produce radical changes in the structure of the iron industry. Eventually the more proficient capital accumulator, the corporation, was to displace the proprietorship and the partnership. And, through the aid of a rapidly expanding rail net with its voracious appetite for iron, and the subsequent reduction in transport costs, the iron trade expanded, while local market areas, so long monopolized by small charcoal furnaces, were eventually bound together into a national market with a web of iron rails. These same rails also permitted a concentration of iron furnaces at sites near the important coal deposits now so essential for the

---

[64]Swank, <u>Iron in All Ages</u>, p. 455.

production of iron. By 1855 the new locational pattern was already quite in evidence as more and more furnaces were constructed in the Schuylkill, Susquehanna, and Lehigh river valleys as well as in the region of the Connellsville coal fields.

While this change was being made more pronounced, the seed for a still greater change had been planted, a change which would reduce the merchant pig iron industry to a position of insignificance and would finally result in its total elimination. That change was the development of the integrated iron works at Brady's Bend and Johnstown. Almost by chance the owners of the blast furnaces at these two points had combined pig iron production with pig iron refining and fabricating. Forced, by the peculiar market conditions of the period, to find an outlet for pig iron being produced with coke, the operators of the Brady's Bend iron works were soon to discover that there were valuable economies to be gained through the form of integration they had adopted. But for at least another twenty years the anthracite furnaces, merchant pig iron producers in the main, were to be the leading producers of pig iron.

CHAPTER V

INITIATION AND ORGANIZATION OF THE THOMAS IRON COMPANY

The Corporation

During the month of January, 1854, No. 1 anthracite iron at Philadelphia was quoted at $37 a gross ton. This was almost the highest price offered for this type of iron since the commencement of its production in 1839. The price was $5.00 more than had been offered in December and was $17 higher than the low which had been offered in July, 1850. Through that four-year period anthracite pig iron prices had shown a continuous upward movement which gained momentum in 1852 and showed signs of rising even more by January, 1854.[1] This period seemed to offer a golden opportunity for anyone, with an available supply of capital and an enterprising spirit, who was willing to speculate on the growth of the economy of the United States.

On February 2 of that same year the Easton Argus reported that the Allentown Iron Company had decided to build another large anthracite furnace at its location and that it also planned to erect a rolling mill nearby.[2] At that time there were sixteen anthracite iron furnaces in the Lehigh Valley. Moreover, there were some parties in the valley quite willing to venture even more capital in the industrial progress of the

---

[1]Swank, The American Iron Trade in 1876, p. 184.

[2]Easton Argus, Feb. 2, 1854.

times. Several weeks later the same newspaper reported that new iron works were to be constructed on the west side of the Lehigh River, about a half-mile above the Crane Iron Works. These new furnaces were to be constructed by "a number of gentlemen possessing plenty of capital and enterprise," who had organized a company the previous week and subscribed some $200,000 to finance the initial stages of construction.[3]

This news item was the first public announcement of a meeting, attended by eighteen men of diverse interests, which had been held at White's Tavern in Centre Square, Easton. At that meeting plans had been projected to establish two iron furnaces somewhere in the Lehigh Valley. The organization of the meeting and the plan of the project were evidently brought about by David Thomas, who, through personal experience, was conscious of the considerable opportunity offered by the continuing expansion of the iron industry to venturesome and acquisitive individuals who were prepared to grasp the opportunity. Because of his efforts in organizing the company, and in recognition of his past success in the anthracite iron industry, the new business firm was named The Thomas Iron Company. Anxious to commence the business at hand, the eighteen men subscribed to the capital of the new company and appointed a committee of seven men to obtain a charter from the Pennsylvania Legislature and purchase a site for the furnace.[4]

---

[3] Ibid., Feb. 23, 1854.

[4] B. F. Fackenthal, Jr., The Thomas Iron Company, 1854-1904 (New York, 1904), p. 7. This publication was issued to commemorate the fiftieth anniversary of the founding of The Thomas Iron Company.

Two weeks later, at a second meeting, it was decided to organize as general partners rather than as a corporation. At the same time a provisional board of managers of seven men was appointed to decide upon the purchase and location of the furnace site. Officers were elected and an advisory committee selected to take on the responsibility of the construction of the furnaces. Why the deviation from the original plans was made is not known. Possibly delay on the part of the legislature to act on their charter led the men to this decision, for when word was received that the government had granted the group a special corporate charter the scheme for co-partnership was hastily dropped and the corporate charter adopted.[5]

The new corporation had a capital stock authoriziation of 4,000 shares, each share having a par value of $50 or a total of $200,000, all shares being transferable. Under this special corporate charter the company had the right to manufacture and sell iron, but for this purpose it could only hold 500 acres of land. The legal life of the corporation was to be but twenty years; this could be extended, however, through legislative action. There were also limitations as well as privileges. Among the former were the following: (1) the company was to have no banking privileges and (2) all of the stockholders were to be jointly liable for all debts incurred by the company.[6] It must be remembered, however, that

---

[5]Minute Book of The Thomas Iron Company, pp. 2-4. This work will hereafter be cited as Min. Book - The Thomas Iron Co.

This material is in the collection of the Lehigh University Library, Bethlehem, Pennsylvania.

[6]*Pennsylvania Laws* (1854), pp. 677-79.

this corporate charter could be changed or supplemented by legislative action upon application for any such change by the corporation, and in a very short time changes were to be requested to enable the company to expand its facilities.

On April 4, 1854, by-laws were adopted by the stockholders. They established a board of seven directors, as specified by the charter, as well as officers for the company, including a president, secretary, treasurer, and superintendent. Also two committees, a finance committee and a committee on accounts, were established. The former was to supervise moneyed operations and the latter was to act as an auditing body.[7]

Thus The Thomas Iron Company began. It was a business firm fabricated out of high expectations from a favorable price situation, the advancing technological processes of the iron industry, and the further hope of continued industrial expansion of the economy. Molded by an enterprising group of men, the company was to operate, in a few short years, the most important collection of merchant furnaces in the iron industry. In a similarly short period of time the firm was to drop from its position of predominance. The purpose of this study, as has been pointed out previously, is to determine why the company's activities declined and eventually disappeared in history. The story of the growth of this business firm is interlaced with the process of technological development and its decline was identified with the same factor. That relationship is the issue or our problem.

---

[7] By-Laws of The Thomas Iron Company (New York, 1854), n.p.

<u>Sources of Venture Capital</u>

The furnaces contemplated by the founders of The Thomas Iron Company were to be larger than any constructed at that time. Thus in the interest of technical requirements a sizable sum of capital was necessary to commence operations. Also the continuing problems of economic instability within the iron indstry necessitated the employment of a large fund of working capital. Some of these funds would be needed to hire the necessary numbers of skilled furnace workers required to maintain the continuous process of operation. Further, the danger faced in the possibility of depressed industrial activity entailed an essential supply of capital to permit the carrying of a heavy supply of raw materials and finished products through any such situation. These requirements precluded the use of a small fund of working capital such as might have been accumulated by a single r oprietor. Instead it was generally conceded that it all required the use of the corporate form of business organization.

Though the use of a co-partnership had been contemplated, it has already been noted that such plans were dropped when legislative acceptance was given to the corporate charter. By using the corporate form of organization the stockholders would be provided the opportunity of transferring their stock, if the occasion for personal liquidity was required, without dissolving the company. Also the corporate organization eliminated the problem of reorganization if one of the owners was to die, as would have been required under the co-partnership. However, as noted earlier, each stockholder was still confronted with the problem of unlimited liability for any debts incurred by the company.

The original capital of $200,000 was subscribed for by nineteen of the original organizers and eight other capitalists. Most of these men were not directly involved in the iron trade, the larger number being local businessmen, bankers, or professional men. The activities carried on by many of the stockholders, before and after the organization of The Thomas Iron Company, show that many of them were men of more than ordinary business capability and daring.

Among the original stockholders directly interested in the iron trade was David Thomas. He subscribed $10,000 for 200 shares of stock. By 1854 he had served fourteen years as superintendent of the Crane Iron Works after previously serving in a similar position at George Crane's furnaces in Wales. In 1855 Thomas was retired as a furnace operator and indulged in many other business pursuits. He was to serve a number of years as a director of the Lehigh Valley Railroad as well as president of the Catasauqua and Fogelsville Railroad. And at the same time he organized and operated the Lehigh Fire-Brick Company and the Catasauqua Rolling-Mill Company. Meanwhile, he maintained an active interest in the organization of The Thomas Iron Company and the Carbon Iron Company. The last named company, located a few miles above the Crane Iron Works, was established by Thomas and others at the same time as The Thomas Iron Company.

There was also Samuel Thomas, David's son, who was but twenty-seven years of age when the company was established. He had begun to participate in the development of the iron industry in the Lehigh Valley when he was nineteen years of age. Commencing his career at the Crane works, he later moved to Boonton, New Jersey, to superintend the construction of a blast furnace. Returning to Pennsylvania, he became a small shareholder in The Thomas Iron Company but an active participant in the operation of the works. Later he helped organize the Lock Ridge Iron Company and devoted a numer of years of his life to the development of iron production in Alabama. His brother John was also a shareholder and an active participant in the field of iron production. When David Thomas resigned his position as superintendent of the Crane Iron Company, John was appointed to that position; he was then twenty-five years of age. Later he held the same position with The Thomas Iron Company. Both of these young men subscribed $2,500 for shares in the corporation.

One other subscriber to the stock of The Thomas Iron Company who was actively interested in the iron industry was B. J. Leedom of Philadelphia, secretary and treasurer of the Crane Iron Company. The other suscribers were either businessmen active in other fields of endeavor or professional people.

Among these subscribers we find a C. A. Luckenbach, a local Bethlehem citizen and a large landowner in what was to be called South Bethlehem. In 1852, he had organized the Bethlehem Gas Company and was later to be instrumental in the construction of the Bethlehem Railroad, the First National Bank of Bethlehem, and the Bethlehem Iron Company. He subscribed for 300 shares in The Thomas Iron Company and was very shortly to be elected president of the company, in which position he served until 1864.

There was also John Drake of Easton, who, with Derrick Hulick and Samuel Drake, other subscribers, owned and operated a successful wholesale grocery business in Easton. John Drake was also active in the organization of the Carbon Iron Company and later the Delaware Rolling Mill Company.

S. R. Chidsey of Easton, and originally from New England as a number of the other subscribers were, was a successful merchant at the time The Thomas Iron Company was established. Later Chidsey assisted in the establishment of the Warren Foundry and Machine Company in Phillipsburgh, New Jersey, and was an active incorporator of the Farmers' and Mechanics' Bank of Easton. He also took an active interest in the development of western mines and railroads. His subscription to The Thomas Iron Company consisted of 200 shares of stock.

Mathew Krause of Bethlehem was the president of a local fire insurance company, while Augustus Wolle, also of Bethlehem, ran a general store and produced machine-made paper bags. In a few years Wolle was to become one of the most active participants in the organization of the Bethlehem Iron Company (Bethlehem Steel Corporation), and at the same time he operated a slate company in the slate belt area above Easton.

Peter Michler, who was to become the president of the First National Bank of Easton, and C. F. Randolph, also of Easton, were both active in the coal business of the upper Lehigh Valley.

There were others connected with the Lehigh Coal and Navigation Company and the Morris Canal and Banking Company. Both of these companies would be large carriers of ore, coal, and other materials for the iron company. Among this group were E. A. Douglas, superintendent and engineer of the Lehigh Canal, and John Brown, who later became manager of the same canal company. Then from New Jersey there was William Talcott, superintendent and engineer of the Morris Canal, as well as Ephraim Marsh, New Jersey state legislator, judge, and president and manager of the Morris Canal Company.

The other subscribers included William Reed, a lumber merchant at Mauch Chunk; Thomas Butz, a local farmer; Daniel Whitesell, an Easton hotel manager; Henry Singmaster, a tannery operator from Stroudsburg; and I. V. Williamson of Philadelphia and Benjamin Clarke of New York, both merchants. The professional men included Dr. Jacob Scholl, a dentist; the Reverend John Gray, pastor of the First Presbyterian Church of Easton; and Dr. Henry Detwiller, physician and scientist.[8]

Of these twenty-six subscribers only five came from outside the Lehigh Valley. However, as already noted, a number had originally migrated to the valley from other areas; some from New England, New York, Wales, and Europe.

The sums subscribed by each man varied between $2,500 for 50 shares and $15,000 for 300 shares. Only two purchased 300 shares, while the greater number invested $5,000 to $10,000. David Thomas subscribed to but 200 shares while his two sons each held but 50 shares. Under the

---

[8]Fackenthal, _The Thomas Iron Company, 1854-1904_, pp. 7 ff. Other sources used for this biographical information include W. J. Heller, _History of Northampton County and the Grand Valley of the Lehigh_ (New York, 1920), II, III, _passim_. Mathews and Hungerford, _Lehigh and Carbon Counties_, _passim_.

voting procedure established by the corporate charter, the group of investors from Easton maintained the greatest number of votes, a fact which may partially explain the location of the company's main office in Easton though its first furnaces were built a number of miles distant from that city.

Prior to the blowing in of the new furnace in 1855, it was found that the original $200,000 was not enough to construct the works and to operate them. Thus a supplement to the charter permitting $500,000 of capital was requested. The legislature granted the proposed supplement in March and subsequently $75,000 of additional stock was sold to new parties interested in the venture and to some of the original stockholders. Among these new shareholders were additional people with interests in the Lehigh Coal and Navigation Company, the Crane Iron Works, and the Lehigh Valley coal trade.[9]

The first stock issued by The Thomas Iron Company was to expand to a total of 50,000 shares with a par value of $2,500,000. At no time in the history of the company was its stock traded in the stock exchange; instead it generally remained in the hands of the families and descendants of the original subscribers or in estates managed by banks or trusts. By 1912 there were to be 622 stockholders as compared with the original 26 of 1854.

The source of venture capital for the new iron works was the local business community. The individuals that provided the funds were men who

---

9*Ibid*., p. 13.

had already developed some business interests from which they could accumulate savings, savings which could be released for further capital investment. The surplus from their business activities could have been used for further capital accumulation in the same sector from which they were drawn, but the conditions of the iron trade of 1854-55 seemed to offer greater profit expectations for these men. Anxious to exploit the techniques that had been developed earlier by David Thomas and others, probably stimulated by discussion with this very successful and experienced ironmaster, and apparently predisposed to create more productive works because of the economic conditions of the times, these men turned from their coal or canal business, grocery or banking exploits, to enter an entirely new field of endeavor in their quest for profits.

In the first few years a policy of capital accumulation was established which was to continue throughout the early years of the company's history. One of the first pronouncements made by the directors was that the company would follow the policy of appropriating "a part of the net proceeds" to augment the capital of the company.[10] This meant that the stockholders would receive stock dividends instead of cash dividends; while the stockholder's cash income would sometime be limited, his equity would increase over the years. Though forced upon occasion to resort to borrowing money for purposes of operating the iron works, most of the expansion programs of the company were financed through the use of

---

[10]The Thomas Iron Company Financial Records for Fifty Years, p. 7. This work will hereafter be cited as The Thomas Iron Co. Fin. Rec. This material is in the collection of the Lehigh University Library, Bethlehem, Pennsylvania.

retained earnings. Enough of these earnings were reinvested to permit the expansion of the works from two furnaces in 1855 to eleven furnaces by 1893.

Location of the Iron Works

By 1854 the Lehigh Valley had become a very prosperous and progressive industrial area as the coal trade and the anthracite iron industry continued to expand. In that year there were 1,207,186 tons of coal shipped from the valley's coal mines as compared with the 365 tons shipped in 1820. Among other businesses that had been built up in the various communities along the river were numerous foundries and machine shops, factories producing agricultural implements, mills of various kinds, carriage factories, tanneries, stove manufactories, axle production, a rolling mill, iron ore mines, and lime works. Also there were the usual number of breweries and distilleries as well as sixteen anthracite blast furnaces built along the banks of the Lehigh River. Much of this growth in economic activity had been actively supported or developed by the Lehigh Coal and Navigation Company or induced through the improved transportation facilities created by the company and the continued expansion of population.

At the same time the construction of The Thomas Iron Company was undertaken, a revolutionary change in transportation was rapidly taking shape in the Lehigh Valley. Asa Packer's Lehigh Valley Railroad was driving to the end of a long and difficult period of railroad construction. The completion of this railroad meant that Mauch Chunk would be connected with Easton by a surer and more adequate transportation system than had yet prevailed. Moreover, the new railroad would provide connections with railroads reaching into the New York area and Philadelphia. Earlier (1852) the New Jersey Central Railroad had been completed between Phillipsburg and Elizabethport, New Jersey, while the Belvidere-Delaware Railroad, which connected Phillipsburgh and Philadelphia, had been completed in 1854.[11] This great new transportation system meant that the shippers in the valley would be offered new and competitive rates for transit of goods to New York and Philadelphia. Previously the shippers had been forced to rely upon the canals (the Lehigh, Delaware Division, and Morris) which in the past had held a somewhat favorable situation, for there was little to compete against but wagons and poor roads which entailed relatively high costs. Further, the railroads brought the valley closer, in travel time, to those two great market areas, Philadelphia and New York. Instead of a two-day trip to these two cities it would now take a few hours.

The location of a new merchant iron furnace in the Lehigh Valley can be readily understood, for near at hand were four of the basic elements which determine the location of a manufacturing plant. These new works, with the valley's new transport system, had adequate access to market, accessible stores of raw materials (coal, iron ore, and limestone) within a few miles of each other, a supply of power (water or coal), and, as already seen, a growing supply of capital. Further by 1854 there was a group of experienced and disciplined furnace hands

---

[11] Henry, History of the Lehigh Valley, pp. 150-51.

ready to provide the necessary skills to operate the furnaces as well as the brawn to load the furnaces and mine the local ore deposits the company might own. Interestingly enough, the work force was generally of Scotch, Welsh, or "Pennsylvania Dutch" origin and relatively conservative; for a number of years it was to offer practically no labor troubles to the iron company.

The question then arises as to the selection of the particular furnace site of about 185 acres of ground near Catasauqua on the Hokendauqua Creek and the Lehigh River. There adequate land was purchased at a cost of $37,112.50 or about $200 an acre, which evidently was considered a "fair" price.[12] At that site there was ready access to the canal and the railroad then being completed. By selecting this location the company obtained an unsettled portion of land which it could develop not only as a furnace site but as a separate company-controlled community. Building in one of the already settled communities of the valley would have required the company to surrender certain elements of what it considered valuable prerogatives. The organizers of the company seemed to be convinced that it was desirable to continue the traditional practice of the charcoal ironmasters, to build and control their own town site. There they could regulate all the property and would be able to influence and establish the political privileges of the workers which would have been fully established and irrevocable in an already settled community. Of course, there were certain economic implications involved as well, for by

---

[12] Fackenthal, <u>The Thomas Iron Company, 1854-1904</u>, p. 9.

having land to build homes upon the company could attract the workers necessary to operate their iron works. However, we will find that when the organization of the community was first being developed some of the plots of ground were sold to a few of the stockholders and shortly thereafter they were repurchased, for "it was found desirable that the Company should own and control the entire property . . . ."[13] In this way the company, in some manner bound by tradition, preferred to maintain some of those feudal characteristics of the previously mentioned Hampton furnace.

By 1854 most of the Lehigh Valley's new iron works were being or had been constructed in the lower end of the valley, where they were more distant from the coal deposits but within easier access to local and New Jersey ore deposits as well as the New York and Philadelphia markets. The anthracite coal, unlike bituminous coal, was not as susceptible to deterioration in transit; thus it could be shipped, without much loss, for greater distances. Further, the coal mined near Mauch Chunk was moved from the mines to the canal by rail and then by barge via the canal to the furnaces along the canal, or shortly would be hauled all the way from mine to furnace via the Lehigh Valley Railroad. All of this must have served to reduce the transport costs of this raw material.

Though the canal barges, as we have already seen, carried enormous quantities of ore from mines to the furnaces, all of the evidence available seems to indicate that most of this raw material carried via the canal was magnetite ore which was shipped into the Lehigh Valley via the

---

[13] Ibid., p. 31. Mathews and Hungerford, Lehigh and Carbon Counties, p. 502.

Morris Canal in New Jersey to the Lehigh Canal at Easton. At the valley furnaces this ore was mixed with the brown hematite from the local mines to produce the foundry iron demanded by the iron trade at that time. The hematite ores generally were hauled by team and wagon to the furnaces. The reason for this is evident when one locates the iron mines being exploited and relates the distances between the mines and the canal and the mines and the furnaces. Considering the handling problems involved in transporting the ore via the canal to the furnaces and the relative location of the mines, it seems consistent that hauling the ores overland to the furnaces was the more economic method rather than employing the canal. Unfortunately there seem to be no statistics available on the relative costs for such an operation.

Hence, when approximately equal amounts of ore and coal were mixed with a small amount of flux, transportation costs considered, the more economic location of a furnace site within the Lehigh Valley would be influenced by the proximity of the ore and the type of ore that was to be used.[14] Thus if a great amount of magnetite ore from New Jersey was to be used, relative to the brown hematite ores, the more economic location of the furnace site within the valley would be closer to the hematite mines at Easton and on the Morris Canal in New Jersey. But if more brown hematite ore was to be smelted, relative to the magnetite, the location near the more abundant local ore deposits would have been

---

[14]The approximate amounts of coal, ore, and limestone used to produce a ton of iron in No. 1 furnace of The Thomas Iron Company in 1855 were: 2 tons 8 2/10 cwts. of coal, 2 tons 12 3/10 cwts. of ore, and 1 ton 11 cwts. of limestone. See The Thomas Iron Co. Fin. Rec., p. 4.

advisable because of the difficulty of transporting that ore via wagon. As The Thomas Iron Company used, for the moment, a greater quantity of the brown hematite ore relative to the magnetite, its furnace location north of Allentown and a very few miles from the nematite mines indicates that some consideration had been given to this cost problem.

The problem of procuring the local hematite ore was of such enormity that before the first furnace was blown in The Thomas Iron Company managers thought it economically expedient to solve their transportation problem by obtaining some other more expeditious manner of transport than wagon and team. To this end they planned to engage in the construction of a rail connection between the hematite mines and their furnaces. But more on this later.

It seems fair to conclude that the selection of the furnace site of The Thomas Iron Company was influenced by economic considerations as well as traditional preferences, but there might be one further reason for locating in the neighborhood of Catasauqua and the Crane Iron Works. Possibly the role of technical adviser to be played by David Thomas could be transacted most effectively if the works were located in the proximity of his regular business and home, a factor which could account for this location at Hokendauqua. A further consideration is the location of the Carbon Iron Works, another company that David Thomas helped to organize. These works were located a few miles above Hokendauqua on the Lehigh River.

This idea is purely speculative, though it is strange that, while the main office of the company was to be maintained in Easton, a site for the furnace could not have been located near that community on the Lehigh

River. Such a site would have been closer to markets in New York and Philadelphia and closer to the magnetite ores of New Jersey while still within the proximity of a supply of the local ores.

As for the particular plot of ground selected for the furnace site, it was a rather small but flat cut on the west bank of the Lehigh River a few miles north of Allentown. The canal was on the opposite side of the river; this required the building of a bridge to connect the works with that means of transportation. On the west side of the river, and alongside the very works, ran the new Lehigh Valley Railroad Company's tracks, which certainly offered an important advantage over the Crane Iron Company's works across the river and had been so located to take advantage of the location of the canal. In 1855 the 185 acres of land in sheltered cut seemed to provide adequate space for the construction of the iron furnaces of that day and age. Later, however, when the problem of integration and expansion arose, the site was to have certain disadvantages that presented an unfavorable situation that was apparently unsolvable. These very problems played a part in the final decision to withdraw the firm from production in 1922.

The Construction Program

The first president of the corporation was Peter Michler and C. F. Randolph was appointed treasurer and secretary. The superintendent of the works was Samuel Thomas, who was also responsible for the construction of the furnaces, though he was to receive invaluable guidance from his father. His salary was $2,000 with perquisites consisting of a home, the remodeled Butz farmhouse, and fuel. Also, a bookkeeper, almost as important as the superintendent, was hired with an annual salary of $550.[15] Only the latter two positions were full-time jobs.

Once the furnace site had been selected, these men initiated the building program by advertising for bids for the construction of the furnaces. By April orders had been placed with Bunce, Esler, and D. B. Cobb for boilers and with the West Point Foundry at Cold Spring, New York, for two steam blowing engines. The engines were to have steam cylinders 56 inches in diameter and blowing cylinders of 84 inches in diameter. The order for cast metal parts of the furnace was placed with I. P. Morris, Towne and Company of Philadelphia, the Southwark Foundry. Finally, in May a contract was made with Samuel McHose of Allentown to erect the heavy brick and masonry work for the furnaces.[16]

The furnaces, when completed, were the largest and most powerful works yet constructed in the Lehigh Valley. They were both 60 feet high, with boshes 18 feet in diameter. Their gas chambers were placed at the top of the furnace in order to utilize the waste gases from the stack to heat the air for the blast, the heat of the blast being raised to 600° Fahrenheit with the use of the hot gases. The presure of the blast was 7½ pounds to the square inch, the greatest blast pressure used by any furnace yet built. Once again David Thomas's inclination to experiment is observable. Each furnace had twelve tuyeres through which entered the blast blown by one of the largest steam-operated blowing machines then

---

[14]Min. Book - The Thomas Iron Co., pp. 4 ff.

[16]Fackenthal, The Thomas Iron Company, 1854-1904, p. 11.

ILLUSTRATION 4

SECTIONAL VIEW OF THE THOMAS IRON COMPANY
BLAST FURNACE, 1855

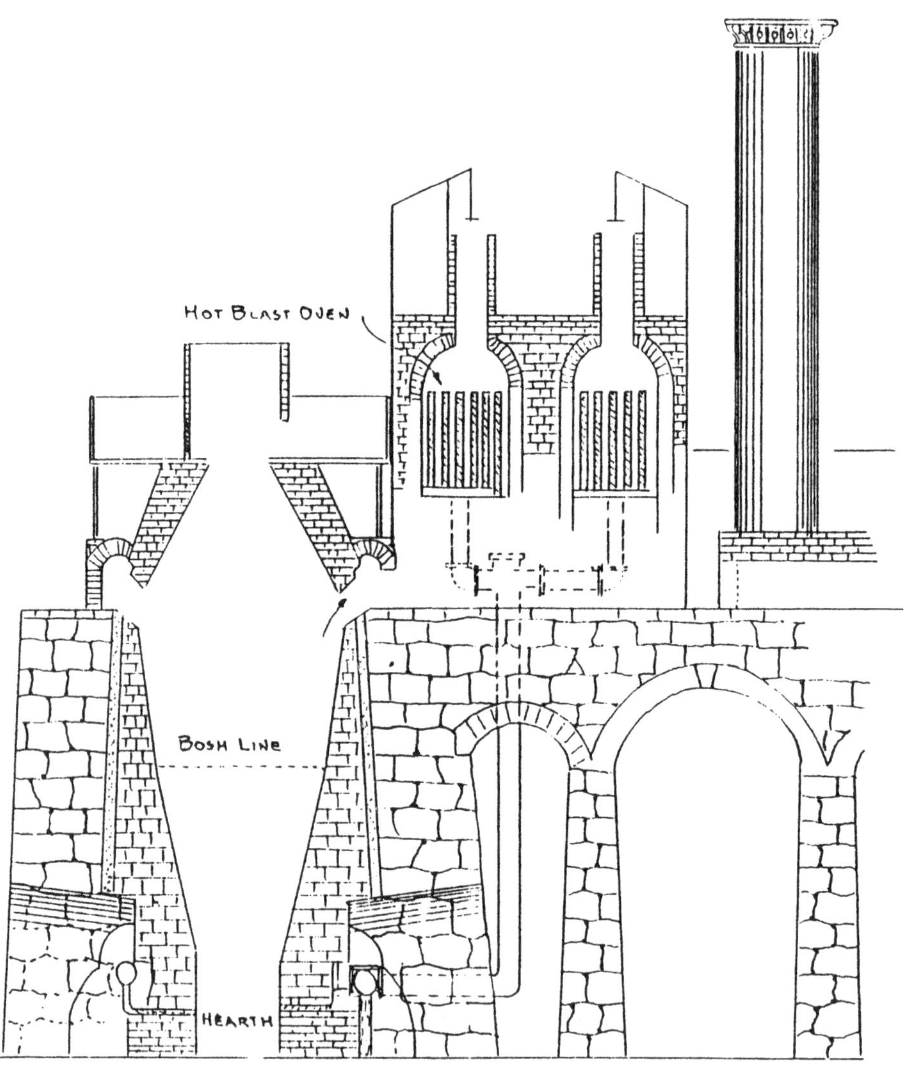

Source: J. Percy, Metallurgy: Iron and Steel, Appendix.

employed in the iron industry. With these facilities it was estimated that the annual capacity of the furnaces would be about 10,000 tons of pig iron per annum.[17] Up to that time David Thomas's furnaces at the Crane Iron Works were estimated to be capable of producing only 8,000 tons per annum.

To digress a moment in order to expand on the technological implications of these new furnaces, it is to be noted that by 1854 the construction of blast furnaces had been undertaken with a greater awareness that changes in the structural design of the furnace might provide greater operating efficiency. The notion was that by improving the interior furnace lines waste gases and fuel could be used more efficiently. Thus more forethought was given to the interior design and the height of the furnaces in order to attain an additional increase in output and possible reductions in the consumption of coal, at the same time improving the quality of the iron. It is true that the basic structure of the blast furnace remained the same, with the typical furnace being made up of "two truncated cones, joined by their bases." The upper cone, and the more acute of the two, was called the stack while the lower cone, which was generally shorter and more obtuse as well as inverted, was called the bosh. The bosh was extended downward to the ground level, forming what was called the hearth or crucible of the furnace in which the molten materials were collected below the level of the tuyeres or pipes through which the hot-blast was introduced. The sides of the

---

[17]Daddow and Bannan, Coal, Iron, and Oil, p. 684.

hearth were generally perpendicular and from 6 to 8 feet high or even higher.[18]

The Thomas Iron Company's furnaces were no different in these respects from any other furnaces, and like others the top of the furnace or the throat was surrounded by a platform for purposes of charging the furnace and a short chimney was attached to lead off the flame escaping at the throat. The furnaces built by the company, however, did differ in their over-all dimensions. The furnace was 60 feet tall; the boshes were extremely high in comparison with other anthracite furnaces and had extremely steep bosh angles which, it was believed, would enable the furnace operators to increase the productivity of their furnaces.

To explain the greater efficiency of these furnaces, it is desirable to explain briefly the function of the various parts or sectors of the blast furnace. In the very early charcoal or air furnaces, when a low hearth was used, a portion of the iron ore was reduced to a metallic state at a relatively low temperature. The other part of the ore combines with the silica present to form a basic slag. The excess of carbon was taken from the spongy metallic material when the blast, introduce through a single tuyere, combined with the oxidizing agency of the slag.

The development of the high blast furnace was an outgrowth of attempts by furnace managers or ironmasters to use the waste heat of the

---

[18]E. M. K. Talcott, "The Manufacture of Pig Iron," _American Society of Civil Engineers Transactions_, I (1867-71), 195. This work will hereafter be cited as Talcott, "The Manufacture of Pig Iron," _ASCE Trans._, I. See also H. Bauerman, _A Treatise on the Metallurgy of Iron_ (New York, 1868), p. 138; J. E. Johnson, Jr., _Blast Furnace Construction_ (New York, 1918), pp. 2-3.

low furnace to reduce the fuel required in the production of iron. When this type of furnace was in blast, it was filled to its top or throat with alternate layers of fuel, ore, and flux, these being mixed in such proportions as to produce the most fusible combinations of earthy materials. Also a constant blast of air was passed through the tuyeres at a sufficient pressure to enable air to penetrate through the materials in the furnaces. Part of the fuel was burned, forming carbonic acid, and the material immediately adjacent to the fuel was melted and fell to the hearth where it separated into the metal and the slag; the latter, being lighter, rose to the surface. The carbonic acid formed in the first situation, upon encountering fresh fuel, was changed to carbonic oxide, with a great absorption of heat. This carbonic oxide, when brought into contact with an oxide of iron at a red heat, was oxidized to carbonic acid and simultaneously the oxide of iron was reduced to metallic iron, which was carburetted by its contact with carbonaceous matter in its descent toward the hearth.

The alternate reproduction of carbonic acid and carbonic oxide was continued in the upper reaches of the furnace so long as the termperature remained sufficiently high and the quantity of the former gas was continually augmented through the decomposition of the limestone flux. At the top of the furnace as the carbonic acid remaining in the waste gases came into contact with the air, it formed a great body of flame. If this gas was not permitted contact with the air but collected in some manner, it served as a valuable fuel for the operation of accessory elements of the furnace. It was this gas which was used to heat the hot-blast. In this way the furnace shaft or stack performed the functions of several furnaces. The hearth was devoted to fusion, the middle section was a concentration chamber, and the top, when raw coal and flux were used, combined the functions of a coke oven and limekiln.[19]

The taller shaft furnaces required a column or stock of materials which could be penetrable by a considerable volume of gas, the more dense the fuel the greater the pressure of the blast. If the gases did not move up through the stack, there was the danger of scaffolding (adhesion of the materials to the side of the furnace) or some other obstruction which slowed up the chemical process and the downward delivery of the solids. Charcoal fuel was probably the most efficient fuel because its porosity required a lower blast pressure, but its friability deterred the furnace managers from building their charcoal furnace stacks too high. Anthracite coal, a much denser fuel, required a much higher pressure blast and, as pointed out previously, required a pre-heated blast. Because of the density of the fuel, however, it could support a heavier load and thus permit the anthracite furnace operators, as seen in this instance, to build furnaces 20 to 30 feet higher than the ordinary charcoal furnace.

Thus it is obvious that The Thomas Iron Company's higher furnace stack, which would carry a heavier load than most furnaces, would require the heavier blast pressure in order to avoid as much as possible the

---

[19]Bauerman, _A Treatise on the Metallurgy of Iron_, pp. 136-37. J. E. Johnson, Jr., _Principles of Operation and Products of the Blast Furnace_ (New York, 1918), pp. 1-4. This work will hereafter be cited as Johnson, _Prin. of Operation and Prod. of the Blast Furn_.

danger of scaffolding and to force the hot gases to the top of the stack. At the same time the taller furnace permitted the more efficient capture of the hot gases passed on by the smelting process. The high bosh provided a greater concentration area and of course increased the capacity of the furnace. It might be mentioned that these works were later selected by John Percy, an authority on metallurgy and author of one of the most comprehensive works on iron production, as the most pre-eminent anthracite works in the United States.[20]

To return to the construction program, in a June edition of the Easton Argus there was an advertisement for bids on "the erection of twelve dwelling houses, to be either brick or frame, and to be ready for occupancy the the 1st day of October next."[21] In November the town had been laid out and the streets named. When completed in 1855, the community of Hokendauqua consisted of twelve brick tenement homes for the workers and one completed street. The homes were provided with spring water pumped through water pipes laid by the company. Also, lots were provided for a schoolhouse and church, their construction commencing that same year.

The following March the legislature passed an act to supplement the corporate charter of The Thomas iron Company. This modification permitted the corporation to invest in a railroad running from the works to the ore mines in Berks County. The same act also permitted the issuance of

---

[20] Percy, Metallurgy: Iron and Steel, p. 382.

[21] Easton Argus, June 22, 1854.

$300,000 more in capital stock, and by April $50,000 of this stock had been sold to the original stockholders. Still later $25,000 more was sold at $50 per share.[22]

Prior to this event President Michler, burdened by his duties which detracted from his coal and banking business, declined re-election as president and C. A. Luckenbach was elected to that office. President Michler received $700 for his year of service, but Luckenbach was to receive $1,500 annually. His responsibilities would become heavier and more complex as the furnace neared completion. John T. Knight was appointed treasurer and C. F. Randolph retained the position of secretary.[23]

Under these new administrative officers the construction program continued with new questions arising which required answers. The completion of the furnaces carried the business firm closer to its function as a producer and seller of pig iron, and the new questions that cropped up pertained to furnace operation and sales. One of the first problems was the appointment of a sales agent for the company; in April, 1855, R. S. Chidsey, one of the stockholders, was appointed as the first sales agent at an annual compensation of $1,500, with the additional payment of certain expenses. Meanwhile, the first coal for the blast furnaces was purchased from J. F. Randolph and Company for $2.20 a ton at Mauch Chunk.[24]

---

[22]Min. Book - The Thomas Iron Co., pp. 25 ff.

[23]Ibid., p. 25.

[24]Ibid., p. 27. The company that sold the coal to the iron company was the same company that J. F. Randolph, secretary of The Thomas Iron Copmpany, held a major interest.

At approximately the same time the question of constructing the mine-to-furnace railroad was settled; it was resolved to build the Catasauqua and Fogelsville Railroad to nearby Rothrocksville. The building of the railroad, however, was dependent upon the acceptance of part of the construction cost by the Crane Iron Company.[25]

As the time approached to put the furnace in actual operation, a labor force was gathered together and the first wage contract was signed by the furnace workers on June 1, 1855. This document, which is among those records of The Thomas Iron Company still in existence, was signed by twelve men who were to be the keepers, helpers, and fillers at the furnace. Only five could affix their signatures; the others used their marks. Each worker was to be paid on a piece-work basis, the rate varying with the make of iron as given:

Keepers	For every ton of	No. 1 iron (2,2540 pounds	9¢
"		No. 2 iron	8¢
"		No. 3 iron	7½¢
Helpers	For every ton of	No. 1 iron	7¼¢
"		No. 2 iron	6½¢
"		No. 3 iron	6¢
Fillers	For every ton of	No. 1 iron	6¢
"		No. 2 iron	5 3/4¢
"		No. 3 iron	5¼¢

The stipulations which followed are such that they are reproduced in part to furnish some indication of the attitude of the management to labor's responsibilities. It also offers evidence of the strong paternalistic attitude toward labor on the part of the management. Possibly

---

[25] *Ibid.*

this may be taken as a further indication of the stockholders' anxious desire to maintain a separate community along the traditional lines of the charcoal iron works.

> The foregoing prices to be paid from the first day of June 1855 to the first day of October 1855 and for the other three months from the 1st October 1855 to the first day of January 1856 10 per cent less than the aforementioned [sic] prices. And The Thomas Iron Co reserves the power to termnate this agreement at a less period than one year, should the price of Iron be so low as to make a general reduction herein before stipulated necessary. And we further severall [sic] agree to receive 90 per cent of the aforementioned [sic] prices at the regular four weekly pay days, and the other 10 per cent to remain in the hands of the Company untill [sic] the Agreement is faithfully performed and fulfilled on our part respectively. And it is distinctly understood that if anyone of us shall get in the habit of drinking liquors or should neglect their work by reason of intoxication or shall absent himself and leave his work (sickness excepted) without having procurred [sic] a sufficient substitute to the satisfaction of the furnace overseer then and in either of said cases such one shall forfeit his situation in the employ of said Company and the said 10 per cent.
>
> And we further severally agree that if through carelessness or inattention we break any part of the Company machinery that we shall be held responsible for the cost of repairing the same . . . .[26]

First Blast

Two days after the labor contract was signed the No. 1 furnace was blown in and 74 tons of foundry iron were made in the first week. By June 29, 399 tons of pig iron had been run out, an average of about 15 tons a day. Total output by December 31 was 6,445 tons, with an average

---

[26]The Thomas Iron Company: Papers and Documents, p. 1. This work will hereafter be cited as The Thomas Iron Co.: Papers and Doc. This material is in the collection of the Lehigh University Library, Bethlehem, Pennsylvania.

daily yield for each furnace of 23.18 tons. These figures included the product of furnace No. 2, which had been put in blast in October.[27]

In the meantime the price of No. 1 anthracite foundry iron in Philadelphia had dropped to approximately $27.75 a ton.[28] That November the company's sales agent was authorized to sell foundry iron delivered for $27.50 a ton.[29]

With the estimated cost of production being $20.57 a ton, the price of $27.50 per ton still provided a sizable tonnage profit. The cost of a ton of iron was divided as follows: coal, $7.57; ore, $9.49; limestone, 98 cents; and labor, salaries, supplies, etc., $2.45. But with profits of only $23,708.53 for the year, the return on the investment of $298,200 was not nearly as great as the tonnage profit. Considering that such returns were on the productive use of capital for a six-month period, however, the shareholders were probably quite satisfied with management's efforts, even though dividends were not paid that year.

By December the balance sheet of The Thomas Iron Company indicated that the managers had established quite a sizable business. Though not quite as impressive as the Brady's Bend iron works near Pittsburgh, with its integrated plan consisting of mines, blast furnaces, rolling mills and foundry, representing an investment of $1,000,000, The Thomas Iron Company's works were probably the most complete merchant iron

---

[27]The Thomas Iron Co. Fin. Rec., p. 4.

[28]Swank, The American Iron Trade in 1876, p. 184.

[29]Min. Book - The Thomas Iron Co., p. 32.

establishment in the eastern area at that time.[30]

By the end of 1855 The Thomas Iron Company had completed the construction of two of the largest furnaces in the country. The works as a whole consisted of the furnaces, railroad equipment within the premises used to handle ore, coal, and limestone in addition to horses, wagons, carts or barrows, scales, and other implements which had cost approximately $240,732. There were also wharves at the works and at Allentown to handle the raw materials, as well as an office building at Hokendauqua, twelve tenement homes, and the superintendent's home, all valued at $42,039. Also the company had accumulated inventories of raw materials valued at $76,687.88.[31]

Before the year had drawn to a close, the minute book indicated that further operation problems were arising which seemed to require further extension of the firm's business activities. Plans were already under way for the purchase of ore deposits in both New Jersey and Pennsylvania, and the construction of the Catasauqua and Fogelsville Railroad was beginning to require immediate attention. Slowly a pattern of growth was emerging, a growth that was to have far-reaching consequences in the history of The Thomas Iron Company and the iron industry of the Lehigh Valley, a significant segment of the American economy at the time.

---

[30] Clark, History of Manufactures in the United States, I, 446.

[31] The Thomas Iron Co. Fin. Rec., p. 4.

CHAPTER VI

THE AGE OF ANTHRACITE PIG IRON, 1855-1875

Business Conditions and Iron Production

As noted previously, the expansion in the production of anthracite pig iron between 1849 and 1854 was hastened by a period of business prosperity. These business conditions had been accentuated by the acceptance of the "railroad idea" by businessmen and the general public; people had finally been convinced that the building of railroads offered great profit opportunities.[1] Discoveries of gold, improved banking facilities, and better credit instruments, as well as an increased flow of capital from England and Europe, provided the necessary finanacial means to facilitate this development. A continuing and relatively rapid influx of immigrants provided an increasing supply of labor for the construction of these railroads and the raising of many new factories and furnaces. But most important was the stimulating effect of the unprecedented expansion of railroads upon the country's business activity. It enhanced the opportunities for other enterprisers and induced them to carry out the expansion of older ventures or develop new ones. Furthermore, this railroad development furnished the opportunity for locational, structural, and organizational alterations among particular firms, industries, and

---

[1]Leland Jenks, "Railroads as an Economic Force in American Development," as found in J. T. Lambie and R. V. Clemence, eds., Economic Change in America (Harrisburg, 1954), pp. 52-53.

regions.

As business activity increased under the pressures of the railroad program, there were also a rapid price rise and growth in speculation, especially in land sales. This speculation was quickened by railroad development and an increase in the volume of agricultural exports, which makes it difficult to place the cause for the rise in land prices on any single factor. In 1854 a panic in the New York Stock Exchange brought the price rise to a halt and caused the failure of a number of business ventures. Shortly thereafter, however, this condition was remedied and once again there was a resumption of speculation which continued throughout the next two years.[2]

Railroad expansion and the increasing use of steam power in other industrial sectors of the economy called for a complementary growth in iron production. Consequently, throughout these years there was a continuing increase in the number of anthracite furnaces, and an ever-increasing amount of pig iron produced. By 1854 the annual production of anthracite iron had been raised to 339,435 net tons, and at the end of the next year the total output from anthracite furnaces exceeded the total product of the more numerous charcoal furnaces scattered throughout the nation. While the total domestic pig iron output was raised to 784,178 net tons, anthracite iron made up 48.6 percent of this total and

---

[2]Elmer C. Bratt, <u>Business Cycles and Forcasting</u> (1st ed.; Chicago, 1948), pp. 258-59. Smith and Cole, <u>Fluctuations in American Businss: 1790-1860</u>, pp. 81 ff. Harold M. Somers, "The Performance of the American Economy, 1789-1865," as found in Harold Williamson, ed., <u>Growth of the American Economy</u>, p. 322.

charcoal iron 43.4 percent. The other 8 percent was produced by a few raw bituminous coal and coke furnaces.[3]

In 1856 there was a further extension of output from the anthracite furnaces as it moved up to 443,113 net tons.[4] But this growth in production was halted quite abruptly by the panic of 1857 and the resulting depression.

During the year of the panic there was a sudden contraction of credit in the United States brought about by unfavorable specie flows and certain banking difficulties. Simultaneously, railroads, which had been extended beyond favorable market areas, found themselves with insufficient income to maintain their fixed costs. A number of these roads were unable to meet their interest payments, and in their failure they proceeded to drag into bankruptcy a number of banks which had become entangled in their railroad expansion program. Shortly thereafter, specie payments were suspended and railroad expansion declined precipitously. With the reduction in the growth of this industry, there followed a drop in output in related industries. Then, as the general price level dropped and the speculative atmosphere of the business world was replaced by an air of unrest, there was a further decline in business activity.[5]

These economic conditions prevailed for a relatively short period

---

[3]American Iron and Steel Association, _Statistics of the American and Foreign Iron Trade for 1876_ (Philadelphia, 1877), p. 12.

[4]_Ibid_.

[5]Bratt, _Business Cycles and Forecasting_, p. 259. Somers, "The Performance of the American Economy, 1789-1865," p. 323.

of time, but it was time enough to bring about the failure of approximately 5,000 business firms; a number of these firms had been in the iron smelting business.[6]

With the revival of the financial sector of the economy, more prosperous conditions returned to the rest of the economy and only slowed down briefly as open warfare between the North and the South commenced. Then, as the federal government's expenditures increased, the earlier caution held by the businessmen in 1860 was swept away, production was increased, and income levels rose once again. For the next few years almost all sectors of the northern economy prospered under the favorable effects of the government's expansionary fiscal policy which included heavy expenditures and borrowing.[7]

Throughout this period of conflict the iron industry brought forth an ever-increasing flow of metal so necessary for the waging of a war which had created numerous uses for iron in guns, rifles, ironclad ships, railroads, wagon wheels, various machines, machine tools, and hardware. This growth in demand carried pig iron prices upward, and, as prices rose, pig iron output was increased until it finally reached 1,135,996 net tons in 1864.[8]

---

[6] Ibid.

[7] Ibid. Somers, "The Performance of the American Economy, 1789-1865," pp. 324 ff.

[8] Swank, The American Iron Trade in 1876, p. 12. American Iron and Steel Institute, Annual Statistical Report for 1922, p. 9. Swank, Iron in All Ages, p. 526. This iron output was a level which had been attained by the British ironmasters in 1836.

With the close of the military conflict in 1865, there was a reduction in government expenditures and a contraction of greenbacks. These adjustments, plus the appearance of surplus revenues in the Federal Treasury and a business panic in England in 1866, served to push the general price level downward.[9] Business activity, on the other hand, was not seriously affected by the economic readjustment, nor did the continuing but gradual decline in wholesale prices up to 1871 restrict the country from enjoying somewhat prosperous business conditions for the next seven years.

During that period which extended from 1866 to 1873 the economic activity of the nation was maintained at a prosperous level of activity by a very active program of railroad expansion. Geared to railroad expansion, the iron industry enjoyed a period of prosperity which stimulated a further growth in the number of furnaces and an increase in the number of tons of pig iron produced.

While railroad mileage was being doubled, from 36,827 miles in 1866 to 72,623 miles in 1874, the iron industry tried to meet the demand through the construction of new facilities, in some cases following the more modern techniques of furnace construction that had been developed in England in the 1850's.[10] Also, pig iron tonnage, which had dropped below

---

[9] Bratt, Business Cycles and Forecasting, p. 260. Harold Somers, "The Performance of the American Economy, 1866-1918," as found in Harold Williamson, ed., Growth of the American Economy, p. 648.

[10] American Iron and Steel Association, Statistics of the American and Foreign Iron Trade for 1875 (Philadelphia, 1876), p. 20.

1,000,000 tons in 1865, was soon pushed beyond the peak period production of 1864 and was continually increased until it had reached a new peak in 1873 of 2,868,278 net tons.[11] But the expansion in output was interrupted in 1873 as railroad construction fell once again when the flow of capital so necessary for its continuance was shut off by disturbed financial conditions.[12] Pig iron, so essential in the production of rails, boiler plate, car axles, wheels, spikes, and other railroad equipment, had been smelted in ever-increasing quantities, but now, as the demand declined, output was reduced somewhat. However, at this stage of development the decline in pig iron production was not as precipitous as the drop in new railroad mileage. (See the chart on the following page.)

Pig iron prices, which had generally moved downward from 1864 to 1870, moved upward quite sharply in 1871 but then proceeded to drop again in 1873 and they were destined to fall to a low of $17.62 in 1878.[13] As prices declined, iron production was reduced and the number of new blast furnaces being constructed fell to an extremely low level. Of the 713 completed blast furnaces of all types in existence in 1875, only 293 were reported in blast, and their total output was less than one-half of the estimated capacity of all the furnaces, being only 2,266,561 net tons.[14]

---

[11] _Ibid._, p. 8.

[12] Bratt, _Business Cycles and Forecasting_, p. 260. Somers, "The Performance of the American Economy, 1866-1918," pp. 648 ff.

[13] Swank, _Iron in All Ages_, p. 514.

[14] _Ibid._, p. 376. Swank, _The American Iron Trade in 1876_, p. 169.

CHART I

RELATIVE CHANGES IN NEW RAILROAD MILEAGE, PIG IRON PRODUCTION PIG IRON IMPORTS, AND PIG IRON PRICES, 1854-77

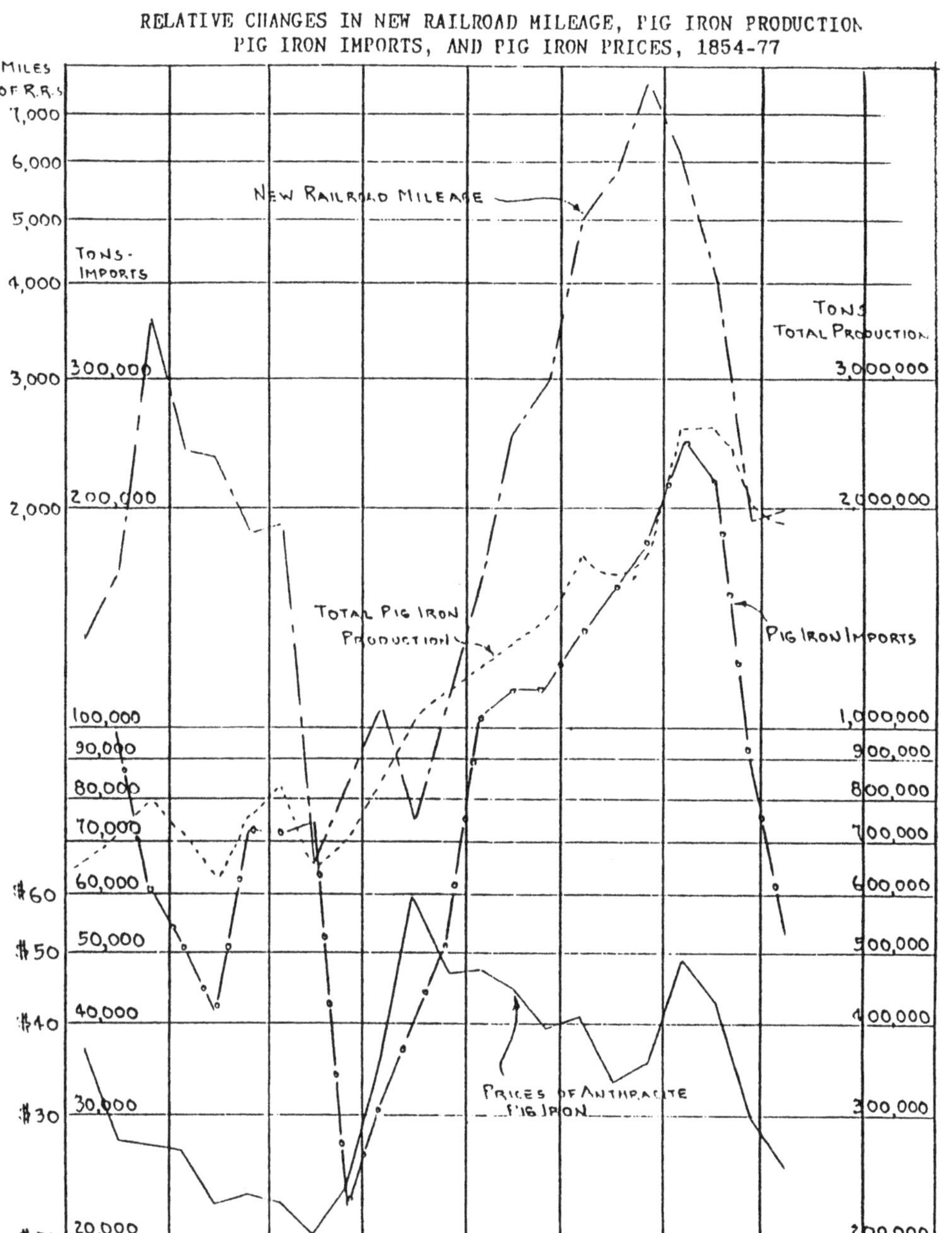

Source: J. M. Swank, The American Iron Trade in 1876 (Philadelphia, 1876), passim.

From this brief discussion of the conditions of business between 1855 and 1875 it is quite evident that the pig iron industry was subject to extreme fluctuations in demand, a condition that arose from the extreme fluctuations in railroad activity which was somewhat speculative in nature. It must be recognized, however, that important changes had taken place in the iron industry during these years, for, despite the general downward movement of pig iron prices, there had been, until 1873, a continual expansion in the production of pig iron. The growth in production suggests that improvements, either in furnace practice or equipment, plus the improvements in the railroad network of the nation, must have reduced the unit cost of pig iron production and enabled ironmasters to obtain profits despite declining prices.

Tariff Policy and the Iron Trade

Nothwithstanding the continuing expansion of output in the iron industry, the domestic production was not voluminous enough to meet the needs of the more rapidly expanding railroads of the nation. Railroad construction throughout this period not only called for more miles of rail but also demanded heavier rails, a change which called for more iron per mile than previously used. As a consequence of this demand and the inability of the domestic iron industry to satiate it, there was a continuous expansion of iron imports which first commenced to grow in 1861. This import trade was sustained until 1872, despite the relatively high import duties established during the war period.

Prior to the outbreak of war in 1861, there had been a reversal of the protectionist policy maintained in various forms between 1832 and

1842. Then the policy of protection was modified somewhat in 1846 when duties on pig iron were reduced to 30 percent *ad valorem*, and later, in 1857, reduced again to 24 percent. During these later years anthracite pig iron output was continually increased despite the lower duty, but charcoal furnaces, in many instances, were forced to shut down as pig iron prices declined.

It is interesting to note that the pattern of change for iron imports show more rapid movements than the change in domestic production. For example, after 1855 the volume of imports dropped continually until 1858 when there was a slight expansion which, however, was wiped out in 1860 and 1861. On the other hand, domestic iron production did not fall as sharply as iron imports and once business activity was rejuvenated domestic production moved to a new peak.

With the commencement of war, the volume of iron imports began to expand once again and continued to increase until 1872, but then, as the number of new miles of railroad dropped, iron imports dropped quite as rapidly. Pig iron imports increased despite the levying of higher duties in 1862, when the proponents of the protective tariff system used the need for revenues as the excuse for the higher barrier to trade. By that date the specific duty on pig iron and scrap was $6.00 a ton while bar iron was taxed $15 a ton.[15] In retrospect such a tax seems difficult to reconcile with the problem of keeping war expenditures at a minimum, for they served to keep the price of domestic iron above the actual cost of

---

[15]American Iron and Steel Association, *Statistics of the American and Foreign Iron Trade for 1871* (Philadelphia, 1872), p. 39.

imported iron.

At first these duties were regarded as temporary expedients, but they were retained, increased, and finally welded into a system of extraordinary protection. By 1864 the specific duty on pig iron had been raised to $9.00 a ton, though an internal tax measure was adopted which placed a charge of $2.00 on every ton of pig iron produced domestically. The excise tax served, in part, to counteract the higher costs of domestically produced iron, a consequence of the "protective" tariff. By that time the "statesmen" who had prepared the tariff acts did not attempt to conceal their desire to protect home industries, although they continually used the urgent need for revenues as a means of carrying out their protective policy.[16]

The internal tax of $2.00 a ton on pig iron was removed in 1866, but it was some five years after the war had ended before any effort was made to remove or lower the import duty, long after the need for revenue had passed. By 1870 the free traders' cry for reduced tariffs and the embarrassing growth in government revenues led Congress to reduce the pig iron duty by $2.00. Momentarily the reduction allayed the growing demand to the complete removal of the duty; yet it still served as a protective barrier for the domestic iron industry.

When a further 10 percent "horizontal" reduction in all duties was made in 1872, the free traders felt sure that they had made another step forward, but the protectionists were just as certain the victory was

---

[16]Taussig, <u>Tariff History of the United States</u>, pp. 155 ff.

theirs.[17] Whatever the direction of change, the method used to reduce import duties was most indiscriminate.

As for the iron industry, the reduction in duties was made during a period of rising pig iron prices; consequently, the specific duty became relatively smaller as a percentage of the value of the imports. Still the American importer had to pay transport costs, the duty, and the cost of foreign iron; thus it seems quite probable that the profits of the domestic ironmasters could have been sizable. As pig iron prices began to drop in 1873, the specific duty became, as a percentage of the value of the imports, a relatively higher barrier to trade. This result seems to suggest that the protectionists had maintained their position.

At the time that the reduction in duties was made, there seems to have been little outcry, but with the decline in pig iron prices after 1872 numerous blast furnaces were forced to stop production. A new plea for higher duties was projected through the trade journals and meetings were called by various groups of furnace operators. This hue and cry was made although the specific duty had become more restrictive at the lower price and imports had dropped very rapidly. Blast furnace owners throughout the country called for further protection against imports, and the eastern owners were the most vociferous in these demands. Furnace owners also sought voluntary reductions in domestic output and prepared an appeal to Congress for the further subsidization of the railroad

---

[17] Ibid., p. 189.

building program.[18] But their most urgent request was for additional protection against the "excessive" importation of foreign goods.

The import statistics of the period indicate a situation somewhat different from that conjured up in the minds of these businessmen. While imports of iron and iron products had increased continuously from 1862 to 1872, the expansion of these imports was sustained in spite of declining prices and the increasing burden of the specific duty at the lower price. Furthermore, though pig iron imports continued to rise and prices declined, domestic iron production expanded at a rate of growth comparable to the growth in imports. Only when the rapid expansion in new railroad mileage declined did the domestic furnace men believe that foreign imports had become a dangerous source of competition. However, the volume of imports of iron and iron products declined much more precipitously than the domestic production of iron when new railroad mileage was reduced in 1872.[19]

When the cries for the extension of protection for the domestic iron producers reached the rather sensitive ears of Congressmen, the 10 percent reduction of 1872 was revoked with little opposition. The protectionists in the iron industry had won their battle. Arguments of the few producers who had been calling for improvements in technology in order to reduce costs were ignored for the moment; the higher duties would protect the iron industry once again. The increased duty, however,

---

[18] Iron Age, Vol. 13 (June 4, 1874), 11; Vol. 14 (Dec. 17, 1874), 5.

[19] Swank, The American Iron Trade in 1876, pp. 165 ff.

did not sustain the prices of pig iron, for they continued to fall. At that time British exports to the United States dropped to their lowest level in years.

Comparative Pig Iron Production Statistics, 1855-1875

After the statistics of iron production for 1855 had been tabulated, it was evident that anthracite pig iron had been widely accepted as a substitute for charcoal iron. By that date anthracite iron made up approximately 49 percent of the total pig iron output, whereas charcoal furnaces had declined in number and their output had declined to but 43 percent of the total. This meant that almost one-half of the pig iron produced in 1855 had been produced in approximately 121 blast furnaces while the major portion of the other 50 percent had required the production of 396 charcoal furnaces. The remaining 8 percent was produced in approximately forty-three coke and raw bituminous coal furnaces located in western Pennsylvania, Maryland, and Ohio.[20]

Although the charcoal furnaces were still producing a very large proportion of the total pig iron, there was a very decided difference in the rate of increase in output from the different types of furnaces during the 1850's. By 1860 anthracite pig iron production had been raised to new heights, with a total output of 519,211 net tons. This tonnage figure indicates an increase in anthracite pig iron of 16 percent over the 1855 tonnage, but the total pig iron production for all furnaces had been increased only 9 percent during the same time period. Part of

---

[20] Lesley, *The Iron Manufacturer's Guide*, p. 747.

this increase in anthracite iron was due to the conversion of charcoal furnaces to anthracite fuel, but the more important change was due to the construction of new and somewhat larger anthracite furnaces which were operated with hotter blasts and higher pressures.[21]

In conjunction with the increased capacity of these newer blast furnaces there came an increasing demand for the raw materials needed to operate them. One of these furnaces alone consumed many times the materials used in an ordinary charcoal furnace; consequently, there was a new locational pattern which gradually evolved during these years. Furnaces more distant from the anthracite coal fields or in the areas of depleted woodlands and inadequate transportation facilities had to be gradually abandoned as unprofitable. Other areas which had the fortuitous combination of the necessary raw materials - coal, iron ores, and limestone - were soon growing into prosperous industrial communities as improved transportation facilities opened them for exploitation and capital flowed in to take advantage of the economic opportunity at hand.

Of the 121 anthracite furnaces constructed in this country by 1856, 93 were located in the Lehigh, Schuylkill, or Susquehanna valleys. The Lehigh Valley alone contained twenty-one, and four more were located in New Jersey in an area contiguous to this valley. By that date all three of the areas were being served by much improved rail and canal facilities; in numerous instances these transportation companies provided aid of some sort in order to attract new furnace owners into their service area.

---

[21] _Ibid._, p. 751.

Three other anthracite furnaces were situated in Massachusetts, fourteen in New York, one in Connecticut, and six in Maryland. The latter works were only able to operate because of the improved transportation facilities from the coal fields to the seaports, which reduced the cost of moving anthracite fuel from the coal fields of Pennsylvania.

The coke and raw bituminous coal furnaces were also located very near important coal fields. Twenty-seven such furnaces were located in western Pennsylvania in the Shenango Valley and in the Pittsburgh region by 1856. The rest of the forty-three coke and bituminous coal furnaces were situated near coal fields in Maryland and in the Mahoning Valley in Ohio.[22]

Numerous charcoal works were still scattered throughout the country, though there was a heavy concentration in Pennsylvania. In that state alone there were 150 such works while Virginia had 39; Tennessee, 41; and Kentucky, 30.[23] Meanwhile, there was a rapid decline in the number of charcoal works in many other areas.

During the war the number of new blast furnaces constructed was reduced somewhat relative to the earlier expansion, but furnace operators maintained a continual increase in the output of pig iron throughout these years. A large part of that iron production was diverted to war use rather than railroad construction, but with the shift back to railroad expansion there was an increase in the number of new furnaces and a

---

[22] *Ibid.*, pp. 747 and 759. Swank, *Iron in All Ages*, p. 370.

[23] *Ibid.*, *passim*.

TABLE 4

NUMBER OF BLAST FURNACES IN SELECTED YEARS

Year	Anthracite	Bituminous Coal and Coke	Charcoal	Total
1810	-	-	153	153[1]
1840	6	-	796	804[1]
1850	57	11	309	377[1]
1856	121	43	416	680[2]
1872	192	150	247	589[3]
1873	207	171	279	657[4]
1875	225	207	281	713[4]

Source: 1. T. Dunlap, Wiley's American Iron Trade Manual, passim. J. M. Swank, Iron in All Ages, p. 510.
2. J. P. Lesley, The Iron Manufacturer's Guide, pp. 747 and 759.
3. American Iron and Steel Association, Statistics of the American and Foreign Iron Trade for 1873 (Philadelphia, 1874), pp. 48-49.
4. J. M. Swank, The American Iron Trade in 1876, pp. 169-70.

continuation of the shift in plant location. More and more furnaces were built within easy reach of coal supplies.

Again, in the post-war period as in the 1850's, anthracite pig iron was produced in continually larger quantities, while charcoal iron became a smaller portion of the total pig iron produced despite the continual expansion in the total quantity produced. The most notable change in the production statistics during the later years of the period was the enormous increase in the volume of iron manufactured with coke and bituminous coal.

By 1873 the production of all types of pig iron had been raised to

CHART II

NUMBER OF FURNACES BUILT EACH YEAR, 1835-95

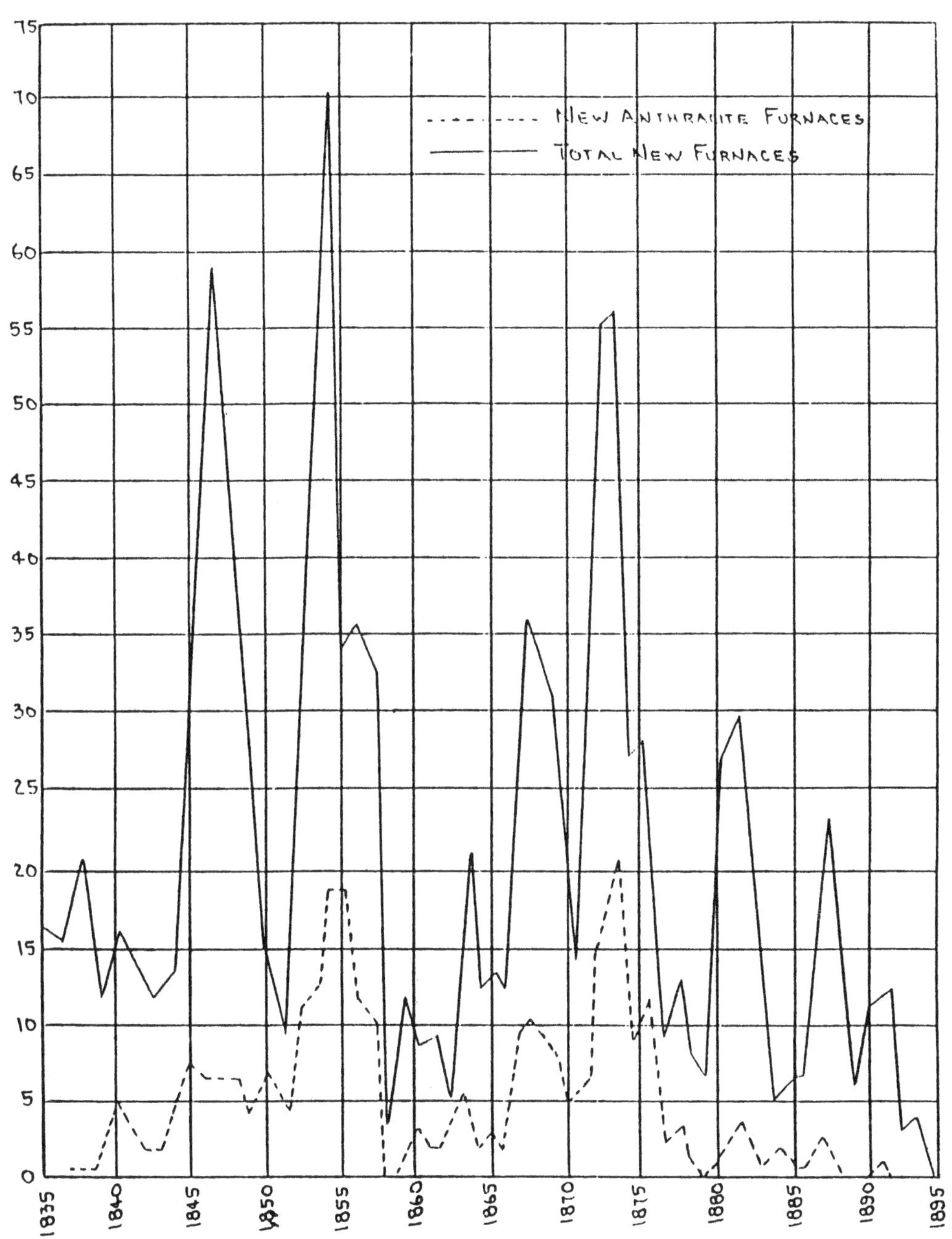

Source: Ralph H. Sweetser, "Anthracite Pig Iron," Iron Age, Vol. 152 (Dec. 30, 1943), 37.

2,868,278 net tons, a large part of which could be accounted for as the product of improved furnace design, more efficient operations, and the selection of high grade ores. Where, in 1840, it had required 804 furnaces - 798 charcoal works and 6 anthracite furnaces - to produce 283,000 net tons of pig iron, it required, thirty-two years later, only 657 furnaces to produce 2,868,276 net tons of pig iron.[24] Most of this pig iron was being produced by approximately 207 anthracite furnaces and 171 coke and bituminous coal works. There were still 279 charcoal furnaces in blast, but by 1873 either the anthracite or the bituminous coal and coke furnaces could produce more pig iron than all of these charcoal furnaces.[25]

Once again the regional statistics indicate a further concentration of iron furnaces near the coal fields, with the eastern district still having the heaviest concentration. Of the 207 anthracite furnaces, 149 were located in either the Lehigh, Schuylkill, or Susquehanna valleys. In the Shenango Valley and the Pittsburgh distrct there were seventy-four of the bituminous coal or coke furnaces; twenty-nine were situated in the Hanging Rock and Mahoning Valley districts.[26] Still the most important of these regions was the Lehigh Valley.

For twenty years or more the Lehigh Valley had maintained leadership in the production of pig iron, with a continuous increase in output

---

[24]Swank, The American Iron Trade in 1876, p. 170. Swant, Iron in All ages, p. 536.

[25]Ibid.

[26]Ibid.

as more anthracite furnaces were built along the river. From the single furnace built by David Thomas in 1840, the number of works had been raised to twenty-one in 1856 and to forty-seven in 1873. By 1875 there were fifty furnaces in the Lehigh Valley, although there were only twenty-five of these in blast during the last month of that year.[27] The production of pig iron had also increased over the years as the 120,386 net tons produced in 1856 was multiplied several times until it reached a peak of 449,663 net tons in 1872. With the poor business conditions of the next few years this output slackened and in 1875 it was only 280,360 net tons;[28] this output was still the largest for any single district in the nation.

Probably the most striking development in the production of iron during this period was the very rapid rate of expansion in the bituminous coal and coke pig iron output. Whereas in 1856 this type of pig iron was of little importance, in the 1870's it had become the most important branch of the industry. At first the growth of production had been very slow; then it was suddenly accelerated in 1870 and 1871. In 1874, as output of anthracite iron dipped a bit, that of the bituminous coal and coke furnaces continued to expand. Finally, in 1875, the total production of iron from furnaces using these fuels had surpassed the product from the anthracite furnaces, the actual figures being 947,545 net tons

---

[27] _Ibid_.

[28] _Ibid_.

and 908,046 net tons respectively.[29]

Upon examining the statistics of pig iron production for these twenty years, one is persuaded to describe this period as the age of bituminous coal and coke rather than the age of anthracite. Even though anthracite iron production was maintained at a substantial lead throughout most of the period, it was the bituminous coal and coke furnace operators who made the greatest progress as the following statistics indicate.

TABLE 5

PIG IRON BLAST FURNACES FOR SELECTED YEARS, 1856 and 1872

Year	Anthracite	Charcoal	Bituminous Coal and Coke	Total
1856	121	416	43	580[1]
1872	192	247	150	589[2]

Source: 1. J. P. Lesley, *The Iron Manufacturer's Guide*, pp. 759-60.
2. American Iron and Steel Association, *Statistics of the American and Foreign Iron Trade for 1873*, pp. 48-49.

These statistics indicate a more rapid expansion in the number of bituminous coal and coke furnaces than in the number of anthracite furnaces. Although the latter type furnaces had increased approximately 58 percent by 1872, the bituminous coal and coke furnaces were increased by 250 percent. The number of charcoal furnaces, however, had been reduced by almost 40 percent. Meanwhile, the increase in the number of coal

---

[29]*Ibid*., p. 169.

CHART III

RELATIVE CHANGE IN PIG IRON PRODUCTION
BY FUEL TYPES, 1855-75

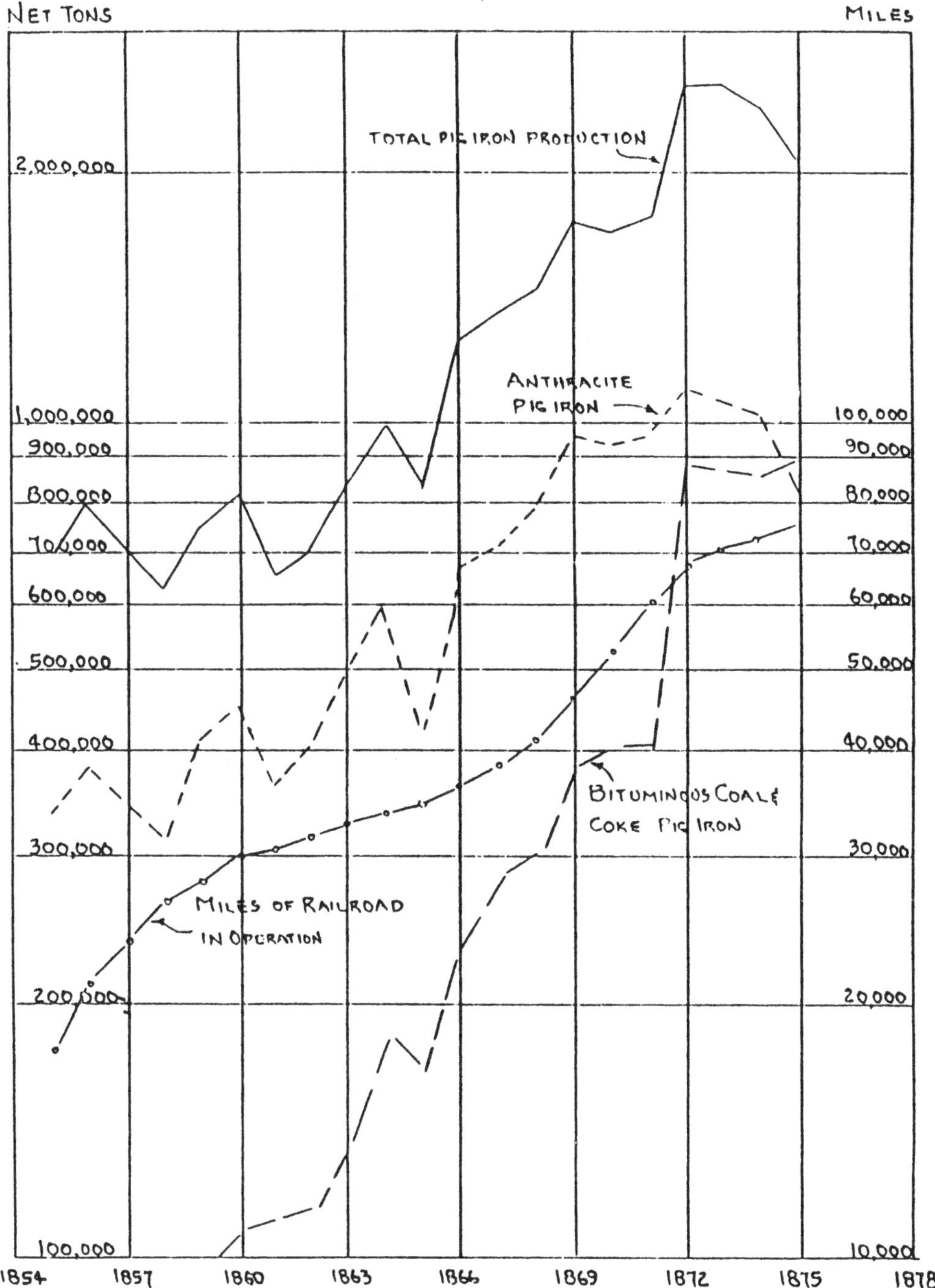

Source: J. M. Swank, The American Iron Trade in 1876, p. 164.

TABLE 6

PIG IRON PRODUCTION, 1855-75
(Net tons)

Year	Anthracite	Bituminous and Coke	Total
1855	381,866	62,390	784,178
1856	443,113	69,554	883,137
1857	390,385	77,451	798,157
1858	361,430	58,351	705,094
1859	471,745	84,841	840,627
1860	519,211	122,228	919,770
1861	409,229	127,037	731,544
1862	470,315	130,687	787,622
1863	577,638	157,961	947,604
1864	684,018	210,125	1,135,996
1865	479,558	189,682	931,582
1866	749,367	268,396	1,350,343
1867	798,638	318,647	1,461,626
1868	893,000	340,000	1,603,000
1869	971,150	553,341	1,916,641
1870	930,000	570,000	1,865,000
1871	956,608	570,000	1,912,608
1872	1,369,812	984,159	2,854,558
1873	1,312,754	977,904	2,868,279
1874	1,202,144	910,712	2,689,413
1875	908,046	947,545	2,266,581

Source: Swank, Iron in All Ages, p. 376.

furnaces brought forth an increasing amount of pig iron, though there were fewer furnaces in operation in 1872 than there were in 1856.

TABLE 7

PIG IRON PRODUCTION FOR SELECTED YEARS
(In net tons)

Year	Anthracite	Charcoal	Bituminous Coal and Coke	Total
1856	443,113	370,470	69,554	883,137
1872	1,369,812	500,587	984,159	2,854,558

Source: J. M. Swank, Iron in all Ages, p. 284.

From the above information it can be seen that, though all sectors of the pig iron industry had increased their output, the most important development was the rate of change in the bituminous coal and coke sector. Anthracite pig iron production had been increased approximately 285 percent, but bituminous coal and coke iron output had been increased over 1400 percent. Charcoal iron, on the other hand, had been increased tonnage-wise despite the reduction in the number of furnaces. But in the latter case production had been raised only 35 percent.

These figures also indicate that the increasing use of coal and coke, along with other technological innovations and improved blast furnace practice, had provided for a sizable increase in output from individual furnaces. The greatest improvement, once again, was made by furnaces in which bituminous coal and coke were used. The average annual capacity of these furnaces had been raised from approximately 1,617 net tons in 1856 to 8,561 net tons in 1872. This was an increase in furnace capacity of more than 300 percent. The production of the average anthracite furnace, on the other hand, while still capable of producing more tons per annum than the average bituminous coal or coke furnace, had not equaled the change in efficiency of the average coke furnace. In 1856 the average output from the anthracite furnace was 3,662 net tons; by 1872 this figure had been raised to 7,132 net tons, an increase in output of less than 200 percent. During this same period the production of the average charcoal furnace had been increased slightly more than 200 percent, a growth in the average capacity from 890 net tons in 1856 to approximately 2,000 net tons in 1872.

Thus, it might be said that the age of bituminous coal and coke iron had arrived in the early 1870's. By 1876 it was quite evident that the age of anthracite iron had passed and the iron industry had moved into a new period of economic and tehnological development.

Advanced Technology and Blast Furnace Practice

From the statistics reported above it is evident that the continual increase in the tonnage of pig iron produced by the iron industry throughout the 1860's and early 1870's was largely an outgrowth of a rather slow adaptation of more efficient furnaces and furnace practice. Generally, however, the new techniques were first developed in foreign countries prior to their application in the United States. And now, more often than in the past, many of these technological innovations in iron smelting were the end product of scientific investigation, though greater reliance was placed on the scientific method in Great Britain, France, and Germany than in the United States. Among those countries there were different areas of exploration which were based largely upon the particular resource and cost problem of the region, but always the intent or purpose of these labors, whatever the direction of research, was to discover new methods of reducing fuel and ore consumption per ton of iron produced. Any development along these lines would obtain for the iron smelters further reductions in the cost of raw materials and/or labor per ton of pig iron.[30]

For years the blast furnaces employed in Great Britain had endured without great alteration in their external shape or improvement of construction materials until the commencement of iron production in the Cleveland district in the 1850's, when revolutionary furnace designs and practices were inaugurated. There the furnaces were mere shells of iron plate which encased a lining of firebrick; the whole stack was supported at the base by a series of cast-iron columns. These furnaces, it was found, reduced the quantity of construction materials required and permitted easy to the hearth and tuyeres sections of the furnace.[31]

Very soon thereafter other British furnace owners commenced more thorough studies of the blast furnace design and operations, and through their constant experimentation they were able to reduce what had been for so many years an art into a science. The rule of thumb and the acquired

---

[30]Ralph Sweetser, "Anthracite Pig Iron," as found in *Iron Age*, Vol. 152 (Dec. 30, 1943), 33 ff. Johnson, *Blast Furnace Construction*, pp. 1 ff.

[31]D. Forbes, "Quarterly Report on the Progress of the Iron and Steel Industries in Foreign Countries," *Journal of the Iron and Steel Institute*, Vol. 2 (London, 1872), 278 ff.

habit were now subjected to careful scrutiny, and the operation of the furnace was gradually set up as a mathematical and chemical calculation. Furnaces of 45 and 50 feet gave way to furnaces of 75 and 100 feet, while the hot-blasts of 600° to 700° Fahrenheit were replaced with blasts heated to more than 1000° Fahrenheit. The effect of such studies was the creation of a much more efficient blast furnace.

The ironmasters on the Continent were splendid imitators and very soon made their works as efficient as the British facilities. In France and Germany ironmasters pioneered in other facets of fuel economy - improved coke-making and refinements in the utilization of waste gases and heat from the furnace. In France scientific control over the furnace process and materials was carried out very precisely, with the resulting production of a more uniform product of predetermined specifications.[32]

Reports of the innovations in iron production from the Continent so alarmed the British that they set about to develop more intensive research programs in chemistry and engineering.[33] Unfortunately for the United States, the British state of alarm was not contagious and, despite the numerous reports of improvements in smelting techniques from both Great Britain and the Continent, most ironmasters in this country indicated little concern for such developments. Only very slowly were the advanced techniques adopted in the domestic iron industry and then by

---

[32]D. L. Burn, The Economic History of Steelmaking, 1887-1939; A Study in Competition (Cambridge, England, 1940), p. 5. This work will hereafter be cited as Burn, The Economic History of Steelmaking.

[33]Ibid., p. 3.

only a few furnace operators.[34]

The reasons for this apparent unconcern with the new developments in Europe probably arose out of the prosperous conditions within the industry which prevailed until 1873. The remunerative returns on the already sunk costs and the relative shortage of capital in the United States must have delayed somewhat the construction of new furnaces by many firms. Also, the very nature of the durability of the old furnaces delayed rapid replacement programs. In other instances, however, some ironmasters seem to have become creatures of habit for they showed little recognition of the new economic opportunities that might have been derived from the adaptation of the new furnace design and techniques. This would seem to be the only reason for the failure of some firms to adopt the new innovations when they built new works but continued to use older furnace designs. Whatever the causes, the iron industry only very slowly made the changes.

Even as the reports of improved working materials could be obtained in the larger boiler plate furnaces were made, some uncertainty, in both Great Britain and Europe, was expressed as to the advisability of continually raising the height of furnaces. Many believed that the still larger furnaces would not produce a gain equal in proportion to the

---

[34]American Iron and Steel Association, Bulletin, Vol. 1 (Jan. 16, 1867), 154; Vol 2 (Sept. 25, 1867), 17. One example of the advanced British design was the Ferry Hill furnace. This furnace was 102 feet tall and was operated with a blast heated to 1100° Fahrenheit. By 1867 it was reported that 50- and 60-foot furnaces were gradually disappearing and were being replaced by furnaces 75 and 100 feet in height, with boshes widened to 27 feet.

increase in the size of the furnace. Lowthian Bell, one of Great Britain's leading ironmasters, was quite convinced that furnace managers may have been, by 1867, in "danger of carrying the 'improvements' a trifle too far."[35] At the same time others contemplated the possibility of securing further reduction in fuel and ore costs through wider experimentation with the temperature of the hot blast.

By 1871, however, further British developments in furnace structure and raising of hot-blast temperatures seemed to have reached a point where the rewards of further success were not large enough to compensate for the effort. Innovations and small cumulative improvements in other directions seemed to offer greater returns. Thus the outburst of technological development originating in the Cleveland district in 1850 came to a close. By that date the larger and more productive ironclad coke furnace had been thoroughtly tested and proved, though larger furnaces and hotter blasts were still to be tried and not without further success.[36]

Ever anxious to reduce costs, British and European ironmasters did not stop at this juncture but instead endeavored to improve other blast furnace accessories, such as the hot-blast stove, and improve the

---

[35] Ibid. (May 22, 1867), p. 120; Vol. 2 (Sept. 25, 1867), 17. That very same year the furnace owners in the Cleveland district reported "that with an increase of 100 degrees in the temperature of the blast above 750 degrees, a saving of one hundred-weight of coke on the ton of iron could be effected."

[36] Isard, "Some Locational Factors in the Iron and Steel Industry Since the Early Nineteenth Century," p. 209.

utilization of the waste gases from the blast furnaces.[37] Concurrently European steel producers commenced experiments in the direct use of molten pig iron in the Bessemer converter. First used in France in 1871, the method was discussed by British operators in 1874 and by 1876 a number of British steel mills were using a ladle car to carry molten metal directly from the blast furnace to the Bessemer converters, a practice which provided fuel economies in steel production.[36]

In conclusion, it is noted that British ironmasters could produce iron cheaper than their American competitors, though time and competitive conditions would tend to make costs equal in the two countries. Throughout these twenty years the British furnace owner held a number of advantages over his American counterpart; among them were economies of large-scale production, lower transportation costs, and probably a better and more systematized administration, the outgrowth of more years of experience with large-scale production. His furnaces were technically superior to those in this country, while his capital supply was more abundant, and

---

[37] American Iron and Steel Association, Bulletin, Vol. 5 (Feb. 4, 1871), 173.

[38] Journal of the Iron and Steel Institute, Vol. 2 (London, 1874), 356 ff.; Vol. 1 (1876), 12 ff.; Vol. 2 (1876), 420 ff.; Vol. 1 (1877), 20 ff. John B. Pearse, A Concise History of the Iron Manufacturing of the American Colonies up to the Revolution and of Pennsylvania Until the Present time (Philadelphia, 1876), p. 256. This work will hereafter be cited as Pearse, A Concise History of Iron Manufacturing.

Pearse reported that the Bethlehem Iron Company was one of the first steel firms in the United States to use molten pig iron in the production of steel. The Bethlehem Iron Company's minute books indicate the first use of this technique was made by the firm in 1876.

consequently he had lower interest charges,[39]

While the British and Continental ironmasters were endeavoring to increase the output of their blast furnaces and reduce their costs of production through the application of the scientific method, the iron-masters in this country seemed to have little inclination to achieve those goals via such methods. The blast furnace used in the 1860's had little more capacity than those of the 1850's, and up to 1869 the blast furnaces of this country were generally the same massive structures of masonry developed thirty years previously.[40] Also the brick gas chamber used to heat the hot-blast was still situated at the tunnel head, its operation having been improved very little over the years. Only very slowly did the pig iron smelters of this country venture to extend the height of their furnaces to measurements comparable to those of the British works.

One of the first experiments along these lines was made in 1869 by William Firmstone, manager of the Glendon Iron Company's furnaces in the Lehigh Valley. The furnace he constructed was made of brick and was raised to a height of 73 feet. At about the same time a second such experiment was made at Stanhope, New Jersey. There Ario Pardee, a substantial coal mine owner, had a furnace built which was 85 feet high and

---

[39]American Iron and Steel Association, Statistics of the American and Foreign Iron Trade for 1875. p. 20.

[40]Talcott, "The Manufacture of Pig Iron," ASCE Trans., I, 201.

22 feet at the top of the bosh.[41] Frank Firmstone reported that both of these furnaces worked with less coal per ton of pig iron than the smaller furnaces at Glendon and Stanhope.[42]

Despite the potential fuel economy to be obtained in the operation of such a furnace, most merchant furnace operators in the anthracite regions persisted in using the stone structures with which they were so well acquainted.[43] As late as 1873 the management of The Thomas Iron Company constructed two new furnaces with the same materials and design as their earlier furnaces despite the proven advantages of the taller boiler plate furnace.[44]

By that date, however, a number of western furnace owners had built their furnaces with the advanced engineering techniques used by their British and European counterparts. As early as 1865 a small number of coke furnaces had been constructed along the lines of the foreign works,

---

[41] _Ibid._, p. 196. Thomas Dunlap, _Wiley's American Iron Trade Manual_ (New York, 1874), pp. 28 ff.

[42] Frank Firmstone, "A Comparison Between Certain English and Certain American Blast Furnaces," _Transactions of the American Institute of Mining Enginerrs_, I (1871-73), 314 ff. Pearse, _A Concise History of Iron Manufacturing_, p. 256. Pearse reported the Bethlehem Iron Company used brick stacks banded by iron straps as early as 1876.

[43] Dunlap, _Wiley's American Iron Trade Manual_, pp. 32 ff. Johnson, _Blast Furnace Construction_, p. 237.

Up to 1873 there were very few anthracite furnaces that were over 60 feet high and just a few were fabricated with boiler plate shell and firbrick linings. The first such furnace using anthracite coal was built at Fort Henry, New York. That furnace was 70 feet tall and 16 feet at the bosh. Another had been constructed at Marquette, Michigan, and a third was built in Philadelphia in 1873.

[44] _Iron Age_, Vol. 109 (May 5, 1922), 1222. The Thomas Iron Co. Fin. Rec., pp. 71-73.

and then, as the years passed, more and more of the boiler plate and brick-lined furnaces were built in the West.[45] These coke furnaces, though at first not notably taller than the older furnaces, were constructed, like the British works, with iron columns supporting a large cast-iron ring upon which was built the iron shell stack. The interior lines of such furnaces varied with the quality of the fuel and ore employed and the fashion prevalent in the local area. Outwardly these furnaces resembled a huge brewer's vat.[46]

Although the materials used to build these furnaces were reported to be as costly as those used in the stone furnaces, they possessed an advantage in the ease of construction and, once completed, offered ready access to the entire circumference of the furnace base. Furthermore, these furnaces provided economy in fuel consumption for each ton of pig iron produced.[47]

Not until 1871 and 1872 were further improvements in domestic furnace design made, when the height of the new coke furnaces was gradually increased to 70 or 75 feet. Meanwhile, continual changes were being made in the interior lines of furnaces that also provided for additional economies in fuel consumption.

---

[45] American Iron and Steel Association, Bulletin, Vol. 2 (Aug. 7, 1867), 389; Vol. 3 (June 17, 1868), 321.

[46] Ibid., Vol. 5 (Nov. 16, 1870), 84

[47] Talcott, "The Manufacture of Pig Iron," ASCE Trans., I, 201. I. Lowthian Bell, "Note on a Visit to Coal and Iron-Mines and Iron Works in the United States," Journal of the Iron and Steel Institute, Vol. 1 (1875), 115. This work will hereafter be cited as Bell, "Note on a Visit to Iron Works in the United States."

Outstanding models of the advance in design and operation were the Isabella furnaces in Pittsburgh. Both these furnaces were fabricated with plate iron shells and firebrick linings. They were built to a height of 75 feet and had boshes 18 feet in diameter. The average annual capacity of each furnace was originally placed at 21,000 tons of pig iron. With slight alterations in the interior lines and an increase in the hot-blast temperature, their output was raised to over 31,000 tons per annum or over 600 tons per week.[48] The more efficient of the older furnaces in the United States produced about 300 tons a week while British works of the same dimensions produced only 500 tons per week.[49]

In addition to the improvements contained in the furnaces, there were several other engineering advances worthy of mention in other furnace equipment. For example, the lower part of the furnace hearth was encircled by a hollow cast-iron ring through which passed a continually circulating flow of water to cool the hearth wall. This device was called a "water basket." Around the throat of each furnace were overhanging charging platforms supported by iron braces. From these platforms the materials were dumped into the furnaces by hand, though the top of the stack was capped by a cup and cone arrangement to facilitate the charging and also to capture more of the waste gases. All of the

---

[48]Dunlap, _Wiley's American Iron Trade Manual_, pp. 49 f. Pearse, _A Concise History of Iron Manufacturing_, p. 141. J. H. Bridge, _The Inside History of the Carnegie Steel Company_ (New York, 1903), pp. 54 ff.

[49]Bell, "Note on a Visit to Iron Works in the United States," p. 118. The increased output was attributed to the use of a blast pressure which was rated at 8 to 9 pounds per square inch.

materials used in the furnace were raised to the charging platform by vertical pneumatic lifts which carried, with each ascent, a barrow containing either coke, ore, or limestone.[50]

These were truly exemplary works, matched only by the Lucy Furnace constructed by Kloman, Carnegie and Company, but they were merely replicas of British furnaces which had been in operation for a number of years. Moreover, though they were the most up-to-date works in this country, they did not utilize the most modern blast furnace accessories. True, the Player hot-blast stoves that were used were superior to the stoves used by most of the furnace operators in the smelting branch of the industry; they were not, however, as efficient as the Siemens-Cowper-Cochrane stove, forerunner of the modern regenerative stove, then being used in Great Britain and Europe.

The hot-blast stoves used by most furnace operators in the United States at that time consisted of brick chambers housing a series of pipes in the shape of inverted U's, in which the air was heated by the hot waste gases from the blast furnace. This type of stove was located at the top of the furnace; the hot air was conducted to the tuyere region of the furnace by a single conduit. The extreme temperatures of the hot gases exerted on the series of pipes in the stoves caused them to burn out quite often and necessitated frequent and expensive replacements.[51]

---

[50] Dunlap, *Wiley's American Iron Trade Manual*, pp. 49-52.

[51] Swank, *Iron in All Ages*, p. 453. Talcott, "The Manufacture of Pig Iron," *ASCE Trans.*, I, 197. Percy, *Metallurgy: Iron and Steel*, pp. 400 ff.

The temperature of the hot-blast from such a stove could be raised to 600° Fahrenheit and even up to 1000° Fahrenheit.

This fact does not mean that all furnaces were using hot-blasts at these high temperatures. Lowthian Bell reported that the Lehigh Valley furnaces were still being operated in 1874 with hot-blasts which were unable to melt zinc, which fuses at several hundred degrees below 1000° Fahrenheit.[52] The Thomas Iron Company presumably was smelting with a blast of over 700° Fahrenheit. But in the Susquehanna Valley some furnaces were still operated with a blast temperature of 400° to 500° Fahrenheit.[53] The consequence of such conditions was a greater consumption of coal per ton of pig iron produced than might have been necessary.[54]

John Player's hot-blast stove obviated the frequent need to replace the pipes in the brick chamber, for he employed a deep combustion chamber under the oven with narrow flues leading into the pipe chamber, a technique which limited the amount of flame reaching the pipes. Furthermore, his stove was located at the base of the furnace, the waste gases being conducted to it from the tunnel head by means of a flue. With this stove, economy in pipes was obtained and hotter blasts secured because of the reduced distance the hot-blast had to travel to the tuyeres.[55] Player's

---

[52] Bell, "Note on a Visit to Iron Works in the United States," p. 114.

[53] Clark, _History of Manufactures in the United States_, II, 78.

[54] Burn, _The Economic History of Steelmaking_, p. 44. Swank, _Iron in All Ages_, p. 354.

[55] American Iron and Steel Association, _Bulletin_, Vol. 5 (Feb. 4, 1871), 175. Talcott, "The Manufacture of Pig Iron," _ASCE Trans._, I, 198.

hot-blast stove was more efficient than others, providing a sizable increase in output for the furnace master who employed it. This type of stove was used at both the Isabella and Lucy furnaces.[56]

While the Player stove was very gradually being adopted in this country, furnace owners in Great Britain and Europe had completed a period of experimentation with the Siemens-Cowper-Cochrane stove or stoves similar in design, which were finally brought together under a single patent in 1870.[57] These regenerative stoves could be cleaned quite easily and had a relatively large air capacity with a uniform radiation which permitted the raising of the blast temperature to 1500° Fahrenheit. Such a high temperature provided a saving of four hundredweight of coke for every ton of iron produced, and it was attended with a further increase in the yield of iron without additional labor costs. The savings in coal, when this stove was used, would permit for the

---

[56] Dunlap, Wiley's American Iron Trade Manual, p. 47.

[57] American Iron and Steel Association, Bulletin, Vol. 4 (Feb. 16, 1870), 185: Vol. 13 (July 16, 1879), 178. In 1857 E. A. Cowper was granted an English patent for a stove which heated the air by means of a regenerator enclosed in an airtight iron casing. The stove consisted of brickwork chambers which were filled with loose firebrick. The firebricks were heated from below with coal fires and, after the chamber was thoroughly heated, the fire was shut out and a cool blast of air was passed into the chamber. In the chamber the cool air absorbed the heat imparted to the brickwork. Meanwhile, a companion stove was heated in the same manner. The Cowper stove offered the economic advantage of using cheap firebrick instead of costly iron pipes.

Cowper's stove was later modified by Thomas Whitwell so that the waste gases from the blast furnace could be used to heat the air. Then, in 1870, Siemens, Cowper, and Cochrane were given a patent for an improved regenerative stove which had dust catchers, was easy to clean, and was quite durable.

payment of the stoves themselves in a very short peiod of time.[58]

While advances in blast furnace design and hot-blast stoves were made more rapidly in Great Britain and Europe than in the United States, there was one innovation which could be said to have originated in the United States. This was the use of a heavier blast pressure than previously used by blast furnaces in any part of the world. Many furnaces in this country used blast pressures ranging up to 8 or 9 pounds per square inch as compared to the British level of 2 to 5 pounds.[59] But this practice had been developed in the 1840's by David Thomas, and now it was being carried to other regions by furnace men trained at the eastern furnaces.

Generally speaking, however, the iron industry of the United States had little influence, competitively or technically, outside the country. Only after 1875 were more rapid strides made in the development of production techniques in the iron industry, but these, it should be noted, were more closely allied with the mass production of steel than the smelting of iron ores. Invariably the old techniques seemed to suffice, and most iron ores continued to be smelted in comparatively small furnaces with relatively low temperature hot-blasts.[60]

---

[58] _Ibid_.

[59] Bell, "Note on a Visit to Iron Works in the United States," pp. 114 ff.

[60] Clark, _History of Manufactures in the United States_, II, 255.

Scientific Training and Applied Science

While furnace owners in the United States only gradually grasped the economic advantages that could accrue through the application of the above-mentioned innovations, contemporary academic engineers and scientists seemed to have been more fully aware of the economies to be derived from these advanced techniques already proven by British and European ironmasters. A reading of the engineering journals and bulletins of this period reveals the great concern held by many academicians for the future progress of the iron industry.[61]

On the other hand, the somewhat tardy adaptation of the advanced techniques by the "practical" businessman would seem to indicate that he was either very pessimistic about the ability of the trained engineer to help him in his work or that he, the ironmaster, was very optimistic about his own capabilities. It is true that a number of successful and visionary businessmen had endowed scientific institutions for the purpose of training personnel for industry, but the general practice seems to have been to rely on the old techniques and ignore the new developments.[62] Despite the interest of the few in the training of technicians,

---

[61] These include: Transactions of the American Institue of Mining Engineers and American Society of Civil Engineers Transactions.

[62] Ruhl Bartlett, "The Development of Industrial Research in the United States," as found in J. T. Lambie and R. V. Clemence, eds., Economic Change in America, pp. 207 ff.

In the Lehigh Valley, where a slow rate of adaptation prevailed, there were two schools endowed by successful businessmen that were developing scientific training programs. Asa Packer, builder of the Lehigh Valley Railroad, provided funds to build Lehigh University. Ario Pardee, coal mine operator and blast furnace owner, gave funds to Lafayette College for the specific purpose of training engineers.

businessmen in general showed little interest in hiring them. Most furnace owners, in times of economic stress or otherwise, did not search for new ways of reducing costs but seemed to prefer the less demanding method of maintaining their profits - tariff protection and the restriction of output. For most furnace operators the elimination of competition seems to have been the preferred solution to their economic problems.[63]

Observation of the forward strides in furnace practice development in the iron industry of the United States after 1876 elicits evidence which suggests that these twenty years between 1855 and 1875 provided a necessary gestation period before the advantages of the technical training could bear fruit. If this is true and this thought were to be extended a little further, it would seem that society owes a great debt to the unrecognized achievements of the academic scientists who led the way and trained those men who were to be instrumental in introducing metallurgy, chemistry, and mechanics into more fertile areas of exploration during the next twenty years.[64] One might say that the period extending from 1875 to 1905 was the culmination of many long years of practical experience joined with the scientific method as a catalyst.[65] But it was

---

[63] Ibid., p. 213 f.

[64] Clark, History of Manufactures in the United States, II, 144 f.

[65] Bartlett, "The Development of Industrial Research in the United States," pp. 214 f. Professor Bartlett suggests that the scientist was not interested in the application of his findings to industrial processes, but upon reading the engineering journals of the period, especially in reference to developments in the smelting of iron ores, this writer is disinclined to accept such findings. In numerous reports the engineers reported on their findings and also urged more rapid application of new techniques.

only very slowly that scientifically trained personnel were hired by the iron industry throughout these years being reviewed, and then it was a policy that was adopted under economic pressure as the problems of increasing pig iron production became more complex, too complex for the practical furnace man.

Prior to the introduction of the Bessemer converter there was little positive knowledge available pertaining to the chemical composition of iron ores and iron. Pig iron produced in most furnaces was not standardized, and the steel made in the Bessemer converter was a rather haphazard product. Presumably it was this very imperfect control over the raw materials going into pig iron which delayed the adoption of the Bessemer process. When Captain E. S. Ward built the first experimental converter in Wyandotte, Michigan, he was forced to hire the services of a chemist to analyze the quality of the pig iron from the various merchant furnaces in order to produce a marketable steel. With the further expansion in the use of the Bessemer process, a number of iron merchants persuaded J. Blodgett Britton to establish a laboratory for the purpose of analyzing their iron ores, pig iron, slags, and furnace cinder.[66] Then, as blast furnaces were called upon to produce more and more pig iron for sale to steel mills using the Bessemer process, there arose the need for a more thorough analysis of the ores and finished product at the works in order to assure the proper specifications for Bessemer pig iron. Because

---

[66]Clark, _History of Manufactures in the United States_, II, 78. Bartlett, "The Development of Industrial Research in the United States," pp. 218 ff. American Iron and Steel Association, _Bulletin_, Vol. 1 (Feb. 27, 1867), 211.

of this, merchant furnace companies began in the late 1860's to hire their own chemists and build their own testing laboratories.[67]

Though the period from 1855 to 1875 had provided little in the way of innovations in the domestic iron smelting industry, it must be recognized nevertheless that as the period drew to a close the advance in method and technique had gained some momentum. The iron age had passed into the age of steel. The anthracite furnace had lost its position of predominance, and the age of anthracite iron was at an end. Gradually the American ironmaster discovered, as the British, French, and German ironmasters before him had, that science and business, when mixed in the proper proportions, provided sizable rewards. But these were only first steps. For these twenty years it was the British and European ironmasters that led the way, while the American ironmaster followed the path only haltingly.

Further Changes Affecting the Pig Iron Industry

The full impact of numerous other changes in the iron industry during this period on the merchant pig iron furnaces was not made evident until the next twenty years, when they served to bring about the gradual elimination of merchant furnaces and the use of anthracite coal in iron manufacturing. As the story of the introduction of the Bessemer converter has been written numerous times, it will be omitted here, though it must be recognized that this innovation ushered in the age of steel and the

---

[67]Bridge, The Inside History of the Carnegie Steel Company, p. 65. Bartlett. "The Development of Industrial Research in the United States," pp. 220 f.

integrated steel mill.[68] As will be pointed out later, this development had a great deal to do with the elimination of the merchant furnace industry. Also adopted at about the same time as the Bessemer converter, the regenerative furnace was not accepted as readily by steel producers but, like the Bessemer converter, it was to lead to extensive changes in plant organization and the elimination of merchant furnaces.[69]

Other changes which affected the anthracite merchant furnaces of the eastern region in particular were the development of the anthracite railroad combination and the organization of the Workingmen's Benevolent Association, a coal miners' union. When at the end of the war the producers in the hard coal region discovered that there had been a creation of excess capacity which caused prices to fall, they began to monopolize the ownership of the mines in order to restrict output. The miners, without whose help no coal could be had, were disinclined to allow the employers to obtain too large a share of the price and organized a union to obtain a larger share for themselves. In 1869, 1871, and 1875 there were extended strikes, with a suspension of output. Also, the railroads endeavored to raise the rates for transporting coal.[70] The consequence

---

[68]Clark, History of Manufactures in the United States, I, 415. W. Kaempffert, ed., A Popular History of American Invention, II (New York, 1924), 15-21. R. S. Forbes, Man the Maker: A History of Technology and Engineering (New York, 1950),pp. 224 ff.

[60]The first open-hearth furnace built in this country was an experimental furnace constructed by Abram Hewitt at his rail mill in Trenton, New Jersey. Allan Nevins, Abram S. Hewitt with Some Account of Peter Cooper (New York 1935), pp. 249 f. Swank, Iron in All Ages, PP. $!(FF.

[70]Peter Roberts, The Anthracite Coal Industry (New York, 1901), pp. 74 ff.

of this restriction of output and the rise in the price of coal was a resorting to a mixture of coke and anthracite on the part of the furnace owners. Upon adopting this fuel mixture, they found it to be an economical substitute for straight anthracite coal. Then, in the next twenty years, more and more coke was used by the eastern furnace operators. More will be said on this change in the next chapter, but for the moment it must be recognized that the influence of these monopolies in the coal industry was to have a tremendous repercussion on the anthracite furnaces, no less than the improvement in transportation of the rich hematite ores from the Great Lakes region to Ohio and the Pittsburgh region.[71]

Organizational Developments

By 1875 the organization of the iron industry had not changed markedly over the pattern of the previous twenty years. Just as they had thirty or so years earlier, some firms operated blast furnaces in conjunction with their rolling mills, but generally most firms operated a single plant performing one function, the processing of iron. Merchant furnaces were the largest producers of pig iron, as they continued to produce the semi-finished material for foundry men, iron converters, and commission men. Relatively heavy transportation costs still contributed somewhat to the division of the nation into individual pig iron markets located in widely separated parts of the country, markets which were distinct in terms of competitive price conditions and the quality of the

---

[71]American Iron and Steel Association, Bulletin, Vol. 9 (April 2, 1875), 92; (Mary 7, 1875) 132. Iron Age, Vol. 15 (April 15, 1875), 28.

iron produced.[72]

Wiley's Trade Manual for 1874 listed 735 blast furnaces owned by 556 firms located in twenty-four different states. There was a heavy concentration of these furnaces in Pennsylvania (152 anthracite furnaces, 44 charcoal furnaces, and 73 bituminous coal and coke furnaces), but there was no great concentration of ownership in this branch of the industry, nor did any one firm produce a large share of the total product. Most firms held but one furnace, and only a few firms operated as many as three furnaces. The Thomas Iron Company, the largest pig iron producer in the nation at that time, owned and operated eight blast furnaces, but the total output from these works made up only 2 percent of the pig iron produced in 1874. While the seven largest firms in the industry controlled some forty furnaces, they produced only 9 percent of the total pig iron output that year.[73]

A few firms which had developed a degree of vertical integration made their appearance in the 1860's, but by 1874 they had not ventured very far in the process. Among these firms was the Bethlehem Iron Company, which had commenced operations in 1864. Originally organized to produce anthracite iron and rolled iron rails, it had extended its

---

[72]Swank, *The American Iron Trade in 1876*, pp. 169 ff.
Swank reported iron production for three different types of fuel and for ten major areas of production. The American Iron and Steel Association's *Bulletin* contained reports on the prices of iron at New York City, Philadelphia, St. Louis, Chicago, and Pittsburgh.

[73]Dunlap, *Wiley's American Iron Trade Manual*, pp. 27 ff.
Dunlap listed some 310 rolling mill companies, 8 Bessemer works, 11 locomotive shops, and numerous car shops and bridge works.

operations into Bessemer steel production by 1873.[74] By that date Kloman, Carnegie and Company had extended its control over blast furnaces, converters, and rolling mills.[75] Meanwhile, the North Chicago Rolling Mill controlled furnaces, converters, and rolling mills valued at \$3,000,000.[76] The largest merchant furnace company controlled eight blast furnaces; it held no converting or rolling units, but it did own numerous ore mines and shared the ownership of several short railroads which had been constructed to haul ore. Earlier the company had owned coal mines but had found it cheaper to buy coal than mine it. These works were capitalized at \$2,000,000.[77] But these firms were the exception rather than the rule; most companies performed only a single process, and very few were capitalized at figures comparable to those given above.

Thus, despite the problems of business crises, the continuing threat of foreign competition, and the tendency toward cutthroat competition in the industry, there were no indications of the great combinations that would appear in the next thirty years. This fact, however, does not mean to imply that no thought of combination existed in the minds of some of the ironmasters. As one writer observed during the prosperous and somewhat difficult supply period of 1878:

---

[74] _Ibid_., p. 29

[75] _Ibid_., pp. 47 ff.

[76] _Ibid_., pp. 173 f.

[77] The Thomas Iron Co. Fin. Rec., p. 82. Dunlap, _Wiley's American Iron Trade Manual_, pp. 27 f.

> The time will come when there will be less separation of these interests. The pressure of this season has developed strong efforts toward their combination. Every day almost, furnace and mill owners are looking over Lake Superior mines to obtain, if possible, such an interest in their working as will guarantee them a regular supply of ore of uniform quality. The inevitable is approaching very rapidly.[78]

The crisis of 1873 was not, however, the most propitious period in which to form such a combination. Beset by a shortage of capital, with the consequential high rate of interest, and supplied with abundant quantities of raw materials at relatively low prices, the stronger merchant furnace companies evidently saw little reason to develop any type of integration at that time. But the periodic oscillations between prosperity and depression which marked the iron trade continually provided strong motivations to organizing the members of the industry into a combination of sorts for their mutual protection against the dangers of cutthroat competition among themselves and competition from overseas.

As early as 1855 the American Iron Association had been formed to provide a central body for the collation of production data and imports, as well as to act as a lobbying agency to obtain protective duties for the industry. Upon the dissolution of this association in 1864, the American Iron and Steel Association was established. Like its predecessor, the new organization served as a clearinghouse for iron and steel production statistics as well as a channel for the mutual interchange of practical and scientific knowledge, "and, generally, to take all proper

---

[78] American Iron and Steel Association, Bulletin, Vol. 7 (Sept. 11, 1872), 9.

measures for advancing the interests of the trade in all its branches."[79] This last seems to cover the policy maintained by the association to spread before the public the need for high tariff duties on imported iron of all types, including the raw materials and a varied group of finished products.[80]

When protective duties did not provide an answer to the industry's cost-price relationship, various groups were formed to try to regulate domestic prices by reducing output. In 1872 pig iron producers, organized as a national group, tried to obtain a voluntary agreement to restrict output; the attempt resulted in failure.[81] When 300 of about 700 furnaces were out of blast in 1874, the merchant furnace operators of the Lehigh Valley met to discuss the possibility of restricting their output. Reaching no agreement among themselves, they turned to a wider group of eastern furnace owners to co-operate with them. In December of that year this larger group prepared a resolution calling for a mutual effort on the part of furnace owners throughout the nation to reduce the output of

---

[79]American Iron and Steel Association, Proceedings for 1873 (Philadelphia, 1873), p. xiv. Clark, History of Manufactures in the United States, II, 280.

[80]Ibid., p. 25. The argument for protection was reasoned in a most circular fashion; yet it served the industry for a number of years. The argument proceeds in the following manner: Protection tends to increase wages; high wages increase the cost of production; increased costs of production lead to the substitution of machinery, which quickens the inventive faculties of mechanics. The increasing use of machinery enables the payment of high wages and permits competition with low wage exporters. The greater the mechanical resources, the more intense the competition and this will tend to reduce the degree of monopoly in the industry.

[81]Clark, History of Manufactures in the United States, II, 281.

their furnaces by one-half. The resolution was not to be binding until two-thirds of the furnaces in the United States agreed to restrict output.[82]

This combination movement which developed among the pig iron producers was similar in nature to the growth of combinations in other industries. In all instances the agitation seems to have arisen from the chaotic price movements and destructive competition caused by the widening of markets, the increased productive capacity, and depressed business conditions. But unlike other industries, anthracite coal mining and oil production, the movement in the pig iron industry did not develop into combinations on the grand scale until the 1890's.[83] Needless to say, with approximately 556 pig iron firms throughout the nation, and no single company large enough to control a large share of the market, the resolution to restrict output went unheeded by most pig iron producers. Paradoxically, despite the depressed state of the iron industry and the seeming necessity to ask for voluntary output restrictions, furnace companies in the Lehigh Valley and other regions readied themselves for future improvements in business by building new furnaces and repairing old ones.[84]

---

[82] Iron Age, Vol. 8 (June 4, 1874), 11; Vol. 9 (Dec. 3, 1874), 15; (Dec. 17, 1874) 5. Journal of the Iron and Steel Institute, Vol. 2 (1874), 445 f.

[83] Ralph W. Hidy and Muriel E. Hidy, Pioneering in Big Business, 1882-1911 (New York, 1955), pp. 9 ff. Roberts, The Anthracite Coal Industry, pp. 78 ff.

[84] American Iron and Steel Association, Bulletin, Vol. 10 (March 8, 1876), 74. Journal of the Iron and Steel Institute, Vol. 2 (1874), 453.

A further outgrowth of this alternation between good and bad times was an attempt made to establish a commodity exchange for pig iron. The movement toward this organization was an effort to duplicate a similar practice that had been practiced in Scotland since 1850. There it had become a common practice among the ironmasters to store their surplus product with a warehousing firm which provided certificates or "pig warrants" that were negotiable. Presumably this warehousing practice served to stabilize pig iron prices and seemed to offer a solution to the unstable price conditions in the iron industry.[85]

As a first step toward the creation of a similar commodity exchange in this country, the Pennsylvania Warehousing and Safe Deposit Company was formed in 1874. The storage company planned to open a number of warehousing points, distant from the seacoast, to which pig iron could be shipped and held until the right price prevailed. And as in the Scottish system, upon receipt of the pigs, warehouse receipts would be issued; these receipts, it was hoped, would become negotiable paper. The first warehouse was to have been established at Allentown in the Lehigh Valley.[86] Unfortunately for the company, the eastern iron producers

---

[85]Clark, History of Manufactures in the United States, II, 305. R. H. Campbell, "Fluctuations in Stocks: A Nineteenth-Century Case Study," Oxford Economic Papers, Vol. 9 (Oxford, England, 1957), 41 ff. Campbell reports that the iron producers found the warehousing system beneficial in the short run, but in the long run the system created excessive capital investments and struggles over wage reductions. Also, the stability of prices attracted into the trade "some of the less desirable elements of the commercial life in Britain."

[86]Iron Age, Vol. 9 (Dec. 24, 1874), 11. American Iron and Steel Association, Bulletin, Vol. 8 (Dec. 31, 1874), 400.

showed little interest in the scheme and the company only survived for a short time.

Nothwithstanding the efforts of those most concerned with the price problem, little was accomplished in providing any sort of control over prices or output. Prices continued to fall and, as they dipped, production declined. Marginal firms were precipitated into bankruptcy, less efficient furnaces were torn down, and few new ones were constructed.[87] Anxiously furnace owners awaited more prosperous times, meanwhile lobbying for higher import duties and subsidies for railroad expansion. As wages, prices of raw materials, and freight rates dropped, some furnace owners were able to produce pig iron and still make a profit. But it was the bituminous coal or coke furnace owners who seemed to be able to hold their own, while anthracite iron production shrank.[88]

Conclusion

As the first decade of this period opened, the eastern merchant furnaces held certain economic advantages over the western ironmasters that led to a much more rapid growth of the iron industry in the vicinity of the anthracite coal fields. The initial expansion of the eastern sector, once the necessary technological innovations had been made, was hastened by the superiority of the transportation system connecting the coal

---

[87] American Iron and Steel Association, Bulletin, Vol. 7 (Feb. 19, 1874), 61; Vol. 10 (Jan. 12, 1876), 13.

[88] Ibid., Vol. 10 (June 28, 1876), 177; (Sept. 20, 1876) 253. American iron and Steel Association, Statistics of the American and Foreign Iron Trade for 1875, p. 18.

fields and the eastern seaboard markets. The early canals and railroads that had been built into the coal fields provided for a continual reduction in the cost of transporting fuel and finished product, while new feeder lines to ore fields provided additional reductions in material costs. Meanwhile, the growing demand for anthracite coal brought numerous coal producers and miners into the coal fields, and these men proceeded to exploit the better and more advantageously located deposits. These conditions aided substantially to decrease the price of coal, and consequently more pig iron producers and related manufacturers were attracted into the region.

As railroad transportation had not reached as high a level of efficiency in other parts of the nation, the eastern merchant furnaces held their comparative advantage over the western furnaces for some years. This advantage, plus the high import duties maintained on iron imports, provided the anthracite furnace operators with a propitious opportunity to realize sizable profits without facing the burdensome problem of adapting new techniques in iron smelting.

The next decade was a period in which western transportation facilities were rapidly expanded and improved. The western iron market grew with the expansion of these facilities; furnaces were increased in number and size as new sources of raw materials were exploited. Specialized ore boats and more serviceable freight cars were used to carry the increasing supplies of rich hematite ores from the Lake Superior region to western furnaces. The Connellsville coal fields were exploited under high competitive conditions, and the price of coke dropped to new low levels that helped to reduce the cost of pig iron.

While the West was gaining its comparative advantage, the eastern area furnaces were losing their earlier established advantages. The ores used by the eastern furnaces were not at all comparable to the Lake Superior ores in mineral content, nor could they be effectively used for Bessemer steel because of their high phosphorous content. Furthermore, as western coke prices were continually dropping, anthracite prices were relatively stable. The coal fields had gradually been brought under monopoly control by the anthracite railroads in order to avoid the dangers of price-cutting and destructive competition. The producers were quite anxious to maintain the high prices prevalent during the war. Of course, there were other advantages derived from the combination such as reduced marketing costs, the elimination of the high cost collieries, and centralized management, but the strongest force was the maintenance of the price. Meanwhile, households were also using an increasing amount of this fuel for heating, a fact which tended to keep the price of anthracite coal at high levels.[89] These cost conditions placed the eastern furnaces in a much less advantageous position cost-wise and would soon force some furnace operators to search about to find means to right their cost-price situation so that profits could be obtained as previously.

The tardiness on the part of the pig iron producers to innovate or adopt new innovations developed elsewhere during these twenty years reveals a slow response to technological change. Only a very few furnace

---

[89]Roberts, The Anthracite Coal Industry, pp. 78 ff.

operators, East and West, showed a readiness to imitate their British or European counterparts; most iron producers were quite cautious in adopting new techniques, even though proven to have economic value. Only upon recognition that not to imitate would result in excessive losses did the majority of furnace owners proceed to improve their furnace equipment and techniques. This somewhat slow advance on the technological front seems to indicate that the furnace owners were a conservative group of men.

At the same time, there may be some compelling reasons which led them to follow this conservative policy. Throughout a very large part of this period, relatively high transportation rates prevailed; this factor limited the size of a firm's market. High duties restricted imports somewhat. Under such limitations and the prevailing prosperous conditions, it would seem that there was little need to innovate; as long as markets were not easily penetrated by competitors, a conservative policy could be followed. However, once the output of western and southern producers began to find its way into the eastern market, the anthracite iron manufacturers would find reason to imitate the more advanced furnace practices or perish.

Probably a more important reason for the lag was the inflexibility and long life of the iron furnaces, which prompted the entrepreneur to defer the adoption of new techniques and continue to use his old facilities until they were fully depreciated. Add to this inflexible character of the equipment the shortage of capital with high interest costs and there was a well-established barrier to rapid replacement programs. But these economic conditions do not explain why, when new facilities were constructed, newer innovations were not adopted.

It has been suggested that because the immediate problems of the era were not those of producing economically but rather the problem of acquiring resources, transporting them, and training of labor, there was little necessity of using the most advanced technique. As long as the demand was high enough to provide a profitable price, and these were the predominant problems, the entrepreneur could give very little time to considering the improvement of production techniques. Anyway, when business conditions were bad, and profits threatened, there were always higher import duties to offset the threat of overseas competition.

There were many lessons which had to be learned about the science of iron production and the management of a large-scale business firm. By 1875 some of the lessons had been learned, and there were indications that great improvements were to be made very soon by some of the less conservative proprietors, the willing imitators. Economies had already been obtained through reduced costs of transportation, the better selection and preparation of ores, lower costs for coal, application of hotter blasts at higher pressures, and the use of more capacious furnaces. And no less important than these changes, there had been an accumulation of twenty more years of experience in furnace operation and business management.

In order to obtain some idea of the progress that had been made in the anthracite iron industry and to try and indicate why technological development in that sector of the pig iron industry was not more rapid during these twenty years, the next section of this work will open, once again, the books of The Thomas Iron Company. Possibly these reports will provide enough information for a more precise explanation of why so many entrepreneurs in the anthracite iron industry delayed imitating the more advanced innovations.

CHAPTER VII

THE THOMAS IRON COMPANY, 1856-1875

Expansion - Mines and Railroads

In the twenty years following the establishment of The Thomas Iron Company, an expansionist policy was pursued in such an ambitious manner that at the close of the period the company held the greatest conglomeration of furnaces in the United States. Growth was achieved in spite of the unstable market conditions which marked the period and the depressing effect of the decline in pig iron prices during most of the latter half of this epoch. The expansion of furnace facilities was not a haphazard development but rather the result of a policy enunciated by President Luckenbach in 1857. Whether the idea was Luckenbach's alone or the product of deliberation among the board of directors is not ascertainable, but as an accepted policy of the board there can be no doubt. As time elapsed the program was extended and the amount of plant, real estate, and mining property was increased well beyond the level envisioned in that policy statement of 1857.[1]

When The Thomas Iron Company was organized, the founders seemed to have been quite sure that they would be able to avoid heavy outlays in

---

[1]The Thomas Iron Co. Fin. Rec., p. 7. President Luckenbach envisioned that the accretion of capital for the expansion program would not exceed $500,000. The year after he had retired the capital stock of the corporation had been raised to $1,000,000 and before the twenty years had passed it had been increased to $2,000,000.

the purchase of mines and machinery to work them, and they had not considered it expedient to obtain or construct railroads for the carriage of such raw materials. However, and in spite of these earlier impressions, before the firm was many months old, it was discovered that two of the most immediate problems to be met were the procurement of essential supplies of ores and the transportation of the same to the furnaces.

By the time the second annual report had been submitted in January, 1857, the railroad program had already been in preparation for several months, and now the further problem of procuring sufficient supplies of ore had arisen. Suddenly it had become evident that it would be a rational policy for the company to purchase ore fields with proven reserves as soon as possible. As President Luckenbach wrote:

> . . . it has become apparent that it is a wise policy of iron manufacturers to become possessed of valuable ore mines; and that those who thus secure a permanent and sufficient supply of ore will find themselves in good condition to prosecute their business steadily and advantageously, while others, less providing or less fortunate, may be struggling with almost insurmountable difficulties in that regard.[2]

With this President Luckenbach reported that the company's management had thought it a wise decision to purchase the McFarlan Mine situated in Morris County, New Jersey. The property consisted of 80 acres of land and cost the company $32,000. The ore to be obtained was largely magnetic iron ore, which had a mineral content of about 60 percent.

This purchase, however, was only the beginning of the company's

---

[2]*Ibid*., p. 8.

efforts to obtain ore sites. Already other expenditures were impending, and before President Luckenbach retired from office in 1864, the company procured, through lease rights or outright purchase, the control over approximately 267 acres of ore properties valued at $145,641.91.[3] The more important of these acquisitions were the McFarlan or Richard Mine, valued at $27,085.26, and Taylor mine, valued at $23,077.17. These properties were both located in Morris County, New Jersey, and together consisted of approximately 160 acres of potential ore-bearing land. The ore was high grade, but both mines required expensive shaft mining techniques, with heavy costs for timerbering and pumping machinery.[4]

In Pennsylvania the company purchased a number of brown hematite (limonite) mines, the most important being the Balliet Mine. Another, Albright Mine, was held jointly with the Lehigh Crane Iron Company. The total value of these two properties was $75,595, and the total acreage encompassed by them was 128 acres. The ore was relatively low in mineral content, ranging from 40 percent to 35 percent iron. Like the New Jersey mines, these deposits required shaft mining with all of the heavy costs involved in providing roof supports and removing water which continually seeped into the mine.[5] By 1864 a number of small mines had been purchased, mined out, and the land returned to farming, facts which emphasized the immediacy of the problem with which the company was confronted

---

[3] Ibid.

[4] Ibid., pp. 251 ff.

[5] Lesley, The Iron Manufacture's Guide, pp. 566 ff. Miller, Allentown Quadrangle pp. 33 ff.

in its quest for sufficient supplies of ore. These mines were certainly not comparable to the great ore deposits of the Lake Superior region.

Ten years later the number of inidividual mine holdings had been increased considerably in number and value. In all, there were twenty-three separate ore properties and three limestone quarries held by the company. These properties extended outward from Hokendauqua into York County in southern Pennsylvania and north into central New Jersey and southern New York. The total properties were valued at $503,952.54 and provided the company with two types of ores, magnetic and brown hematite.[6] The former, the high grade ore, when mixed with the more readily obtainable Pennsylvania ores, served to produce a marketable foundry iron. Both ores, however, contained phosphorous which precluded their use in the manufacture of Bessemer pig iron.

While most of the purchases of ore properties seem to have been made with great discrimination, there were two instances in which it seems that costly errors of judgment were made. The first such case was the purchase of ore fields in York County, Pennsylvania. There an investment of $98,897.40 was made in order to secure a larger supply of ore to feed the six furnaces then owned by the company.[7] The purchase of the 260 acres was made with the approval of a committee that had visited the area and made what was supposedly a careful study of the mines. After the deposits had been mined a short time, it was discovered that the ore

---

[6]The Thomas Iron Co. Fin. Rec., p. 78. The company held two mineral deposits at Lake Champlain in Essex County, New York.

[7]Min. Book - The Thomas Iron Co., p. 175.

was a low grade product and contained from 1 to 2 percent phosphorous. Furthermore, the cost of mining was expensive and the shipping charges heavy. Because of these difficulties, the mining operations were discontinued. After extensive litigation the property was returned to its original owner with a loss to the iron company of $33,258.32.[8]

The second error in judgment was in the purchase, in 1873, of the South Mountain Iron Company. Because of the impending completion of two additional furnaces at that time, the directors deemed it advisable to secure more ore lands for the company's future requirements. After "careful examination," the board of directors concluded that the South Mountain Iron Company's assets consisting of 20,000 acres of land, a charcoal furnace, and several buildings, plus a short railroad line connecting with the Cumberland Valley Railroad at Carlisle, would be "desirable property" for The Thomas Iron Company to own. The cost of these assets was $408,000. At that time it was believed that there was an almost unlimited supply of high quality ore available on the land, and if the iron company ever desired to expands its smelting facilities, the site would prove to be a most advantageous holding.[9]

With the panic of 1879 and the continuing depressed business conditions, the South Mountain Iron Company venture was quickly turned into a fiasco and necessitated the issuance, in 1875, of over $500,000 in

---

[8]The Thomas Iron Co. Fin. Rec., p. 260.

[9]_Ibid._, p. 66. J. W. Harden, "The Brown Hematite Ores of South Mountain," _Transactions of the American Institute of Mining Engineers_, I (Philadelphia, 1873), 136 ff.

first mortgage bonds. The total loss to The Thomas Iron Company, when the situation was finally cleared from its books, was $601,885.27.[10] It is difficult to ascertain whether the company had committed an error, for there were reports published at that time providing evidence of valuable ore deposits on the property. If there was an error, it appears that the engineer who provided the scientific evidence to prove the availability of the ore had committed it. The Thomas Iron Company, however, suffered the loss. Fortunately the management's choice of railroad projects was made with more prudence and greater success.

In order to reach a number of the local ore mines and its limestone quarries, The Thomas Iron Company participated in the construction of two feeder lines from mines to mainlines of railroad. The first project, the Catasauqua and Fogelsville Railroad, originally planned as a plank road, was built with the assistance of the Lehigh Crane Iron Company, and the Mount Hope Railroad in New Jersey was built with the aid of other mining companies in the area of the Richard Mine.

The Catasauqua and Fogelsville Railroad's original destination was Rothrocksville, a distance of 9 miles from the Lehigh Valley Railroad track just below The Thomas Iron Company's furnaces. By 1857 the railroad was extended to Alburtis; there it made a junction with the East Pennsylvania Railroad.[11] The Thomas Iron Company's share in the venture totaled $170,725. At first the road paid no dividends and annually

---

[10] Ibid., p. 237.

[11] Mathews and Hungerford, Lehigh and Carbon Counties, p. 111.

required more and more capital, but by 1867 it had paid its first dividend and it continued to pay them for the next fifty-five years.

In New Jersey the ores from Richard Mine were originally carted to the Morris Canal by means of wagon and mule. Because the company desired to reduce the costs of carriage and increase deliveries of the ores, it was decided in 1859 to join with other companies to build a more efficient system of transportation to connect the mine and canal. That year these companies attempted to obtain a charter for the Mount Hope Railroad, a horse railroad.[12] As a consequence of some irregularity in the process of obtaining this charter, it was not until 1862 that the New Jersey Legislature permitted the construction of the railroad. By that time the plans had been changed and road was built for a steam locomotive and was to connect with a nearby railroad instead of the canal. But it was almost five years later before any expenditures were made for purposes of constructing this railroad, and it was not until 1869 that the railroad was fully completed. The iron company had invested $44,100 in the venture.[13] By 1872 this railroad was also paying dividends to the various companies holding its capital stock. Dividends from this venture were passed only three times in the next twenty-nine years.[14]

The problem of obtaining the necessary limestone flux seems to have been easily satisfied through the exploitation of nearby deposits of the

---

[12]Min. Book - The Thomas Iron Co., p. 83.

[13]The Thomas Iron Co. Fin. Rec., p. 51.

[13]*Ibid.*, p. 272.

ubiquitous material, and for a number of years the coal requirements were readily provided by the growing number of mines in the Lehigh coal region. Throughout the years there had been a steady influx of miners and mining companies into that coal region which were served by an ever expanding transportation network. Consequently, the price of anthracite coal dropped continuously between 1855 and 1863. Then with the increase in the demand for fuel during the war, coal prices began to rise, just as the cost of transportation increased.[15]

Confronted with a coal shortage in 1862, the company planned to build up reserves of the fuel for handling future emergencies.[16] Shortly thereafter members of the board of directors visited a number of coal mines in the area of the upper reaches of the Lehigh River in order to determine the feasibility of purchasing a colliery to secure their coal supplies.[17] Though the superintendent of the furnaces was forced to blow out one of the furnaces at this time because of a coal shortage, the directors found it inexpedient to purchase any one of the several mines they had inspected.

As the directors vacillated in making their decision, coal prices continued to rise. From a price of $3.23 a ton f.o.b. in 1863, the cost

---

[15] Ibid., p. 271. Min. Book - The Thomas Iron Co., p. 89.

[16] Min. Book - The Thomas Iron Co., p. 106.

[17] Ibid., pp. 112 f. The Bethlehem Iron Company began a similar quest for coal supplies in 1874. See Bethlehem Iron Company, Stockholders Minutes, n.p. This material is held by the Bethlehem Steel Corporation Library in Bethlehem, Pennsylvania. This work will hereafter be cited as Beth. Iron Co. Stockholders Min.

moved to $5.32 a ton in 1864 and finally reached $6.67 a ton in 1865.[18] In the latter year, three years after the coal problem had been mentioned in the minutes of the board of directors' meetings, the company finally obtained several lease agreements from Charles Parrish for the operation of two collieries in Luzerne County, and the charter of the company was changed in order to permit it to own and mine coal lands for its own use or for sale.[19]

For the next few years the company seems to have succeeded in securing an adequate supply of coal for its furnaces. Meanwhile the regional output of coal increased and prices commenced to decline. Anxious to stabilize prices, a few mine operators and railroad companies in the area began to concentrate control over many of the numerous coal properties. By 1869 this group of owners was planning to meet in New York City to discuss the fixing of coal rates.[20] At the same time the miners began to organize a labor union in order to obtain a larger share of the coal revenues; as a consequence, the period was replete with labor

---

[18]The Thomas Iron Co. Fin. Rec., p. 271. The figures given are prices per ton prior to transportation to the furnaces. The price of a ton of coal at Philadelphia, including the cost of carriage, was $6.06 in 1863. The following year, 1864, the price of coal was $8.39 a ton and in 1865 it was $7.86 per ton. See Swank, _The American Iron Trade in 1876_, p. 192.

[19]Min. Book - The Thomas Iron Co., pp. 127 ff. Marvin W. Schlegel, _Ruler of the Reading; The Life of Franklin B. Gowen, 1836-1889_ (Harrisburg, 1947), p. 75. President Parrish of the Wilkes-Barre Coal and Iron Company held one-half interest in each of the collieries. The coal and iron company was soon brought under the control of the Central Railroad of New Jersey, one of the members of the anthracite coal combination.

[20]Roberts, _The Anthracite Coal Industry_, p. 72.

troubles, which finally culminated in a long strike in 1871 and another in 1875.

Presumably the company's coal mines were free from these conditions of unrest, but it was reported in 1871 that five furnaces were shut down because of a fuel shortage. At the same time the iron company was faced with costly repairs to one of its mines as a consequence of an explosion. Hindered by these difficulties and discovering, after six years of mining and consuming the coal, the quality of the fuel was not suitable for making iron, it was deemed advisable to dispose of both mines. One mine, Sugar Notch Colliery, was sold to the Lehigh Coal and Navigation Company. The records indicate that the iron company assumed a loss of $41,253.99 in the transaction.[21] During the same year a loss of $41,320.28 was reported in the operation of the Pine Ridge Colliery; however, The Thomas Iron Company made an agreement with the Delaware and Hudson Coal Company to continue the operation of that mine.[22] The coal mining company was to sell the coal and make payment to the iron company for the privilege. In 1873, after a disagreement with the Delaware and Hudson Coal Company over the mining of the property, the board of directors decided to withdraw from all coal mining operations and bring to a close their abortive attempt to carry out another phase of vertical integration.[23]

---

[21] Min. Book - The Thomas Iron Co., pp. 192 ff. The Thomas Iron Co. Fin. Rec., p. 58.

[22] Ibid., p. 195

[23] Ibid., pp. 207 ff. The Thomas Iron Co. Fin. Rec., p. 67.

Blast Furnace Production

These almost ceaseless efforts to unearth new and more reliable sources of fuel and raw material are reflections of the company's addition to its productive facilities which had increased, in this span of twenty years, from two to eight blast furnaces. As early as 1860, after the above-mentioned sources of ore had been secured, it became evident to the directors that several more furnaces could be used to advantage, and plans were made at that time to erect two additional stacks.[24] Slow and heavy work that it was, almost three years passed before both furnaces were in production; furnace number three being put in blast in 1862, and furnace four was blown in the next year.[25]

The new structures, like the original works, were constructed of local stone with boshes 13 feet across, but, unlike the original furnaces, they were only built to a height of 55 feet instead of 60 feet, and only nine tuyeres were used instead of twelve. The temperature of the hot-blast was still maintained at 600° Fahrenheit and the blast was blown into the furnace under a pressure of 7½ pounds per square inch. Also, as at the first furnaces, the hot-blast stoves were situated at the tunnel head with the hot air conducted to the tuyeres by a single hot-blast main.[26]

In no way do these works provide any evidence of the management

---

[24] *Ibid.*, pp. 65 and 72.

[25] The Thomas Iron Co. Fin. Rec., p. 45.

[26] Daddow and Bannan, *Coal, Iron, and Oil*, pp. 684 ff.

pioneering in improved techniques of smelting. Such furnaces as these had been tried before and found serviceable. There seems to have been little urgency to change the design or substitute other materials in fabricating the stack. By that date the Cleveland district ironmasters in Great Britain had proven the greater efficiency of the taller boiler plate furnace.

With the further expansion in the demand for iron in the middle 1860's, and after the extension of control over additional sources of ore, The Thomas Iron Company, at the urging of members of the board of directors, purchased the Lock Ridge Iron Company in nearby Alburtis.[27] Though the new furnace had not been completed at the time of purchase, it was soon prepared for operation, and plans were set afoot to build still another furnace at the same site.[25] When they were finally constructed, these furnaces were duplicates of the company's earlier works with the heavy masonry wells, hot-blast stoves at the tunnel head, and built to a height of 55 feet.

At that time the western ironmasters were adapting the advanced British furnace designs and the boiler plate shells with their firebrick linings. In the Lehigh Valley, experiments in using the taller furances had been undertaken at the Glendon iron works, and the Bethlehem Iron Company had built and successfully operated a boiler plate stack with

---

[27]Min. Book - The Thomas Iron Co., pp. 153 ff.

[28]*Ibid.*, p. 162.

anthracite coal.[29] For some reason, however, the management of The Thomas Iron Company held fast to what were becoming outmoded techniques of smelting iron ore.

Just why the decision to use the stone stack was made is difficult to determine. Possibly it was more economical to use the stone; however, as time went on, the company persisted in using stone, while all about them other furnace companies were building their furnaces with boiler plate shells. Such a policy as this would seem to suggest that whoever was responsible for providing technical advice to the board of directors must have held rather strong opinions on the use of the stone structures and must have maintained little interest in the possibility of experimenting with tried innovations.[30]

Before 1870 the company had commenced the construction of two more furnaces at Hokendauqua, but as economic conditions became difficult, some stockholders censured the management for continuing the projects. Nevertheless, enough votes were mustered by the interested stockholders to gain support for the directors' policy.[31] The board then proceeded to complete the works and put them in blast in 1873 and 1874. With these

---

[29] John Fritz, Autobiography of John Fritz (New York, 1912), pp. 142 f.

[30] American Iron and Steel Association, Bulletin, Vol. 2 (Jan. 22, 1868), 154. At that time the company had adopted the Lurman closed furnace front. The device closed the hearth of the furnace and permitted the maintenance of a blast pressure of greater weight than previously secured.

[31] The Thomas Iron Co. Fin. Rec., pp. 61 ff. Min. Book - The Thomas Iron Co., p. 183.

furnaces The Thomas Iron Company became the largest single merchant pig iron firm in the United States, but the firm was the owner of eight somewhat outmoded furnaces.

The company's works no longer represented the most advanced techniques in smelting as had the first furnaces built in 1855.[32] Not one of the furnaces was built to a height over 60 feet, and all were fabricated with stone. Though the temperature of the blast had been increased, it had not been raised to the temperatures being used by some western furnace companies. Output from each furnace was approximately 37 net tons a day or 259 tons a week. This level of output was below the capacity of a number of new furnaces located in the western iron centers which were capable of producing over 300 tons of pig iron a week.[33]

In spite of these differences in average furnace capacities, The Thomas Iron Company had attained the topmost rank among the nation's pig iron producers. Between 1856 and the peak production year of 1872, the firm had succeeded in expanding its total output from approximately 19,059 net tons to 81,324 tons, an increase in production of 326 percent. In that peak year the output of The Thomas Iron Company was equivalent to 3 percent of the total pig iron production in the nation and 18 percent of the output of the Lehigh Valley.

The major portion of the additional tonnage can be credited to the

---

[32]Lesley, _The Iron Manufacturer's Guide_, p. 8. Percy, _Metallurgy: Iron and Steel_, pp. 383 ff.

[33]Firmstone, "Sketches of Early Anthracite Furnaces," _Trans. AIME_, III (1874-75), 156. Talcott, "The Manufacture of Pit Iron," _ASCE Trans._, I, 196.

expansion in the number of furances, while another segment resulted from additional operating days. There was, however, one other reason for the increased furnace output; the average daily output for each furnace had been raised from 29.56 net tons to 37 tons, an increase in daily furnace output of 25 percent.[34]

An examination of the available operating data seems to indicate that the reason for the rise in daily furnace output rests on several improvements in furnace practice. First, and probably most significant, was the employment of higher grade ores in the furnaces. For example, the mineral content of the ore in 1856 had been 38.56 percent iron, but by 1872 the increasing use of the righer magnetic ores had raised the average mineral content of the ore mixture to 45.60 percent.[35] Concurrent with this improvement in the ore mixture the temperature and the pressure of the blast were both increased slightly to account for another part of the improvement in daily furnace output.[36] It might be added that sixteen years of experience with the same type of furnace must have helped to improve the efficiency of the labor force and management.

From Chart IV and Table 8 it can be seen that the company's output

---

[34]The Thomas Iron Co. Fin. Rec., p. 230.

[35]Ibid., p. 271. American Iron and Steel Association, Bulletin, Vol. 6 (Nov. 29, 1871), 97. David Thomas reported the mixture of ores generally used in the furnaces was approximately 70 percent hematite and 30 percent magnetite ores.

[36]Ibid. Improvements in furnace technique aided in increasing output and also reduced fuel consumption per ton of pig iron. Coal consumption per ton of iron fell from a little more than 2 tons 7 cwts. to 1 ton 17 cwts.

CHART IV

RELATIVE CHANGE IN LEHIGH VALLEY AND THE THOMAS IRON COMPANY PRODUCTION, 1856-75

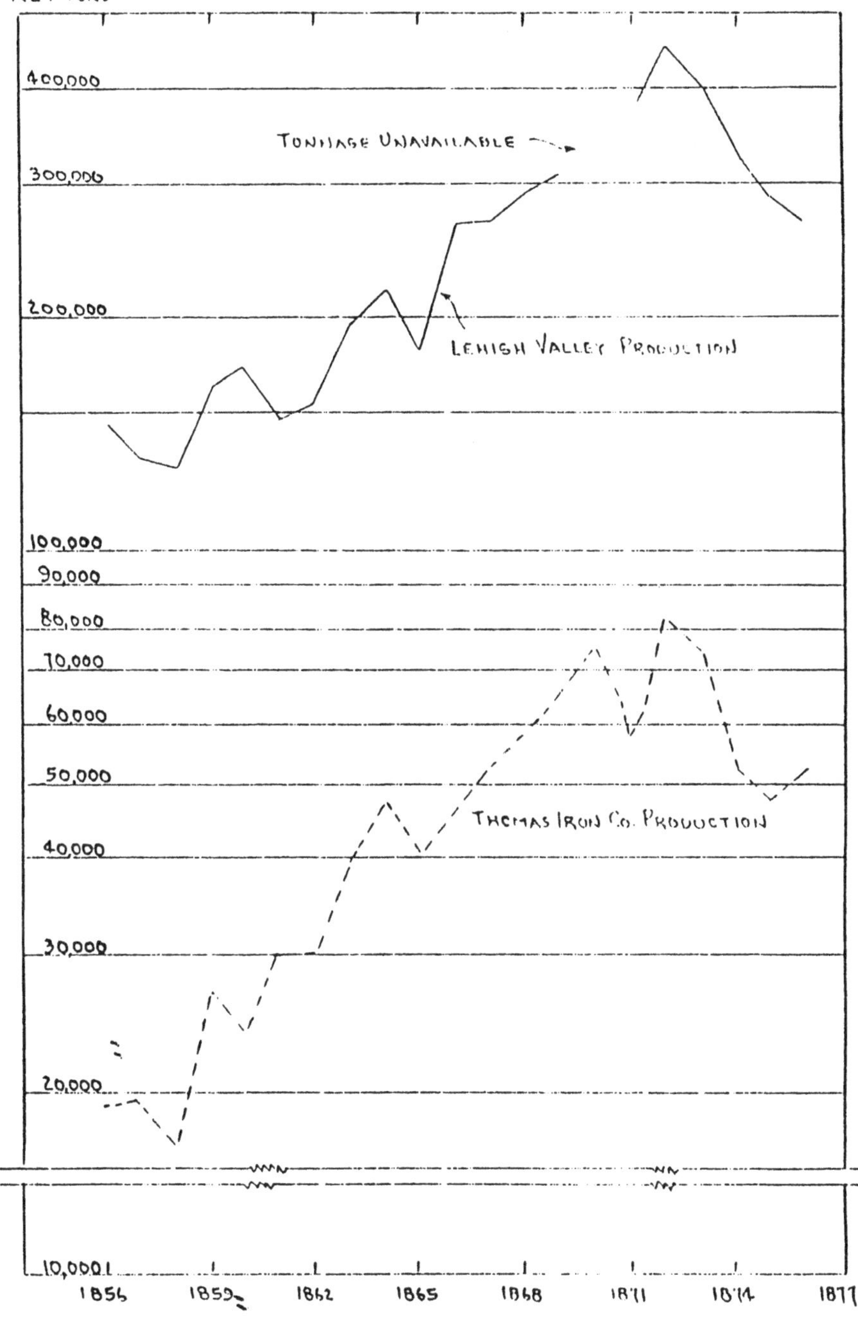

Source: The Thomas Iron Company Financial Records for Fifty Years, p. 271; American Iron and Steel Association, Statistics of the American and Foreign Iron Trade (1871-76).

TABLE 8

LEHIGH VALLEY AND THE THOMAS IRON COMPANY
PIG IRON PRODUCTION, 1856-75
(Net tons)

Year	Lehigh Valley Furnaces	Lehigh Valley Production	The Thomas Iron Company Furnaces	The Thomas Iron Company Production
1856	23	145,161	2	19,059
1857	23	131,078	2	19,421
1858	23	127,839	2	17,131
1859	23	161,431	2	26,905
1860	23	173,075	2	24.169
1861	25	147,418	2	30,197
1862	26	156,696	3	29,748
1863	26	192,740	4	39,054
1864	28	214,093	4	47,085
1865	30	177,438	4	39,736
1866	30	257,016	4	45,572
1867	33	262,000	4	51,144
1868	36	287,200	5	57,345
1869	41	300,916	6	63,012
1870	43	Unavailable	6	74,712
1871	43	372,009	6	55,797
1872	44	449,663	6	81,324
1873	47	389,969	7	72,723
1874	47	316,789	8	51,474
1875	50	280,360	8	47,664

Source: The Thomas Iron Company Financial Records for Fifty Years, p. 271; American Iron and Steel Association, _Statistics of the American and Foreign Iron Trade for 1871_ (Philadelphia, 1872), p. 11.

grew at a faster rate than the total production of the Lehigh Valley. Like other producers, The Thomas Iron Company suffered setbacks in production during the several periods of business depression in 1857, 1861, and 1873-75. The reduction output in 1864 and 1871 was a consequence of fuel shortages; in the latter instance the shortage arose because of the coal miners' strike. Again, in 1875 a second coal miners' strike caused a further loss in possible production; however, an attempt was made to substitute coke for anthracite coal, and production was maintained.[37]

Never, during these twenty years, were the company's furnaces shut down because of labor disputes. This statement does not mean to imply that there were not any troubles arising over labor problems. David Thomas hints that there were increasing difficulties in labor-management relations after 1861 when he wrote:

> The chief difficulty I have experienced in the manufacture of pig iron in our part of the country is the want of experience in the men employed, as well as the difficulty of managing labor, more especially since the breaking out of the unfortunate war in 1861. In my opinion it should be one of the chief studies of iron men, as well as manufacturers generally, to continue to use machinery as a substitute for manual labor, as it can be shown that the cost of making pig iron 96 per cent. consists in labor.[38]

Also, in nearby Catasauqua, at the Lehigh Crane Iron Company's works a strike was reported among the workers in 1874, but the strike did not

---

[37] Ibid., p. vii. American Iron and Steel Association, Bulletin, Vol. 9 (April 2, 1875), 92. The Thomas Iron Company was the first firm to substitute coke for anthracite coal, but the company did not continue to use the fuel regularly until 1883. Coke was employed between 1879 and 1882 but it was "used only as a medicine" for the furnace.

[38] American Iron and Steel Association, Bulletin, Vol. 6 (Nov. 29, 1871), 97; Vol. 8 (May 28, 1874), 164.

extend across the river to Hokendauqua. In the business records, however, there is little evidence of increasing labor-management problems.

Costs of Production

The firm's cost of producing a ton of pig iron generally fluctuated with the business conditions of the period, but the make-up of the total cost varied somewhat over time. For example, fuel costs, which made up about one-third of the total cost of a ton of pig iron in the 1850's increased to about one-half the cost in early 1860's. The rise in fuel cost was attributable largely to the much more rapid rise in the price of coal during the war years. Only after coal prices declined in the latter half of that decade did fuel costs gradually drop to one-third of the cost of a ton of pig iron. Then, in the early 1870's, improved furnace operations seemed to have reduced the cost of fuel for a ton of pig iron to about one-fifth of the total cost.

Ore costs, like the cost of fuel per ton of iron, were influenced by demand conditions and consequent price fluctuations, but, as the production of iron ores increased, their cost moved upward because of the ever increasing difficulties in mining the rather small deposits. The ore mines owned by the company required ever increasing expenditures of labor to timber the mines and wash the ores. Also, there were additional costs arising from the continual seepage of water in the mines. The extraction of the ores was done by laborers using picks and shovels, a slow and tedious job considering the size of the veins of ore found in most of the mines. And while the furnaces required approximately 300 men to operate them, the mines required about 1,600 or more men to provide the ores necessary to keep the furnaces in blast.[39] Because of such physical limitations, ore costs became an increasingly larger and larger portion of the cost of a ton of pig iron.

Though labor costs at the furnace are not readily available in the records because they have been integrated with the cost of supplies, the available data seems to indicate that labor costs per ton of pig iron generally remained near one-fifth of the cost of smelting a ton of iron throughout the twenty years. Wage rates were subject to fluctuation with the changing conditions of demand and supply, though it appears that wages lagged behind other price changes in most instances. This variable cost, however, appears to have been one which management, as could be assumed under the competitive conditions prevalent in the industry, adjusted quite readily when trade conditions became depressed. For example, in 1857 the company paid the workers with provisions rather than in cash. Again, in 1871 wages were reduced about 10 percent, an action taken simultaneously by all of the other furnace companies in the Lehigh Valley.[40] Then in 1874, as trade conditions continued to decline after the panic of 1873, the company's employees, both management and furnace workers, had their wages reduced on the average of about 12½ percent. In this adjustment management and supervisory personnel had reductions made amounting to 20 percent of their wages, while the worker's wage was

---

[39]The Thomas Iron Co. Fin. Rec., p. 266. Miller, Allentown Quadrangle, pp. 37 ff. Mathews and Hungergord, Lehigh and Carbon Counties, p. 502.

[40]Easton Argus, April 18, 1871

CHART V

THE THOMAS IRON COMPANY
RELATIVE CHANGES IN FACTOR COSTS FOR ONE TON OF PIG IRON, 1856-75

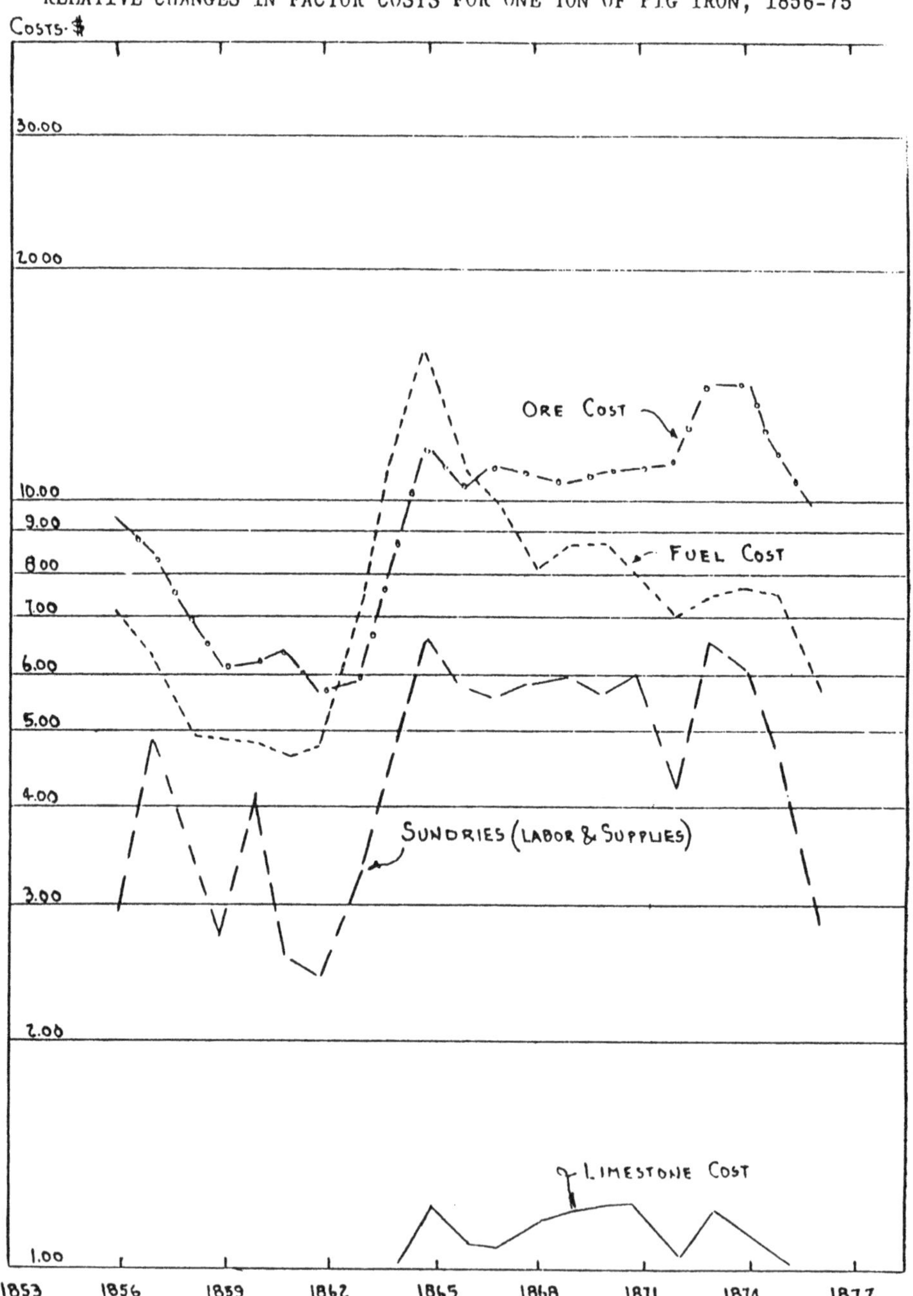

Source: The Thomas Iron Company Financial Records for Fifty Years, p. 271.

dropped about 10 percent.[41]

Throughout most of the twenty years the cost-price relationship for the firm was generally excellent. The spread ranged between $13.13 in 1867 to $1.43 in 1871, and the average spread was $6.44. Only in 1875, when wages, limestone, and fuel costs seemed to lag behind the general price changes, was the company placed in a precarious position. At that time the cost-price spread was but 47 cents on a ton of pig iron. The next year, however, adjustments were made in all of these costs, and a margin of $1.34 was secured on each ton of pig iron. For a somewhat clearer picture of these developments, see Chart VI on the following page.

Marketing

The pig iron produced in the furnaces was a foundry iron which found a market in the immediate vicinity and along the coastal region from Virginia to Maine. Though the quality of the firm's iron was reputed to be excellent, very little effort was made to secure uniformity in quality through chemical analysis of the raw materials or the finished product. Generally the grading of the pigs was done by the fracture method in which the internal crystalline structure of the pig indicated the approximate character of the iron. Records were maintained for only three grades of iron, No. 1X, No. 2X, and No. 3 foundry iron.[42] Because

---

[41] American Iron and Steel Association, Bulletin, Vol. 8 (May 28, 1874), 164. The Thomas Iron Co. Fin. Rec., pp. 278 ff.

[42] Charles W. Sisson, The ABC of Iron (Kentucky, 1893), pp. 37 ff. No. 1X was a foundry iron with a fracture dark in color, with rough, open grain, and low tensile strength. No. 2X did not have as wide a grain as

CHART VI

THE THOMAS IRON COMPANY
RELATIVE CHANGE IN COST, PRICE, OUTPUT, AND SALES, 1856-75

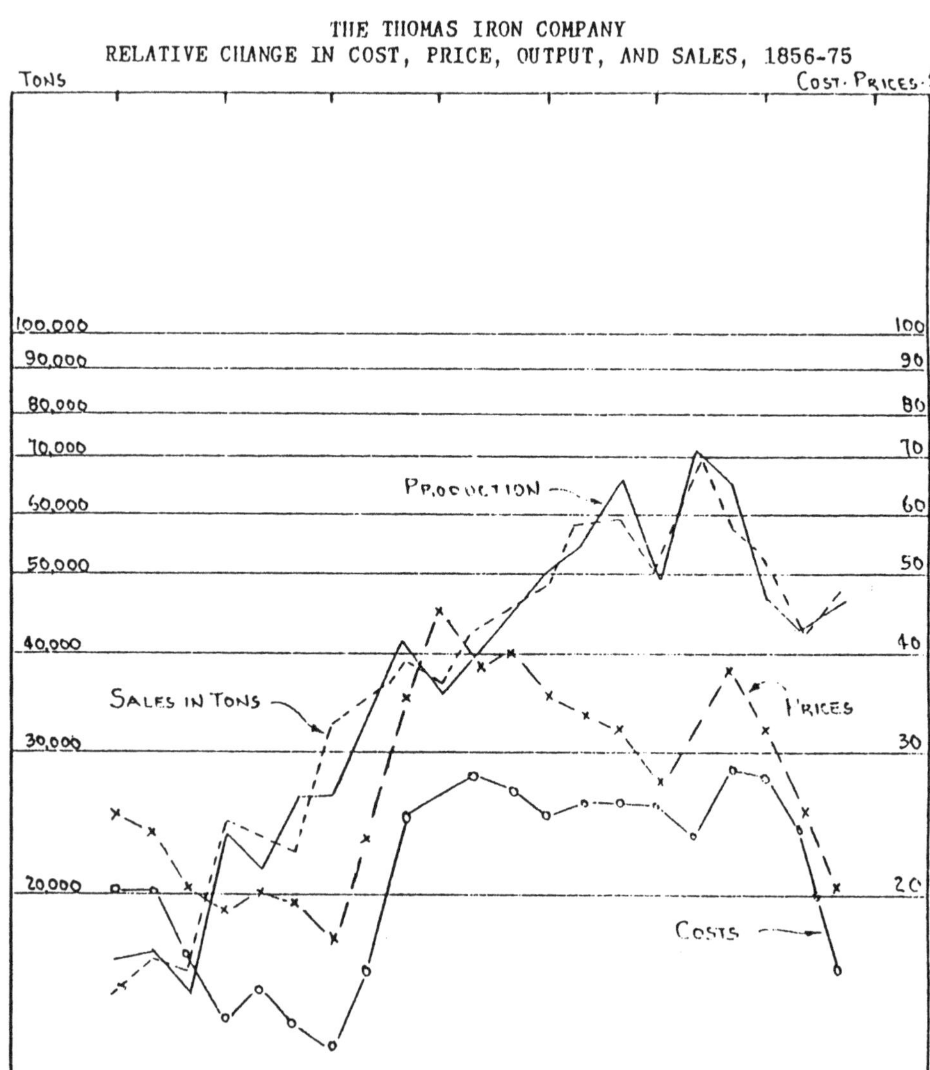

Source: The Thomas Iron Company Financial Records for Fifty Years, pp. 271-72.

of its phosphorous and sulphur content, the pig iron was not adaptable to the Bessemer process, nor was there any effort made to secure ores which could have been smelted for that purpose.

Sales of iron were made to the consumer through a commission house in Philadelphia and a sales representative of the firm in New York City. It was common practice in the industry for the merchant furnace companies to extend a long line of credit to their customers and The Thomas Iron Company followed the same practice. Sometimes credit terms extended over a six-month period.

For several years the New York sales representative, who was paid 6½ cents commission on each ton of pig iron sold, plus a small salary, was given almost complete jurisdiction over the firm's sales policy. His functions included the pricing and the determination of allowances as well as credit terms. He maintained all the records of his transactions and was held responsible only to the board of directors in Easton. When a series of bad account losses appeared during several seasons, it was decided to change this method of control and the jurisdiction of the sales agent was reduced considerably. At that juncture the price and credit policies were placed in the hands of the directors.[43] After that

---

No. 1, but the iron was harder than No. 1 although less tough and more brittle. These two grades of iron became very liquid and could be used in the finest castings. No. 3 iron was a finer grain metal and was used both in rolling mills and foundries. An iron of this quality was better adapted to heavy castings, being less tough and more brittle than the other two grades.

[43]Min. Book - The Thomas Iron Co., p. 121. The Thomas Iron Co. Fin. Rec., pp. 17 and 219A.

change the sales agent's activities are not too clearly pictured through the available records. Because so little information is at hand, it can only be assumed that the practices employed were sufficient and thus called for little discussion. As there is even less information available on the action of the commission house in Philadelphia, Lyman and Company, it must be assumed that the same holds true in that case.

The price policy of the company was to follow the market price. Little else could have been done, for the industry was quite competitive. Only on one occasion is reference made in the minute book to price policy, and then it merely refers to a proposed meeting with the Lehigh Crane Iron Company and other firms "to confer about prices."[44] The meeting was to have been held at a time when prices of pig iron were declining. Again, as nothing more was recorded on this matter and prices continued to fall, it can be assumed that nothing was accomplished.

In 1874 and 1875, when the state of the iron trade was quite depressed, efforts were made by several furnace owners in the Lehigh Valley to restrict production in order to stabilize the price of pig iron. The Thomas Iron Company was not one of the participants in these discussions. Furthermore, at the very time that the discussions were held and furnace owners were calling for reduced output, The Thomas Iron Company was reported to have reduced its price to meet the shift in demand. The company reduced its price to $25 a ton at a time when other firms were

---

[44] Ibid., p. 168.

charging $26.[45] Action such as this suggests that the company preferred to maintain an independent position as far as prices and output were concerned. Management probably recognized that under the competitive conditions of the merchant pig iron trade - the number of firms, the homogeneous nature of the product, and the relative freedom of entry - little could be done to control prices by such stratagem as long as only a small portion of the industry was in agreement on such a practice.[46]

There was, however, one area of business in which the company could exert some pressure and obtain certain reductions in its costs. The highly competitive nature of the transportation system in the Lehigh Valley led to the practice, on the part of the transportation companies, of providing rebates on tonnage carried. Prices for iron were furnace prices; the purchaser paid freight charges. Thus, any drawbacks from the railroads or canals meant larger profits for the favored company on each ton of pig iron shipped.

---

[45] Iron Age, Vol. 15 (March 4, 1875), 17.

[46] Min. Book - The Thomas Iron Co., pp. 119 and 172. Minute Book of the American Iron and Steel Association, n.p. This material is held by the American Iron and Steel Institute Library, New York City.

It is interesting to note that while The Thomas Iron Company was not instrumental in organizing the American Iron and Steel Association, as the Bethlehem Iron Company and Lehigh Crane Company were, it maintained its membership in that organization until 1873. Moreover, Samuel Thomas, president of The Thomas Iron Company from 1865 to 1882, was appointed to the original board of managers of the Association and served in that capacity for a number of years.

The Thomas Iron Company's minute book mentions several instances when the board of directors decided to withdraw from the Association, but it was not until 1873 that the step was finally taken. There is no record of the company's membership fees being paid from that date to 1894. From 1894 until 1910 the company maintained its membership in the Association.

Fully aware of the competitive character of the transportation companies within the valley and especially between the lines going to tidewater ports, the iron company, on several occasions of record, negotiated with various shipping companies to obtain favorable rate changes and in several instances sought and received rebates on iron and ore shipments. In 1859 the company received a favorable rate change with the Central Railroad of New Jersey, and the rate per ton of pig iron was dropped from $1.80 to $1.60 per ton for carriage to Elizabethport, New Jersey. The agreement included a rebate of 5 cents on a ton of pig iron.[47]

In 1860 the Morris Canal and Banking Company provided a rebate of 8 cents on each ton of pig iron shipped to tidewater over its route. Immediately thereafter the iron company received what was recorded as an "acceptable" rate adjustment from the Central Railroad of New Jersey for shipments of pig iron to Elizabethport.[48] Whether the agreement provided an equal rebate is difficult to report, though it appears easy to assume some such adjustment was made to meet the competitive price.

Then in 1862 the company requested a rebate from the Lehigh Coal and Navigation Company on shipments of iron ore coming over from the Morris Canal which was already providing a rebate. By that date the competitive conditions of the canal had been increased considerably. Despite the established policy of the canal company to exlude drawbacks on iron ore ascending the canal, the iron company obtained a rebate of ½

---

[47] _Ibid_., pp. 53 ff.

[48] _Ibid_., p. 70.

cent per ton per mile on its ore shipments from New Jersey.[49] Though there is no further record in the next fifteen years of any more rebates being received, it is entirely probable, in the light of the railroad development within the Lehigh Valley, that the iron company was favored with further advantages of that sort.

Financing Expansion

To finance the expansion program there were several possible schemes at hand, among them being the selling of additional stock, debt financing, or the reinvesting of earnings. The stratagem of financing the replacement of equipment through depreciation allowances, so popular today, was not available to the board of directors, for they had not provided the firm with such reserve accounts in their accounting records, nor did they seem to indicate any recognition that such a method might have been used.[50]

At the outset the directors resorted to the investment of retained earnings as the most expedient strategy, never considering the possibility of incurring debt for that purpose.[51] Then, as time and conditions

---

[49]Brzyski, "The Lehigh Canal and its Effect on the Development of the Region Through Which It Passed, 1818-1873," pp. 103 ff.

[50]The Thomas Iron Company did not institute a system of depreciation accounting until 1917, five short years prior to the transfer of the company's property to the Reading Coal and Iron Company. The Bethlehem Iron Company adopted depreciation accounting in 1864, one year after it had commenced its production of iron. See Beth. Iron Co. Stockholders Min.

[51]The Thomas Iron Co. Fin. Rec., p. 7. President Luckenbach wrote on the matter of investment as follows:

"To accumulate such amount of capital two modes presented themselves; the one, by the selling of additional stock; the other by

changed and the schemes for expansion became more grandiose, other strategies were used.[52]

Reasons for adopting the reinvestment of earnings as the "most eligible" method are not provided in the records, but it seems that it had been used in preference to the other techniques in order to avoid the difficulties which might arise with the other sources of funds. Though the retention of earnings deprived the stockholders of immediate cash dividends, it promised an expansion of assets that appeared to offer rich rewards and assured the stockholders of record that the then established shares of control would not be disturbed, as they might have been with additional stock sales. The incurring of additional debt would not only present a prior claim on the earnings but would also have required a higher rate of return on capital investment in order to maintain the return to the stockholders and pay the fixed interest charges.

Because of changing conditions the other methods of financing were resorted to before the end of the period under consideration. For example, in the financing of the purchase of the Lock Ridge Iron Company's works in 1868, the records suggest that a small "in group" received a

---

appropriating a portion of the net proceeds to the augmentation of the capital. The latter mode was deemed the most eligible, and it is here believed the true policy of our Board of Directors, hereafter, to declare cash dividends not exceeding 6% per annum, until the increase of the capital to the amount above stated [$500,000] shall have placed the Company upon its own resources."

[52]Min. Book - The Thomas Iron Co., pp. 38 f. The company had issued bonds in 1856 in order to raise the cash necessary to build the Catasauqua and Fogelsville Railroad.

sizable windfall gain and a strengthened voice in the operation of The Thomas Iron Company through what appears to have been the equivalent of a stock sale.

In 1867 several stockholders in The Thomas Iron Company commenced the building of a blast furnace at Alburtis under the corporate charter of the Lock Ridge Iron Company. The stockholders included David and Samuel Thomas, B. G. Clarke, John Drake, all members of the board of directors. Also, there were several other stockholders that were also shareholders in The Thomas Iron Company, two of them being among the management personnel of that company. The following year the Lock Ridge furnace was purchased by The Thomas Iron Company upon the transference of 2,750 shares of stock of that company to the owners of the Lock Ridge works. Other shareholders of The Thomas Iron Company, in this instance, did not participate in this particular stock issue; consequently, the transaction, the equivalent of a stock sale, resulted in dilution of control in the shares held by some stockholders while a few others had an accretion of control.[53] Upon adding these shares of stock and the shares previously purchased or paid as dividends to these shareholders, there was a relatively large accumulation of stock in the hands of members of the Thomas family and a few others, who, it seems, gained some control over The Thomas Iron Company's operations.

---

[53]The Thomas Iron Co. Fin. Rec., p. 45. The major recipients of these shares of stock were: David Thomas, 343 3/4 shares; Samuel Thomas, 412½ shares; John Thomas, 269½ shares; John Drake, 275 shares; Theodore Sturgis, 137½ shares; Joshua Hunt, 253 shares; and Valentine Weaver, 137½ shares. Eight other individuals outside of the company shared the remainder of the 2,750 shares but in smaller amounts.

The issuance of this stock, however, was not carried through without question. In the Senate of the Pennsylvania Legislature, where a supplement to the company's charter to permit the issuance of the 2,750 shares of stock was debated, a member of the Senate from Northampton County contested the policy being established by and in favor of a few interested stockholders holding shares in both companies. To Senator Brown the payment in stock was the product of Wall Street machinations "gotten up for the purpose of taking out of the hands of the present stockholders all this appropriation of stock, and the management of the company."[54] In regard of the latter charge, there can probably be no disagreement, but there seems to be no evidence to substantiate the claim that the plan was the product of a scheme devised by a group of Wall Street financiers.

The windfall gain harvested by the group was clearly evident in the difference in the dollar value of the stock received and the dollar cost of the plant surrendered. The Lock Ridge furnace cost The Thomas Iron Company 2,750 shares of stock at par value ($50). The purchase price was entered in The Thomas Iron Company's books at $137,500, the par value of the stock. At that time the company's stock was valued at $100 to $106 per share in the market place. The Lock Ridge plant had cost approximately $200,000 to construct, a circumstance which resulted in a windfall profit of $75,000 or more.[55]

---

[54]Pennsylvania Legislative Record (Feb. 20, 1868), p. 422.

[55]Ibid.

On other occasions it was found necessary to borrow money through the issuance of notes or bonds in order to carry to completion projects previously planned and only partially consumated.

The company had two furnaces which had been placed in the capital expansion program in 1869 and were only partially completed by 1872 and were in danger of going unfinished for some length of time because of the losses suffered by the iron company during the coal strike of 1871.[56] In order to provide the necessary funds to complete these furnaces and purchase more ore lands, the company, in 1873, issued short-term notes for approximately $300,000. The fact that these were short-term notes indicates that the directors held high expectations for sizable profits within the next few years. Meanwhile, the coal mines purchased a few years previously were sold, a move which provided additional funds.[57] That same year total improvements to the company's facilities cost approximately $703,577.[58]

When the following year proved to be difficult and profits dropped from $799,611 to $117,616, the directors were placed in a very uncomfortable position. The short-term notes were due, and additional plant improvements had been made that would require more cash payments in a very short time.

In order to extricate the firm from this situation, two solutions

---

[56]The Thomas Iron Co. Fin. Rec., p. 63.

[57]*Ibid.*, p. 66.

[58]*Ibid.*, p. 65.

were offered. One was to sell additional shares of stock to the existing stockholders at par value, and the second was to issue convertible bonds, convertible into the stock of the company at par value any time up to 1880.[59] Before either one of these plans could be used, business conditions became even more unfavorable; profits fell to almost nothing ($6,270.28), a condition very unlikely to induce people to purchase the company's stock or convertible bonds. Because of this exigency, the board decided to float a bond issue with a mortgage lien.[60] Thus, under what appear to be rather stringent economic circumstances, and faced with the payment of debt incurred through what seems to have been a somewhat inadvisable expansion program, the board of directors was forced to resort to methods of financing other than through the reinvestment of earnings.

Dividends and Profits

Dividends for the whole period amounted to about one-third of the income, though the payments in the first ten years were smaller by 6 percent than the total paid in the second ten years. The payment of a low rate of cash dividends reflects the very heavy capital accumulation program and the rather extensive effort made to accumulate raw material sources. This distribution of funds is apparent in Chart VII which has been derived from the financial records of the company.

---

[59] *Ibid*., p. 73.

[60] *Ibid*., p. 77. The mortgage loan was made for $600,000 with an interest rate of 7 percent. The Farmers Loan and Trust Company of New York City acted as trustee for the bondholders.

CHART VII

THE THOMAS IRON COMPANY
SOURCE AND APPLICATION OF FUNDS IN TWO PERIODS

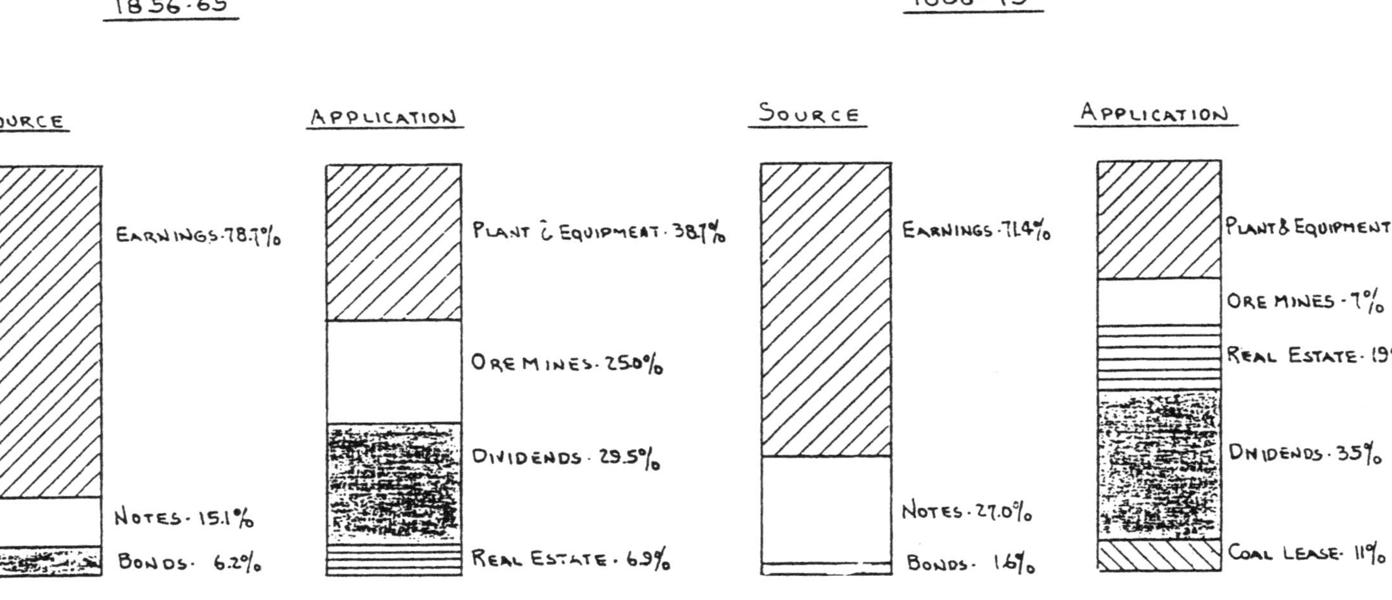

Source: The Thomas Iron Company Financial Records for Fifty Years, pp. 5 ff.

There were five years when dividends were passed - 1856, 1858, 1861, 1870, and 1875. There was but one year, however, when cash dividends exceeded profits; that was in 1871 when a coal strike interfered with production. Stock dividends were issued in eight of the twenty years, and four of these were years in which no cash dividends were issued.

Though the directors had announced the establishment of a policy to pay only 6 percent cash dividends when accumulating capital resources, they seemed to have forgotten the policy in a very short time or were forced by conditions to proceed under quite a different policy. After paying 6 percent on the book value of the capital stock in 1857, there was a predisposition to pay more and more in the way of cash dividends until the difficult times of 1875 interefered and the rate dipped to 3 percent. For the full twenty-year period the rate of return on capital stock (par value) averaged 8.5 percent, though in the fifteen years in which payments were made the average rate of return on the capital stock was 11.3 percent. The highest cash dividend amounted to a 27 percent return on the capital stock. That payment was made in 1867.

During the twenty years a number of stock dividends were issued that supposedly were equal to total cash payments of $1,473,845. Such stock dividends helped to increase the outstanding stock of the corporation from 4,000 to 40,000 shares.

Profits, earned income, averaged about 20.3 percent return on the gross fixed assets of the firm, though they amounted to only 14.6 percent of the net worth.[61] Relative to the 6 and 7 percent interest rate paid by the company for borrowed money, these earnings represented a fair return on the firm's assets. These measures provide an index of profitability; yet, as there is a lack of comparative earnings by like firms, it is quite difficult, if not impossible, to make any judgment of the relative efficiency of management. That is to say, it is difficult to determine whether the profits were the product of managerial policies or merely the result of the economic conditions of the times.

To venture a guess it appears that a large portion of the profits were the product of the economic events of the time. But this is not meant to detract from the success of the board of directors and management in their expansion program. Certainly the expansion of the plant at this particular period had a great deal to do with the increase in the absolute amount of profits. Also, the fact that this company, and not some others, was able to operate its furnaces through the business depression of the 1870's and make business profits indicates that the managers were relatively more efficient than some other management groups. It might be concluded that the managers of The Thomas Iron Company turned in a better-than-average record for the short run period. The long run success is another matter.

Profit receipts, as could be expected, were quite unstable, for they were duly affected by the fiscal policy of the federal government and railroad expansion just as they were affected by coal strikes and

---

[61] Net worth included bonds, capital stock, and surplus.

banking conditions. But, as indicated in Chart VIII, despite the instability of profits, and as long as it appeared that there would be profit opportunities, the board of directors persisted in continuing their expansion program.

Another interesting aspect of finances depicted in Chart VIII is the heavy volume of current assets maintained by the company. The magnitude of these assets is explained by the heavy inventories carried by the company and the rather long credit periods provided customers. Inventories consisted of both raw materials and finished products. Weather conditions which hampered mining often required the storage of relatively large quantities of raw materials, while the policy of maintaining production during certain periods when demand was slack often led to the accumulation of a large stock of pig iron. It should be noted, however, that these supplies were quite often sold at more favorable prices when more prosperous conditions prevailed.

As previously mentioned, credit periods of extensive duration were extended to customers, a practice that necessitated the carrying of a large volume of accounts receivable. When business conditions became quite active in 1862, there was some agitation among iron manufacturers to reduce the credit period to four months.[62] As nothing more was reported on the matter and the firm's accounts receivable continued to grow, it is difficult to ascertain whether any agreement was reached.

---

[62] Min. Book - The Thomas Iron Co., p. 89. The minutes indicate that a meeting of the iron manufacturers was held in Philadelphia to consider the reduction of the credit period from six to four months.

CHART VIII

THE THOMAS IRON COMPANY
RELATIVE CHANGE IN TOTAL ASSETS, GROSS FIXED ASSETS,
AND PROFITS, 1856-75

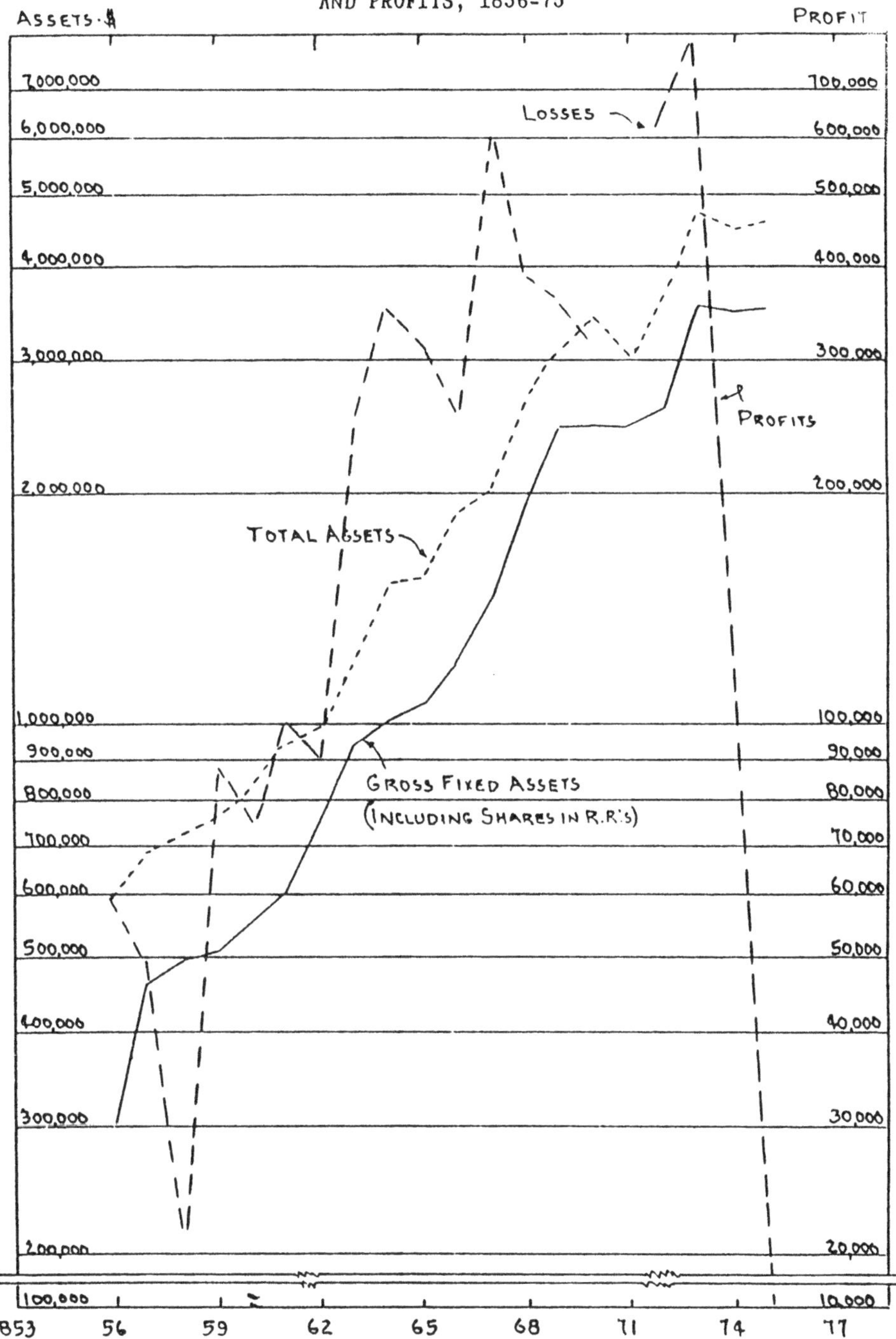

Source: The Thomas Iron Company Financial Records for Fifty Years, pp. 5 ff.

Both of the above-mentioned practices required the use of a relatively large supply of working capital and resulted in tying up a large portion of the company's funds that might have been used for more productive purposes. But as long as the other firms in the industry persisted in maintaining such a policy, The Thomas Iron Company had to follow the same practice or lose customers.

In order to provide a clearer picture of the burden of these policies, Table 9 provides the working capital ratios for the years between 1856 and 1875.

TABLE 9

THE THOMAS IRON COMPANY
RATIO OF CURRENT ASSETS TO CURRENT LIABILITIES, 1856-75

1856	'57	'58	'59	'60	'61	'62	'63	'64	'65
7:1	8:1	4:1	7:1	5:1	6:1	5:1	3:1	4:1	6:1

1866	'67	'68	'69	'70	'71	'72	'73	'74	'75
6:1	5:1	5:1	5:1	5:1	4:1	5:1	5:1	7:1	9:1

Source: The Thomas Iron Company Financial Records for Fifty Years, pp. 1 ff.

As Table 9 indicates, working capital ratios for the firm were relatively high when compared to the common accounting practices of today which usually suggest a ratio of current assets to current liabilities of 2:1. The lower ratios during the most active business periods indicate a more rapid turnover in inventories and a more rapid payment of accounts receivable by customers anxious to make sure they had a source of supply of pig iron. The expansion of the ratio in the period of slower business activity indicates an effort on the part of the iron company to increase its sales through the extension of credit, as well as the storing of inventories of raw materials and finished goods.

Administrative Changes

Partially as a consequence of the long credit period provided, but largely as a result of inadequate administrative practices established at the commencement of business, the company suffered a series of losses arising from bad accounts. In 1858 the managers wrote of $5,914.92 in bad accounts and an additional sum of $17,951,43 the following year.[63] Then, in 1862, after a number of foundries, both in the North and in the South, had defaulted on their debts, the company was forced to write off another $38,000.[64] This loss was equivalent to 31 percent of the company's profits on pig iron sales for that year.

The major reason for these losses seems to have been the inadequate controls exerted by the management over the sales agent in New York City. Having the power to make contracts, receive payments in cash or notes, and made deductions as he thought proper, while being required to report his operations only once every six months, this individual had been placed in a position of great responsibility. At the same time such procedures made it almost impossible for the board of directors to supervise or determine what part of the business was well done. They could not

---

[63] The Thomas Iron Co. Fin. Rec., pp. 14 ff.

[64] *Ibid*., p. 29.

determine very readily whether the money received was paid over to the treasurer when received, whether allowances or deductions were properly made, or whether such other matters were handled to the best interests of the company. This business practice provided one individual entire control of the company's resources, and numerous errors could have been committed while the other officers of the company were in complete ignorance of the situation.

As the business grew and further bad debts were reported, the board of directors exhibited a great concern over these somewhat lax administrative practices. Previously, when the demands of economy had prevailed, the treasurer and the secretary of the corporation were appointed as part-time employees, but it had now become evident that to maintain proper controls it would require at least one full-time employee. Shortly thereafter John T. Knight was appointed as a full-time secretary and treasurer. Through his appointment many of the tasks formerly performed by the sales agent were centered in the office of the treasurer, and the detailed operations of the business were subjected to the daily scrutiny of the officers and directors of the company.[65] From this date to 1875 the reported bad debts declined.

In conjunction with this administrative adjustment, there also came a reduction of the powers and duty of the sales agent, a change that placed him in what today would be considered his legitimate province. R. S. Chidsey, the sales agent, no longer collected moneys or issued

---

[65] Ibid., p. 26.

credit and allowances. Now, through a system of vouchers and suitable order blanks, all sales, remittances or allowances, freight charges, and commissions were handled by or through the office of the treasurer. The salesman's function was to contract for sales and deliveries of iron. Any price changes and allowances to customers were made only after consultation with an executive committee of the board of directors.[66]

While the superintendent of the works was already required to pay all bills incurred in his operations through drafts on the treasurer, it was now incumbent upon the treasurer and president of the company to confer and concur prior to the negotiation of notes and the drawing of checks. In this way it was felt that errors would be far less likely to occur without detection than they could under the earlier administrative methods.

These administrative modifications did not merely shift power from one man to another. Instead the board of directors was given jurisdiction over operations and sales policy. A rather close check was placed upon management through the operation of various committees made up of the board of directors, just as cross checks were established between the different departments of operation.[67]

---

[66] Ibid.

[67] The Thomas Iron Company and Ironton Railroad Company, Charters, By-Laws, n.p. This material is held by the Lehigh University Library in Bethlehem, Pennsylvania.

Though little else was achieved in the way of improvements in administration, there were further additions made to the powers of the corporation itself. Nine supplements were added to the original charter by the Pennsylvania Legislature during the twenty years. These supplements permitted the coproration to issue additional shares of stock, and

Though the policies of the company emanated from the board of directors, the actual administration of policy was left in the hands of President Luckenbach, one of the members of the board. Shortly after President Luckenbach assumed office, and before the financial credit of the company had been fully established, his mettle was tested by the trying conditions of the panic of 1857. The president was forced to halt all cash payments, extend further credit time to customers, settle some accounts at 50 percent, and accept total losses on a number of others. Though output was maintained, it was done only at a very low level until additional credit sources could be obtained and more raw materials purchased.[68]

President Luckenbach emerged from that situation only to face the problem of securing funds necessary for the expansion program. In that year (1857) he established, evidently at the board's behest, the practice of reinvesting the company's earned income in new ore deposits and additional railroad and plant facilities. Later, in 1862, after the company's sales of pig iron had been raised from $394,317.58 to $2,074,223.35, President Luckenbach proposed the administrative changes already described, and prior to his retirement in 1864 he had instituted

---

authorized the firm to construct railroads for hauling of ores, to own coal fields, and to own properties in counties other than those specified in the original charter. Also, the New Jersey Legislature passed enabling acts which permitted the company to own and mine ore deposits in New Jersey as well as operate the Mount Hope Railroad.

[68]Min. Book - The Thomas Iron Co., p. 48. When the iron company did secure crdit from the local banks, it was provided to the company only after the board of directors personally endorsed the corporation's notes.

the necessary controls to administer the policy. Meanwhile sales had risen to $13,768,825.61, and production had been increased to 42,000 tons per year.

Just why Mr. Luckenbach elected to resign in 1864 is difficult to determine. He had directed the firm quite successfully through a most trying financial situation into a period when sizable gains had been made in both output and profits. Then, during an interval of very active demand when all of his accumulated skills and knowledge were required to push the firm ahead, he chose to drop the reins. And just as perplexing was his sale of the stock he held in the corporation at the same time that he quit his office. Possibly his many other business interests and real estate ventures in South Bethlehem were demanding more and more of his time. Again, it might have been for reasons of health, but this is mere speculation, for C. A. Luckenbach did not die until 1882, eighteen years later. The fact that he sold his shares of stock just as cash dividends were rising and great strides had been made in building new facilities could also mean that he harbored some dissatisfaction in the new policies planned by the board of directors. As there is little in the way of evidence to point the way to an answer, the question must be left in the air.

After the resignation of C. A. Luckenbach, Samuel Thomas, then about thirty-six and superintendent of the works, was appointed as the third president of the company and general superintendent. Young as he was, he brought considerable experience in the industry to this position of management in The Thomas Iron Company. Having spent his youth in training for such work under his father, David Thomas, at the Crane Iron Company's works, he soon set out on his own, in 1848, to supervise the construction of a blast furnace at Boonton, New Jersey. Then, returning to work at the Lehigh Crane Iron Company's furnaces, he was called upon to superintend the construction and operation of The Thomas Iron Company's furnaces at Hokendauqua in 1855. Though not as outstanding an ironmaster as his father, he achieved some success and recognition for his improvement of the design of the hot-blast stove. His innovation did not, however, provide any revolutionary change in iron smelting.[69]

Samuel Thomas's salary reflects, to some extent, the increasing responsitility he held over the twenty-three odd years that he served as president of the company. In the 1850's, as superintendent he had received a salary of $2,000 to $3,000 plus perquisites. Then his salary was increased to $4,500 in 1863; when he was elected president and a director of the company, his salary was raised to $5,000.[70]

It was, perhaps, in recognition of Samuel Thomas's value to the company that he was voted an additional payment of $1,500 in both 1865 and 1866. Then in 1867 his salary was raised to $10,000.

Under Samuel Thomas the company increased its property holdings considerably, expanded its Hokendauqua works, experienced a brief attempt at coal mining, bought the Lock Ridge Iron Company's works, and in 1882 gained control over the Ironton Railroad. In several instances during

---

[69]Mathews and Hungerford, Lehigh and Carbon Counties, pp. 242. f.

[70]The Thomas Iron Co. Fin. Rec., p. xxxii.

Samuel Thomas's presidency, serious and rather costly mistakes were made in the purchase of properties. Whether these purchases were made at his suggestion is not definitely known; it is only known that they were passed on by the board after an inspection by a committee of directors had been made.

The more serious error does not rest on President Thomas's action; rather it is the result of his inaction. there is no evidence that he made any suggestion to introduce new technological changes, and all improvements or additions to the furnace works indicate a relatively conservative policy in this regard. To prove that the delay or hesitation or conservatism rested with him is almost impossible, but certainly as president and general superintendent, and a member of the board of directors as well as an experienced ironmaster, which C. A. Luckenbach was not, Samuel Thomas does not seem to have provided dynamic leadership. He did not adopt tedchnological innovations and other policies designed to keep his company in or near the front of a dynamically changing iron and steel industry. In short, Samuel Thomas was not another John Fritz, or Alexander Holley, nor was he the image of his father, David Thomas.

Despite his shortcomings Samuel Thomas retained the respect of the board of directors of The Thomas Iron Company for a number of years. On two occasions he resigned for reasons of health, and in each instance he was reappointed president of the corporation. It is essential to remember, however, that three members of the Thomas family held over 2,000 shares of stock and thus had quite some importance in the appointment of officers. Their influence became even more effective after 1875, when the Pennsylvania Legislature changed the corporation laws and gave a vote for each share of stock held. Then, with approximately 10 percent of the shares, plus the support of friends and other relatives, the Thomas family was able to exert some control over a relatively large block of stock.

Submitted as evidence of such a possibility is the apparent nepotism which prevailed for some years in the management of the company. A number of sons, nephews, and in-laws served as superintendents or assistant superintendents at the various furnaces; at one time or other more than nine members of the family served in some supervisory capacity in the company's operations up to 1907. Even as late as 1899 the family owned approximately 10 percent of the total shares, still the largest single block of stock in the corporation.[71]

Evaluation

In spite of the ill-advised purchases of mineral and coal deposits, the apparent unwillingness to adapt new smelting techniques, and the appearance of nepotism, the board of directors succeeded in directing the company to the topmost rank among the pig iron producers of the nation. Continuously during the first twenty years production, sales, and profits had been raised to new levels. The going-concern value had also been augmented, even as the number of shares of capital stock was increased from 4,000 to 40,000 units to take account of reinvestment and earnings. Also, the total book value of the firm's assets, which had been $472,005.27 in 1855, had been raised to $4,557,798.18 at the end of the

---

[71]The Thomas Iron Co.: PAPERS AND Doc., p. 142.

period.[72]

There is no evidence that management showed any unique ability in developing business procedures, expanding sales, or in developing technical innovations. While adapting a few new techniques for smelting, such as improved pipe arrangement in the hot-blast oven and the Lurman closed front, management responded very slowly to the revolutionary changes that were taking place about them. Despite the extensive program of reinvestment, it is quite apparent that the management and the board of directors had not "kept up with the times" as the company moved to the top. Continually they preferred to "bet" on the older method and avoid the uncertainty of the new. If, however, Joel Dean's proposed criterion of a firm's innovation, the magnitude of reinvestment, is any measure for evaluating the firm's contribution to progress, it would seem that tentative evidence of innovation was provided in substantial amounts.[73] Also, the expansion of production, sales, and profits, previously proposed as criteria of success, give further evidence of some ingenuity in meeting the daily problems of production and management.

Lehigh Valley Iron Production, 1856-75

The economic development of that branch of the iron industry located in the Lehigh Valley during these twenty years is an exceedingly

---

[72]The last figure probably does not contain an adequate measure of the value of the company's fixed assets for they were all recorded at original cost. The firm did not maintain depreciation accounts nor did it revalue its assets each year. The heavy maintenance expenditures seem to indicate that the property was kept in good repair.

[73]Joel Dean, Managerial Economics (New York, 1951), p. 11.

interesting illustration of Alfred Weber's general theory of regional concentration and the operation of the "agglomerative forces."[74] At its inception the industry's growth was accelerated by advances made in transportation facilities and improved smelting techniques. Then the region gradually evolved into an iron center of great magnitude as a consequence of the momentum induced through the economies of production originating in the initial advance. The economic advantages of large-scale production worked in its favor; secondary industries ready to consume large supplies of pig iron were established nearby, gradually a fully developed labor force appeared, and marketing facilities were improved as large supplies of raw materials and semi-finished or finished goods were bought and sold. Momentarily the agglomerative forces prevailed. Eventually, as other areas gained the special advantages previously held by this region and incipient enterprises began to rise in new aspiring localities, the "deglomerative forces" eclipsed the "agglomerative forces," gained precedence, and the Lehigh Valley's iron industry slowly retreated before the economic pressures of the new age. The latter development will be covered later, but during the epoch at hand the "agglomerative forces" were in operation in the Lehigh Valley. Transportation facilities had been improved and transportation costs reduced. Large-scale production had been established and secondary industries had appeared, all prepared to consume increasing quantities of pig iron.

Throughout the twenty years the railroad mileage of the Lehigh

---

[74]Carl J. Friedrich, Alfred Weber's Theory of the Location of Industries (Chicago, 1929), pp. 124 ff.

Valley was continuously augmented as new railroads were constructed and old ones extended or double tracked. Rail systems were developed that carried goods to tidewaer ports; the Lehigh Valley Railroad gradually penetrated into New Jersey, and the Central Railroad of New Jersey obtained control over the Lehigh and Susquehanna Railroad which had been built into the coal fields by the Lehigh Coal and Navigation Company. In the coal fields a few short lines of railroad were built into a web of tracks leading to numerous collieries, while in the lower reaches of the valley a number of feeder lines were constructed to tap the slate, limestone, and iron ore deposits.[75] There seemed to be a never ending quantity of coal, iron ore, and pig iron, among other commodities, to haul for the iron industry, a factor which consequently reinforced the growth of the railroads. No longer was it a matter of the railroad expansion leading to the growth of the iron industry, but rather there was a mutual interaction that provided the impetus for further growth in both industries.[76]

---

[75]A very large part of the story of railroad development in the Lehigh Valley is provided in the _Report_(s) _of the Board of Managers of the Lehigh Coal and Navigation Company_ and _Annual Reports_(s) _of the Board of Directors of the Lehigh Valley Railroad Company_. This latter work will hereafter be cited as _Rpt. Bd. Dir. LVRRC_.

[76]An interesting comment on this development is presented in _Lehigh Valley Railroad Company, Annual Reports of Superintendent and Engineer, 1855-1863_ (New York, 1899), p. 5.

"The Lehigh Valley Iron Works, Allentown Iron Works and Lehigh Zinc Works situated in such close proximity to your road, and with excellent opportunities for unloading their coal and ore, must eventually get all their supplies by railroad.

"With all these avenues open there can be no doubt but that upon the completion of the second track of the Beaver Meadow Road your road

A few statistics on mileage and tonnage provide some notion of the extent of this mutual development. The Lehigh Valley Railroad increased its main track facilities from 46 miles in 1856 to 101 miles in 1874, and where it had carried 165,740 tons of coal toward tidewater ports in 1856, in 1874 it was capable of hauling 3,016,636 tons from the coal fields toward tidewater.[77] In that same year the Lehigh and Susquehanna Railroad, with 105 miles of track, and the Lehigh Canal reported the shipment of 3,071,487 tons of coal over their lines. In 1856, before the Lehigh and Susquehanna Railroad had been constructed, only 1,187,084 tons of coal had been shipped via the canal.[78]

As a further indication of the expansion of railroad capacity and the production of the iron industry, the following statistics on shipments of ore and pig iron are presented. The Lehigh Valley Railroad reported in 1860 that it had hauled an aggregate of 186,774 tons of ore and pig iron. By 1866, the last year that the company's reports provide a clear breakdown on these shipments, the railroad carried about 347,440 tons of pig iron and ore from furnace to market or from connecting lines to furnaces.[79] Meanwhile, the Lehigh Canal Company reported shipments of over 47,000 tons of iron and 104,000 tons of ore in 1860, and in 1866

---

will be filled with business. In view of this, active measures should be taken at once to supply a sufficient amount of rolling stock to meets its requirements."

[77] _Annual Report of the Secretary of Internal Affairs of the Commonwealth of Pennsylvania for 1874-5_, Part III (Harrisburg, 1876), pp. 411 ff.

[78] _Ibid_.

[79] _Rpt. Bd. Dir. LVRRC_, 1861, p. 37; 1867, p. 32.

these shipments had been reported as 10,000 tons of iron and 95,599 tons of ore.[80] These statistics indicate an increase of 33.5 percent in the shipment of such materials in a matter of six years.

Two of the important feeder lines in the lower reaches of the Lehigh Valley were built by 1861 and performed heavy duty in the carriage of ore and limestone to the main lines. By that date the Catasauqua and Fogelsville Railroad had constructed some 2C miles of rail, while the Ironton Railroad Company had built 11 miles of track into the ore fields west of the Lehigh River and Hokendauqua.[81] Both lines carried the ore to the Lehigh Valley Railroad, which, in turn, carried the ores to the furnaces. To obtain some idea of the routes of these railroads, see the map on the following page which as been inserted to provide some indication of the growth in transportation facilities in the valley.

As the railroads grew, the number of furnaces was increased. By 1875 the Lehigh Valley contained fifty completed blast furnaces, an increase over the twenty-one furnaces of 1856 of 138 percent. The furnaces were owned by eighteen different companies; the largest firm, The Thomas

---

[80] Rpt. Bd. Mgrs. LCNC, 1861, p. 8; 1867, p. 24.
The drop in the tonnage indicates the decline in the use of the canal to haul ores. The location of the Lehigh and Susquehanna Railroad on the east bank of the Lehigh River placed that company in an unfavorable location for providing services to the iron industry; the majority of the furnaces were on the west bank.

[81] Annual Report of the Secretary of Internal Affairs of the §Commonwealth of Pennsylvania for 1874-5, Part III, p. 411.
The Ironton Railroad was built by Tinsley Jeter and financed by Jay Cooke and E. W. Clark and Company of Philadelphia for the purpose of mining and transporting iron ore to the local iron furnaces. See Henrietta M. Larson, "Cooke's Early Work in Transportation," Pennsylvania Magazine, Vol. 59 (1935), 372.

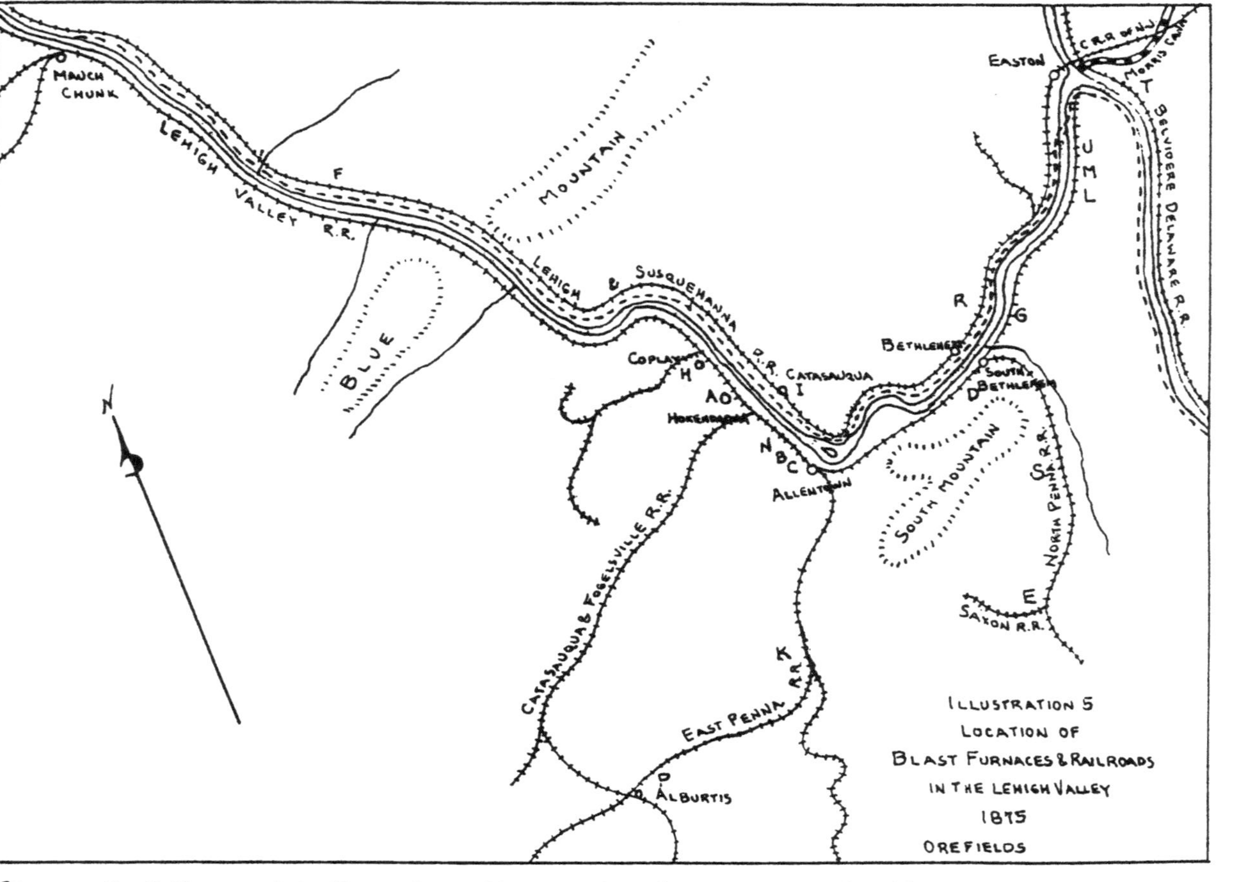

Source: A. Mathews and A. Hungerford, History of Lehigh and Carbon Counties, p. 1.

IRON FURNACES IN THE LEHIGH VALLEY - 1875
(To be located on the map by letters)

A - The Thomas Iron Company
1 - 1855
2 - 1855
3 - 1863
4 - 1863
5 - 1873
6 - 1873

B - Allentown Iron Company
1 - 1846
2 - 1846
3 - 1853
4 - 1854
5 - 1872

C - Roberts Iron Company
1- 1864
2 - 1864

D - Bethlehem Iron Company
1 - 1863
2 - 1867
3 - 1868
4 - 1875
5 - 1875
6 - 1875

E - North Penn Iron Company
1 - 1870

F - Carbon Iron Company
1 - 1853
2 - 1864
3 - 1869

G - Coleraine Iron Company
1 - 1869
2 - 1872

H - Coplay Iron Company
1 - 1853
2 - 1862
3 - 1868

I - Lehigh Crane Iron Company
1 - 1839
2 - 1842
3 - 1846
4 - 1850
5 - 1850
6 - 1867

K - Emaus Furnace
1 - 1872

L - Glendon Iron Company
1 - 1843
2 - 1844
3 - 1850
4 - 1852
5 - 1869

M - Keystone Furnace
1 - 1876

N - Lehigh Iron Company
1 - 1869
2 - 1872

P - Lock Ridge Furnace
1 - 1867
2 - 1869

Q - Macungie Furnace
1 - 1874

R - Northampton Furnace
1 - 1872

S - Saucon Furnace
1 - 1866
2 - 1870

T - Andover Iron Company
1 - 1848
2 - 1848
3 - 1848

U - Lucy Furnace
1 - 1872

Iron Company, operated eight of these furnaces. Two other firms owned six furnaces each, two, five each, while the others held either one, two or three. Several of the firms also operated rolling or rail mills in conjunction with their blast furnaces and held ore fields near their plant or in New Jersey.[82]

Probably the outstanding plant in the Lehigh Valley at that time was the one operated by the Bethlehem Iron Company, which had been organized in 1860 but had not entered into production until 1863. By 1875 that company, under the guidance of an able plant superintendent, John Fritz, and what seems to have been a very alert board of directors, had built six blast furnaces, erected two five-ton Bessemer converters as well as rolling and rail mills,[83]

There were five more rolling mills in the Lehigh Valley at this time, two of them having an average annual capacity of 20,000 tons

---

[82]Dunlap, Wiley's American Iron Trade Manual, passim.

[83]Ibid. Beth. Iron Co. Stockholders Min., and Bethlehem Iron Company Board of Directors Minutes. The latter work will hereafter be cited as Beth. Iron Co. Bd. Dir. Min.

The Bethlehem Iron Company's works were reputed to be the finest and best arranged works in the Lehigh Valley. The growth pattern of the company indicates that the management of the company was made up of a group of men quite capable of solving problems that others could not solve, or preferred to disregard. The management was made up of willing adapters and innovators in their own right. The Bethlehem Iron Company was one of the first companies to build a Bessemer converter (1873), and the first, in this country, to use molten pig iron directly from the blast furnace for conversion to steel.

When the company's sales of iron rails fell, the management proceeded to shift to steel rails; and when the demand for steel rails declined, the company moved into the production of armor plate and brought into use the first open-hearth furnaces in the Lehigh Valley.

apiece.[84] They produced bars, rod, plate, sheet iron, and rails. There were one car wheel and axle works in Catasauqua, two iron pipe and tube works, one stove manufacturer, and an iron bridge works in Phillipsburg. There were also numerous foundries, machine shops, several agricultural implement manufacturers, boiler makers, and shovel manufacturers.[85]

To meet the needs of this cluster of iron fabricators and processors, the Lehigh Valley ironmasters poured forth a continuing stream of pig iron until they reached a peak production period in 1872. Then, in the next two years, production fell by 30 percent. This drop in output was the greatest decrease for any region in the nation, and in the next year it dropped even lower.[86] The next year, 1875, was the year of the second coal strike and the agitation by some of the area producers for a restriction on output.[87] That year the production of anthracite pig iron was surpassed by the production of the bituminous and coke furnaces.

---

[84] Dunlap, *Wiley's American Iron Trade Manual*, pp. 152 ff. One of these mills, the Catasauqua Manufacturing Company, was organized in 1863 by David Thomas. The organizers of the company originally planned to produce armor plate and rails, but after the war a shift was made to the production of boiler plate and sheet iron. Later a bar train was added to the works. This company also controlled the Ferndale Rolling Mill, a producer of bar and skelp. Both mills seemed to have had a close working arrangement with The Thomas Iron Company. See Mathews and Hungerford, *Lehigh and Carbon Counties*, p. 343.

[85] *Ibid*.

[86] *Annual Report of the Secretary of Internal Affairs of the Commonwealth of Pennsylvania for 1874-5*, Part III, p. 344.

[87] *Iron Age*, Vol. 14 (Dec. 17, 1874), 5. The firms that seemed to be the strongest agitators for output restrictions were owners of the smaller works. None of the owners of the larger works appear to have participated in the discussions.

It appears that at that point the Lehigh Valley iron industry had reached its zenith. A few years hence and the iron producers of the region would begin to lose their forward momentum, and the valley's special attractions would disappear. Gradually, as local fuel and ore costs increased, the Lehigh Valley iron producers would be forced to reach out farther and farther to obtain their requisite supplies of ore and coke. Soon improved transportation facilities and advanced smelting technology would permit rival areas to send their products out to complete with the iron from the Lehigh Valley. Also, by 1875 the mold for the integrated steel mill seems to have been cast; gradually the merchant furnaces would become a phenomenon of the past.

CHAPTER VIII

IRON TO STEEL, 1875-1919

Introduction

Prior to proceeding further with the history of The Thomas Iron Company and the Lehigh Valley's iron industry, it may be helpful to make a contributory inquiry into the development of the national iron industry between 1875 and 1919. No attempt will be made to provide a detailed coverage of this topic; that task goes beyond the limits of this dissertation. But to better understand the gradual elimination of the merchant furnaces in the Lehigh Valley, as well as the eventual disappearance of anthracit pig iron, it is essential to observe the changes in the steel industry.

From 1875 on, there was a rather rapid shift in the type of fuel employed to smelt iron ores. As new iron furnaces were constructed, they were generally designed to burn beehive coke. Anthracite furnaces, on the other hand, began to decline in number and importance. Also, with the change in the fuel used to smelt iron ore, there was a further adjustment in the geographical location of the major pig iron production centers. The increasing use of coke took place rather gradually at first, but by 1893 the rapid rise of the coke furnace iron had reduced the anthracite iron output to a relatively small portion of the total output. The last iron smelted with anthracite coal alone was recorded in 1914. For a short time thereafter, some anthracite coal mixed with coke was used in a few furnaces, but by 1923 even that production had been halted.[1] The decline in the use of anthracite coal occurred because it was an inferior blast furnace fuel relative to coke, a fact arising from its physical structure. But more will be said in another section of this essay relative to this matter. The changes suggested above can be seen quite clearly in Charts IX and X on the following pages.

Probably the most important development in the over-all history of the iron industry in these years was the gradual reduction in the use of iron, puddled, rolled, or cast, and the rapid expansion in steel consumption. The new industrial age was truly an age of steel, as technological developments called for and produced a metal admirably suited to the high speeds and heavy strains of modern industrialism. Bessemer and open-hearth steel became the formidable competitors of puddled iron, while foundries using open-hearth steel gradually replaced the older iron foundries. Products once cast in iron were replaced by steel castings made directly from open-hearth furnaces; for example, cast-iron car wheels. In 1892 there were eighteen such open-hearth foundries prepared to make numerous types of steel castings. Two years later the number had been increased to twenty-eight.[2] This shift in steel consumption and production reduced the demand for foundry iron from the merchant furnaces,

---

[1] Ralph H. Sweetser, "Blast Furnace Fuels: Their Regional Influences," as found in Iron Age, Vol. 134 (Nov. 29, 1934), 25. In 1923 the Carbon Iron Company, at Parryville in the Lehigh Valley, used an anthracite coal and coke mix.

[2] James Swank, "Progress of the Iron and Steel Industries of the United States in 1892 and 1893," as found in David T. Day, ed., Mineral Resources of the United States, 1893 (Washington, D. C., 1894), p. 18.

CHART IX

RELATIVE CHANGES IN NUMBER OF BLAST FURNACES
1876-1900

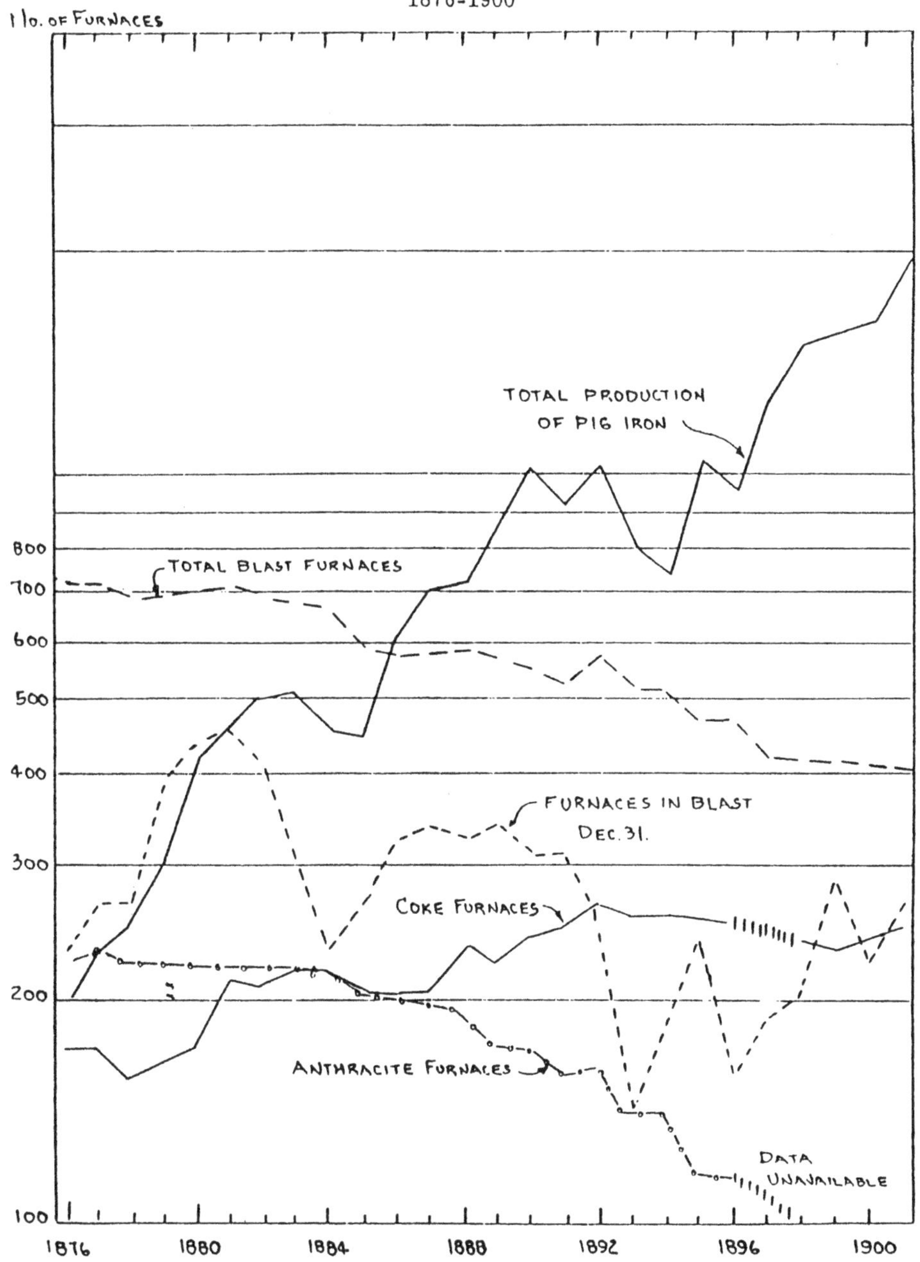

Source: American Iron and Steel Association, Statistics of the American and Foreign Iron Trades.

CHART X

RELATIVE CHANGES IN NUMBER OF BLAST FURNACES
1900-1922

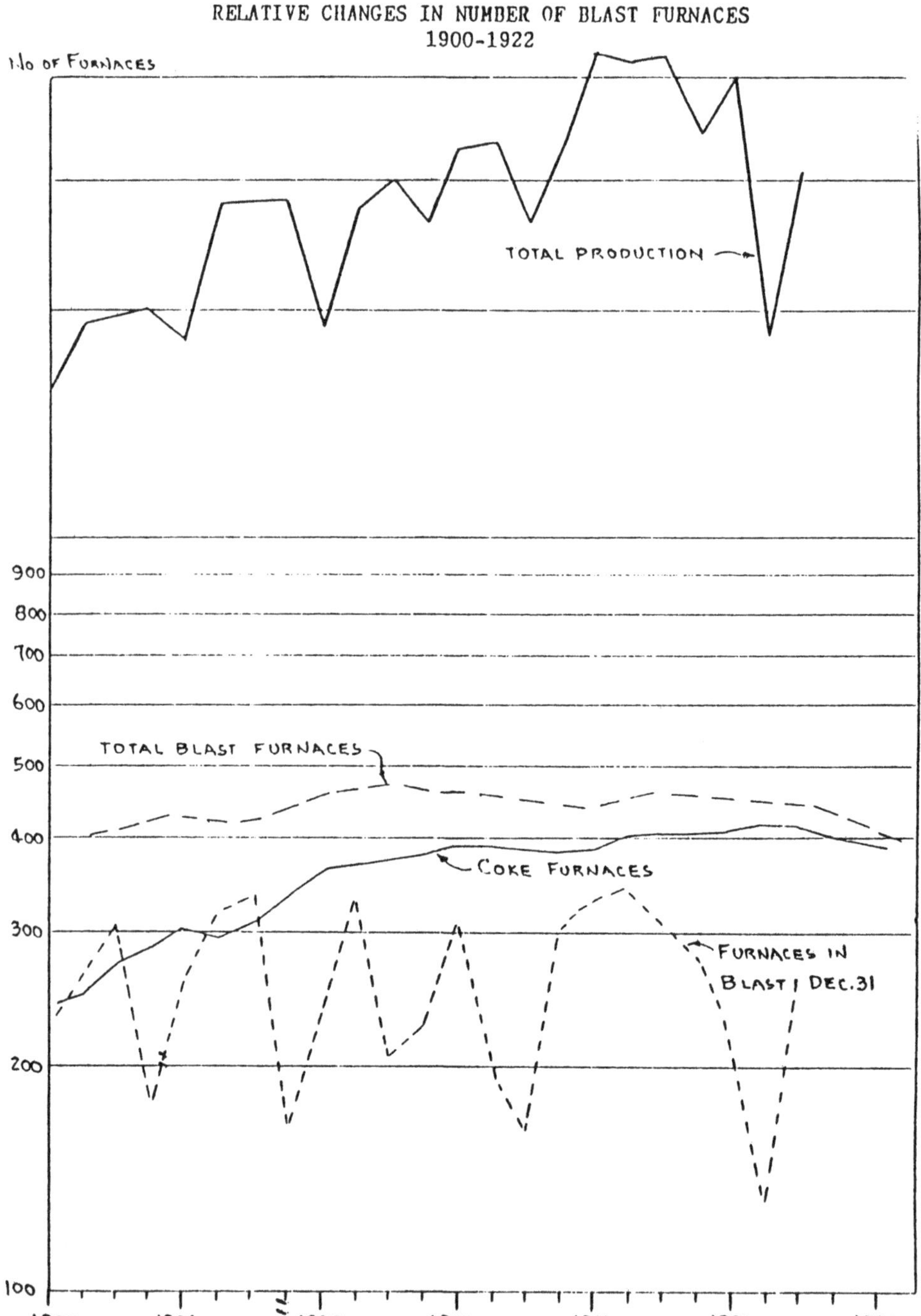

Source: American Iron and Steel Association, Statistics of the American and Foreign Iron Trades; American Iron and Steel Institute, Annual Statistical Reports.

especially those furnaces producing pig iron unsuitable for conversion to steel, although their iron had been quite acceptable for iron castings.

In conjunction with the above developments, there was a continuing adjustment in the organizational pattern of the iron industry. Gradually the industry was altered from one of many separate branches containing numerous processing firms to a single industry containing a few firms in control of integrated plants and combinations of mining companies, railroads, coking ovens, blast furnaces, rolling mills, foundries, wire and rod mills, bridge works, and forges. By 1920 the age of the merchant furnace had passed, and once famous iron works were being demolished or were awaiting their eventual destruction.

With the elimination of the merchant furnace trade, the number of iron furnaces in the Lehigh Valley was reduced, but many of the furnace companies would probably have been eclipsed even though integration of production had not developed. A rapidly expanding transportation system had opened up the national market to the more efficient coke furnaces of the South and the West, just as it had prepared the way for the exploitation of the Lake Superior iron ores and had opened up the Lehigh Valley for exploitation. Meanwhile, in the eastern iron regions which had flourished for a few years, the furnace operators found their less efficient fuel and furnaces too costly to operate in competition with the new producing centers. In order to compete, some anthracite furnaces were remodeled to permit the use of coke. Also, many eastern ore deposits which, in some instances, had been exploited for 160 years or more were being rapidly depleted and ores had to be shipped into the region from

Lake Superior mines or overseas. These changes increased raw material costs for the local furnace operators and enabled the outside producers to compete successfully with eastern pig iron in what had once been the exclusive market of eastern furnaces.

Business Conditions and Iron Production

In the course of these years the economy of the United States was transformed into a mature industrial state, with its agriculture, transportation, communications, and manufacturing intensively organized and capable of making the nation largely self-sufficient. Agriculture declined in relative importance, while manufacturing increased under the stimulus provided by a rapidly expanding population and a concomitant growth in the size of markets. Additions and improvements in transportation facilities widened the market for numerous products and made the various sectors of the economy more interdependent. These changes, in conjunction with improved financial and business management techniques, enabled businessmen to extend the use of machine technology and mass production into radically new forms of industrial organization; the iron and steel industry was an outstanding example of the change.

With the expansion and improvements in manufacturing, transportation, and agriculture, there also came a series of panics and depressions arising largely from speculation and probably a too rapid rate of investment in railroads and plant expansion. These were developments symptomatic of a naturing economy. Instead of panics and depressed business conditions arising from external causes, the forces leading to depressed economic conditions seemed to have originated within the economy. For example, investments in railroads and manufacturing plants fluctuated with the expansion and contraction of the supply of credit.[3]

Almost continuously, from 1875 to 1897, wholesale prices moved downward and business conditions seemed to worsen. Numerous business firms went into receivership, while others, the more fortunate or persevering, overcame the price difficulties by reducing their costs.[4] Then, between 1897 and 1919, the secular trend of wholesale prices was upward. Many businessmen, however, continued their search for more productive manufacturing methods. Meanwhile, in order to avoid the dangers of competition when burdened with heavy fixed costs, some businessmen proceeded to integrate their works or created combinations of similar or related producing units in order to reduce competition. Thus, out of the vigorous competitive conditions prevailing betwen 1873 and 1897, the age of business combination in the iron industry was born. The rapid expansion of this combination movement was aided to a great extent by the increased and improved credit facilities of the nation, as well as by a much more effective system of communications.[5]

In the course of this long secular price movement, there were alternating periods of good and bad times. The first few years were years of

---

[3]Somers, "The Performance of the American Economy, 1866-1918," pp. 646 f.

[4]N. S. B. Gras and H. M. Larson, Casebook in American Business History (New York, 1939), pp. 715-24.

[5]*Ibid.*, pp. 726 ff. William C. Kesler, "Business Organization and Management," as found in H. Williamson, ed., Growth of the American Economy, pp. 604 f.

depression, the aftermath of the panic of 1873. By 1877 signs of revival only appeared when crop shortages in other parts of the world and large exports of agricultural commodities from this country provided prosperous conditions for the agricultural sector of the economy. As agriculture prospered, railroad mileage was increased once again, and general manufacturing was stimulated.[6]

The pig iron industry was not an exception, for it felt the influence of this expansionist development. The increasing demand for new railroad mileage and agricultural equipment pressed the domestic iron and steel industry to increase its output as similar developments in the past had influenced the iron industry. In 1882, when a record 11,596 miles of new railroad track were built, the nation's blast furnaces produced 5,178,122 net tons of pig iron.[7] The larger portion of the tonnage was melted with beehive coke (2,438,078 net tons), but anthracite pig iron output was also increased and it reached a new peak of 2,042,138 tons.[8]

When railroad construction mileage dropped approximately 50 percent in 1883, there were repercussions on pig iron prices and output as both fell off. This reduction in iron output was further accentuated by the panic of 1884 and the following depression.[9] Only the economic revival

---

[6]Bratt, Business Cycles and Forecasting, p. 262. Somers, "The Performance of the American Economy, 1866-1918," p. 651.

[7]American Iron and Steel Association, Statistics of the American and Foreign Iron Trade for 1883 (Philadelphia, 1884), pp. 23 ff.

[8]Ibid.

[9]Bratt, Business Cycles and Forecasting, pp. 262 f.

commencing with the renewal in investment in more railroad mileage permitted the iron industry to recover its forward momentum. As railroad mileage expanded, the iron industry regained its vigor. In 1887, with the construction of a record 12,812 miles of new track, the pig iron furnaces in the nation were used to produce a record output.[10]

After 1888, however, when new railroad construction fell, the market conditions for the iron industry had changed considerably. Instead of the demand for iron moving downward simultaneously, it remained steady and production was expanded during the next two years. The industry produced a record 10,307,028 net tons in 1890.

This maintenance of the demand for iron resulted from the growing needs for iron and steel in industries other than the railroads. More and more iron was being employed in the production of machinery, stoves, ranges, domestic utensils, wagons, plows, mechanics' and laborers' tools, cast- and wrought-iron water and gas pipes, as well as bridges. Next to these primary demands, created in part by an expanding population and the rapid growth of cities, was the extensive use of iron in locomotives, passenger and freight cars, iron and steel railroad bridges, plus the material required to build the new American navy. There was also an increased demand for steel for structural purposes, not least among these projects being the iron and steel required to produce the growing number of iron works in the southern states.[11]

---

[10] American Iron and Steel Association, Statistics of the American and Foreign Iron Trade of 1889 (Philadelphia, 1890), p. 71.

[11] Ibid., 1888, p. 14.

The tight money situation existing after the Baring crisis in 1890 delayed further railroad expansion and resulted in the failure of a number of business firms in the iron industry. Then a restriction in the production of coke in 1891, arising from a strike in the Connellsville coal region, reduced pig iron output momentarily, but it did not halt a downward movement in iron prices. Several pools and gentlemen's agreements among the producers of iron and iron products did little to alleviate the price situation; in fact, they only seemed to heighten the competition from southern pig iron producers. More and more iron firms fell by the wayside; generally, however, they were firms poorly situated or operating furnaces with antiquated design and an insufficient supply of capital.

For several years production of pig iron remained below 8,000,000 short tons under the stress of the difficult conditions of the trade. In 1897, however, production from the nation's blast furnaces was advanced to 13,186,806 net tons, an unprecedented tonnage figure.[12] This new production peak was achieved under the influence of a renewed agricultural prosperity and an increased money supply, a stimulant to the general wholesale price level. From that date pig iron output was continually expanded, contracting only momentarily in 1904. Three years later, in 1907, a new high of 28,399,747 tons of pig iron was smelted. But the panic of that year, which left a number of railroads in the hands of receivers and caused numerous other business failures, resulted in a

---

[12] Ibid., 1897, p. 68.

drastic reduction in blast furnace output. During that single year iron production shrank from 28,399,747 tons to 17,504,512 tons in 1908, a decline of approximately 62 percent.

During this period of years (1897-1907), foundry iron prices at Philadelphia had continually increased until they reached a high of $23.89 a long ton in 1907, the highest price paid for iron following the high of 1880. With the panic and the rapid decline in demand that occurred, the price of pig iron dropped to $17.20 a ton in 1908, at which level it remained for the next two years. Between 1910 and 1914 pig iron prices continued the decline started earlier, and in 1914 foundry iron was quoted at $15.21 a gross ton at Philadelphia. At the same time, foundry iron produced in Birmingham was priced at $13.42 a ton.[13] It is noteworthy that while pig iron prices had fallen, the general price level had risen. And more, despite this peculiar price relationship between the general price level and prices in the iron industry, the tonnage of pig iron increased, though more steel than pig iron was produced. The latter change in the statistics of the trade was indicative of the new forces pressing upon the merchant furnace trade. The price and production movements are seen a little more distinctly in Chart XI on the following page.

With the advent of World War I, production efforts in the industry were intensified, and in 1916 iron manufacturers turned out 44,166,972

---

[13]American Iron and Steel Institute, _Annual Statistical Report for 1917_ (New York, 1918), p. 81. The prices quoted are based upon _Iron Age_ reports. In 1914 the _Iron Trade Review_ quoted a price of $10.32 per long ton for foundry iron in Birmingham.

CHART XI

RELATIVE CHANGE IN PIG IRON PRODUCTION
BY FUEL TYPE, STEEL PRODUCTION, AND IRON PRICES
1876-1900

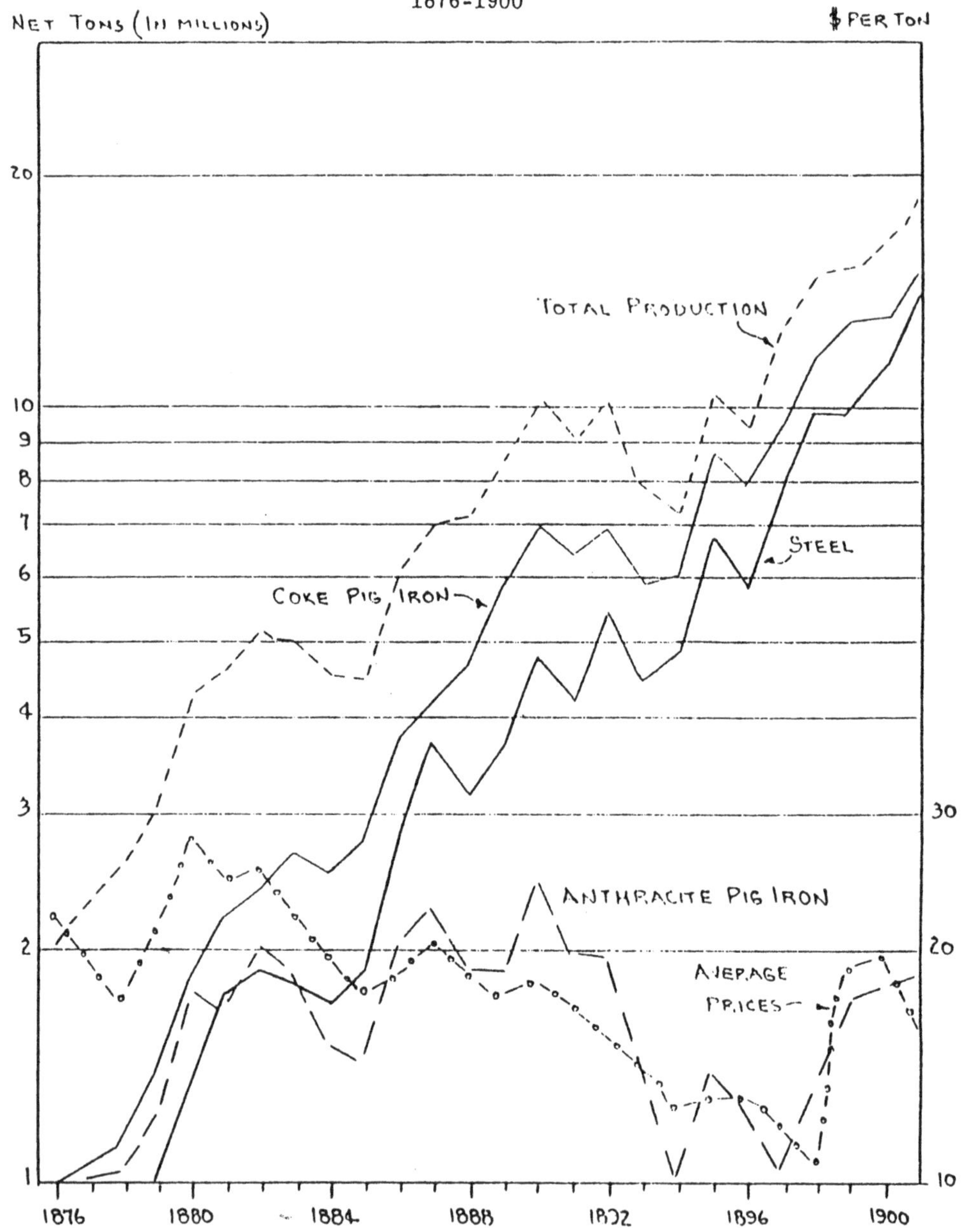

Source: American Iron and Steel Association, <u>Statistics of the American and Foreign Iron Trades</u>.

CHART XII

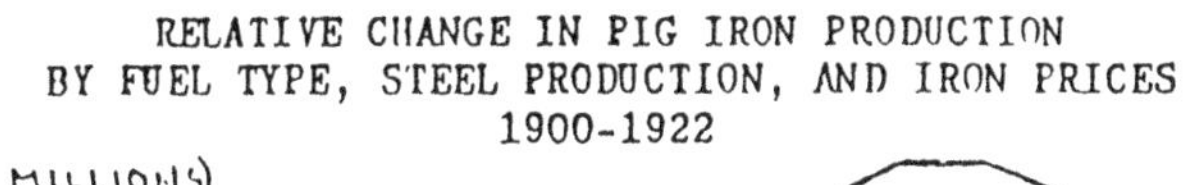
RELATIVE CHANGE IN PIG IRON PRODUCTION
BY FUEL TYPE, STEEL PRODUCTION, AND IRON PRICES
1900-1922

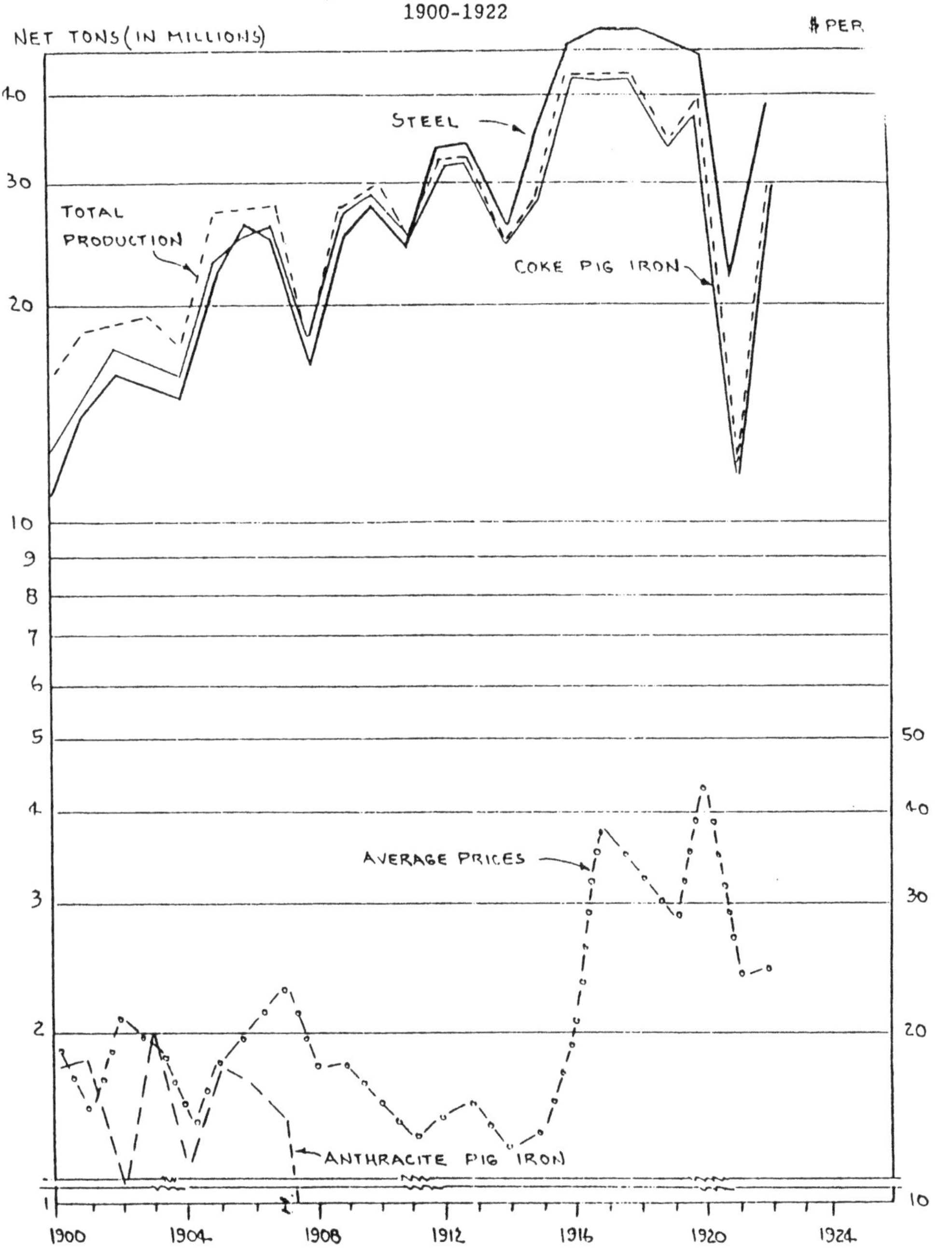

Source: American Iron and Steel Association, Statistics of the American and Foreign Iron Trades; American Iron and Steel Institute, Annual Statistical Reports.

net tons of pig iron. Then in the next two years over 43,000,000 tons of pig iron were smelted in each year, but before the war had ended the output figures began to diminish.[14] By 1919 the total annual output had been reduced by some 8,961,125 tons. With a rise in the price of both foundry and basic pig iron in 1920, the loss in output was recovered; however, the 1921 recession resulted in a swift abatement of this production. That year the tonnage figure dropped approximately 55 percent.[15]

The above statistics indicate that the long-time tendency or secular trend for pig iron production was continually upward, increasing more rapidly in some periods than others, but the mere recitation of these production figures does not provide the complete story of the changes that had arisen in the iron industry during those years. To present a clearer picture of the changes, these statistics must be related to others that are available.

As the aggregate production of pig iron was augmented, there was a distinct but very gradual reduction in the total number of blast furnaces available for production, a change, as will be shown in Table 10, indicative of the continuous accumulation and adaptation of improvements in

---

[14]*Ibid.*, 1922, p. 10. The production statistics reported by the Institute are in gross tons. For purposes of maintaining continuity with the previously reported data, these figures have been converted to net tons.

[15]*Ibid.*, *passim*. The price of foundry pig iron in 1920 was $46.92, but in 1921 it had fallen to $25.14. Production figures for the same years were 41,357,105 and 18,690,701 net tons. Most of the tonnage for the latter year consisted of basic iron for conversion to steel in open-hearth furnaces. Foundry iron for sale made up approximately 12 percent of the total figure. Probably a large portion of that iron came from the steel companies' furnaces.

furnace design and practice. The greatest gains in productivity were made between 1883 and 1907.

Returning to the period between 1872 and 1883, the total number of furnaces was increased by 71 units, rising from 612 to 683 furnaces, a gain of 12 percent. Production during those years was increased only 45 percent. In the next twelve years, despite a 2 percent reduction in active furnaces, production was raised to 10,579,864 tons, a gain of 105 percent in product over the 1883 output. From 1895 to 1907 the number of active furnaces fell another 5 percent, but this time production increased approximately 168 percent. The proportional gain made between 1907 and 1918 was much smaller, a mere 54 percent, but during that period there was an increase of 4 percent in the number of active furnaces over the number of furnaces in use in the former year. The decline in the rate of expansion in production, while effected by the larger base figure, also indicates or suggests a slowing down in the accumulation of more productive smelting techniques. It almost appears that leaders of the steel industry, having developed their improvements, were prepard to sit back and administer their business firms as other less dynamic businessmen were conducting theirs.

The statistics reported in Table 10 are based upon the total number of furnaces available for production in the respective years, but in many years a relatively large number of furnaces remained idle, and in some instances were out of blast as long as two or three years. Such a condition meant that a number of furnaces included in the active list probably should not have been recorded, but the very durability of the facilities

TABLE 10

RELATIVE CHANGES IN TOTAL FURNACES AND PIG IRON PRODUCTION FOR SELECTED PERIODS

Years	Change in Furnaces	Percentage Change in Furnaces	Percentage Increase in Production
1872-1883	+ 71	+ 12	45
1883-1895	- 15	- 2	105
1895-1907	-25	- 5	168
1907-1918	+ 16	+ 4	54

Source: American Iron and Steel Association, *Statistics of the American and Foreign Iron Trades*; American Iron and Steel Institute, *Annual Statistical Reports*.

enticed a large number of firms to maintain their old works despite the unstable business conditions.[16] It is to be noted, however, that between 1883 and 1907 old furnaces were abandoned more rapidly than new furnaces were constructed, a sign of the difficult times for the marginal furnace companies. That production increased rapidly during the same years suggests that the technological innovations made during the period were highly productive. Only as conditions in the trade improved did the construction of new furnaces proceed at a much more rapid pace, and fewer furnaces were dismantled. Yet, the increase in production was not near

[16]American Iron and Steel Association, *Bulletin*, Vol. 18 (Dec. 3, 1884), 313. A contemporary writer in the *Bulletin* questioned the validity of the number of "idle" furnaces listed by the industry. He pointed out that when high prices prevailed, in 1881, there were 255 idle furnaces, an indication that some operators found it unprofitable to blow in even under good conditions.

as great as in the earlier years. This further diminution in the rate of increase in production suggests that innovations in blast furnace practice had slowed considerably.

One factor which permitted many merchant furnace companies to delay the dismantling of their furnaces during the later period was the rate at which new steel furnaces were constructed. Though steel manufacturers found economies in producing their own pig iron, in the early historical stage of development of the steel industry, the capacity of the steel companies furnaces was in excess of the capacity of their blast furnaces. partially as a consequence of this maladjustment in the steel production facilities, on a number of occasions prior to the war runaway markets for pig iron occurred.[17]

It has been estimated that steel capacity, between 1898 and 1907, was increased at an annual rate of 9.6 percent, while blast furnace capacity only increased at an annual rate of 6.5 percent. Over a period of ten years this difference was sufficient to produce a disparity in total capacity of 140 percent for steel and 82 percent for blast furnaces.[18] The maladjustment, while it prevailed, enabled some merchant furnace owners to continue the use of their equipment for a longer period

---

[17] O. W. Blackett, "Some Price-Determining Factors in the Iron Industry." Review of Economic Statistics, Vol. 7 (1925), 204 f.

[18] Ibid., p. 203. American Iron and Steel Association, Bulletin, Vol. 26 (Sept. 2, 1892), 275. One writer in the Bulletin reported that the rapid increase in blast furnace capacity had done much to take the pig iron trade out of line with other branches of the industry. However, he believed that the development, checked momentarily by the low prices, would adjust to meet the requirements of the industry.

than more balanced conditions of growth in the integrated steel plants might have allowed.

Unfortunately for the merchant pig iron companies, every additional blast furnace constructed by a steel manufacturer reduced the market for merchant iron and left more merchant furnaces to complete with each other in the smaller market. The less efficient merchant furnaces were continually being forced to withdraw their productive capacity as such companies had to concentrate on a smalller share of the total market. After 1880 the eastern furnaces found their competition growing more difficult, as Carnegie and other steel manufactureres built their own blast furnaces. Merchant works in both the South and the West, which had been supplying the steel mills, now began to concentrate their sales in the market the eastern furnaces had controlled for such a long period of time. As a consequence, the older and less efficiently located eastern plants began to crumble before the onslaught of this growing competitive force. Every new depression period found more of the eastern furnace companies dropping out of the industry, and even the more efficient furnaces in the East found their conditions of survival were quite precarious.

Tariff Policy and the Iron and Steel Industry, 1875-1919

Throughout this forty-year period, the attitude of the iron and steel industry toward the protective tariff changed considerably from that held during earlier years. The change in posture was a sign of the maturing of the industry and a consequence of the abundant gains in production made in most sectors of the industry. After the depression of 1875, the furnace owners in the United States had proved quite receptive to technical changes as they sought economies in production. And these economies derived from large-scale output and improved technical appliances were probably secured to a greater extent in the United States than in Europe or Great Britain. The improvements in technology, technical training, and improved management practices showed themselves in reduced costs of iron and minimized the urgency of the old tariff arguments. This development does not mean to say that continuous demands for protection were not made. As long as James Swank remained general manager of the American Iron and Steel Association, its publications continued to carry lengthy statements pertaining to these matters of protection. Swank's arguments against the free importation of iron, however, had less influence over Bulletin readers, for free trade seemed to hold less danger for the domestic iron and steel producers.

While the duty on pig iron had been raised from $6.30 a ton to $7.00 in 1875, by 1883 this duty had been reduced to $6.72. Again, in 1894, the duty on pig iron was pared to $4.00, a rate which was continued in the Dingley Tariff of 1897. The Payne tariff bill of 1909 eliminated another $1.50, and reduced the duty to $2.50; at the same time the duty on foreign ores was lowered to 15 cents or 25 cents a ton, depending upon the type of ore imported. Also, the duty on scrap iron and steel, a raw material of growing importance in steel production, was reduced from $4.00 to $1.00 a ton. By 1913, the duty on pig iron had been eliminated.[19]

---

[19]American Iron and Steel Association, Statistics of the American and Foreign Iron Trade for 1911 (Philadelphia, 1912), p. 85. F. W. Taussig,

Though the latter development may have created some uncertainty among iron producers relative to their future market prospects, it appears that most producers showed little concern over the change. By that date the domestic market for pig iron had become rather limited. About three-quarters of the blast furnace product of the industry was produced and consumed by integrated steel plants, with the molten iron being moved directly from the blast furnaces to converters or now, more often, to open-hearth furnaces. It appears that the only producers that might have been affected by the elimination of the duty were the few companies that were still producing pig iron for the open market. And, because of freight costs, it seems that only the merchant furnaces still remaining in the northeastern sector of the nation faced any competitive threat from imports. The declining numbers of merchant pig iron producers, however, left them in a vulnerable political position, for they were unable to secure the support so essential to maintain protective tariffs.

The year after the pig iron duty was removed, pig iron prices dropped, but at the same time the volume of imports declined. Then through the war years, exports of pig iron increased and were in excess of imports. Though there was always a certain amount of iron imported because particular grades could not be produced advantageously from domestic ores, the volume of imported iron was but a small part of the total amount of pig iron produced for sale in the open market. As

---

Some Aspects of the Tariff Question (Cambridge, Massachusetts, 1934), p. 394.

Taussig wrote, "the time had gone by when the protective system was of real consequence for the iron and steel industries. For good or ill, it had done its work."[20]

Improved Blast Furnace Operations

As previously pointed out, the economies of production in iron manufacture secured during these years were quite considerable. By 1900 the cost of producing a single ton of pig iron had been reduced so effecttively that iron producers from other parts of the world turned to the United States to observe and study the seemingly superior technical facilities and organizational practices used in the industry. These economic successes were achieved in spite of, or because of, the rather unstable business conditions of the era. It must be borne in mind, however, that this success was not shared equally among the various geographic areas of production.

Mention has already been made of the industry's much improved capacity in pig iron production in the aggregate, but such a measure, at best, presents a somewhat distorted impression of the actual level of achievement. In using the aggregate figures, the extremes of individual furnace output are clouded over, as are the differences between fuel types. To clarify the difference between anthracite furnaces and coke furnaces, an effort will be made here to segregate some of these statistics. For this purpose it is desirable to move back to the data for 1883, the first year beehive coke fired furnaces produced more pig iron than the output of

---

[20] Taussig, Tariff History of the United States, p. 442.

both charcoal and anthracite furnaces.

From 1856 to 1871 the quantity of anthracite pig iron had continually exceeded the combined production of furnaces utilizing bituminous coal and coke, and charcoal iron. Between 1872 and 1880 anthracite users produced nearly the same amounts of iron as users of bituminous coal and coke. Then, by 1883, the accumulation of innovations at the coke burning furnaces had enabled such furnace operators to push their total output beyond the product of the anthracite furnaces. At that time, furnaces producing 30 tons of iron a day were technically quite outmoded; the modern beehive coke burning furnace was often capable of producing 80 tons of pig iron in a single day.

The number of plants using bituminous or anthracite fuel, in 1883, were practically equal (221 bituminous coke furnaces and 222 anthracite furnaces), but the output from the coke furnaces was 2,689,650 net tons while the latter produced only 1,885,596 tons.[21] These figures indicate that the average annual capacity for the anthracite furnaces was approximately 8,493 net tons per year, and the coke furnaces were capable of producing about 12,170 tons a year. But that year was one of business depression, and the percentage of furnaces in blast was probably less than would have been employed under more prosperous conditions. By dividing the output figures by the number of each type of furnace actually in blast, a more meaningful figure may be obtained. However, even that method of correction is subject to error, because in a period of

---

[21] American Iron and Steel Association, Statistics of the American and Foreign Iron Trade for 1883, pp. 23 ff.

depression the small, less efficient furnaces would be out of blast, and the number of furnaces in blast would only be for a specific day and not the entire year. Despite these difficulties, the following estimations are presented in Table 11, but they are included with some apprehension.

TABLE 11

AVERAGE OUTPUT OF FURNACES IN BLAST
December 31, 1883

Furnaces	Number in Blast Dec. 31, 1883	Pig Iron Production 1883 (net tons)	Average Annual Output 1883 (net tons)
Anthracite Furn.	118	1,885,596	15,979
Bituminous Coke	105	2,689,597	25,616

Source: American Iron and Steel Association, _Statistics of the American and Foreign Iron Trade for 1883._

In order to indicate the progress that had been made, these figures, when related to those of 1873, show that gains of greater magnitude had been made through the use of beehive coke.

TABLE 12

AVERAGE OUTPUT OF FURNACES IN BLAST
December 31
(1873 and 1883 Compared)

Furnaces	Number in Blast Dec., 1873	Pig Iron Production 1873 (net tons)	Average Output 1873 (net tons)	Average Output 1883 (net tons)	Percentage Gain
Anthracite	137	1,312,254	9,582	15,979	67
Bituminous	83	977,904	11,782	25,616	117

Source: American Iron and Steel Association, _Statistics of the American and Foreign Iron Trade of 1873._

The question now arises as to the cause for those gains in production, especially the outstanding expansion in the average annual output of bituminous coke furnaces. From the information at hand, the increased efficiency appears to have arisen from an accumulation of refinements in furnace design and practice rather than the introduction of any revolutionary innovation.

A number of older anthracite furnaces had been dismantled and replaced with new works having greater dimensions, larger hot-blast stoves, and more powerful blowing machines. Quite often, though, the older anthracite furnaces were merely altered internally. Closed fronts were employed by most furnace companies, and sometimes the bell and hopper system at the tunnel head was installed as an aid in charging the furnace and capturing more of the hot gases from the furnace. Charging the furnace was still done by laborers, the so-called "top fillers," and many of the furnaces continued to use iron pipe hot-blast stoves; only a few companies had settled upon the use of regenerative stoves. The temperature of the pre-heated blast delivered by these stoves was slowly raised above the 600° or 700° Fahrenheit previously obtained; sometimes an air pressure as high as 14 pounds to the square inch was employed.

A number of the newer anthracite furnaces were built with wrought-iron shells and refractory brick linings. As a rule the slope of most of the furnace boshes was designed with steeper angles, while the height of the furnaces was generally somewhat taller than those built in the earlier period.

More and more the chemist became an indispensable feature of furnace management. He was hired to assure the company the best product possible through an analysis of the materials prior to their being smelted. In numerous instances the chemist commenced the study of the chemical reaction within the stack. On the basis of these studies, interior lines were changed and materials improved for smelting in an effort to multiply the product of the furnace. A result of these efforts was the adaptation of ore crushers to reduce the ore and limestone into uniform sizes prior to charging it into the furnace. Many times the ore was roasted or calcined to produce a higher concentrate in the raw material.[22]

The majority of the new furnaces were located near the important coking coal fields in Alabama, western Pennsylvania, and eastern Ohio. Like the newer anthracite furnaces, these works were taller than the older furnaces, though they had not been raised to the 90- or 100-foot heights common in British iron centers. Most of these furnaces were built about 75 feet high, though some were extended to 80 and 85 feet. They were invariably designed with steeper boshes, as were many of the new anthracite furnaces. More often than at the anthracite furnaces, the hot-blast stoves were of the regenerative type. The gas flues or "downcomers" were improved, and in many cases the gases from the furnaces were being washed or condensed in the downcomer in order to remove the deleterious flue dust prior to the entry of the hot gases into the regenerative

---

[22]John Birkinbine, "American Blast Furnace Progress," as found in Albert Williams, Jr., ed., Mineral Resources of the United States, 1883-1884 (Washington, D. C., 1885), pp. 296 ff.

stoves.[23]

As the western furnaces were charged with a high grade Lake Superior ore, the furnace operators were not concerned with the problems of concentrating ores; however, the chemist was quite as essential in the operation of their works as at the eastern furnaces. Like his eastern counterpart, the chemist made careful analyses of fuels, flux, ores, and gases, but more often he interested himself in the study of the proper proportions of the furnace, the volume, pressure, and temperature of the blast in an effort to secure interior furnace lines and chemical actions capable of providing a larger output from the fixed capital. Many times the success of this applied science went beyond the greatest expectations.[24] With the first triumphs in these efforts, the day of "fast driving" and higher furnace output was initiated. The temperature of the hot-blast was advanced to over 1000° Fahrenheit, and the pressure of the blast was continuously augmented. Though these improvements were amazingly productive in terms of the productivity of capital, they did not economize in fuel consumption as earlier technological innovations had.

The outstanding achievements made by means of these improved techniques of furnace operation were the amazing records established at the Edgar Thomson steel mills in Pittsburgh; projects conducted by Captain William R. Jones and Julian Kennedy. Their first success was

---

[23] Ibid., p. 302

[24] Ibid., p. 303.

accomplished at Carnegie's A furnace in 1880, when they raised the furnace's weekly output from 537 tons to 671 tons, a remarkable achievement, considering the fact that the furnace was only 65 feet high and 13 feet at the bosh. The improvements in output resulted from the use of a blast heated to 1500° Fahrenheit and blown into the furnace under a pressure of 10 pounds per square inch. The blast was pre-heated in Siemens-Cowper-Cochrane regenerative stoves.

The second furnace at the same works produced as much as 4,722 tons in a single month. During its first twelve months of operation, this single furnace was driven hard enough to enable the firm to produce 48,179 tons of pig iron. Only ten years previously 80 tons a day or approximately 29,000 tons a year was considered an extraordinary feat of production.[25]

The record output was not accompanied by reduced costs for all the factors of production per ton of iron. Fuel consumption per ton of iron, according to Bridge's record, was actually increased in some instances.[26] Also, the increased output probably helped to reduce labor costs per ton of iron, but the larger furnaces required the employment of more labor. At this time the furnace charging was handled by labor, and with the increased weight of material to move the need for labor was maintained. Great reductions in the cost of labor would have to wait for the

---

[25] American Iron and Steel Association, Bulletin, Vol. 19 (Nov. 11, 1885), 299.

[26] Bridge, The Inside History of the Carnegie Steel Company, p. 89.

development of labor-saving, material-handling machines.

That there were savings in capital outlay is quite evident, but this saving was only applicable to the furnace itself. The greater quantity of air and hotter blast required for these operations necessitated the enlargement of the blowing apparatus and hot-blast stoves. Moreover, there was an additional cost of maintenance in the increased wear of the furnace lining, for the hard driving of a blast furnace reduced the length of time a lining could be used.[27]

Regardless of the economic shortcomings of the method, these first efforts pointed the way to further economies in iron smelting. In the next twenty years, the attention of the enterprising furnace managers was taken up mainly with the problems of reducing costs and secondly with the further expansion of output. But these first records mark the beginning of a modern era in iron production. As the British Iron Trade Commission reported:

> Modern iron making in America began when in 1881, the long-doubted rumour became a certainty, that the late Captain William R. Jones and Julian Kennedy had, by means of high heats and large volume of blast succeeded in more than doubling the output of the Edgar Thomson furnaces, without altering the plant.[28]

---

[27] Sir Lowthian Bell, "On the American Iron Trade and its Progress During Sixteen Years," as found in _The Iron and Steel Institute in America in 1890_ (London, 1890), p. 174. Bell reported British furnace linings could be used continuously for almost seventeen years when low blast pressures were used. American furnaces, on the other hand, had to have the lining replaced about every three years because of the hard driving techniques employed by the steel producers.

[28] James S. Jeans, ed., _American Industrial Conditions and Competition_ (London, 1902), p. 399.

At the end of the next ten years, furnace production had been increased once again. This time the anthracite owners made greater efforts to raise their furnace output than they had in the earlier period. But, the gains made during the same period at the coke furnaces were even greater.

TABLE 13

AVERAGE OUTPUT OF FURNACES IN BLAST
December 31
(1883 and 1892 Compared)

Furnaces	Number in Blast Dec.,1892	Pig Iron Production 1892 (net tons)	Average Output 1892 (net tons)	Average Output 1883 (net tons)	Percentage Gain
Anthracite	72	2,012,766	27,955	15,979	75
Bituminous	141	7,040,928	49,935	25,616	91

Source: American Iron and Steel Association, Statistics of the American and Foreign Iron Trade for 1902 (Philadelphia, 1903).

Again the outstanding individual furnace records were made at the Edgar Thomson works. By 1887 James Gayley, the works manager, had operated one furnace in such a manner that he was able to obtain 8,398 gross tons of pig iron in a single month. The best weekly mark was the production of 2,161 tons, and the best single day's output was 414 tons.[29] Two years later he had raised the monthly record to 10,603 tons. At that time, the furnaces were about 15 feet taller than the 65-foot A furnace,

[29]American Iron and Steel Association, Bulletin, Vol. 21 (Feb. 9, 1887), 36.

in which the first records had been established.[30]

In 1892 another Carnegie furnace was driven to higher production levels and for a time held the coveted broom of the Carnegie works, indicating that the furnace had swept away all previous records. The record from F furnace was 511 tons on the best day.[31] This furnace was 80 feet high with a 22-foot bosh, then lowered to within 22 feet of the hearth; older furnace boshes were about 30 feet from the hearth. Also, improvements had been made in the regenerative stoves, permitting the maintenance of a hot-blast at higher blast pressures. For example, the blast pressure used at F furnace was equivalent to 20 pounds per square inch, a sizable increase over David Thomas's first blast at Catasauqua of 5 to 6 pounds per square inch.

The further advantages derived from the improved furnace practices and facilities was a reduction in the cost of a ton of pig iron. A portion of the cost reduction, however, arose from the external economies that had gradually developed as the iron and steel industry expanded, but more will be said on these economies in another section of this study. In Pennsylvania, as the following data indicate, the gains made through internal and external economies were considerable.

---

[30] Bridge, _The Inside History of the Carnegie Steel Company_, p. 89. William Colquhoun, "Notes on the Iron and Steel Industries in the United States," as found in _The Iron and Steel Institute in America in 1890_, p. 241.

[31] American Iron and Steel Association, _Bulletin_, Vol. 26 (Feb. 10, 1892), 33.

TABLE 14

COMPARATIVE COSTS OF PIG IRON IN PENNSYLVANIA, 1880-90

Year	Average Quantity of Coke Used Per Ton of Pig Iron	Cost Per Ton of Ore	Percent Yield Per Ton of Ore	Wages Per Ton or Ore	Average Output Per Worker	Average Total Cost
1880	2.0 tons	$4.60	48.86	$2.40	143 tons	$15.50
1890	1.4 tons	$3.70	54.36	$1.50	304 tons	$11.10
Percent Change	- 80	- 20	+ 5.50	- 38	+112	- 28

Source: J. S. Jeans, ed., American Industrial Conditions and Competition, pp. 113-23

The number of labor units used to operate a blast furnace was only reduced very slowly for there was a continuing need for a great amount of human effort to keep a blast furnace in operation. As late as 1892, little consideration had been given to the reduction of the amount of labor required to fill the furnaces or load the wagons employed in hauling raw materials. At the Edgar Thomson furnaces, for example, it required eight "top fillers" to keep one furnace charged, and it necessitated a special staff of men to keep the dandies filled.[32] The furnace hoist was still the vertical structure used in earlier years, though electric power units had replaced the older water-balance technique.[33] The skip hoist and automatic charging machines were only developed after

[32]The dandies were wagons designed to haul raw materials from the stockyards to the furnaces.

[33]Colquhoun, "Notes on the Iron and Steel Industries in the United States," pp. 254 ff.

1892.

While the western furnaces had been considerably improved and their costs of production reduced, the eastern anthracite furnaces had also gained some advance in these directions, though they were not comparable. Because little had been done to change the furnace equipment in the eastern plants, the reduction in costs and increased capacity can only be accounted for in improved furnace practices. Lower costs were secured through the application of science to the study of materials and the concentration of ores.[34] Of course, the eastern furnaces also obtained the same benefits from the external economies of scale that had developed as the western furnace companies.

By 1902, after more than 50 percent of the blast furnace plants in operation in 1892 had been abandoned and many of their places taken by modern furnaces, there was a further increase in total output and average furnace production.[35] The available data, however, does not indicate equivalent gains in the two sectors of the industry under consideration, the coke furnaces and the anthracite furnaces. Actually the average output for the anthracite furnaces dropped by approximately 14 percent.

The reduction in average furnace capacity for the anthracite furnaces may be accounted for by the anthracite coal miners' strike and the transportation problem of that year. In 1901 railroads had increased

---

[34] American Iron and Steel Association, <u>Bulletin</u>, Vol. 26 (June 1, 1892), 155.

[35] Jeans, ed., <u>American Industrial Conditions and Competition</u>, p. 437.

TABLE 15

AVERAGE OUTPUT OF FURNACES IN BLAST
On December 31
(1892 and 1902 Compared)

Furnaces	Number in Blast 1902	Pig Iron Production 1902 (net tons)	Average Output 1902 (net tons)	Average Output 1892 (net tons)	Percent Gain
Anthracite	52	1,249,076	24,021	27,955	- 14
Bituminous	222	18,274,298	82,316	49,935	+ 65

Source: American Iron and Steel Association, _Statistics of the American and Foreign Iron Trade for 1902_.

their supply of rolling stock considerably in order to handle their expanding business, but once all the new cars were placed on tracks, congestion occurred. The congestion presumably resulted in delays in the delivery of ore and coke to eastern furnaces; producers were consequently forced to bank their furnaces on numerous occasions, a factor that tended to reduce their output. Not until the spring of 1903 was this transportation situation relieved.[36]

Ten years later, in 1912, the average output for coke furnaces had been increased once again, whereas the anthracite works merely regained the ground lost prior to 1902. The number of active anthracite furnaces dropped to ten, and most of them were using some coke mixed with the anthracite coal. The average annual output of the anthracite furnaces

---

[36]American Iron and Steel Association, _Statistics of the American and Foreign Iron Trade for 1902_ (Philadelphia, 1903), p. 18. Clark, _History of Manufactures in the United States_, III, 29.

was approximately 24,021 tons. This output was approximately one-third of the average output of 82,316 tons produced by 282 coke furnaces. While the anthracite furnace output had been increased approximately 15 percent, there was actually no gain in average furnace capacity over that in 1892. The coke furnaces, however, showed a further gain in average capacity of 41 percent, but this expansion indicates a diminishing rate of change.[37]

Other developments during this twenty-year span consisted of rather extensive improvements in plant arrangements, the application of labor-saving mechanisms and furnace apparatus. Also, there were continuous gains derived from the external economies provided by the introduction of amazing new material-handling devices. The latter improvements tended to reduce costs of raw materials to all furnaces alike, while the gains from the other innovations varied among the plants of different size and location. Improvements in yard arrangements and labor-saving devices were adopted more often by the larger steel companies and a few of the merchant furnaces in the South and West. Generally the eastern merchant furnace operators in the older iron areas did little to improve the efficiency of their plants, or what little they did was done too late. The freedom of such companies to make changes within the industry became more and more limited as the giant steel corporations gradually began to

---

[#&] American Iron and Steel Institute, <u>Annual Statistical Report for 1913</u> (New York, 1914), pp. 14 ff.

dominate the market.[38]

At the older eastern furnaces, the loaded freight cars coming in from the mines, quarries, or coke ovens were generally pulled or pushed to a trestle or elevated track, and the cars' contents dumped into storage bins below through openings in the bottom of the cars. The materials were transferred by hand shovelling or gravity into charging barrows. The loaded barrows were then raised to the furnace tops via a vertical hoist where their contents were charged into the furnace by hand labor.

At the modern blast furnaces, to accomplish the task of handling the enormous quantities of raw materials required to keep the large furnaces in blast, three new pieces of equipment had been developed. These devices included the car-dumper or tipple, the bridge-crane, and the automatic skip hoist.[39] The initial investment in such equipment was quite high, but at the larger works such investments reduced considerably

---

[38]Clark, History of Manufactures in the United States, III, 22 ff. Frank Popplewell, Iron and Steel Production in America (Manchester, England, 1906), pp. 64 ff. Axel Sahlin, "Production of Coke and Anthracite Pig Iron in the United States," as found in Jeans, ed., American Industrial Conditions and Competition, pp. 339 ff.

[39]Popplewell, Iron and Steel Production in American, pp. 69 ff. Sahlin, "Production of Coke and Anthracite Pig Iron in the United States," pp. 464-76.

The car-dumper was a huge platform on which the freight cars were guided, clamps fastened to their wheels, and the complete platform tipped to discharge the contents of the car into storage bins below the platform.

The bridge-crane was employed by companies using Lake Superior ores. The crane had a dependent grab bucket that could be moved from one end of the bridge over the storage pile to the bins near the blast furnace. From the bins the material was moved by gravity into electrically propelled cars that were transferred to the skip hoists. At the skip hoist the materials were automatically elevated to the furnace top and the materials discharged into the furnace. The skip hoist was operated by a single man at the bottom of the furnace.

the necessary time for handling a specific amount of material, eliminated demurrage charges on freight cars, and economized on labor.

After the ore was smelted, the further problem of tapping and casting required a great deal of labor time at the old furnaces. The more modern works, however, had begun to use mechanical tapping machines as well as mechanical casting machines. Furnaces at steel mills were generally tapped, and the molten metal was moved directly to the converters by means of ladle cars. This was a technique that reduced both fuel as well as labor costs. A few of the larger merchant furnace companies adopted casting machines of one sort or another; these had almost become a necessity at some furnaces, for iron cast in sand could not be used in the basic open-hearth furnace, and many buyers of foundry iron would not purchase sand castings.[40]

The smaller merchant furnaces found the casting machines an expensive luxury, but many did employ the Brown pig breaker. When this machine was used, the iron was cast in sand, or, if basic pig iron, it was cast in coke or dolomite dust and then permitted to cool. When cooled sufficiently, the sow, with pigs attached, was removed to a site

---

[40] *Ibid*., pp. 67 ff. Sahlin, "Production of Coke and Anthracite Pig Iron in the United States," pp. 481 f.

One casting machine, designed by E. A. Uehling, consisted of an endless chain of cast-iron molds, coated with a spray of lime prior to tapping, that received the molten metal directly from the furnace. The pigs were permitted to cool in the molds for about nine minutes, then dropped on a conveyor, and carried into a water-filled tank for further cooling. Once cooled the pigs were moved automatically to a loading platform or to storage yards.

A second casting machine, the Davis machine, consisted of circular track to guide the molds from the furnace to a conveyor belt. The conveyor moved the pigs into a water tank and then to a loading platform.

where the pig breaker, consisting of a steel frame to hold the cast in place, and two hydraulic plungers, was used to break the pigs free and break the sow into desired lengths.[41]

Great economies were also passed on to the iron and steel companies through the introduction of technological innovations in satellite industries, but it was probably in the shipping and handling of iron ore that some of the greatest economies were achieved. Where the transportation of local ores had only required the utilization of regular railroad equipment for its transit, the movement of Lake Superior ores necessitated much more, for it had to be handled several times prior to its arrival at final destination. First, the ore was moved from the mines to the loading docks at the upper end of the lakes; then it was transferred to ore boats, to be carried to the lower lake ports. Once at these ports, it had to be unloaded and reloaded once again into freight cars going to the furnaces.

With the increasing use of Bessemer steel, more of the lake ore was demanded and more was shipped. But even as late as 1889 the method of loading and unloading was rather crude; either hand shoveling or simple processes of gravity were employed. For example, in unloading a boat, the ore was shoveled into buckets which were raised and lowered by windlass or steam power. Once on deck the bucket was emptied into barrows, and they were wheeled from the deck to be loaded into freight cars,

---

[41]Sahlin, "Production of Coke and Anthracite Pig Iron in the United States," p. 482.

sometimes by steam shovel and at other times by gravity.[42] The freight cars originally used to haul the ores from the mines to the ore docks were also improved and enlarged. The first cars had a capacity of 7 or 8 tons, but these were discarded for 30-ton cars which, by 1904, were being replaced by 50-ton cars. Ore trains were run directly over the ore piers, the bottoms of the cars were opened, and the ore deposited in storage bins by gravity. Ore ships of 5,000- or 7,000-ton capacity could then be loaded from these storage bins by gravity in a very few hours.[43]

The "whaleback ore boat" of the earlier period eventually gave way to much larger and more serviceable vessels. The new ships had perpendicular sides which were strongly reinforced, while their steel decks were perforated by a series of hatches through which the ore was loaded. One such ship, the "Augustus B. Wolvin," was 560 feet in length, 56 feet wide, and 30 feet deep, large enough to carry 10,000 to 11,000 tons of iron ore. This load was equivalent to 333 carloads or 11 train loads of ore. A ship of such proportions represented a high degree of economy in transportation.[44]

Upon arrival at the lower lake ports, unloading machines were employed to remove the ores from the ships. These machines could remove as much as 95 percent of the load, using the labor of only seventeen men.

---

[42] Popplewell, _Iron and Steel Production in America_, p. 59.

[43] Sahlin, "Production of Coke and Anthracite Pig Iron in the United States," pp. 409-12.

[44] _Ibid_. Popplewell, _Iron and Steel Production in America_, p. 58.

An ore boat arriving at one of these ports in the morning was able to return to the upper lake region by evening.[45]

The economy of such handling devices is made evident in the price changes and the increase in the movements of Lake Superior ores. In 1895 ore shipments from the Lake Superior region totaled 8,112,228 tons. By 1905, after the development of these mechanical handling devices, the annual shipments had reached a total of 28,941,259 tons; five years later the figure of shipments had reached a total of 34,042,897 tons. Meanwhile, ores which had cost $8.00 a ton in 1858, at the lower lake ports, dropped to $4.00 a ton in 1902.[46]

Overland transportation of ores was equally improved through the use of automatic loading devices, larger freight cars, heavier rails, and more powerful steam locomotives. These innovations continually reduced labor costs, permitted larger trains to run between the lake ports and the furnace sites, and conserved fuel by reducing the number of motive units required to haul the ore. The handling of materials in this manner tended to reduce the costs to all furnace operators, whether large steel producers or merchant furnace firms.[47]

---

[45] Ibid., pp. 416 ff. The first such improvement was the bridge-crane designed to move along rails on the dock. The bucket on the crane was filled by hand and then raised over the dock and the materials dumped into the cars. In 1898 the Hulett Loader was introduced. This crane was capable of dipping into the hatchway and filling itself automatically.

[46] American Iron and Steel Association, Statistics of the American and Foreign Iron Trade for 1910 (Philadelphia, 1911), p. 35. These figures represent shipments to Lake Erie ports only.

[47] Popplewell, Iron and Steel Production in American, pp. 50 ff.

For a time a combination of lake ore interests sought to control the price of the ore, but by 1904 the combination had gone out of existence, having been replaced by a much stronger control group. The very nature of the nation's ore deposits tended to encourage large-scale steelmaking operations; the long haul costs of ore transportation were cheapened by the employment of high capacity mechanical equipment which had to be used intensively, hence control fell to a few large companies with adequate funds for the heavy capital reuirements. Smaller firms were sometimes forced to pay tribute to those companies, while larger firms set about to avoid these payments by controlling their own mines, ore ships, and railroads. By 1904 less than 35 percent of the lake ores entered into the open market; this market situation considerably reduced the economic freedom of the remaining eastern merchant furnaces and forced them to rely to some extent upon local ore deposits or foreign imports.[48]

Finally, it should be noted that equally important improvements were made in mining and handling of coal during these years. Coal cutting machines, car tipples, and automatic coal handling devices were employed by an increasing number of coal companies, and these provided economies in mining and shipping. Of course, the exploitation of new coal fields, in West Virginia and especially the Connellsville field near Pittsburgh, considerably increased the available supply of fuel for blast

---

[48] Ibid., p. 53. Burn, The Economic History of Steelmaking, pp. 268 ff.

furnaces. As the supply of coal increased, the price of coke dropped; beehive coke which sold for $3.00 a ton at the ovens in 1870 was sold for $1.50 in 1900.[49] These improvements in mining and coke manufacturing and the consequent price reduction had a great deal to do with the displacement of anthracite coal as a blast furnace fuel.

Georgraphy of Iron Smelting

In response to the continual improvements in transportation and the continuous westward movement, there were very extensive readjustments in the distribution of the major iron smelting centers in the nation. The most significant of these developments was the rapid expansion of production of iron and steel in western Pennsylvania. There were also important gains made by the iron manufacturers in the South, while in the East there was a relative decline in the importance of the three valley regions, the Susquehanna, the Schuylkill, and Lehigh, as well as in New Jersey. Meanwhile St. Louis, which had displayed great promise in the 1870's, faded with the failure of Missouri's ore mines to yield adequate supplies.

In Pennsylvania's Allegheny County the number of stacks quadrupled between 1874 and 1913. This extraordinary expansion in the number of blast furnaces in that region arose from several factors. An already established iron milling industry provided impetus for pig iron production as the demand for heavy products for railroad construction in the

---

[49] F. W. Taussig, "The Iron Industry in the United States," Quarterly Journal of Economics, XIV (February, 1900), 143-70. Popplewell, Iron and Steel Production in American, pp. 34 ff.

West increased. As those same transportation facilities were improved, Lake Superior ores moved into the area at lower costs and were joined with the coke made nearby from the Connellsville coal. The area also contained a substanial supply of enterprise and skills, an increasing supply of capital, and a diversity of manufactures which provided further means of increasing iron production.[50] Eventually the region came to hold iron-producing facilities, enough to produce about one-fourth of all the pig iron made in the United States. The trend of production in the area continually increased between 1886 and 1906, but from that latter date until 1916 the rate of increase diminished. Since 1916 the rate of change in production in the region has been downward. This development reflects the further shift in iron and steel production to growing centers located at lake ports.[51]

Another of the outstanding regional developments was that expansion of pig iron production in the South. There the remarkable combination of fuel, ore, and limestone within a few miles of each other made it possible to produce pig iron at a cost low enough to permit its shipment to distant markets. Despite the unstable business conditions of the 1880's, the production of the southern furnaces continually expanded. The area's stacks were constructed upon the most advanced design, and most of them were equipped with modern hot-blast ovens, as well as strong blowing

---

[50]E. N. Montague, "The Pig Iron Industry in Allegheny County, 1872-1931," as found in Pittsburgh Business Review (Feb. 28, 1933), pp. 14 ff. Clark, History of Manufactures in the United States, III, 23.

[51]Ibid., p. 15. Isard, "Some Locational Factors in the Iron and Steel Industry Since the Early Nineteenth Century," pp. 203 ff.

machines. Labor was paid relatively low wages compared to the northern furnace wages; however, the workers were inexperienced and consequently less efficient. Railroads of the region, anxious to promote their services, reduced freight charges to a level which enabled the southern pig iron producer to compete quite effectively in the northeastern iron market.[52]

As the southern pig iron found its way into the eastern markets, St. Louis, Chicago, and other western cities, it created disturbances in the market which threatened the very existence of many of the older merchant furnace companies. But as depressions in the iron trade occurred and competition sharpened, some of the southern firms lacking adequate supplies of capital and sufficient management personnel also failed.[53] To offset this instability arising from the region's unbalanced market structure, attempts were made to produce steel. But the region lacked a good Bessemer ore; consequently, it found steel production costs quite high. Also, as the southern market for steel had not developed, and efforts to compete with the other areas proved quite futile, the southern iron producer preferred to remain in his most efficient area of production, foundry iron. Later, when the United States Steel Corporation took over the largest consolidation in the South, the Tennessee Coal, Iron, and Railroad Company, many of its works were shifted to the production of

---

[52]American Iron and Steel Association, Bulletin, Vol. 19 (March 4, 1885), 8.

[53]Ibid., Vol. 21 (July 13, 1887), 189; Vol. 23 (Dec. 11, 1889), 339.

basic pig iron for that corporation's open-hearth furnaces.[54]

As the demand for steel continued to expand and the technical innovations already mentioned were put into practice, there was gradual expansion in the number of new furnace facilities along the lakes. Also, as additional fuel economies were obtained through the use of scrap metal in open-hearth furnaces, a further impetus was given to the expansion of the steel plants located closer to the very large eastern markets, where large supplies of scrap metal could be obtained. The relative decline in Pittsburgh's share of the total production of steel was, in part, a consequence of its lack of an abundant supply of scrap metal.[55]

While the eastern steel mills continued to prosper, the merchant furnaces of the region found it continually more difficult to survive. Anthracite coal had been found to reduce the efficiency of the blast in the furnaces because of its density, and the fuel had a tendency to spall or decrepitate under the action of the heat in the furnace, causing a great deal of scaffolding.[56] At the same time the limited supply of the fuel, its cleanliness, and freedom from smoke, which made it an ideal domestic fuel, caused its price to remain at a relatively high level.

---

[54] Clark, History of Manufactures in the United States, III, 24 ff. Sahlin, "Production of Coke and Anthracite Pig Iron in the United States," pp. 435 f. Colquhoun, "Notes on the Iron and Steel Industries in the United States," pp. 322 ff. Between 1893 and 1903 the expansion of the South's pig iron production seems to have reached its peak. After that date its share of the total pig iron output declined.

[55] Isard, "Some Locational Factors in the Iron and Steel Industry Since the Early Nineteenth Century," pp. 211 ff.

[56] Popplewell, Iron and Steel Production in America, p. 36. Johnson, Prin. of Operation and Prod. of the Blast Furn., pp. 1 ff.

The result of these conditions was an extension of the eastern furnaces' supply lines into western Pennsylvania and West Virginia as they sought coke to replace or mix with anthracite coal. Also, as the small deposits of local ores upon which these furnaces had relied so long began to run out, additional supply lines had to be extended to the Lake Superior ores and foreign imports. By 1900 the major advantage that remained to the merchant furnaces of the region was their proximity to market; however, the continual expansion in open-hearth furnace steel and the ability to substitute scrap metal for pig iron caused that market to shrink.

The shifts in the predominance of the various sectors or geographic regions are quite apparent in Table 16. The expansion of production of pig iron in the Eastern Distric moved ahead much more rapidly than in the Southern District, but it was largely the result of the expansion of production at the Bethlehem Steel's two plants in Bethlehem, Pennsylvania, and the Lackawanna works at Buffalo, New York. By 1920 the merchant furnaces in the area were disappearing quite rapidly.

Organizational Changes

While the above review of the iron industry's development has been rather sketchy, it has demonstrated that the growth was quite rapid, production was increased to unimagined quantities, and the industry was beset with periodic but temporary depressions. These factors were not without their influence upon the character of the industry.

The rapidity with which iron output was expanded in new areas of production, whatever the reasons, enabled the industry to take advantage of past experience and incorporate improvements in new methods and

TABLE 16

PRODUCTION OF PIG IRON BY DISTRICTS IN THE UNITED STATES
FOR SELECTED YEARS
(In thousands of gross tons)

	1872	1880	1885	1890	1895	1900	1910	1920
Eastern District (Eastern Pennsylvania, New York, New Jersey)	1,217	1,610	1,312	2,342	1,390	1,911	4,409	5,424
Western Pennsylvania	387	772	1,081	2,561	3,549	4,922	9,066	11,160
Central District (Western Pennsylvania, Ohio, Illinois	849	1,502	1,874	4,517	6,019	8,756	17,494	22,975
Southern District (Alabama, Virginia, Maryland, Tennessee)	127	238	539	1,554	1,491	2,327	3,118	3,628
Other States	356	485	319	790	546	795	2,282	4,898
Total United States	2,549	3,835	4,044	9,203	9,446	13,789	27,303	36,925

Source: American Iron and Steel Association, *Statistics of the American and Foreign Iron Trade*; American Iron and Steel Institute, *Annual Statistical Report for 1921*; F. W. Taussig, "The Iron Industry in the United States," *Quarterly Journal of Economics*, XIV (February, 1900), 143 ff.

The figure for eastern Pennsylvania, up to 1900, is for iron smelted with anthracite, or anthracite and coke mixed, while that for western Pennsylvania is for bituminous (coke) pig iron. For 1900, the eastern Pennsylvania figure is production in the Lehigh Valley, Susquehanna Valley, and Schuylkill Valley. The remainder produced in the state is credited to western Pennsylvania. The figure under Other States moved up very rapidly in the last two periods because of the extraordinary expansion of production at the Gary plant of the United States Steel Corporation in Indiana.

facilities. Each new plant that was built contained the latest equipment, and its management generally employed the most up-to-date furnace practices. This rapid development also provided incentive to experiment and led to a growing mass of smaller technical innovations. As each new plant that was built was more efficient, the older plants became outdated and required modification or renewal if the firm hoped to remain in business; this was a condition presumed to have been conducive to rapid replacement of outmoded equipment.

There were times of prosperity, when supply lagged behind demand, and the marginal plant could obtain some economic sustenance. However, with a return to normal circumstances, when the capacity available was more than that needed, the older less efficient firms were eliminated in the resulting competitive struggle. The outcome of this rather rapid technological change and explosive growth in capacity was the appearance of large-scale production, accompanied by an increase in the size of the firm, a product of integration and combination.

In 1900 the greater portion of the pig iron produced in the United States was converted into steel either by the Bessemer or open-hearth processes, and with the expansion in the production of steel came the integrated steel mills. Advantages derived through such arrangements were a greater control over the quality of the steel producer's raw material, pig iron, and a tremendous saving in heat energy by using molten pig iron. The evidence of the value of such integration sppears in the rapid growth of similar arrangements in most steel plants.

The larger steel works provided opportunity for the further

division of labor, the economy of skill, and the use of applied science. Modifications in technical processes, furnace construction, and handling equipment were made at these larger works more often than at the merchant furnaces. Integration reduced the necessary business contacts for the firm and consequently economized in certain business activities. For example, economies were supposedly obtained in the buying and selling of raw materials and finished goods. In some cases there was a fusion of other branches of the industry in the hands of a single firm. Mines, railroads, shipping facilities, coke furnaces, and processing or fabricating works were acquired in order to make the firm independent and self-sufficient for raw materials and to guarantee sales of semi-finished or finished products.

The growth of steel firms of this order of magnitude required an expansion in the range of management skills, the application of machinery, and the reduction of many management procedures to routine and system. Technical education provided a wide array of trained assistants for this purpose - engineers, chemists, mineralogists, electricians, accountants, and others. It was to these skilled workers that the routine steps were delegated, and the processes that once required the watchful eye of the ironmaster himself were managed by hired help. Those ironmasters willing to swim against the stream of change now developed new powers and resources of managerial ability.

The appearance of the large-scale steel plant was accompanied by periods of severe competition in an era of expanding markets and reduced transportation costs. Numerous companies, once isolated because of an inadequate national transportation system, found themselves deprived of monopolistic positions and faced with competitors from more distant locations. The combination of declining iron prices and widening markets, joined with the depressions of the period, subjected individual iron and steel firms to a rather formidable competitive situation.[57]

This competitive struggle, in conjunction with the problems of heavier fixed costs that had arisen with the technical advances of the period, resulted in various efforts to restrain the competition which seemed to endanger each firm's existence. Several attempts were made, through temporary pools and agreements, to stabilize the prices of various iron products; among these efforts were the Western Bar Iron Association and the Eastern Bar Iron Association.[58] In 1896 a steel billet pool was formed in the Pittsburgh district and a wire nail association was formed, though its existence was quite short.[59] A combination of southern pig iron manufacturers collapsed after a very brief existence of two months. The Eastern Pig Iron Association, formed in 1883, was somewhat more successful in maintaining its existence, but it was not any more successful than the others in maintaining the price of pig iron sold in the open market.[60]

---

[57]American Iron and Steel Association, Bulletin, Vol. 18 (Oct. 1, 1884), 253; Vol. 22 (June 20, 1888), 195; Vol. 23 (May 22, 1889), 138; (Dec. 11, 1889) 339.

[58]Ibid., Vol. 29 (April 1, 1985), 77.

[59]Ibid. (Nov. 1, 1895), p. 245; Vol. 30 (July 1, 1896), 149.

[60]Ibid., Vol. 18 (Jan. 17, 1883), 12; Vol. 32 (May 1, 1898), 69; (June 15, 1898) 93; Vol. 42 (Jan. 1, 1908), 5.

Each voluntary association was held together by rather tenuous and informal agreements, many times ambiguous in nature and possessing no means of enforcement. As a consequence of this informality, they proved to be devices of a temporary nature which had questionable value to their members. Because of the temporary nature of these combinations, some of the industry's leaders who were a little more ambitious sought a form of more lasting and stronger business organization. The outcome of their quest was the formation of what were then considered gigantic corporations. The combination movements resulted in the merging of like firms into a single corporation or a complex of firms under a single holding corporation.

The advantages of such a business organization as seen by one contemporary writer were:

> In America, in addition to the advantage of putting private businesses into corporate form, the benefits of consolidated management are obtained and the advantages of larger aggregations of capital and ability are thus secured.
>
> If the writer were asked what these are, the answer would be difficult only because the list is so long. The following are the principal ones: Raw material bought in large quantities is secured at a lower price; the specialization of manufacture on a large scale in separate plants permits the fullest utilization of special machinery and processes, thus decreasing cost; the standard of quality is raised and fixed; the number of styles reduced and the best standards are adopted; those plants which are best equipped and most advantageously situated are run continuously and in preference to those less favored; in case of local strikes or fires the work goes on elsewhere, thus preventing serious loss; there is no multiplication of the means of distribution; a better force of salesmen takes the place of a large number, and same is true of branch stores; terms and conditions of sale become more uniform, and credits through comparisons are more safely granted; the aggregate of stocks carried is greatly reduced, thus saving interest, insurance, storage, and shop wear; greater skill in management accrues

> to the benefit of the whole instead of a part; and large advantages are realized from comparative accounting and comparative administration.[61]

Notably lacking from this rather extensive list of advantages was the advantageous elimination of competition, but the leaders in this movement would deny that such was the end result of their vast new organizational schemes. Once established, the specialized firm might dismantle the less efficient and poorly located plants for the purpose of economy, and they could build, in more favorable locations, larger and more adequate facilities. In several instances, however, a single firm gained a virtual monopoly over its area of production, though most combinations resulted in the new firm gaining only a larger proportion of the trade, while the rest of the market was left to a few rivals.[62] The smaller firms specializing in separate processes of production discovered that their business decisions were being severely restricted; many were left with a single choice, to withdraw their facilities from production.

A union of similar companies or related units of manufacturing had not been uncommon in the iron industry prior to 1880, as evidenced by the history of The Thomas Iron Company, the organization of the Albany and Rennsselear Iron and Steel Company in 1875, or the union of the North and

---

[61] _Ibid_., Vol. 33 (Oct. 15, 1899), 179.

[62] Clark, _History of Manufactures in the United States_, III, 45 ff. Commissioner of Corporations, _Report on the Steel Industry_, I (Washington, D. C., 1911), 61 ff.

According to the Commissioner's report the major reasons for consolidation were, first, to restrict competition, then the advantages of integration, and the creation of inflated securities. The first reason, however, was considered "the most potent."

South Chicago rolling mills prior to 1880. However, effective competition had not been endangered by these organizations, for none of the firms were able to exert any substantial control over the market. The consolidation movement, after 1880, however, became much more ambitious as the combinations became larger in capacity, number of employees, share of the market, and degree of integration. More often the new firms drove the smaller firms out of business or reduced them to impotence.

By the early 1900's the peak of this revolutionary development seems to have been reached, but by that time the whole structure of the iron industry had been changed. Now, instead of an industry with a number of almost independent branches of manufacturing, each containing numerous firms, the competitive situation had given way to the rivalry of gigantic integrated steel firms.

There were a number of important combinations or mergers in this period, but none was quite as dramatic or meaningful for the steel industry as the creation of the United State Steel Corporation in 1901[63] At its conception the Steel Corporation had over three-fifths of the nation's steel production. With its blast furnace capacity of 7,400,000 tons, it controlled 44 percent of the total production of basic and Bessemer pig iron, but it produced only 3.4 percent of the total foundry iron. The company also controlled 45 percent of the iron ore output in

---

[63]The history of the United States Steel Corporation's creation and its early years is available in numerous sources, among them being: Commissioner of Corporations, Report on the Steel Industry; Arundel Cotter, United States Steel, A Corporation With a Soul (New York, 1921); E. D. McCallum, The Iron and Steel Industry in the United States (London, 1931), pp. 112 ff.

that year and was the owner of the best and largest coking coal deposit in the nation.[64] Though the firm was primarily a manufacturer of finished steel products, it did not produce any steel castings. Furthermore, despite its immense capacity to produce pig iron, the firm was a buyer, rather than a seller, of that raw material.

The major portion of the rest of the iron and steel production was controlled by another twenty-five large producers which were in no way connected to the corporation. Those companies were also integrated companies, though none had such a diffused ownership of properties as the United States Steel Corporation. Within this group were two companies which were purely merchant furnace operations, The Thomas Iron Company and Empire Steel and Iron Company, but their continued existence was rather precarious. Twenty of these companies owned 114 of the nation's 406 blast furnaces, while the Steel Corporation owned another 78.[65]

The ownership of these 192 furnaces by 21 firms placed almost 50 percent of the industry's blast furnaces under the control of a very small portion of the firms in the industry. Such concentration of control was a very radical change from the conditions of 1874, when the 735 blast furnaces then available for production had been owned by 556 firms, and the larges firm had controlled only 8 of those furnaces.

The fact that merchant furnaces continued to be important was

---

[64] Commissioner of Corporations, <u>Report on the Steel Industry</u>, I, 109, American Iron and Steel Association, <u>Bulletin</u>, Vol. 36 (August 25, 1902), 126.

[65] <u>Ibid</u>. Cotter, <u>United States Steel. A Corporation With a Soul</u>, p. 32.

mainly a consequence of the continued maladjustment between the industry's steel and pig iron capacity and the continuance of iron casting of fairly large proportions by firms which did not own their own blast furnaces. As long as those conditions prevailed, the merchant furnaces served a useful function. As the maladjustment was corrected and the steel firms gained a more effective control over their pig iron sources, the merchant furnaces' importance diminished.[66]

The merchant furnace companies' market was further weakened by the continual expansion in the production of open-hearth steel. Though introducted at about the same time as the Bessemer process, the open-hearth furnace did not come into vogue in the steel industry until about 1890. Even then, such production as there was lagged behind the Bessemer process beyond the close of the century. Not until 1908 did the production of open-hearth steel outdistance that of the Bessemer converters.

The change from Bessemer steel to open-hearth steel was occasioned by the growing demands from the consumers of steel plate or structural steel forms for a more perfect steel. Bessemer steel plate often contained many imperfections. But open-hearth steel not only replaced Bessemer steel; it also proved to be an excellent substitute for cast iron, which Bessemer steel had never been.[67]

The application of the basic process to the open-hearth furnaces resulted in a very sudden increase in the flow of steel from open-hearth

---

[66] Clark, History of Manufactures in the United States, III, 63 and 90.

[67] American Iron and Steel Association, Bulletin, Vol. 28 (May 23, 1894), 108.

furnaces; in a single year production was increased by as much as 44 percent, and in a few years more open-hearth steel was produced than Bessemer.[68] The adaptation of the basic process widened the available sources of raw materials for the steel industry, for a wider variety of pig iron could be used and scrap iron could be employed as readily as pig iron. The latter development led those who sought to disparage such steel to refer to the open-hearth furnace as the "scavenger" of the industry.[69] Soon, however, even the iron foundries were shifting to steel castings and mixing scrap metal in their charge, sometimes using as much as 50 percent scrap, a condition which continually reduced the market for merchant pig iron.[70]

The more frequent use of open-hearth furnaces and the increasing use of scrap metal produced tremendous economies for the steel industry. The practice of using this once waste material netted savings in coal consumption and prevented the more rapid depletion of the nation's iron ore resources. The use of scrap also provided a portion of the impetus for a further reorientation in the location of the major centers of steel production, but that development is not a topic to be covered by this

---

[68] Ibid., Vol. 30 (Dec. 10, 1896), 276. American Iron and Steel Institute, Annual Statistical Report for 1921, p. 23. By 1921 the production of open-hearth steel ingots had reached 15,589,802 gross tons as compared to 4,015,936 tons of Bessemer steel.

[69] Ibid., Vol. 28 (May 23, 1894), 108.

[70] Boylston, An Introduction to the Metallurgy of Iron and Steel, p. 146.

dissertation.[71]

The preceding discussion, it is hoped, has made it evident that the location of the iron industry in the United States, in the years under observation, was the result of a complex of forces. With changes in the strength of one or more these forces, the pattern of location was altered as the industry moved toward a new equilibrium. The most pertinent consequence of the change, relative to this study, was the gradual, or sometimes quite rapid, elimination of the merchant pig iron trade and the once numerous furnaces making up that sector of the iron industry. To obtain an idea of how these forces affected one firm in the trade, the remaining chapters of this study will be concerned with the decline and demise of The Thomas Iron Company.

---

[71] Isard, "Some Locational Factors in the Iron and Steel Industry Since the Early Nineteenth Century," pp. 203 ff.

CHAPTER IX

THE GROWTH OF COMPETITION, 1876-1893

The Home Market Invaded

In the two decades preceding the panic of 1893, the market for pig iron grew quite rapidly, but the Lehigh Valley furnaces, as a group, were unable to maintain their former share of total sales against the competition of southern and western producers. Prior to the panic of 1873 and the six years of depression which followed, the Lehigh Valley had been the most important iron-producing district in the United States, and its furnaces were all, or nearly all, running and presumably making money. But in the ensuing competitive struggle, despite the pre-eminence enjoyed by their product, few of the valley's merchant furnace companies escaped unscathed. By 1893 many of the once flourishing companies had succumbed, and a number of furnaces that had been in blast in 1873 had been abandoned or dismantled.

The Lehigh Valley furnaces were unable to maintain their position for a number of reasons. Relatively high railroad rates and the increasing necessity of hauling their raw materials from more distant areas placed a handicap on these companies that they could not readily overcome. The displacement of iron by steel, as a consequence of the rapid development of the Bessemer process, placed the merchant furnaces at a further disadvantage, for the region lacked suitable ores for the production of Bessemer pig iron. Meanwhile, the development of the immense ore deposits in Alabama, where the cost of assembling raw materials was very low, led to an increase in the total production of foundry iron and resulted in the overcrowding of the market for that type of iron in the North. Attempts by northern producers to disparage the southern iron proved a valueless defense against the competition. More founders and mill owners soon discovered that the southern iron was quite as workable as that from northern furnaces.[1]

While other furnace men had refined their furnace design, increased the blowing capacity of their works, and improved their hot-blast stoves, many of the Lehigh Valley furnace companies continued to operate with their outmoded equipment. Any reduction in costs secured by the various companies in the region were generally a consequence of the more careful selection and concentration of local ores. The only advantage the valley continued to retain was its location in relation to the eastern centers of consumption. But for most of the local companies, this single advantage was not enough to permit their competing successfully against the western and southern manufacturers whose furnaces were modern and well equipped and had the further advantage of cheap ore, coke, and labor as well as low railroad rates to eastern markets.[2]

In order to eliminate the competitive pricing which occurred with the increase in the supply of foundry iron, suggestions for combination were put forward by some producers; others, however, faced with the same

---

[1]American Iron and Steel Association, Bulletin, Vol. 18 (Dec. 17, 1884), 321.

[2]Ibid., Vol. 19 (March 4, 1885), 8.

competitive conditions, frowned upon such schemes. The suggested combination required the furnaces making the greatest quantity of iron to blow out their stacks first, giving an advantage to the less efficient works. Such a scheme was quite unacceptable to the larger and more efficient producers.[3] To the companies that were still making profits, the only sensible way of reducing output and sustaining prices was for the less efficient firms to blow out their furnaces when it was no longer possible for them to make profits.[4] In the competitive struggle that followed, there was no thought of adopting a policy of "live and let live." Because of these circumstances there was little success in securing any cooperation or constructing a combination.

During these years the American Iron and Steel Association's Bulletin carried numerous reports of the difficult times faced by most of the Lehigh Valley furnaces and the reorganization of others. For example, the Lehigh Valley Iron Company was reorganized in July, 1879, as the

---

[3] Ibid., Vol. 13 (Feb. 5, 1879), 31.

[4] Ibid. (Jan. 29, 1879), p. 22. A series of letters signed "Pig Iron" and "Vulcan" carried on an extensive argument on the methods to be used to maintain the price of pig iron. One of the last letters in the series presented the following:

"There is only one sensible and legitimate way to stop overproduction and make a healthy market, and that is, just as soon as producers of pig iron can not make and sell it at a profit they should shut down - as sooner or later they must, whether willing or not. When they find they can make two ends meet, let them blow in; if this creates overproduction, out they must go again. If they can not afford this and others can, then they have no business in this branch of the trade, and the sooner they get out of it, or go to the wall, the better for themselves, their friends and every one else."

Coplay Iron Company after the first named company had become insolvent.[5] Later Uhler Furnace, at Glendon, was sold at a sheriff's sale for $45,000. The furnace had been built six years previously at a cost of $90,000.[6] Other furnaces were blown out, and with the difficult conditions during the depression of 1883, more furnaces were sold. In 1883, the Carbon Iron Company, the Coplay Iron Company, the Emaus iron works, and the Bingen iron works were all sold, while three other Lehigh Valley companies were obliged to mortgage their property to secure essential working capital.[7]

The onerous trade conditions prevailing during the latter part of this period finally drove the pig iron producers in the eastern sector of the United States into a combination of sorts. Even the firms that had resisted previously capitulated as their profits were endangered. Thus, the Eastern Pig Iron Association, made up of companies that sold pig iron in the open market, was organized in 1883. Established for the mutual protection of the economic interests of its members, it proposed to seek legislation by Congress for furtherance of the members' trade.[8] The fact that they were meeting together to discuss matters pertaining to their advantage suggests that some contrivance to raise the price of pig iron was discussed. As price conditions did not change in their favor, there

---

[5] _Ibid._, p. 30; (July 16, 1879) p. 16.

[6] _Ibid._ (Nov. 19, 1879), p. 293.

[7] _Ibid._, Vol. 17 (Feb. 14, 1883), 43.

[8] _Ibid._ (Jan. 17, 1883), p. 12; (March 28, 1883) p. 85.

is little evidence to suggest that any achievement in this direction was secured.[9]

As the price of pig iron showed no tendency to advance, but only continued to fall, it became more difficult for the marginal firms to survive. More and more of the pig iron from Alabama and Virginia furnaces found its way into the Philadelphia market in direct competition with the greater portion of the Lehigh Valley's pig iron.[10] As a result of these competitive pressures, one more of the valley's iron companies was sold upon the foreclosure of its mortgage. At the same time two of the firm's stacks were torn down.[11] Placed on the defensive, some of the firms attempted to improve their furnace facilities, and all practiced the closest economies.

Efforts were made to obtain reductions in freight rates. Representatives of the Lehigh and Schuylkill iron firms made an appeal to the railroads for reductions in 1888 and shortly thereafter received some relief, but it was not sufficient.[12] Later another plea was made for further reductions in freight rates but without success.

---

[9] It is interesting to quote Adam Smith on a similar situation when, in 1776, he wrote: "People of the same trade seldom meet together, even for merriment and diversion, but the conversation ends in a conspiracy against the public, or in some contrivance to raise prices." Adam Smith, _An Inquiry into the Nature and Causes of the Wealth of Nations_, Modern Library Edition (New York, 1937), p. 128.

[10] American Iron and Steel Association, _Bulletin_, Vol. 18 (August 20, 1884), 210.

[11] _Ibid_. (April 16, 1884), p. 101; Vol. 19 (Sept. 30, 1885), 259.

[12] _Ibid_., Vol. 22 (April 4, 1888), 109; (April 18, 1888) 125; (May 9, 1888) 149.

About the same time the American Pig Iron Storage Warrant Company was established. The organizers of this company proposed to locate storage yards for pig iron on land leased from furnace companies and secondary storage yards at the leading points of consumption, such as New York, Philadelphia, and Boston.[13] Warrants, supposedly negotiable, were to be issued for any pig iron placed in storage. The system would presumably have enabled the weaker furnace companies to obtain working capital in times of need and consequently serve to smooth out the production of pig iron over the business cycle.[14] It seems, however, that most furnace operators in the North and West were prejudiced against such a scheme, and consequently the storage firm played an insignificant role in the years that it operated. Most of its business was done with southern producers.

One reason for the lagging interest in the warrant system arose from the geographical location of the furnaces, the very nature of which provided protected markets for the different iron companies. The further fact that the most economical transportation routes from many furnaces to market quite often did not pass by the few warehousing sites restricted the use of the service. Also consumers had developed traditional preferences in their purchasing of iron; they preferred to buy directly from the original producer. Furthermore, because the yards handled only foundry iron, the few Bessemer steel producers, many of whom controlled

---

[13] _Ibid_., Vol. 23 (Jan. 30, 1889), 29; (Feb. 6, 1889) 35.

[14] _Ibid_.

all the processes of production, had no occasion to use the warehousing services. When they did buy iron, it was generally purchased in large lots directly from the producer. Finally, there was a widespread belief that the institution was likely to introduce a new speculative feature in the iron trade, a factor that led many of the merchant furnace companies to avoid depositing their iron with the storage company. Even the New York Iron and Metal Exchange was viewed as an agency that would depress iron prices, and rumors circulated in the industry that the exchange was in the hands of a bear clique.[15]

In 1890, after the conditions of trade had improved somewhat, furnaces were relighted, many having been out of blast for several years, and momentarily the flow of pig iron from the Lehigh Valley was increased. But the prosperous conditions were quite short-lived, and in the next few years furnaces were blown out again, wages were reduced, mines shut down, and output sharply restricted.

A few days before the year 1893 ended, the Lehigh Crane Iron Company announced its insolvency. Failure, it was claimed, arose from heavy bad-debt losses. Thus, the oldest anthracite iron company in the Lehigh Valley had failed to meet the test after fifty-three years of active participation in the merchant pig iron trade. But that failure was not the last; others were to follow.[16] By December 31, out of forth-three

---

[15] Ibid. (Feb. 27, 1889), p. 60; (Oct. 23, 1889) p. 293; Vol. 39 (Feb. 1, 1905), 19. Clark, History of Manufactures in the United States, II, 306 f.

[16] Ibid., Vol. 27 (Dec. 20, 1893), 361.

furnaces available for pig iron production in the Lehigh Valley, only twenty-two were in blast.[17]

Throughout these difficult years, The Thomas Iron Company had been one of the most uniformly prosperous companies in the district. The company had always been able to operate some of its furnaces, even during the periods of greatest depression.

In the 1880's The Thomas Iron Company, through the influence of its continual success and by reason of its predominance in production, being outranked only by the Edgar Thomson and Cambria iron works, became the "price leader" for the eastern foundry iron producers. For a number of years its monthly quotation letters were means by which foundry iron prices were established.[18] The very movement of The Thomas Iron Company's prices could dampen the hopes of many furnace owners who had hoped to blow in their furnaces with a rise in prices.[19]

But acting in this manner as the "price leader" did not mean that The Thomas Company had a free hand in setting of prices as a

---

[17]American Iron and Steel Association, Statistics of the American and Foreign Iron Trade for 1893 (Philadelphia, 1894), p. 45.

[18]American Iron and Steel Association, Bulletin, Vol. 20 (Jan. 20, 1886), 19; (Dec. 15, 1886) 333. The following report provides evidence of the "leadership" alluded to above.

"The Thomas Iron Company has announced its prices for pig iron for the year 1887. The larger portion of the trade in the Eastern States has been waiting for this even for some weeks. To a certain extent Vice President B. G. Clarke, who is managing director of the Thomas Iron Company, has made the prices for iron for years. He is looked upon as an authority in the trade, and his judgement has proved to be very good and especially so during the past few years."

[19]Ibid.

monopolist might have. Though the firm's established price was followed by other firms, the price was quoted only after careful consideration of the flow of pig iron into the market from southern and western furnaces. Almost any foundry iron could be readily substituted for "Thomas" foundry iron. Thus, the competitive threat from outside furnace probably resulted in a price that would keep that competition at a minimum.[20] Certainly the market was not controlled by the firm. Later, as the competitive pace was increased, The Thomas Iron Company had even less influence on the price of foundry iron. By 1888 the firm's officers had to concede that the troubled trade conditions had made it most difficult for the firm to compete with the furnaces located in the South and West. Because of the growing danger from those sources, the firm's management became active participants in the organized effort among the furnace companies

---

[20] Ibid., Vol. 27 (Feb. 8, 1893), 43. The following report from the Bulletin provides some idea of the influence of southern pig iron on the northern market.

"But what was perhaps the most shocking revelation to Northern pig iron producers was the report of shipments North and East from Southern furnaces. An exceptionally well informed dealer in pig, and owner of a stock in two of the best known Northern furnaces, was asked the day before the results of our investigations were published how much Southern pig iron he thought had come north of Pennsylvania and east of Ohio to compete with Eastern brands within a year, and his reply, after some thought was: 'Well, perhaps as much as 20,000 tons - probably less.'

"His surprise the next day at learning that the total was fully 100,000 tons was only equaled by the astonishment of the entire Eastern pig iron industry. It is sufficient, in order to wind up the reminiscence, to add that the late B. G. Clarke, then at the head of the Thomas Iron Co., marked Lehigh No. 1 iron down from $20 to $18 per ton after reading the report, which, as iron prices went, meant that the showing of an unexpected competition from Southern pig iron manufactures had knocked prices of Northern irons off 10 per cent. within twenty-four hours."

to obtain reductions in railroad rates.[21]

Sales

Despite its reputation as a producer of excellent foundry iron, and its leadership in the eastern market, The Thomas Iron Company gradually began to suffer a relative decline in its share of pig iron sales. Once the company's sales had equaled 3 percent of all the pig iron consumed in the United States; by 1892 the proportion of the firm's sales to the nation's total consumption had been pared to 1.4 percent. Thus, as the nation's consumption of pig iron had increased, the firm's sales had not grown proportionately. The statistics indicate further that national consumption had increased by approximately 272 percent, but the company's sales had only risen by 192 percent.[22]

Probably the most outstanding feature of the change, as suggested by an analysis of iron sales and production statistics, is the limited but relatively successful resistance the firm maintained against the early competitive instrusions of the southern pig iron producers. But it appears that, while the firm was capable of meeting southern competition for some time, it was incapable of resisting the further encroachment on its trade made by steel firms.

Between 1876 and 1880 the company's sales increased from 47,283 gross tons to 91,241 tons, or 93 percent. The nation's consumption of

---

[21] Ibid., Vol. 22 (April 4, 1888), 109.

[22] American Iron and Steel Association, Statistics of the American and Foreign Iron Trade for 1892 (Philadelphia, 1893), p. 40. The Thomas Iron Co. Fin. Rec., pp. 80 ff.

pig iron, through the same period, increased only 63 percent. Certainly the difference between the two figures represents a commendable accretion in sales for the company despite the rise in southern competition. One must also remember that the gain in sales was made during a period of depressed trade conditions.

In the next two years, 1881 and 1882, the company's sales increased again, but this time the gain in sales was not quite as expansive as the increase in consumption. The sales were raised from 91,241 tons to 109,854 tons, a 20 percent increase. Meanwhile the nation's consumption of pig iron had risen to a level 24 percent higher than the consumption in 1880.

During the depression of 1883 and 1884, the company's sales declined approximately 15 percent, but consumption of pig iron dropped by a like amount. The company had succeeded in holding fast to its proportion of the market despite the further influx of southern pig iron into the eastern market. Relative to the position of a number of other firms in the Lehigh Valley, The Thomas Iron Company achieved a commendable record in these two years. Many of the other companies had to blow out all of their furnaces, and several furnaces were sold, under foreclosure proceedings.

Through the next three years, 1885 through 1887, the nation's consumption of pig iron increased about 61 percent; The Thomas Iron Company raised its sales by 80 percent. The expansion in the company's sales at this time seems to offer evidence of the management's ability to meet southern competition in the sale of foundry iron. The next few years, however, brought a reversal of that trend as the company's sales began to lag behind the aggregate consumption of pig iron.

Between 1887 and 1890, the year of the Baring crisis, the company's sales were enlarged by 13,547 tons, an expansion of 8 percent. But the consumption of pig iron, in the very same period, had increased approximately 20 percent. If the full span of years from 1887 to 1892 is considered, there is an even greater difference arising between the two items. After 1890 The Thomas Iron Company's sales declined rather sharply, despite the continued expansion in the over-all consumption of pig iron. The difference in this instance was an increase in national consumption of 37 percent and a decline in the firm's sales of 19 percent.

The change seems to have arisen more from the relatively rapid expansion in the production and use of Bessemer steel rather than the further growth of southern competition. By 1892 approximately 50 percent of the pig iron produced in the nation was converted into Bessemer steel. From 1880 to 1892, the production of that steel had been increased approximately 200 percent. But The Thomas Iron Company did not share in the growth of pig iron sales to steel-converting companies. The reason for the company's failure to share in these gains can be explained by the fact that the firm failed to find sources of ore that would meet the chemical qualifications for such pig iron. Although other firms in the Lehigh Valley were producing Bessemer iron with Lake Superior or imported ores, The Thomas Iron Company continued to produce only foundry and forge iron. While it had prepared a furnace to produce Bessemer pig iron in

1880, no large quantities of the iron were ever produced.[23]

But the failure to meet the growing demand for Bessemer pig iron seems to have been only one of the more important reasons for the relative decline in the company's pig iron sales. Add to that failure the quite rapid development of integrated steel works, where pig iron was produced in conjunction with steel products, and there is further cause for the decline in the company's share of the market.

Tonnage sales throughout most of these years would seem to demonstrate that the management personnel had been quite successful in its operation of the firm, despite the relative decline in its share of the market. But when success is measured by the criterion of earnings, it is apparent that the firm had been somewhat less successfully operated during this second phase of its corporate life than in the first period. For example, aggregate earnings for the earlier period show a total of $4,870,742, for an average of $243,537 per year. During the second phase profits totaled approximately a million dollars less, being only $3,663,207, for an average of $214,622 per year.

The reduction in profits was partially due to the decline in the margin of profit taken on each ton of pig iron sold. While the average profit on a ton of iron sold between 1856 and 1875 was $6.96, the margin in the second period was only about one-third that figure, or $2.08 a ton. During the best year of this second phase, the sales of pig iron brought in fewer returns than in the best year of the first phase. In 1890,

---

[23]Min. Book - The Thomas Iron Co., p. 277.

though total sales reached 205,131 net tons, profits only amounted to $407,823.58 as compared to profits of $625,445.22 made on 80,415 tons in 1872.[24]

For the period as a whole, the earnings ratios were much lower than those of the first twenty years. From 1876 through 1885, the average rate of return on net worth was approximately 4.4 percent, and the return on fixed assets was 6.2 percent. In the next eight years, 1886 through 1893, the figures were slightly higher with the return on net worth being 5.4 percent and the return on fixed assets being 7.3 percent. The earnings for the first ten years were lower because of the depressed trade conditions during the first four years when no profits were received. In the second period there was only one profitless year, 1893.[25] The profit figures and the ratios referred to are provided in Table 17.

If the comments on contemporary sources are any measure of conditions of the times, the lower profits earned by The Thomas Iron Company were not uncommon. By comparison with profit figures for other types of business activity, the management had proved itself quite as capable as other managers.[26] However, there is one problem posed in the use of

---

[24]The Thomas Iron Co. Fin. Rec., pp. 63 and 132.

[25]*Ibid*., pp. 136 ff. The profits in 1891 and 1892 were understated by approximately $134,384.57 and $46,970,91. The reason for the understatement was that certain capital improvements were charged to the cost of producing pig iron. One must remember, however, that all of the company's profit figures were overstated because all extraordinary improvements were charged to the single year of the expenditure.

[26]Gras and Larson, *Casebook in American Business History*, pp. 720-22. Clark, *History of Manufactures in the United States*, II, 171 f. Statistics on profits of various types of business presented by Gras and Larson

TABLE 17

PROFIT AND RATE OF RETURN ON NEW WORTH
AND FIXED ASSETS, 1876-93

Year	Profits	Percent Return Net Worth	Percent Return Fixed Asset	Dividend as Percent Return on Common Stock (Par value)
1876	($58,875)[1]	-	-	2.0
1877	($506,660)	-	-	2.0
1878	($26,949)	-	-	Passed
1879	($3,417)	-	-	Passed
1880	$464,464	12.0	18.0	4.0
1881	299,213	8.0	11.0	8.0
1882	304,186	7.0	10.0	9.0
1883	332,596	8.0	11.0	10.0
1884	195,633	5.0	6.0	10.0
1885	196,889	4.0	6.0	8.0
1886	247,782	5.5	7.5	8.0
1887	195,101	4.4	6.0	10.0
1888	252,951	6.0	7.0	10.0
1889	376,185	8.0	11.0	10.0
1890	410,944	9.0	12.0	11.5
1891	302,191	6.0	9.0	8.0
1892	186,072	4.0	5.5	9.0
1893	($1,055)	-	-	6.5

1. Losses in Parentheses.

Source: The Thomas Iron Company Financial Records for Fifty Years, pp. 80 ff.

these statistics. No depreciation charges were used in the firm's accounting of its profit; thus the profit figures, for managerial decisions, were probably somewhat misleading. All of the company's property was continuously carried on its books at original cost. No adjustment was made to account for wear and tear on the equipment or for changes in the price level or replacements costs.

The rapid growth in the number of new blast furnaces in Allegheny County, Pennsylvania, in Ohio, and in Alabama indicates that profits from smelting iron ore were probably consideably higher in other sectors of the nation than in the Lehigh Valley. For example, it was reported that the earnings of Carnegie's company, between 1881 and 1888, ranged between 20 and 69 percent.[27] But that company's record is an individual case, and it cannot be said to represent all the firms in the area. The only generalization that can probably be made is that profits outside the eastern district were more attractive to investors. The evidence offered is the continual growth of the number of blast furnaces in the new areas and the gradual reduction of the number of furnaces in the older iron areas.[28]

The lower profits earned by iron firms in the eastern district

---

show a range between 12 and 2 percent during the eighteen years. New England textile mill profits covered the whole range. National banks earned between 9.5 and 4.8 percent.

[27] Ibid., p. 721.

[28] During this period the number of furnaces in the Lehigh Valley fell from fifty-one to forty-three. In Allegheny County the number of stacks increased from eleven in 1875 to twenty-seven in 1893. See Montague, "The Pig Iron Industry in Allegheny County, 1872-1931," p. 15.

offer some indication of the competitive character of the iron industry during the years. Up to this period, the costs of entry into the industry were not high enough to diminish competition; thus, with the increase in the number of blast furnace profits were reduced to the level of other trades.

Investment expenditures and Dividends

The Thomas Iron Company's average annual profits differed only by $28,915 between the first and second phases of the corporation's history; there was, however, a considerable difference in the application of those funds between the two periods. During the second period, the reinvestment of earnings was reduced considerably, and dividend payments were increased substantially. Chart XIII provides a comparison of the application of funds between the two periods.

Neither the board members nor the stockholders seemed to have demonstrated any great concern about making extensive investments; nor did the investments, when they were made, appear to have been part of a positive investment policy. No suggestions for modernization of plant facilities or integration with other works were made, and little concern was evinced about the future of the merchant furnace industry. Dividend payments and investment expenditures seem to disclose the prevalence of a mood of conservatism and self-satisfaction among the individuals concerned with the operation of the venture. The dividends received by the stockholders sustained them in a mood of apathy.

No investments were made in new plants, real estate, or mines between 1876 and 1880. Only in the latter year did the board of directors

CHART XIII

APPLICATION OF FUNDS IN TWO PERIODS

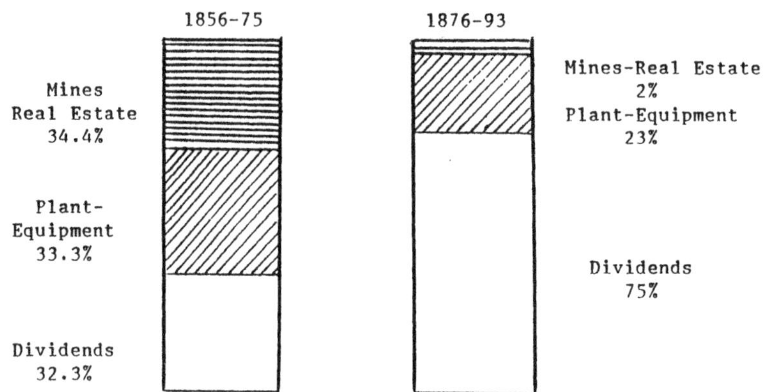

Source: The Thomas Iron Company Financial Records for Fifty Years, pp. 5 ff.

advise the purchase of an additional 125 acres of ore lands in Lehigh County. The total cost was $23,658.44. With the purchase of that property, the iron company held twenty-three ore sites and three limestone quarries having a total value of $500,000.[29]

Not until 1882 was the next investment made when the firm purchased the stock and property of the Ironton Railroad, and the Island Park furnace located in Glendon. The total expenditure in this instance was $375,000.[30]

The Ironton Railroad was a short feeder line that ran from the

---

[29]The Thomas Iron Co. Fin. Rec., p. 95.

[30]*Ibid.*, p. 102.

nearby ore fields west of the furances at Hokendauqua. The purchase was paid for with funds received from the sale of the last coal mine owned by the firm, the Sugar Notch Colliery, which had been sold to the Delaware and Hudson Coal Company.[31] The ownership of the railroad placed the company in control of its ore and limestone shipments from its nearby mines. More important, as the area's cement industry expanded, the railroad proved to be a lucarative source of income, although at the time the road was purchased the cement industry was in its infancy.

With the purchase of the Keystone or Island Park furnace, it appears that the board of directors had once again worked quite closely with certain stockholders of The Thomas Iron Company's board, as in the case of the Alburtis furnaces. The Island Park furnace had originally been built in 1876 by Easton people, and it had been operated for several years by Abraham Boyer and Company. Later, in 1879, the furnace was purchased by D. Runkle & Company, a firm which had been organized by a group of directors of The Thomas Iron Company, including Daniel Runkle, John Knight, Samuel Thomas, and B. G. Clarke. The furnace was put in blast on two different occasions by this company; then it was decided to sell the works to The Thomas Iron Company.[32]

Unlike the firm's earlier purchase of the Alburtis furnace in 1868, when payment was made in the stock of the company, Island Park furnace was paid for with borrowed funds. At this juncture, the board of

---

[31] Min. Book - The Thomas Iron Co., p. 296.

[32] Ibid., p. 298. The Thomas Iron Co.: Papers and Doc., p. 31.

directors demonstrated less concern about borrowing capital and the note holders' prior claim on future income. Evidently, as an established business firm, it had capital more readily obtainable than when it was a new firm in 1868.

The "new" furnace at Glendon was only 65 feet high and had a rated annual capacity of 12,000 tons, or an average daily output of 35 tons. Furnaces of more modern design were capable of producing at least twice that tonnage, if not more, in a single day. The furnace was quite as productive as most of the other furnaces owned by the company.[33]

The last major investment made during this period was the purchase of a second iron company's furnaces, the Saucon Iron Company's property situated in Hellertown, Pennsylvania. The Saucon Company had been organized in the prosperous years of the war period, and with the continuous growth in the demand for pig iron, it had been able to construct two furnaces both over 60 feet high and fabricated with iron shells. These were the first of such works in the Lehigh Valley. Over the company's ten years of operation it had also purchased ore fields in nearby Friedensville and Hellertown and had built a short railroad line in order to connect the Friedensville ore field with the North Pennsyvlania or Philadelphia and Reading Railroad. That railroad ran past the Saucon Company's furnaces in Hellertown. The transportation of ores from the other mines in Hellertown was done by mule and wagon.

When the flush of prosperity disappeared in the 1870's, the Saucon

---

[33] American Iron and Steel Association, <u>Directory of the Iron and Steel Works of the United States</u> (Philadelphia, 1880), pp. 21 f.

Iron Company ran into bad times, and the furnaces were idle for long periods of time. Upon the return to more prosperous conditions in 1879, the owners, evidently anxious to rid themselves of their burden, approached the Bethlehem Iron Company with an offer to sell the Hellertown works.[34] At that time the Bethlehem Company found it inexpedient to make the purchase, although it did purchase a furnace in Bingen at this time. Meanwhile, the Bethlehem Company commenced the construction of two new furnaces at its Bethlehem site.[35]

Four years later, in 1883, the Bethlehem Iron Company was offered the opportunity to buy the Saucon works once again, and at the same time The Thomas Iron Company was invited to submit a bid. By that date, despite the improved market conditions, the Saucon Iron Company had been unable to earn enough to cover interest charges on its debt. For a second time the Bethlehem Iron Company turned down the opportunity to buy this plant, but The Thomas Iron Company, after extended deliberation and the submission of several bids, purchased the property.[36]

The purchase was made at a sheriff's sale for $1.00, but the property was subject to a heavy mortgage which The Thomas Iron Company agreed to guarantee.[37] Presumably the objective in purchasing the property was

---

[34]Beth. Iron Co. Bd. Dir. Min. The offer that was made was $425,000. Payments were to be $125,000 in cash and a guarantee of the Saucon Iron Company's bonds outstanding of $300,000.

[35]*Ibid.*

[36]*Ibid.* Min. Book - The Thomas Iron Co., p. 310.

[37]American Iron and Steel Association, *Bulletin*, Vol. 18 (Dec. 24, 1884), 331. The Thomas Iron Co. Fin. Rec., p. 114.

to secure control of the ore fields owned by that company, though The Thomas Company managers planned to improve the furnaces and put them in blast once again.[38]

There was some difference of opinion among the board of directors in regard to the purchase of the property, although most of the board members supported the investment. Among the financial records at hand, there are two original letters which provide some insight into these differences of opinion. These same letters express something of the general outlook of the board of directors, and for that reason they are inserted below. The first letter was written by William Marsh, a member of the board of directors.

> Referring to the purchase of Saucon Furnaces I have about decided that I cannot vote for it. I think we better 'let well eno [*sic*] alone.' I am sure it is safer for us in the unsettled condition of the Iron [*sic*] business of late years, not to get too much extended. I think there is a little *pride* on the part of some of our Directors to spread out & be known as the *largest* concern of the kind in the U. [*sic*] States. 'Pride sometimes goes before a fall.' I don't want to fall. No, let us look well after what we have and we shall be able to pay regular dividends, and be easy financially.[39]

B. G. Clarke, director and sales agent in New York City, wrote the second letter. Unlike William Marsh, Clarke appears to have been quite satisfied with the idea of purchasing the Saucon Company's furnaces. But, like Marsh, Clarke sought assurance that the purchase would not result in the elimination of regular dividend payments.

---

[38] *Ibid.*

[39] The Thomas Iron Co. Fin. Rec., p. 114.

> I presume the only subject of importance that will come up is the purchase of the Saucon furnaces.
>
> I will be certainly satisfied with either decision you arrive at to purchase or not, if however you think we can continue to pay dividends and also to pay for the Saucon property then would advise doing so.
>
> I feel as tho [sic] there is much value in good Lehigh Valley property and if properly handled there is a future in it but all depends who runs it.[40]

There were enough stockholders in agreement with Clarke's opinion on the Saucon furnaces, and the property was taken into the accounts of The Thomas Iron Company. The financing was done with a cash payment of $50,880 plus the payment of the Saucon Iron Company's outstanding bonds of $249,120. The bonds were to be paid off with future earnings. The acquisition of this property made The Thomas Company the largest producer of pig iron in the East. The total capacity of its eleven works was rated at somewhat less than 200,000 gross tons per year.[41] The company's furnaces, however, were old and not very large.

From this date to 1921 The Thomas Iron Company did not make any further extension of its facilities, and a few short years later it began to reduce the number of furnaces it owned. Throughout these years practically nothing was done to modernize the facilities, and when attempts were made to improve the works, they were done in a piecemeal fashion. As one contemporary commentator observed:

> Its management [The Thomas Iron Company's] has been eminently conservative, and to outward appearance even 'old fogy.' But few alterations have been made in the last 20

---

[40] _Ibid_., p. 115.

[41] _Ibid_.

> years. Only one of the furnaces is equipped with firebrick stoves, and the modernizing of the whole plant is only begun.[42]

The inability of the firm to adapt its operations to the changed data with sufficient speed and thoroughness to avoid a decline in earning power cannot be explained merely by saying that the board of directors and the management were conservative or "old fogy." Instead it is necessary to discover what made these men hesitate. Why were their reactions to the changed conditions so conservative? Perhaps they thought it was impossible to adapt to the changed conditions. Or possibly it was thought that the adaptation could be made, but because of the nature of their capital goods and the company's inability to finance the change, the adjustment could not be made. Or possibly they were just not alert, being bound by tradition and habit. However, before an answer is offered to this question, it is necessary to consider further aspects of the firm's business activities.

Dividends paid to the stockholders from 1876 to 1893 were considerably greater than the total dividends paid out in the first twenty years. The absolute amount was larger, the relative return on capital stock was lower, for more shares were in the hands of the stockholders. The larger absolute payment is associated with the much lower rate of reinvestment already discussed and reflected in Chart XIII on page 336.

In contrast to dividend payments of the earlier period, there were six years in which dividends exceeded profits, 1876, 1877, 1884, 1887,

---

[42] American Iron and Steel Association, Bulletin, Vol. 23 (June 5, 1889), 148.

1892, and 1893. During the first period only one dividend payment exceeded earnings. Dividends were passed twice, in 1878 and 1879, years when the company was recovering from losses incurred through the purchase of the South Mountain Iron Company.

The cash dividends that were paid ranged from 2 percent on the par value of the capital stock in 1876 and 1877 to 10 percent in 1883, 1884, 1887, 1888, and 1889. The average dividend payment was equal to 7.93 percent return on the par value of the stock. In the first twenty years, 1856 through 1875, the average return had been equal to 10 percent on the par value of the stock. However, as there had been sizable amounts of stock issued in lieu of cash dividends, the return on the original investment during this period was considerably larger than in the first twenty years.[43]

Though the payment of dividends per share of stock was lower, it was evidently quite acceptable to the stockholders, for when offered the opportunity to sell their shares to an English syndicate in 1889, they voted to withhold sale unless a price equivalent to $87.50, the book value of the stock, was paid. At that time the par value of the 40,000 shares of stock was $50.[44] A 10 percent return on $50, the rate of return the stockholders had received for several years, seemed to have been adequate. However, it is quite apparent, from the letters quoted previously and the policy of maintaining dividend payments whatever the income,

---

[43]The Thomas Iron Co. Fin. Rec., p. 269.

[44]*Ibid.*, p. 129E.

that the stockholders preferred continual dividend payments in the present to reinvestment in new equipment which might have increased future profits. Their views on dividends were attuned to short-run considerations. The uncertainties of the future evidently gave the owners of the firm little concern.

Management

Samuel Thomas remained in the office of the president of the corporation until 1887. From the available information it is quite difficult to determine the amont of time he spent at this job, his function, and how he influenced the development of the firm. From the minute book records and scattered other sources, it can only be surmised that he acted as the policy administrator and policy adviser. While the board passed on policy, it was Samuel Thomas who provided the guidance and technical advice on policy matters. He did not seem to have a great deal to do with the actual operation of the furnaces; a general manager was appointed to handle that work. Actually the position of the president seems to have been equivalent to that of today's board chairman. Samuel Thomas's responsibility and value to the firm appears to have been quite important, for his salary was continuously increased until it reached $12,000.

In retrospect there is little that can be said in praise of Samuel Thomas's record during these years. There was practically no change in the management of the firm or in its direction over that prevailing in the last ten years of its first period of operation. No new furnaces were built, though several old works had been purchased. There was no attempt made to modify the operation of the firm in order to meet the change taking place in the iron industry. Furthermore, the larger the firm bcame, the wider the web of nepotism spread. As more furnaces were purchased, more supervisory personnel were required, and either members of the Thomas family, or near relations, secured those positions.

The year before Samuel Thomas resigned from the office of president, the assistant to the president and purchasing agent was Edwin Thomas, Samuel's son. The general superintendent or general manager was John Thomas, the president's brother, while the assistant general superintendent was Edwin Mickley, Samuel Thomas's brother-in-law. The superintendent of the Hokendauqua works was William R. Thomas, John Thomas's brother-in-law. The superintendent of the Lock Ridge, Keystone, and Saucon furnaces was David H. Thomas, John's son. Supervisor at the Saucon works was Horace Boyd, the brother-in-law of Edwin Thomas. Also, the accountant at the Easton office was related through marriage to Samuel Thomas. At the New Jersey mines James Mickley, brother-in-law of Samuel Thomas, acted as superintendent.

There is no positive proof that this nepotism had anything to do with the operation problems that arose, but the records indicate that there was a continuous conflict among the board of directors over the management of the furnaces.

In 1880 John Thomas, then general manager of all the furnaces, was called before the board of directors to explain the decline in the proportion of No. 1X pig iron produced by the furnaces.[45] No explanation is recorded; however, at the same meeting it was decided to hire a chemist in order to try to improve the output and maintain the quality of the company's foundry iron.[46] Meanwhile, John Thomas was relieved of his duties as furnace manager for a six-month period.

Four years later the production problem still lingered. The board of directors was still finding fault with John Thomas's management of the furnaces and the proportion of No. 1X iron being produced. Available statistics indicate that No. 2X and No. 2 plain foundry iron were continually produced in larger quantities than No. 1X foundry iron. However, one achievement was reported: an increase in the average daily output of the furnaces. Between 1880 and 1884 the average daily furnace output had been raised by 14 percent as compared to a slight decline in output in the first four years.[47]

When Samuel Thomas resigned in 1887, the board of directors relieved John Thomas of his duties for six months, and later, though he still retained his title of general manager, he was reduced to the position of managing the Hokendauqua furnaces.[48]

In 1898 when Benjamin Fackenthal was appointed president of the corporation, John Thomas resigned as general manager. Meanwhile, the

---

[45] Min. Book - The Thomas Iron Co., p. 285.

[46] Ibid.

[47] The Thomas Iron Co. Fin. Rec., pp. 80 ff.

[48] Min. Book - The Thomas Iron Co., O. 345.

furnaces he had been managing were still smelting more No. 2X and No. 2 plain foundry iron than No. 1X. By 1893 the average daily output of the furnaces had been raised another 18 percent. Output had been raised from 45.03 net tons a day to 53.45 tons, or 374.15 tons a week.[49] But by that date some western furnace operators were producing as much as 500 tons a week in their furnaces.

In the light of these rather poor furnace records and the delay in remodeling the works, it is interesting to note why Samuel Thomas resigned. According to the minute book, the cause for his resignation was the burden of other work. A year previous to his retirement he had taken a leave of absence to tend to the building of two blast furnaces in Alabama. Upon his retirement he continued in business as the vice-president of the Pioneer Iron and Manufacturing Company, which owned two blast furnaces in Thomas, Alabama. But even more important is the fact that these furnaces were of the most modern design. They were both iron shell furnaces, built to a height of 75 feet. Each furnace was operated with an automatic skip hoist, a closed furnace top, and regenerative stoves. Their product, foundry iron, was produced for sale in the open market, in competition with The Thomas Company's iron.[50]

The Pioneer works were certainly in advance of any facilities owned by The Thomas Iron Company, and they demonstrate that under the "right

---

[49]The Thomas Iron Co. Fin. Rec., pp. 83 ff.

[50]American Iron and Steel Association, The Iron and Steel Works of the United States (Philadelphia, 1898), p. 41. Colquhoun, "Notes on the Iron and Steel Industries in the United States," pp. 337 f. American Iron and Steel Association, Bulletin, Vol. 20 (June 9, 1886), 149.

conditions" Samuel Thomas was quite willing to adapt innovations to produce iron. The question is then raised as to why improvements on the older furnaces at Hokendauqua were not requested and carried out during Samuel Thomas's administration. Possibly he had been quite willing to introduce the new techniques, but he faced resistance from the board or his furnace superintendents. Possibly the investment of earnings in such a venture might have interrupted the regular dividend payments and the stockholders resisted any advance. Or perhaps Samuel Thomas saw no advantage in the change because the time and place did not offer the hope of any greater returns than the company was already receiving. With the unsettled conditions in the market, as long as profits could be earned without expensive renovations, there was little urgency to break away from habit and tradition.

When Samuel Thomas resigned, Benjamin Clarke, one of the original founders of the company and the sales agent for the firm in New York City, was elected as his successor. Clarke's acceptance of this administrative position brought several other changes in supervisory personnel, and the first extensive renovation of the furnace facilities was commenced. New hot-blast stoves were built, stock houses extended, compressors and boilers replaced at several plants, and new rolling stock purchased.

These changes were not major revisions, but they were the first step toward the establishment of a new investment policy. Unfortunately for The Thomas Iron Company, Benjamin Clarke was unable to carry out his plans to rebuild the furnaces. In 1892, while on a journey through

Europe, he died before those plans could come to fruition.[51]

Clarke's successor, John T. Knight, another of the original stock owners, proved to have an even shorter period in which to make any changes. Appointed to the office in October, 1892, Knight died within two months. With his death came the end of the management of the firm by the "old-timers."

The sixth president of the corporation was Benjamin F. Fackenthal, the first president to be selected from outside the ranks of the original stockholders. Fackenthal had grown up in the iron industry, holding his first job with the Durham furnace company which was owned by Cooper and Hewitt. While working for the company he had superintended the construction of what was then the largest blast furnace in the United States. By 1893, Fackenthal had had twenty-seven years of experience in the iron industry, but he had no experience in producing steel or rolled iron products. Fackenthal's business habits and traditions were those of the merchant furnace industry.

The change in management meant that the "old guard" had relinquished its control over the company's policy. By that date most of the original owners had either died or retired from active participation in the operations of the firm. Of the original twenty-six subscribers, only three were still alive in 1893; two of these died a few years later. Samuel Thomas was the single original founder that survived beyond the turn of the century. The life of the company, from that date forward,

---

[51]The Thomas Iron Co. Fin. Rec., _passim_.

was in the hands of men who had either inherited their claims to ownership or had purchased the same from one of the older stockholders. Most of these men were interested in other forms of business activity; thus, they did not give their undivided attention to the iron firm or its problems. A number of shares of stock were held in trust funds and were managed by disinterested parties.

Production Problems

Between 1876 and 1890, a peak production period, the company's total output of pig iron was raised from 52,956 net tons to 205,131 net tons, an increase of approximately 288 percent. This addition to output can be accounted for in a number of ways: the use of additional furnaces, an increase in the number of days that the furnaces were in blast, improved furnace facilities and practices, and the better selection and preparation of ores.

As the company owned three more furnaces by 1890 than in 1875, some portion of the increased output was accounted for by the larger total capacity. Furthermore, the average furnace output had been raised somewhat over the years. The improvements in average output per furnace was accounted for by the better selection of ores as well as the preparation of ores prior to their being used in the furnaces.[52] No portion of the

---

[52]American Iron and Steel Association, Directory of the Iron and Steel Works in the United States, pp. 21 f. The Thomas Iron Co. Fin. Rec., p. 230.

The three additional furnaces added approximately 41,144 net tons to the company's estimated capacity. The average daily output of the furnaces had been raised from 38.55 net tons per day to 53.15 tons, an increase of 37 percent.

increased output came from the adoption of new or modern furnace facilities. Moreover, the continued employment of anthracite coal hampered the adoption of the hard driving techniques used so successfully at a number of the coke furnaces in the West. Anthracite coal splintered under intense heat and caused a shifting in the furnace load. Apparently the greater part of the increased output resulted from the more intensive use of the available furnaces. For example, in 1876 the average number of the firm's furnaces in blast throughout the year was 3.7, but in 1890 the average was 10.12 furnaces.[53] There had been eight furnaces available for production in 1876 and thus only 46 percent of the company's facilities were operated that year. On the other hand, in 1890 approximately 92 percent of the furnaces were in blast throughout the year.

Though lake ores were used after 1882, they were never employed in significant quantities prior to 1893. The total consumption of these ores did not reach 9 percent of the total ores used until 1889. During the next three years the lake ore tonnage remained at 13 percent, and only in 1893 did the consumption reach 20 percent.[54] Later, as the cost of lake ores declined, the company continually increased its consumption, but lake ores certainly were not influential in the production of Thomas foundry iron prior to 1893.

Coke, like lake ores, was not consumed in large quantities prior to 1893. Though the company had first used that fuel in 1875, the

---

[53]The Thomas Iron Co. Fin. Rec., p. 230.

[54]*Ibid.*, p. 27.

consumption of coke was never more than 3 percent of the total fuel employed during these years. Throughout the long coal miners' strike of 1888, the company continued to employ anthracite coal, though more coke was purchased at that time than previously. Basically the reason for the continued use of anthracite was the price differential between the two fuels. The shorter haul for anthracite coal enabled the company to purchase that fuel at a lower price than they would have paid for coke. A further reason for the management's persistence in using anthracite coal was the furnace design. The company's furnaces had been designed for the use of anthracite coal, and when too much coke was employed, the operation of the furnaces was disrupted. Finally, the management held that the quality of the foundry iron that the firm produced could only be maintained with the use of anthracite coal.[55]

Production costs fluctuated with the business conditions, though the trend of the manufacturing costs generally moved downward, reaching a low of $12 a ton in 1893. This price represented a drop of 37 percent over the $18.99 cost in 1876.[56] The movement in the company's costs followed the general pattern of prices during the years; however, the company had improved its use of fuel and ores, providing a slight reduction in its costs. For example, fuel consumption per ton of pig iron was reduced 6 cwts., from 1 ton 13 cwts. to 1 ton 7 cwts. Also, ore consumption per ton of pig iron was reduced from 2 tons to 1 ton 16 cwts.[57]

---

[55] Ibid.

[56] Ibid.

[57] Ibid.

Generally the proportion of the total cost for each factor remained relatively stable throughout the eighteen years. Fuel costs made up approximately one-third of the total cost, while ore costs constituted roughly one-half. Sundry costs, which included labor, fluctuated between a low of 12 percent and 18 percent of the total costs. Limestone costs remained about 4 percent of the total cost. All of these figures indicate that the management had done little to improve the operation of the furnaces over the earlier period.

In no single year of the eighteen did the spread between the firm's costs and the prices it received compare quite so favorably with the best years of the first twenty. The most favorable cost-price spread, \$5.20 a ton, was obtained in 1880. By comparison, however, that figure was much less than the remarkable \$13.13 a ton the firm earned in 1867. In 1878 the spread was a mere 22 cents. The average difference between the cost and price was \$2.15 a ton, whereas earlier the comparable figure was \$6.44.[58] While the market structure of the industry required the firm to take the price established through the forces of competition, it might have done something about reducing the costs of production in order to widen that cost-price differential. The management, however, did not make a diligent effort to reduce the average costs of production. Instead, the management obtained larger total profits by producing a greater tonnage with more furnaces. Relative to the problems other Lehigh Valley iron firms faced in obtaining profits, perhaps the

---

[58] _Ibid._

management's ability to earn the profits it did entitled the group to some praise.

As the company extended its plant facilities and increased its total output, the firm's proportion of the total tonnage produced in the Lehigh Valley continually expanded. In 1876 the company produced 20 percent of the total. By 1893, after the number of furnaces in the area had declined from fifty-one to forty-three, 36 percent of the total pig iron production was produced in The Thomas Iron Company's furnaces. Relative to the expansion in output from the Bethlehem Iron Company's furnaces, the gains made by The Thomas Company were not quite as remarkable as they would appear. The Bethlehem firm had produced only 13 percent of the total iron output in the Lehigh Valley in 1876, but by 1893 its proportion had been raised to 35 percent. What was most important was that the product was turned out with only seven blast furnaces.[59]

Between the two companies, they produced 71 percent of the total pig iron output in the Lehigh Valley. The Bethlehem Iron Company,

---

[59]Beth. Iron Co. Bd. Dir. Min. The average furnace output for The Thomas Iron Company was 13,983 tons and 21,573 tons for the Bethlehem Iron Company. These figures have been calculated from total tonnage figures and the number of furnaces owned by the firms; thus, they offer only a rough approximation of the various outputs. It is a fact that neither company operated all of their furnaces during the year in question; thus the average could be quite different.

Crude as these figures may be, they do represent an apparent difference in the quality of the furnace design and practice at the two works. Descriptions of the furnaces indicate that the Bethlehem Iron Company had moved ahead with the changing times and had constructed probably the best equipped furnaces in the Lehigh Valley. See American Iron and Steel Association, <u>Directory of the Iron and Steel Works of the United States</u>, pp. 20 ff.; <u>The Iron and Steel Works of the United States</u>, pp. 8ff.

however, smelted pig iron for its own consumption, while The Thomas Iron Company produced foundry iron for the open market. Only when conditions of trade were slow did the Bethlehem Company sell its pig iron in competition with Thomas foundry iron. Generally the Lehigh Valley furnaces sold pig iron to the Bethlehem Iron Company.

Though The Thomas Iron Company did not achieve the same success in production that the Bethlehem Iron Company had, it seems to have had much less trouble with labor. During the eighteen years, as in the previous twenty, the company's furnaces were never shut down because of a labor strike or lockout. Other firms in the area were not quite so fortunate. The Bethlehem firm in particular was shut down several times by labor trouble. After a long and difficult strike period in 1883, Bethlehem Iron finally forced the Amalgamated Association of Iron and Steel Workers' local to disband.[60]

Probably the reason for The Thomas Iron Company's avoidance of labor problems rests with its rather feudalistic and paternalistic control over the community in which the furnaces were located. The company maintained workingmen's homes in the company town. At Hokendauqua there were about 175 homes of six rooms each, and all were rather substantially built. Each house was provided water pumped in by the company, and each tenant could obtain heating fuel at original cost from the company. The board of directors also built a school, a library, and a church which the local residents were supposed to attend. All 1,000 of the residents were

---

[60]American Iron and Steel Association, Bulletin, Vol. 17 (July 18, 1883), 193; (August 26, 1883) 226.

company employees. By owning all the property in the community, the company had secured the environment against the intrusion of "undesirable" elements, be they labor agitators or saloons. While such a policy would be considered rather paternalistic, it seems to have secured " a sober, steady, contented population." There was little turnover in the labor force, and in 186 fully seven-eighths of the company's employees were men who had been with the company for an extended period of time.[61]

Evaluation

In 1893, as the national economy slipped into another long period of depression, The Thomas Iron Company moved into a new phase in its development. The original founders of the corporation were no longer managing the firm, most of them having died, while the remaining few had retired from active participation in the firm's business. The future of the company had been placed in the hands of new managerial personnel. But what had the old managers left behind? Could it be said that they had managed the firm's business successfully, or had they failed?

Using sales, earngings, changes in going-concern value, and investment as criteria of successful management, it has been pointed out that during the firm's first twenty years, despite the rather slow adaptation of new technical developments, it was eminently successful by all other tests. But during the second period these criteria indicate that the managment was unable to accomplish quite as much as the management had

---

[61] *Ibid.*, Vol. 20 (June 23, 1886), 161. Mathews and Hungerford, *Lehigh and Carbon Counties*, pp. 502 ff.

in the first period. Everything seems to indicate that the firm had attained a stage of maturity and had entered into a phase of stagnation and decline.

Despite the upward trend in the company's sales throughout the years, the proportion of the nation's total consumption of pig iron which the company held began to diminish. The continual and rapid growth in the consumption of steel led to the development of integrated steel works. Increasing quantities of pig iron were carried to the converters in the molten state after having been prepared in the steel companies' own blast furnaces. Meanwhile, though foundry iron sales in the open market continued to grow, they did not keep pace with the more rapid growth in the consumption of pig iron in steel production. As a consequence of these changes, the economic opportunities for merchant furnaces continually contracted.

The continual expansion of foundry iron production in other more favored areas of the United States, especially in the South, made it more arduous to gain the rich rewards prevalent in the earlier era. Thus, though the company's aggregate sales were extended, profits per unit were not as high. The average annual earnings of the firm were below those of the first twenty years, and the earnings, as related to net worth and fixed assets, started to decline.

As dividends were paid almost every year, a much smaller proportion of available funds remained for reinvestment. The magnitude of reinvestment of earnings in mines, real estate, and plant facilities was considerably small relative to what they had than it had been earlier. The application of such funds for reinvestment totaled \$601,154, or an average annual expenditure of \$33,397. These expenditures accounted for only 25 percent of the funds applied for all purposes. Expenditures for new assets between 1856 and 1875 totaled \$2,389,478 for an average annual expenditure of \$110,473, or 77.7 percent of the funds applied for all purposes. Thus, on the basis of the magnitude of reinvestment as a measure of the firm's success, the management made a markedly poorer showing in the second phase of the company's history.

A decrease in the going-concern value of the firm has been suggested by the estimated value placed on the firm's stock when an English syndicate offered to buy the works in 1889. The board of directors had suggested a selling price of \$3,500,000, though many of the stockholders believed the price should have been set at \$4,000,000.[62] While the board had estimated the going-concern value at \$87.50 a share, the stockholders were quite sure it was closer to \$100 a share. The sale was never consummated, although the stockholders had agreed to sell at the lower figure. The only conclusion to be drawn from this turn of events is that the going-concern value was probably below the \$87.50 a share suggested by the board of directors.

Previously it was suggested that the reason for the board's failure to construct larger and more adequate works was a manifestation of the conservative nature of the board's personnel. Though there is no certain explanation for their conservative policy, there are several reasons that

---

[62]The Thomas Iron Co. Fin. Rec., pp. 129A ff.

might account for it. First, it is possible that the directors and the managers, after long years of business activity, no longer had the zeal or the required ability to build and operate modern furnace facilities. But such an explanation cannot be verified, and it is weakened somewhat when one recalls that both Samuel and Edwin Thomas built two quite modern furnaces in Alabama at a time when they were serving as members of the managerial staff of The Thomas Iron Company.

A further reason for the board's continuing use of the older equipment rests in the very nature of the equipment. The furnace facilities used by the company were well built and still reasonably effective. The blowing engines were among the best in the industry, and the boilers and ovens were of ample capacity. With heavy sunk costs in this durable equipment, it apparently seemed more economical to the management to continue its use until fully depreciated. As long as the cost of producing pig iron with the old equipment was low enough to provide some profit, there was bound to be some hesitancy about rebuilding. To rebuild the works would have required the accumulation of new capital, as well as the development of new skills or personnel with the required know-how. Furthermore, larger furnaces would have required the development of new ore sources, for those then employed by the firm could not have supplied enough ore to keep the furnaces continually charged. Then, the ineffectiveness of anthracite coal in the taller blast furnaces would also have required the development of new fuel sources. All these problems, plus the cost of new capital, may have appeared an excessive burden relative to any gains that might have accrued.

Finally, after these many years of productive sales of an excellent quality foundry iron, these men had taken on the attitude of craftsmen. In order to continue to smelt the high grade foundry iron that their customers had become accustomed to receiving, the managers thought it necessary to continue production with the same types of furnace, fuel, and iron ore. Any change in the plant and its operation may very well have resulted in an inferior foundry iron. Having chosen their area of production, specialization in foundry iron, the management preferred to continue in the timeworn paths of the trade.

By taking this position, the board and the management avoided numerous new problems but left the company in a condition that eventually would result in its demise. The continuous expansion in the consumption of steel, and new facilities for the production of iron, the opening of new sources of raw materials, new markets, and the integration of production called for a reappraisal of the firm's progress and purpose for existing. Failing to make the reappraisal, the directors showed that they lacked the ability and the interest needed to adapt the enterprise to new areas of production in order to maintain the higher rate of return earned in the first period of the firm's development. The incompetence was not outwardly observable, and the fortuitous problems of the business cycle and the continuous payment of dividends disguised their failure to meet the challenge of the dynamic changes taking place in the iron and steel industry. The burden of making the decision to adjust or withdraw from production was shifted to the shoulders of those who would follow. Only later were the problems of tehnological change and organizational developments to strike the stockholders and the management as important economic facts.

CHAPTER X

OLD PATHS

Lehigh Valley Iron Production, 1876-1913

Just as The Thomas Iron Company had suffered a loss of prestige and position because of the growth of competition from western and southern iron producers, the Lehigh Valley had been replaced by Allegheny County in western Pennsyvlania as the leading iron producing center in the nation. The energetic western enterprisers brought about the rapid improvement of transportation facilities in the West after 1865, which stimulated the economic development of the area. The improvements in transportation attracted new settlers, reduced the costs of carriage for raw materials and finished products, and opened new markets for western manufactures. In response to these new opportunities and the introduction of the Bessemer process, iron producers proceeded to exploit the almost unlimited supplies of coking coal in Pennsylvania, Ohio, and Illinois as well as the low phosphorous ores of the Lake Superior district.

Gradually the locational pull of the Connellsville coal fields resulted in a concentration of new iron and steel production facilities in that area. Developed only gradually at first, Allegheny County's pig iron output suddenly experienced an unprecedented upsurge in production in the latter part of the 1880's and the early 1890's. Between 1872 and 1882, the county's output grew from 110,599 tons to 358,840 tons. But during this period the expansion in capacity had only elevated the region's share of the national output from 5.2 percent to 6.9 percent. In 1883, with the addition of one new furnace and the development of revolutionary furnace practices, the county had enough furnace capacity to produce 592,475 tons of pig iron, an output that was equivalent to 11.5 percent of the national output of 5,146,972 tons. No other region in the United States had produced as much iron that year. Over the span of twelve years Allegheny County's aggregate output had been increased 360 percent.[1]

During the ensuing depression the county held its own in iron production, and then, with the resurgence of business activity and the consequential growth in the demand of steel, five more blast furnaces were built by 1890. Using these additional furnaces, plus the other sixteen, the iron manufacturers turned out 1,497,786 tons of pig iron, a tonnage that was equivalent to 14.5 percent of the national output of 10,307,028 tons. In the next two years the county gained five new furnaces for a total of twenty-six. In 1892 these furnaces were employed to smelt 1,974,085 tons of pig iron, or 19.4 percent of the nation's total output of 10,255,840 tons. Thus, over the seventeen-year span, from 1876 through 1892, Allegheny County's aggregate output of pig iron had been increased over a thousandfold.[2]

---

[1]Montague, "The PIg Iron Industry in Allegheny County, 1872-1931," p. 15.

[2]Ibid. Between 1876 and 1892 there was an increase in output of 1435 percent. The national increase in production during the same period

The growth in the production of the Lehigh Valley's furnaces presents a sharp contrast to that development in Allegheny County. The local ore supply which had been used for so many years by the iron firms in the valley proved to be unusable for Bessemer pig iron production because of its high phosphorous content. Thus, the expansion of production was limited somewhat by an inadeauate supply of "good" ores for steel production, though the Bethlehem Iron Company, the lone steel producer in the region, solved its ore problem by venturing to import ore from Cuba, Canada, Africa, and Spain.[3] In 1890 the Bethlehem Company commenced the production of open-hearth steel, employing local ores to produce pig iron and substituting scrap metal for pig iron.[4] Most of the furnace companies in the area, however, persisted in relying upon the rapidly diminishing reserves of local ores. In some furnaces, these ores were mixed with small quantities of Lake Superior ore, but the product produced by the merchant furnace companies was generally a foundry or forge iron. A few companies remodeled furnaces in order to produce Bessemer pig iron from Lake Superior ores and coke.

Though beehive coke had proved to be superior to anthracite coal for smelting purposes, most of the furnaces in the valley, including the Bethlehem Iron Company's, were operated with a mixture of anthracite coal

---

had been approximately 390 percent. When the latter is compared to Allegheny County's expansion, one is able to perceive the phenomenal success of that county's furnace owners.

[3]Beth. Iron Co. Stockholders Min.

[4]*Ibid*.

and coke. The predominant fuel in the mixture was anthracite. The hard coal had to be used because the interior lines of most of the furnaces, with their high boshes, hindered them in the use of coke. On the other hand, the physical action of the anthracite coal in the furnace eliminated the use of the fast driving techniques so successfully employed in Allegheny County. As mentioned previously, anthracite coal tended to splinter and shift the furnace load when hard driving methods were employed.

Because of these physical limitations and an apparent unwillingness on the part of most of the furnace companies to reform their blast furnace methods in a revolutionary manner, there was a rather slow rate of expansion of pig iron production in the Lehigh Valley.[5] In 1872 the Lehigh Valley's total output had equaled 12.4 percent of the nation's total of 2,093,236 tons. By 1882, despite a growth in production from 449,663 tons to 609,338 tons, the valley's proportion of national output had declined to 11.7 percent; the output was still the largest for any single region. In 1883, with the decline in business activity, the production in the Lehigh Valley shrank absolutely and the district slipped into second place in the ranks of the leading pig iron producing regions. That year the local companies produced only 575,987 tons of pig iron, 11.1 percent of the nation's total.

The advent of the depression resulted in an elimination of some of

---

[5]Sweetser, "Anthracite Pig Iron," p. 32. Sweetser believed that the failure to improve blast furnace methods arose from the increased cost of anthracite coal and a misunderstanding of the operation of the furnace, in particular the quantity, velocity, and density of compression of the blast.

the old firms; then, in spite of the improved market conditions in the East, there was a gradual elimination of many old furnaces. By 1890 there were only forty-six furnaces still standing, five furnaces having been dismantled between 1882 and 1890.[6] In the latter year the Lehigh Valley furnaces that remained turned out 815,888 tons of pig iron, but now their production amounted to only 8 percent of the national output. In fourteen years, from 1876 to 1890, the Lehigh Valley iron producers had been able to increase their production by 212 percent, but their efforts were not enough to keep pace with the national expansion of 392 percent. Within the next three years the region's share of the total product fell to 5.3 percent of the total 7,979,402 tons produced in the United States. At the same time, however, Allegheny County's share had risen to 23.8 percent of the total.

The wide variance in the reported capacities of the furnaces in the two areas offers some idea of the greater efficiency of the furnaces, furnace facilities, and practices, as well as differences in the ore and fuel used. The reported capacity of the forty-nine furnaces in the Lehigh Valley in 1860 was estimated to be 664,700 tons, while in Allegheny County the fifteen standing furnaces were capable of producing 587,500 tons when used at 100 percent of capacity.[7] Dividing each of these tonnage figures by the number of furnaces provides an approximation

---

[6]Montague, "The Pig Iron Industry in Allegheny County, 1872-1931," p. 15. Six additional furnaces were constructed in Allegheny County between 1882 and 1890.

[7]American Iron and Steel Association, *Directory of the Iron and Steel Works of the United States*, *passim*.

of the average furnace capacity. The Lehigh Valley data indicates an average annual capacity of approximately 13,565 tons, while Allegheny County statistics represent an average output of 39,166 tons per year. A few years later, after the introduction of "hard driving" practices had been employed by several of the furnace operators in Allegheny County, the average was raised another 2,000 tons per annum. These figures, however, do not clearly indicate the actual conditions; some furnaces in both regions were more effeicient than others.

Between the depression years of 1893 and 1913, years that were interspersed with other depression periods in 1900, 1903, 1908, and 1910-11, there were rather extensive readjustments made in the Lehigh Valley's iron production. More of the old blast furnaces were withdrawn from production, never to be blown in again. Many of the companies, because of their very high costs of production, became marginal units, and each time business activity declined, they were forced to blow out all of their furnaces. Some of these works were held in idleness for several years in anticipation of more favorable price conditions, but when "good times" did not return, the furnaces were dismantled. Other firms, those that were apparently a little more efficient, junked some of their furnaces and replaced them with larger and more productive facilities. But, by 1913, after twenty years of readjusting to the changing conditions in the iron and steel industry, only twenty-two blast furnaces remained in the Lehigh Valley out of a total of fifty-one standing in 1876.

Between 1893 and 1895 the Lehigh Valley iron manufacturers suffered severely from the depressed conditions prevailing in the trade; many furnaces were blown out, and several companies went into the hands of receivers.[8] Then, in 1896, after having dismantled two of its furnaces and having operated another two works at a loss for several years, Glendon Iron Company, one of the oldest firms in the Lehigh Valley, withdrew from further production.[9] Meanwhile, the companies that had gone into the hands of receivers were reorganized, and a number of their furnaces were blown in once again by new firms organized about the remnants of the old firm.

Three furnaces were dismantled between 1893 and 1896. The following year six furnaces, which had been idle for several years, were demolished. Another six furnaces were dismantled in 1898, leaving only twenty-nine furnaces in the Lehigh Valley, some old and some new. Gradually other furnaces were abandoned, one at a time, as the iron trade fluctuated from good to bad times.

Over the years the management of the various iron firms was considerably changed as reorganizations took place and the combination movement developed.[10] The Glendon Iron Company, as already mentioned, had been dissolved; the Lehigh Iron Company became the Lehigh Steel and Iron

---

[8] American Iron and Steel Association, Bulletin, Vol. 27 (Jan. 4, 1893), 5; (April 19, 1893) 117; (June 28, 1893) 197; (Dec. 20, 1893) 361; Vol. 28 (Oct. 17, 1894), 237; Vol. 29 (Feb. 20, 1895), 45.

[9] Ibid., Vol. 30 (June 10, 1896), 133.

[10] Ibid., Vol. 33 (Feb. 15, 1899), 25. As one contemporary writer reported: "Year 1899 will be noted as the year in which consolidations of manufacturing and other companies and the organizations of trusts were of almost daily occurrence."

Company;[11] and the Bethlehem Iron Company, which had succeeded in meeting the challenge of economic change while others failed, was leased to the Bethlehem Steel Corporation in 1899 and later sold to the same company.[12] Meanwhile, the Crane Iron Company was taken over by the Empire Steel and Iron Company, a firm that had been incorporated in 1899.

The latter company had been organized "in keeping with the policy of the stronger iron and steel consolidations, to control their raw materials from the ground up." Capitalized at $5,000,000, the company presumably held assets originally valued at $7,250,000. The firm's properties consisted of blast furnaces in Pennsylvania, Virginia, North Carolina, and New Jersey, as well as ore mines in Virginia and New Jersey. The management and organizers of the corporation claimed that, through the company's close affiliation in the partial ownership of the Empire Coke Company situated in the Connellsville coal district, it was assured all the necessary coke supplies that might be required to operate its furnaces. Presumably the firm also had "friendly sources" ready to

---

[11] Ibid., Vol. 31 (Jan. 1, 1897), 5.

[12] Ibid., Vol. 33 (April 1, 1899), 67; (May 1, 1899) 77; Vol. 25 (Sept. 10, 1901), 131. Beth. Iron Co. Stockholders Min. By 1870 the Bethlehem Iron Company had commenced the preparation of facilities for the production of Bessemer steel; the first blow was made in 1873. Then, in 1887, the firm commenced the production of heavy forgings for naval contracts. Earlier, in 1879, the company had begun the production of open-hearth steel.

The Bethlehem Iron Company's works in 1891 consisted of thirty 5-ton open-hearth furnaces plus several 20- and 10-ton furnaces. Huge hydraulic forging hammers had been built as well as a large bending press for form armor plate. All of the firm's blast furnaces had been modernized, while traveling cranes were installed to handle the large quantities of raw materials. These works were compared favorably with establishments such as Manchester, LeCreuzot, and Krupp.

supply the firm with Lake Superior ores for the production of Bessemer pig iron.[13]

Actually the Empire Steel and Iron Company produced no steel, nor did it own any facilities for that purpose. The inclusion of steel in the corporation's title was probably employed to provide whatever possible advantages it might offer in the sale of the company's stock. But even more significant for the purpose of this study is the nature of the claims made in the brochure from which the above information was gathered. By suggesting that the corporation had an "affiliation" with a coke company and "friendly sources" were ready to supply Lake Superior ores, the brochure emphasized the growing burden carried by the merchant furnaces in the Lehigh Valley arising from the diminishing importance of the local sources of supply. The ore deposits there had become more costly to mine as the veins began to thin out. Also, anthracite coal became more costly because of its utility for home heating and the development of an effective combination in the anthracite coal trade.[14]

---

[13] _The Empire Steel and Iron Company: Furnaces and Mines_ (New York, 1899), pp. 1 ff. Popplewell, _Iron and Steel Production in America_, pp. 83 ff. Popplewell reported that Empire's plant in Catasauqua, Pennsylvania (the old Lehigh Crane works), was, in comparison to western furnaces, quite antiquated. The furnaces were small, the mineral content of the ore employed was relatively low, and the fuel consumption was high. The blowing engines were old, as were the hot-blast stoves. The pig iron was still cast in sand beds and moved about by hand, while the amount of labor employed to operate the works appeared to be very high. The one advantage the furnaces could claim was their proximity to the eastern markets.

[14] A more effective anthracite coal combination grew out of the railroad consolidations of the era and gradually led to the elimination of many small coal mine operators. See Jones, _The Anthracite Coal Combintion in the United States_, pp. 59 ff.

In spite of all the economic pressures and the wave of consolidations in the 1900's, The Thomas Iron Company remained under the same corporate name, and nearly all of its stockholders were lineal descendants of the men who had founded the company. Whether it was a sound policy or not, the board of directors of the firm continued to maintain the company's independence and the production of pig iron for the open market. By 1903, however, the company had abandoned several furnaces while continuing to operate, off and on, the nine remaining works, all of them rather inefficient units.

While approximately 50 percent of the forty-three works standing in the Lehigh Valley in 1893 had been dismantled by 1913, several furnaces had been replaced or rebuilt along more modern lines; consequently, the region was capable of producing 1,180,128 tons of pig iron the latter year. This output marked a 40 percent increase over the previous peak year volume of 815,888 tons produced by the greater number of furnaces in 1890. The average annual furnace output in 1913 was 53,642 tons as compared to 13,565 tons in 1880.[15] But the total output from the Lehigh Valley furnaces, in 1913, made up only 3.4 percent of the national total.

---

[15] American Iron and Steel Association, Bulletin, Vol. 40 (Feb. 1, 1906), 18. It should be noted that the use of the average obliterates the tremendous differences in capacity between the older merchant furnaces in the Lehigh Valley and the capacity of the more capacious and productive furnaces owned by the Bethlehem Steel Corporation. For example, in 1906 the steel company constructed a 90-foot furnace which was 22 feet at the bosh. The furnace was equipped with four of the most advanced hot-blast ovens available plus an automatic skip hoist. The rated capacity of the plant was 144,000 tons per year, either foundry or basic iron. If the demand fell for steel, the company could shift the furnace's output into the open market to compete with local merchant furnace products.

For the next seven years the same proportion was maintained; then, as more merchant furnaces were eliminated, the valley's proportion declined once again. By 1922 the major portion of the total iron produced in the Lehigh Valley was smelted in the Bethlehem Steel Company's seven blast furnaces.

For the purpose of contrast, and in order to suggest the further shifts in the locational pattern of the steel industry, the following information is submitted. While many Lehigh Valley furnaces had been eliminated during those twenty years, Allegheny County had had twenty new furnaces added to the twenty-seven already built by 1893. At the same time the county's share of the total product had risen until 1897 when the furnaces in that area produced 2,961,359 tons of pig iron. That production represented 27.6 percent of the nation's total output of 13,186,806 tons. After that year, as pig iron production expanded quite rapidly in northern Ohio and Illinois, Allegheny County, despite the addition of more furnaces and the continual extension of output, found its proportion of the total output had declined. From 1900 to 1915 the furnaces situated in Allegheny County produced only one-fifth of the total pig iron produced in the nation.[16]

The contrast in the rates of change in output between the Lehigh Valley and Allegheny County can be seen quite readily in Table 18 on page 373. The most interesting feature in the table is the contrast between an area in its developmental and rapidly expanding stage and a region

---

[16] Montague, "The Pig Iron Industry in Allegheny County, 1872-1931," p. 15.

TABLE 18

COMPARATIVE FURNACE AND PRODUCTION STATISTICS
LEHIGH VALLEY AND ALLEGHENY COUNTY
1894-1913
(Net tons)

Year	Lehigh Valley		Allegheny County	
	Production	Furnaces	Production	Furnaces
1894	251,109	41	1,981,671	26
1895	434,833	41	2,284,698	27
1896	429,156	41	2,292,131	27
1897	307,575	35	2,961,359	30
1898	300,460	29	3,361,465	30
1899	478,966	30	3,620,313	34
1900	610,621	29	3,468,061	34
1901	546,226	29	4,103,292	34
1902	580,101	29	4,737,975	40
1903	726,679	28	4,683,264	41
1904	510,757	29	4,874,083	41
1905	701,456	27	6,016,909	42
1906	722,100	27	6,341,425	47
1907	861,375	27	6,047,315	47
1908	526,911	-	4,356,747	44
1909	773,346	26	6,113,077	46
1910	850,360	26	5,928,051	47
1911	993,454	25	5,689,483	47
1912	1,066,316	25	6,791,235	47
1913	1,180,128	22	6,671,487	47

Source: E. N. Montague, "The Pig Iron Industry in Allegheny County, 1872-1931," Pittsburgh Business Review (Feb. 28, 1933), p. 15; American Iron and Steel Association, Statistics of the American and Foreign Iron Trade (1894-1913).

that has already reached maturity. In Allegheny County, during its early years of expansion, production was subject to very little fluctuation in the many periods of depression. In the Lehigh Valley, however, it is readily observed that the furnace companies had become quite vulnerable to the influence of the same business fluctuations. Even Allegheny County demonstrates its maturity in this manner in the data for later years.

By 1913 the economic justification for the continued operation and location of merchant furnaces in the Lehigh Valley had been considerably diminished. Their comparative advantages lost, many of the older furnaces fell into disuse, and only the high prices that would appear in the war years would permit the repair and temporary use of those still standing. Just as the other companies seemed to decay or falter, so did The Thomas Iron Company. Constantly the company's management seemed to avoid the important problem of adjusting the firm's facilities to meet the changing economic conditions. Exceedingly cautious and apparently not interested in moving "beyond the range of familiar beacons" to overcome the resistance that might be met in new areas of production, they trod the old paths. Meanwhile, the economic changes tended to reduce the earning power of the firm.

Sales, 1893-1913

In the year that B. F. Fackenthal was elected president of The Thomas Iron Company, the nation's consumption of pig iron had dropped considerably. As a consequence of this adverse development, the company found its sales of foundry iron reduced materially, and integrated steel mills, in some instances having enough capacity to produce all the pig iron they needed and more, were selling their product in competition with merchant furnace companies. Then, as trade conditions improved and the consumption of pig iron began to pick up once again, the company's sales increased. Not until 1894, however, did the firm's sales figure surpass the peak previously achieved in 1890. In that year the company's sales representatives sold 194,550 tons of pig iron. But these sales were only gained as the nation's consumption of pig iron reached a new peak of 13,779,442 tons. Then after further fluctuations in the market, the company reached a peak in sales of 249,782 tons in 1906 and 1907. From that date until 1922, sales tended to move downward, only reviving briefly during the war years.

In each of the depression periods throughout the twenty years, the company's sales fell relatively more than the nation's consumption of pig iron declined and, as the years passed, the company became much more vulnerable to the changes in business activity. For example, between 1892 and 1894 the company's sales dropped 34 percent while the consumption of pig iron had fallen only 27 percent. Again, in the depression of 1907, the company's sales fell about 48 percent, but national consumption dropped only 38 percent. Finally, between 1910 and 1912, after a momentary decline in consumption in 1911, the nation's pig iron consuming industries absorbed 8 percent more pig iron than they had in 1910, but The Thomas Iron Company's sales dropped approximately 53 percent.

Reasons for the increasing vulnerability of the firm to the depressed trade conditions arose from the company's internal policy as well as the structural and technical changes in the iron industry. The company's internal problems will be discussed more fully later, but it may be helpful to look briefly at the external factors which continually subjected the firm to diminishing sales.

Upon investigating their problem, the board of directors recognized the fact that the growth of the integrated steel mills reduced somewhat the demand for their output. But more important, as the western steel mills extended their own blast furnace capacity, they withdrew their demand for the merchant furnace iron in their area; those furnace companies, in turn, began to send their pig iron into the eastern markets. As that iron entered the market, eastern prices fell and many buyers began to purchase western iron. Then, whenever the steel market slumped, the steel mills turned their furnaces to the production of foundry iron only to drag that market down further.[17]

In addition to the foregoing factors, there was a continual growth of iron production in Kentucky, Alabama, Virginia, and Tennessee. As the furnaces in those areas produced only foundry iron, and their own local market was somewhat limited, they shipped most of their iron into the northeastern sector. These furnaces the board of The Thomas Iron Company considered among the firm's worst competitors.[18]

Locally there were other competitors. Both the Swede and Warwick furnaces in the Schuylkill Valley had moved with greater speed than The

---

[17]The Thomas Iron Co.: Papers and Doc., pp. 119 ff.

[18]Ibid.

Thomas Iron Company to meet the new economic conditions; they had built furnaces capable of producing iron at costs which permitted them to compete with the furnaces located in the new regions of production.

The slump in sales following the depression of 1907 came in part from the growth in competition from the above sources, but there were other complicating factors. For several years the company had been selling pig iron for refining in the open-hearth furnaces of the Bethlehem Steel Company and United States Steel Corporation in Pittsburgh. In 1906 Bethlehem Steel increased its own pig iron volume tremendously by constructing a new furnace with a capacity of 144,000 tons per year of basic or foundry iron. Meanwhile, in 1907, United States Steel had taken over the Tennessee Coal and Iron Railroad Company and had turned that company's furnaces to the production of basic pig iron for the Steel Corporation's own furnaces. Both of these changes reduced the potential market for The Thomas Iron Company's product. And from that date to 1921 there was a continual secular decline in the company's sales volume.

By 1911 and 1912 the pressure on the pig iron market was increased as the steel companies finally brought their iron production into line with their steel capacity. In 1911 steel production was in excess of pig iron production, a development made possible through the wider use of open-hearth furnaces and the increasing use of scrap iron and steel in place of pig iron. These changes placed numerous merchant furnace companies in a precarious economic situation, The Thomas Iron Company included. Now the very survival of the merchant iron furnaces rested upon a change in the price of scrap metal or on a sudden and unprecedented increase in the demand for steel which would tax the supplies of scrap metal and the blast furnace capacity of the steelmakers. As this situation developed, The Thomas Iron Company was forced to sell its pig iron below its production costs.[19]

At the first obvious indications of the firm's infirmities in 1893, the management and the directors made no attempt to provide any remedies. They did not explore the possibility of producing new products, nor did they make any extended effort to obtain new business. But when the company's stock dropped to $21 a share in 1896, after an extended period of profitless business, the directors commenced an investigation of the firm's affairs.[20]

The findings of the investigation were that in the "struggle for survival" the firm would have to "crowd the other merchant furnaces out of the market with cheaper iron . . . ." To assure any success in such a struggle, the directors recommended the management use "the utmost economy and the greatest skill and care in operating the furnaces to get the best and greatest product."

All of this must have been quite obvious to the managers, but their problem was to make old and inefficient furnaces operate as effectively as the newer, more ideally located works. On this matter the committee suggested that little success could be achieved until the firm's furnaces

---

[19] The Thomas Iron Co. Fin. Rec., pp. 384 ff.

[20] Min. Book - The Thomas Iron Co., p. 445. The Thomas Iron Co.: Papers and Doc., p. 140.

were "put in the proper shape to do it."[21] There was no recommendation that the furnaces be rebuilt along more modern lines or that some form of integration be established; the only suggestion was to get the furnaces in shape. If cheaper iron could not be produced, it was believed inevitable that the firm would have to close.

Plant Improvements

The directors' plan for survival placed the management in a somewhat difficult position. Prior to 1895 the plant at Hokendauqua, the major works, consisted of six stone stacks that were probably as antiquated as any blast furnaces then in existence. Some improvements had been made in 1895 on stack Nos. 1 and 3, when the old stone stacks were replaced with furnaces having sheet iron shells, resting upon columns. Also new boilers and regenerative stoves had been erected. This reconstruction, however, did not go far enough.[22] To produce enough iron with these furnaces at a cost low enough to force competitors out of business would have been impossible. To compensate for this deficiency, the

---

[21] The Thomas Iron Co.: Papers and Doc., pp. 22 f.

In 1897 the Hokendauqua works consisted of No. 1 furnace, an iron shell furnace that had been rebuilt in 1894. No. 2 and No. 4 furnaces had been dismantled, while No. 3, No. 5 and No. 6 furnaces were old stone stacks with iron pipe hot-blast stoves. Furnaces No. 7 and No. 8, at Lock Ridge, were also old stacks with old blast ovens, but the Island Park furnace, No. 9, was constructed with an iron shell and equipped with regenerative stoves. In Hellertown, furnaces No. 10 and No. 11 were also built with iron shells, though the blasts were heated with old-fashioned iron pipe stoves.

[22] Min. Book - The Thomas Iron Co., p. 418. The Thomas Iron Co. Fin. Rec., p. 339.

rebuilding of the furnaces was continued under the guidance of B. F. Fackenthal, then general manager of all the plants.[23]

Unfortunately for the general manager, while the directors planned to improve the works, they chose to do it in a piecemeal fashion. Evidently they did not consider the firm's economic situation necessitated completing the project as soon as possible. The directors planned to finance the rebuilding program from the profits to be received in the future. As no profits had been earned in two of the three years prior to the study of the firm's situation, it was highly improbable that any great or immediate gains would be made toward improving the works. Gradually the company's sales did increase to the point where profits were adequate enough to finance the rebuilding program, but the work was very slowly completed.

In 1904 President Fackenthal recommended the installation of skip hoists for the rebuilt furnaces, the construction of traveling cranes to handle the ores, and the building of steel ore bins.[24] A year later, 1905, the board acted on the president's recommendations, at which time he was authorized to proceed with the suggested improvements. But again, this program proceeded at a very slow pace and it was not until 1906 that the Brown Hoisting Company was awarded the contract to build ore bins.

---

[23] _Ibid._, p. 450. In 1893 David H. Thomas, grandson of David Thomas, was general superintendent of the works. The later appointment of B. F. Fackenthal to the role of general manager indicates that the board was not prepared to thrust the more responsible work into the superintendent's hands.

[24] _Ibid._

The next year the furnaces were kept quite busy and little time was taken for improvements. Then when the panic occurred in 1907 any thought of expending large amounts of money on improvements were quickly dismissed.[25]

By 1911, the company had invested a total of $1,102,229.58 to repair and rebuild furnaces. The stock yards and trackage about the two new furnaces have been rearranged to facilitate the handling of raw materials. These expenditures, the board assured the stockholders, were justified because they helped reduce the cost of producing each ton of pig iron.[26] The only trouble was that the costs had not been reduced enough. There is evidence that the new furnaces provided additional capacity, but the continual changes being made at other furnaces reduced the relative advantages of these improvements.

While the condition of the iron market should have suggested that a radical change was necessary, the board of directors continued to believe there would always be a demand for its pig iron. As early as 1901 President Fackenthal had recommended that the board consider the construction of an open-hearth furnace in order to use the pig iron the furnaces produced. The suggestion was tabled.[27] Then, just prior to his resignation from the company in 1912, Fackenthal submitted a long report to the board of directors which pointed out that ultimately the economy

---

[25]<u>Ibid</u>. The Thomas Iron Co. Fin. Rec., pp. 318 ff.

[26]The Thomas Iron Co. Fin. Rec., pp. 328 ff.

[27]Min. Book - The Thomas Iron Co., p. 508.

would have to find some means to consume the major portion of the furnace product. At that time he suggested the construction of a cast-iron pipe foundry.[28] The board eliminated the report from the minutes and the matter was never presented to the stockholders for their consideration.[29]

The Thomas Iron Company's directors, it is quite evident, were not inclined to move too far in any direction, especially if the action would hold up the payment of dividends or might require additional funds, new organization, and new skills. Their policy was to concentrate the majority of any expenditures made on the furnaces at Hokendauqua. Meanwhile, the older furnaces were permitted to remain idle, except in periods of excessive demand when repairs and relinings were made in order to blow the furnaces in once again. After the panic of 1907 much less attention and money were given to those furnaces.[30] Irrespective of the rapid depreciation of the plant, dividends were paid regularly every year. In effect, the board was carrying out a process of disinvestment.

Production and Cost Problems

As the refurbishing of some of the furnaces was slowly pushed forward and new blowers and hot-blast ovens were installed, furnace capacity was gradually increased. Finally, after furnace No. 1 had been rebuilt and its height raised to 82 feet, an average daily furnace output of 100 tons a day was attained. When No. 3 furnace was finished, the average

---

[28]The Thomas Iron Co.: Papers and Doc., p. 55.

[29]Min. Book - The Thomas Iron Co., n.p.

[30]The Thomas Iron Co.: Papers and Doc., p. 52.

output was raised to 136 tons a day. But despite the gains made in volume, the average cost of production had not been reduced sufficiently to provide an advantageous cost-price relationship.

The management's failure to reduce the average cost of a ton of iron so that a wider margin of profit could be secured rests on a combination of developments. First and foremost, the furnaces were not equipped with labor-saving skip hoists, and the handling of materials in the yards was not done with overhead cranes or ore bridges. But the building of taller furnaces entailed the handling of larger quantities of ore and fuel which had to be done by hand in many cases.

The successful organization of an anthracite railroad combination raised the price of that fuel, while the use of taller furnaces necessitated the employment of more coke. As the coke had to be shipped in from Pittsburgh and West Virginia, with heavy transportation costs, the firm's fuel costs per ton of iron increased.

The company's nearby ore fields were being rapidly depleted, and Richard Mine, in New Jersey, was not productive enough to supply all the ore necessary to keep the larger furnaces charged. Furthermore, the machinery at that mine was antiquated, and the cost of mining was relatively higher than it might have been if done with modern machinery. Gradually more foreign and Lake Superior ores were used in the furnaces, though both cost more than the local ores. At first lake ores were used in larger quantities than the foreign ores, but as the lake ore increased in cost more than imported ores, the company continually consumed more of the foreign ores.

In 1899 the president considered the ore supply question the most difficult to answer. Because the company lacked "friendly interests" in both ore mining and coke manufacturing, it had become increasingly difficult to secure the requisite supply of raw materials. In his report to the stockholders President Fackenthal wrote:

> The most serious question that is confronting the pig-iron manufacturers throughout the country is that of ore supply. The consolidation of iron interests that have been made, usually include some of the best ore mines, and moreover, many of the furnace companies, particularly those in the Pittsburgh district, have proprietary rights in many of the best mines in the Lake Superior region, which in times of greatest activity precluded outside purchasers from drawing any part of their supply from such mines, whereas, in time of depression, ore is offered freely from all mines. I am glad, however, to state, that we have contracts for a supply of ore at comparatively low prices, to last up to July 1st, 1900, although we are experiencing the greatest trouble and annoyance to get our low priced contracts filled.[31]

The following year the president reported that the Jackson Iron Company had failed to make deliveries on the ore contracted for and other ores had to be purchased from other sources at much higher prices.[32] Meanwhile, a contract for coke supplies made with Hatfield & Hilles, which called for the delivery of all that coke company's output

---

[31]The Thomas Iron Co. Fin. Rec., p. 183. The president's statement of the changing conditions in the iron and steel industry during the boom period seems to support the contention that the advantages of backward integration will be emphasized by boom conditions and forward integration is more likely to be encouraged by a trade depression. See E. A. G. Robinson, _The Structure of Competitive Industry_ (New York, 1932), pp. 129 ff.

[32]_Ibid._, pp. 190 f. The Thomas Iron Company took this breach of contract case to court and a verdict was issued in its favor for $21,890.48. _The Thomas Iron Company v. The Jackson Iron Company_, Michigan Supreme Court (1901), pp. 1 ff.

of seven cars daily, had also been broken. The coke company, like the ore company, failed to make the contracted deliveries because of "labor troubles" and a scarcity of freight cars." Fackenthal was just as sure that the company had been selling the coke to other furnaces above the contract price, which deprived the iron company of an adequate supply of fuel at a time when the market was favorable.[33] From other reports these two cases were not isolated situations, though they were the only contract problems taken to the courts by the iron company.

The company's lack of control over its sources of raw material proved to make the operating conditions of the furnaces quite uncertain and more costly than they might have been otherwise. Then the long anthracite coal strikes in 1902 and 1906 crippled furnace operations, threw the company into an already crowded coke market, and compounded the firm's problems. Meanwhile, after each strike anthracite coal prices were increased, a factor adding a few more cents to the cost of smelting.[34]

Raw material problems were not the only conditions plaguing the managers of The Thomas Iron Company. They also experienced a scarcity of labor. Though the shutting down of furnaces by other iron firms in the

---

[33]The Thomas Iron Co. Fin. Rec., p. 210. Hatfield & Hilles vs. The Thomas Iron Copmpany, 154, Supreme Court of Pennsylvania (1903), pp. 1 ff.

[34]*Ibid*., pp. 211 ff. At this time the president reported to the stockholders that the company's furnaces, because of their old-fashioned construction, could not be operated successfully on all coke. It was, he said, possible to make as large a quantity of iron, but it was impossible to maintain the quality of the iron.

valley released skilled furnace labor, the workers were soon absorbed into the work force at the Bethlehem Steel Corporation's plant, or the rapidly growing cement industry offered employment. Thus, just as ore, coal, and coke prices increased, labor costs also began to rise.[35]

As a majority of The Thomas Company's furnaces were the old-fashioned, hand-charged stacks, they required a relatively larger work force than employed at a more modern automatically charged furnace. With rising labor costs and the necessity of having the larger work force, the company's wage bill must have increased despite the increased productivity at the two new furnaces at Hokendauqua. To further complicate matters, the company apparently tried to pay lower wages than those paid at other furnaces. The minute book indicates an almost continuous turnover in supervisory personnel at the various plants throughout these years. Furthermore, as wages in the area increased, the Pennsylvania-German and Welsh workers left for more remunerative employment. The Thomas Iron Company then proceeded to employ new immigrants, but even the marginal foreign workers were not retained for long periods; better wage opportunities in other areas drew them away from the iron works. During one month in 1906, President Fackenthal reported that the company had employed sixty-five new men to replace an equal number that had found employment elsewhere "at lighter work and often at better wages than blast-furnaces can afford to pay."[36] After 1906 the labor turnover

---

[35] _Ibid_.

[36] _Ibid_.

continued as the continual market fluctuations created an uncertainty in employment, hence probably increasing the unattractive nature of employment at the company's furnaces.

As a result of these cost conditions, the margin of profit on each ton of iron remained quite low relative to the margins attained in the earlier phases of the firm's history. The highest return on a ton of pig iron in this period was earned in the rising market of 1900; the spread between cost and price was $3.26 a ton. During the first eighteen years of B. F. Fackenthal's adminstration the average margin of profit on a ton of iron was 81 cents. For the preceding eighteen-year period, 1876 through 1893, the average had been $2.15 a ton, and in the first twenty years of business the average spread between the cost and price was $6.44 a ton.

By 1912 and 1913 the conditions of operation had reached a most difficult juncture. In those years the average costs of production were $14.87 and $15.08 a ton, but the average prices received were only $14.04 and $14.44 per ton. Thus, despite the company's furnace improvements, it was forced to sell its iron below the costs of production.[37]

Fortunately for the stockholders, as furnace operations became less profitable, the operation of both the Ironton and Catasauqua and Fogelsville Railroad Companies became more profitable. Dividends received from the railroad investments continued to rise as the cement industry in the area expanded. The actual dividend payments from these two railroads

---

[37] *Ibid.*, pp. 272 ff.

ranged from $29,072.50 in 1893 to $117,072.50 in 1911. The total dividends paid by the Ironton Railroad Company over the twenty years was $1,273,000, a sum equivalent to 45 percent of the total profits reported by the iron company over the same period. During seven of those years the Ironton paid more in dividends than the iron company earned through the sale of pig iron. In 1912, when the iron company lost $56,982 in the production of iron, the Ironton paid a dividend of $90,000, and the Catasauqua and Fogelsville paid a dividend of $17,072.50.[38]

Early in 1895, when the iron company had been pressed for funds needed for furnace improvements, the Ironton Railroad was offered to the Lehigh Valley Railroad Company but the bid to sell was turned down.[39] Again, in 1905, after further improvements were planned and working capital had to be replenished, the railroad was offered to the Lehigh Valley Railroad for $2,500,000. With earnings of $120,000 in that year, and assuming a 6 percent interest rate, the capitalized value of the railroad was approximately $2,000,000. Possibly because of the difference between the asking price and the then present worth of the railroad, the Lehigh Valley Railroad Company refused the offer once again.[40]

The cost of refurbishing the furnaces, in this third period of the company's history, consumed more funds than were employed for similar purposes in the second period. Generally the moneys for such purposes

---

[38] Ibid., p. 380

[39] Min. Book - The Thomas Iron Co., p. 417.

[40] The Thomas Iron Co.: Papers and Doc., p. 13.

were obtained through revenue from the sale of pig iron. Thus, all the reconstruction costs were charged to the cost of producing pig iron, a method of accounting for investment expenditures that tends to distort the accounting profits for the various periods concerned. Because of this accounting procedure, much of the following material is presented with some apprehension as to its validity. Another portion of the moneys used to rebuild the furnaces was obtained through the sales of old mining lands. Also, $400,000 of the funds was borrowed through short-term loans and the stock of the Catasauqua and Fogelsville Railroad was used as collateral.[41] The note was later paid off with earnings.

Approximately $4,209,741,58 was applied to the rebuilding of furnaces, acquiring new mining equipment, and the payment of dividends. Twenty-six percent, or $1,102.229.58 of that figure, was employed in furnace construction and repairs at Hokendauqua. Another 5 percent was used to install new mining equipment at Richard Mine in New Jersey, but the largest portion of the money, 69 percent or $2,943,750, was used to pay dividends.

Dividends were paid regularly from 1894 to 1912. During the first five years, when profits were only earned in 1896, the total dividends paid amounted to $418,750, an average payment of 3.3 percent on the $2,500,000 par value stock. From 1899 to 1911, $2,525,000 more was paid to the stockholders. The average rate of return on the par value of the

---

[41]Min. Book - The Thomas Iron Co., n.p. The funds were borrowed in 1906, after the Lehigh Valley Railroad had turned down the right to purchase the Ironton Railroad.

stock was 6½ percent. That was about 1 percent lower than the average for the preceding eighteen years.

Despite the expenditures made on new furnace equipment, the improvements were not very fruitful. The returns on fixed assets, between 1899 and 1903, fluctuated from a low of 3 percent to a high of 19 percent. The year of the high return, 1900, was one in which expenditures on furnace equipment were at a minimum. From 1904 through 1912, the return on the fixed assets of the firm exceeded 7 percent in only two years. The rate of return on fixed assets ranged from 5 percent to 0.2 percent in 1912. No profits were earned in 1913. From 1907 through 1912, the rate of return on both net worth and fixed assets was even lower than the interest rate being paid by the firm on the money it had borrowed to refurbish the furnaces. This profit data is presented in Table 19 on page 391.

Throughout the first ten years, 1894-1904, President Fackenthal maintained the ratio of current assets to current liabilities at approximately the same level held in previous years, about 5:1. In the next ten years, as the iron trade conditions became a little more difficult, the ratio tended to decline and, in the last year he served as president, the ratio of current assets to current liabilities had fallen to 1.4:1. This change offered a distinct sign of the firm's precarious situation. Though not without the ability to pay its debts, if required, the firm, through the pressures of external economic forces and internal disabilities, had moved to a condition in which it had insufficient working capital.

TABLE 19

PROFIT AND RATE OF RETURN ON NET WORTH AND FIXED ASSETS, 1894-1913

Year	Profits	Percent Return Ned Worth	Percent Return Fixed Assets	Dividend as Percent Return on Common Stock (par value)
1894	($58,698)[1]	-	-	5.0
1895	($69,762)	-	-	3.25
1896	$129,826	3.0	4.0	5.0
1897	($58,473)	-	-	1.5
1898	($81,770)	-	-	2.0
1899	98,429	2.6	3.0	6.0
1900	601,810	15.0	19.0	6.0
1901	105,909	3.0	3.3	8.0
1902	289,041	8.0	9.0	8.0
1903	430,337	10.7	13.0	8.0
1904	38,494	1.0	1.2	8.0
1905	238,558	6.0	7.6	8.0
1906	255,640	6.7	8.2	8.0
1907	167,608	4.5	5.0	8.0
1908	152,100	4.2	4.4	8.0
1909	34,548	1.0	1.0	6.0
1910	134,996	3.4	4.0	6.0
1911	101,325	3.0	3.0	4.0
1912	10,230	0.2	0.2	1.0
1913	(Unavailable)	-	-	-

1. Losses in parentheses.

Source: The Thomas Iron Company Financial Records for Fifty Years, pp. 154 ff.

Consolidation Schemes

Further signs of the changing conditions of the iron trade are provided by a number of merger or consolidation schemes that were presented to the board of directors. Though none of the plans were adopted, they indicate quite fully the outlook of the businessmen of the era who had become enamored with the consolidation idea.[42] Furthermore, the correspondence relating to these schemes offers further evidence of the indecisive and almost casual attitude of the board of directors to the problem of the firm's future.

The first inquiry to sell the company's stock came to the board of directors from Archer Brown. He represented the recently formed Empire Steel and Iron Company, parent corporation of the Lehigh Crane Iron Company and several other iron firms.[43] As the board wanted to sell all of the stock of the corporation instead of controlling shares, the scheme was not consummated.[44]

A second inquiry came from T. A. White of Meadville, Pennsylvania. White presumably represented the United States Steel Corporation. As

---

[42] Ibid., pp. 409 ff. It may be noted that on several occasions The Thomas Iron Company was offered opportunities to purchase several iron furnaces. In each instance the offers were rejected. Probably the most significant offer was made by Frank Baird of Buffalo, New York, who put the Buffalo Furnace Company up for sale in 1894. Located on the lake front at Buffalo, the plant was modern in every way and was favorably located for freight rates on Lake Superior ores as well as market location. However, the depressed conditions of the trade seemed to have deterred the directors from making the purchase.

[43] Ibid.

[44] The Thomas Iron Co.: Papers and Doc., pp. 156 ff. Min. Book - The Thomas Iron Co., p. 488.

nothing more than mention of the inquiry is recorded on this matter, it must have been given little consideration by the board.[45]

On two other occasions, first in 1902 and again in 1905, C. H. Zehnder requested an option to purchase controlling interests of The Thomas Iron Company. Again the requests were made on behalf of the Empire Steel and Iron Company. The first offer suggested a selling price of $70 per share, but the second price offer dropped to $65 a share. In both instances, the board of directors was unwilling to accept the option; it was quite sure that the value of the stock was higher than the offered price.[46]

Earlier, in 1901, Noel B. Wittman of Philadelphia suggested to B. F. Fackenthal that The Thomas Company participate in the organization of a corporation which would merge the largest merchant furnace companies in the East.[47] For the next ten years the scheme was discussed through correspondence and at numerous meetings, but the venture was never carried through to completion.[48] The available records indicate that Wittman was the spearhead for the merger movement and, of course, if he had succeeded, he would have received a sizable commission for his efforts. President Fackenthal and the president of the Empire Steel and Iron Company, Leonard Peckitt, were enticed into supporting the merger

---

[45] Ibid.

[46] Ibid., pp. 518 ff.

[47] Ibid., p. 187.

[48] Ibid., pp. 13 ff.

through the offer of responsible positions in the new corporation that would have been made up of the Empire Steel and Iron Company, The Thomas Iron Company, the Warwick Iron and Steel Company, and the Andover Iron Company. The coalition of these companies would have created a corporation capable of producing 4,116,673 tons of pig iron annually. The total valuation of furnaces, mines, and railroads would have amounted to $18,504,770.[49] The ulterior end sought in this case seems to have been merely a consolidation in ownership, not industrial efficiency, for all of the companies concerned were merchant furnace owners; none produced any finished products. The scope of the project required the consent of many business interests, and the long negotiations indicate that no one group was bargaining from a strategic position of strength. In the end, no one was strong enough to maneuver the others into the consolidation.[50]

The objectives of the consolidation were rather poorly defined. Certainly the promoters would, if successful, unite several of the largest producers of pig iron in the North-East, but to what end? Wittman only vaguely hinted in one letter that under a united management the companies would be able "to meet future conditions," whatever that may have meant. Wittman, however, expressed some doubt about the future

---

[49] Ibid., p. 17.

[50] Thorstein Veblen, The Theory of Business Enterprise (New York, 1915), p. 36. Veblen wrote: "If a prospective industrial consolidation is of such scope as to require the concurrence or consent of many business interests, among which no one is very decidedly preponderant in pecuniary strength or in a strategic position, a long time will be consumed in the negotiations and strategy necessary to define the terms on which the several business interests will consent to come in and the degree of solidarity and central control to which they will submit."

possibility of maintaining sales and profits were the firm merely to produce pig iron. "Probably," he wrote, "a considerable portion of the iron would have to be put into more finished form."[51]

In 1910 Noel Wittman and his associates made another attempt to unite only The Thomas Iron Company and the Empire Steel and Iron Company. The combination would have for its main objective "the utilization of property which might otherwise be forced into idleness." At that time the total value of the companies' assets was assumed to be $6,254,770. The syndicate, however, offered the stockholders only $4,136,000 for their stock while the syndicate itself would take another $620,400 worth of stock in the new corporation. The total capitalization for the new combination would have been 44,756,400. It would seem that the promoters, not the stockholders of the two companies involved, would have made the greatest gains.

With the demoralized market conditions for pig iron in 1911, Wittman made one more offer, this time at a lower price than previously. President Fackenthal's reply to Wittman indicated that the majority stockholders, consisting of the directors of the corporation and their families, looked with disfavor upon the negotiations.[52] As no further letters are available on this matter, it can be assumed that no agreement could be reached.

---

[51]The Thomas Iron Co.: Papers and Doc., p. 177.

[52]Ibid., pp. 175 ff.

A New President

The fifty-seven years of business activity of The Thomas Iron Company presented to this point represent, in many respects, the evolution of the anthracite merchant furnace industry, from infancy through years of vigorous manhood into an age of decay and decline. In 1912 the remaining anthracite pig iron producers smelted only 276,840 net tons of anthracite pig iron. That volume was about one-half the tonnage of 1856. Moreover, while the tonnage in 1856 represented 50 percent of the total output of pig iron, the production in 1912 was a mere 0.8 percent of the nation's total output. Furthermore, the number of anthracite furnaces had dropped from 121 in 1856 to 26 in 1912, and in a relatively few years even these would be abandoned. By 1922 there would no longer be any record of anthracite iron production in the United States.

Similarly, The Thomas Iron Company had grown from a small firm to one of relatively large proportions, becoming one of the leading firms in the industry. The economic vicissitudes and crises the company had passed through had placed their imprint upon the firm. Hampered by the depletion of local advantages and believing that it was unnecessary to adopt the technological and organization innovations developed by other more enterprising firms, The Thoms Iron Company tumbled from the ranks of the industry's leaders. In 1912 the firm's very survival was placed in question when it was forced to sell pig iron at prices below its cost of production. At the same time the firm's working capital ratio fell to a dangerously low level.

An evaluation of the company's sales, earnings, and investment policy has already been made, and the criteria indicate, on the whole, that the firm had continued a decline commenced toward the end of the preceding eighteen years. By 1912 the long established policy of paying dividends, whether profits were earned or not, had resulted in the depletion of the firm's working capital and had placed the firm in a rather precarious financial position. Despite the greater magnitude of reinvestment during these years, over the preceding eighteen years the efforts proved inadequate to maintain the value of the company's fixed assets. The company's furnaces were continually operated at relatively high costs because of the heavy maintenance and labor expenses. Meanwhile, the old ore mines were now depleted; the only value of many acres was in their use as farm land. Thus, rapid depreciation, obsolescence, and depletion had taken their toll; the only factor tending to protect the stockholders' investment was the rapid growth of the cement industry in the area. That industry's expansion continually raised the value of the Ironton and Catasauqua and Fogelsville Railroads and returned sizable profits to the firm. By 1912 it must have been quite obvious to the stockholders, board of directors, and the management that the purpose for which the company had originally been formed no longer existed.

Throughout the years of President Fackenthal's administration he seems to have been given a free hand with the operation of the firm. Generally, when he made a recommendation for some improvement, the board of directors gave its approval. On several occasions, however, when Fackenthal had suggested improvements in works, changes that might have taken the firm into new fields of operation, the board exerted its power and refused to accept his suggestions.

Obviously quite concerned over the condition of the firm, Fackenthal submitted a long report to the board of directors in 1912 on future operations. This report proved to be the president's last effort to regain the corporation's lost ground.

After briefly tracing the early history of the firm, he noted, "In the original construction of the works the best and latest methods were employed, and for a long time the company was pre-eminent in the manufacture of merchant pig iron, ..." However, he pointed out, "Since the furnaces were erected, in fact since Nos. 1 and 3 were remodeled in 1894 and 1898, rapid strides and improvements have been made in the construction of blast furnace"; thus, he concluded, "The time has now arrived when some action should be taken toward improving the condition of our plant."[53]

Then, following a rather extensive discourse on the condition of all of the company's furnaces, he drew special attention to the construction dates of all the firm's furnaces; No. 1 was built in 1894, No. 3 in 1899, No. 5 started in 1873, and No. 6 in 1874. Furnaces No. 2 and No. 4 had been abandoned in 1893 and 1902. At Alburtis the company was still operating furnaces that had been constructed in 1868 and 1874, while Island Park furnace was put in operation in 1876. Furnaces No. 10 and No. 11, at Hellertown, were constructed in 1868 and 1870. In this manner he tried to make it self-evident that the company was far behind the

---

[53] Ibid., pp. 49 ff.

times. He also added that, despite the seemingly extensive expenditure of $669,742.48 on repairs and renewals throughout the years of his administration, the furnaces had not been kept in thorough repair.

Finally, President Fackenthal summed up in the following manner:

> If, therefore, the works are to be continued, they will have to be reconstructed along modern line, or we cannot keep up with the procession. I doubt if, taken as a whole, there is a more antiquated plant in the country today.[54]

The recommendation he made to counteract this deplorable situation was that the plant be rebuilt and every consideration be made for ultimately adding manufacturing facilities that would use a portion of the pig iron produced in the new furnaces. He added that, if the board of directors was not prepared to obtain the necessary funds for such a rebuilding and expansion program, the only rational course to pursue was "to consider the question of going into liquidation." Further operations, he thought, would merely jeopardize the value of the funds invested in the business.

Upon hearing Fackenthal's report, the board of directors, all large stockholders, requested that he keep the contents of the paper confidential and no reference to it be placed in the minutes.

After continuous losses were incurred through the further production and sale of pig iron in 1913, and the directors offered little hope that they were prepared to change the works in any manner, Fackenthal submitted his resignation as president and general manager. The contents of

---

[54] Ibid., p. 80.

his resignation indicate that, at that time, Fackenthal was only sixty-one years of age, and his later activities suggest that he was in good health at the time of his resignation. Thus, though the following statement is speculative in nature, it seems that the president, upon losing the support of the board of directors, had resigned in protest. Apparently he had no desire to be a part of what must have appeared to be the almost momentary dissolution of the company.

With President Fackenthal's resignation, Edwin Thomas, Samuel Thomas's son, became the acting president until a successor to Fackenthal could be found. Finally, in July, 1913, Ralph H. Sweetser was elected president and general manager.

The new president came to the company with what the board of directors considered an outstanding record. A graduate of Massachusetts Institute of Technology, he had obtained extensive practical operating experience with the Maryland Steel Company, Everett Furnace, in Everett, Pennsylvania, and Salem Iron Company in Ohio, among others. He came to Hokendauqua from the Columbus Iron and Steel Company in Columbus, Ohio. Presumably a skilled practitioner in the field of iron production, Sweetser was thrown into a situation requiring the specialized skills of a financier and a marketing analyst more than the background of a furnace superintendent. The task of survival called for action, adaptation, or innovation, but Sweetser was to prove incapable of meeting the task.

Evaluation

Thus, during this third phase of The Thomas Iron Company's history, President Fackenthal, with the consent of the board of directors, paid out dividends when profits had not been earned, had depleted the firm's working capital, and had been unable to protect the stockholders' original investment through the development of more efficient facilities and organization. But the most incomprehensible development was the directors' refusal to appraise more judiciously the problem of a declining market for merchant pig iron and the rapid rise of the integrated steel companies. Seemingly oblivious of the significance of the changes in the iron industry, or unwilling to face up to the problem, they continued to operate the firm as though there would always be a strong merchant furnace trade. The alternatives were ignored, or momentarily shunted aside.

Only the shift in the demand for pig iron brought about by the conditions of war would temporarily raise iron prices high enough to permit the firm to obtain short run profits once again. Meanwhile, in the struggle for survival the organized merchant pig iron trade was rapidly being supplanted by the integrated steel firms.[55] More often, the latter form of business organization offered financial rewards that were no longer available to merchant furnace companies. Eventually the directors would have to return to the same alternative choices offered by President Fackenthal, integrate or liquidate.

In retrospect, it would seem that the better choice probably would have been to liquidate, but the very nature of the fixed assets owned by

---

[55]Marshall, Principles of Economics, pp. 596 ff. Marshall wrote as follows: "For as a general rule the law of substitution - which is nothing more than a special and limited application of the law of survival of the fittest - tends to make one method of industrial organization supplant another when it offers a direct and immediate service at a lower price."

the firm probably led the directors to delay making that decision. Because the board decided to continue operations does not indicate that it acted unwisely. But the fact that the board's members believed that the firm would be able to survive as a merchant furnace company, despite the technological and organization changes in the industry, suggests that they were not very realistic in the estimation of the future. By 1913 it was quite obvious that the firm's progress was likely to be arrested unless some change was made; survival required integration.

CHAPTER XI

THE LAST YEARS

Difficult Times

It is quite obvious that the persistent changes in the location, organization, and technology of the iron and steel industry between 1893 and 1913 had diminished The Thomas Iron Company's economic advantages and reduced the firm to the rank of a marginal firm. No longer were the company's furnaces, once reputed to be outstanding works, efficient enough to permit the earning of large profits. Doggedly persisting in clinging to the old processes and course of business, the management found that the firm's furnaces were maintained on an inadequate base of raw materials and most of the furnaces lacked the advantages of modern labor-saving mechanisms as well as the advanced furnace design then being employed by the rising steel firms. The lack of labor-saving skip hoists, the use of low grade ores, and the employment of inefficient furnaces and hot-blast stoves tended to keep the average costs of production high. Thus, whenever the price of pig iron dipped, the firm's profits were reduced considerably and sometimes disappeared.

To add to the firm's problems, the continual expansion in the use of the open-hearth furnaces and the further extension of blast furnace capacity at the integrated steel mills minimized the steel industry's dependence on merchant furnaces. By 1903 approximately 60 percent of the total pig iron manufactured in the United States had been smelted in steel company furnaces; ten years later as much as 75 percent of the total was produced by such integrated works.[1] When periods of slack trade occurred, the steel companies often continued to produce more pig iron than they consumed, and any surplus iron was thrown into the open market in competition with the output from the merchant furnaces. Furthermore, the growing use of the open-hearth steel furnaces, which consumed scrap metal as well as pig iron, introduced a new source of competition, the scrap iron dealers.

Subjected to these new competitive conditions, increasing in intensity during the downswing in business activity in 1913, The Thomas Iron Company closed that year with an operating loss. The firm's management consequently lacked the necessary funds to continue the essential furnace improvements commenced earlier, and plans for rebuilding and reorganizing the plants were dropped momentarily. During the year cash dividends derived from the Ironton and Catasauqua and Fogelsville Railroads were employed to cover the deficiency arising from iron production. Over $100,000 in funds was absorbed for this purpose.[2] Meanwhile, the firm's cash and accounts receivable were contracted considerably, and raw material and finished goods inventories, less liquid assets, were increased. On the liability side of the balance sheet, accounts payable had been

---

[1] Homer B. Vanderblue and William L. Crum, The Iron Industry in Prosperity and Depression (Chicago, 1927), p. 11.

[2] The Thomas Iron Co.: Papers and Doc., p. 83.

advanced by $198,611.[3] These changes in the company's accounts indicate that the company had come upon hard times. The working capital ratio, which historically had been maintained between 6:1 and 4:1, was at a low of 1.4:1 at the end of the year.

In retrospect it would appear that the continued production of iron had been rather foolhardy, for it had only resulted in a diminution of the firm's "quick assets" and resulted in an expansion of inventories. Furthermore, as dividends were not paid to the stockholders, the operation of the works had not provided the opportunity for disinvestment. At the same time furnace operations had consumed income derived from the railroad stock held by the company.

Irrespective of the depressed conditions of the iron trade and the continual decline in the pig iron sales, the directors ventured to find outside funds for the purpose of supplementing their now depleted resources of working capital. The only factor which seemed to be in their favor was the almost continual appreciation in value of the Ironton and Catasauqua and Fogelsville Railroads, essential links to main line railroads for the rapidly expanding cement industry in the area.

In order to borrow this capital, the stockholders were asked to vote on the issuance of bonds for $1,000,000, of which $600,000 would be issued immediately. The remaining $400,000 was to be held in abeyance

---

[3]The Thomas Iron Co. Fin. Rec., p. 390. In 1913 the firm's cash account fell from $180,178 to $83,522. Accounts receivable dropped by $54,000, while inventories were increased by approximately $100,000. As there is no profit and loss statement available for this period, it is impossible to determine the loss from operations.

for use at some later date when further additions to the firm's plant might be made. Collateral for the bonds consisted of a first mortgage on all the plants and equipment of the corporation, as well as the holdings in the Catasauqua and Fogelsville, Mount Hope, and Ironton Railroads. The rate of interest was to be 6 percent.[4]

Financing operations in this manner presumably supposes that more profit can be made on the borrowed capital than the interest charge on the debt. In the financial history of the firm from 1907 to 1913, there was no single year when the company had earned that much on its net worth or fixed assets. Confronted with the uncertainties of the future, the management could hardly have expected to secure adequate marginal returns through the expenditure of these funds to make the borrowing worthwhile. It is a fact that the earnings from the firm's railroad investments had been quite remunerative; however, the borrowed funds were to be employed in pig iron production and only losses had been recorded from these operations in the most recent years.

A group of stockholders who were evidently unimpressed by the future prospects of the pig iron market sought to have the bond issue voted down. To achieve that end, they organized a "Stockholders' Protective Committee" and recommended to all the stockholders that extreme caution be exercised before permitting more capital to flow into the firm's smelting and mining operations. The collective opinion of the group was that, under the economic conditions ruling in the most recent years, the board's

---

[4]The Thomas Iron Co.: Papers and Doc., p. 87.

proposal could only result in a transfer of the firm's property to the potential bondholders.[5] The members of the committee seem to have been firmly convinced that the liquidation of the manufacturing sector of the firm was the proper stratagem at this time, though they believed that the railroad stocks should have been retained.[6]

The insurgent stockholders also petitioned other stockholders to vote for the dissolution of the executive committee which had become more influential in the creation of policy after President Fackenthal's resignation. The protective committee recognized that the only way to void the influence of this executive committee was to do away with the by-law which had authorized it in 1855.[7]

Despite the exhortations of the "Stockholders' Protective Committee," the board of directors found enough support for its rebuilding program to enable the floatation of the bond issue.[8] By the close of that fiscal

---

[5] Ibid., p. 83.

[6] Ibid. At this time all the railroads, the Catasauqua and Fogelsville, the Ironton, and the Mount Hope, were earning substantial profits, but only in the case of the Ironton did the iron company receive all the profits in the form of dividends. The Catasauqua and Fogelsville Railroad never paid its total income out in dividends, but employed extra cash for other investments. This practice tended to appreciate the value of its own stock considerably. Interview with Oliver T. Case, November 19, 1957. (Mr. Case was secretary of The Thomas Iron Company from 1916 to 1922.)

[7] The board of directors was made up of men who were descendants of the original founders of the firm. Most of these men held interests in other business activities and had no great interest in altering the operations of the iron company. They did, however, believe that there would always be a demand for merchant pig iron. Interview with Oliver T. Case, November 19, 1957.

[8] The Thomas Iron Co.: Papers and Doc., p. 86.

period, $271,000 of the bond issue had been purchased by local banks and, once again, the firm's working capital was replenished. Within a short period of time the firm's accounts payable had been reduced by $387,367, but short-term debt had been replaced by long-term debt that would exact a fixed amount of revenue from the future revenue of the company.[9]

Several furnaces were relined that year, and an effort was made to open a "new vein" of ore at Richard Mine in New Jersey. The extraction of this ore was to absorb extensive amounts of revenue for the construction of a completely new mine shaft. Though the project was commenced in 1914, it was not completed until 1920, and after its completion the mining of ore was disrupted by a series of labor disputes and a shortage of labor[10]

Another part of the operations in 1914 consisted of the rebuilding of No. 8 furnace at Alburtis. The elements used in remodeling the old stone furnace, which was built in the 1860's, were castoffs taken from one of the older furnaces at Hokendauqua. The Hokendauqua furnace was dismantled after it had been idle for four years. These changes left the

---

[9]The Thomas Iron Co. Fin. Rec., p. 389.

[10]Iron Age, Vol. 93 (Feb. 19, 1914), 526. Oddly enough, the announcement that a new vein of ore had been discovered at Richard Mine was made at approximately the same time that The Thomas Iron Company began to sell its bonds.

The company reported that the Richard Mine ore contained 0.07 percent vanadium. When smelted, this ore would yield 0.036 percent vanadium in the pig iron. This element had proven to be a valuable ingredient in tool steel; however, its presence in pig iron was of doubtful value. Despite the doubt, the firm's iron was advertised as containing vanadium and sold under the trade name of "Thomas-Vanadium" pig iron. See The Thomas Iron Co. Fin. Rec., The Thomas Iron Company, Sixty-First Annual Report, 1915.

company with eight furnaces, though only six were in a condition of repair and capable of producing pig iron.[11]

No. 7 furnace at Alburtis, another old stone stack originally constructed in 1868, was used for one month in 1914. When the furnace was finally blown out, in order to have it rebuilt, the era of anthracite pig iron came to a close. Never again was pig iron to be produced with anthracite coal alone, though a few furnaces would use a mixture of anthracite coal and coke in their operations until 1923.[12]

The Thomas Iron Company sold approximately 116,308 tons of pig iron in 1914, though only 109,025 tons of iron had been produced. The furnace operations, however, resulted in a loss of about $290,710, although a portion of the loss arose from inventory revaluation. This operating loss was diminished somewhat by the earnings derived from other sources; consequently, the management was able to report a net loss of only $146,716.[13] The very poor returns from operations indicate quite emphatically the difficult times that the firm had run into and suggest that possibly the borrowing of funds was not a very sound business decision.

The curtailment of trade attributing to the disappointing income reports heightened the speculation about the eventual liquidation of the enterprise. The passing of dividends agitated the stockholders and must

---

[11] Ibid. (Aug. 23, 1914), p. 1033.

[12] Ibid., Vol. 152 (Dec. 30, 1943), 33 ff.; Vol. 92 (Nov. 27, 1913), 1218; Vol. 93 (April 16, 1914), 985. In 1914 the largest weekly output of the Alburtis furnace was 459 tons. The old stone stack was still being blown with blowing equipment that had been constructed in 1868.

[13] The Thomas Iron Co. Fin. Rec., "Analyses of Profit and Loss Account for 1914," n.p.

have discouraged the management. At this juncture the expansion of the war in Europe brought what appears to be an unexpected boon to the firm, for it stimulated the demand for United States' manufactures, pig iron included.

As 1915 unfolded, however, the financial condition of the firm did not improve as quickly as expected. Despite the rise in the nation's consumption of pig iron, The Thomas Iron Company's sales dropped from 116,308 tons to a mere 63,694 tons, a decline of 45 percent. Then, as supplemental expenditures were made for repairs and renewals of blast furnaces, only two furnaces out of the eight the company still owned were put in blast. Production that year amounted to only 58,974 tons, or a mere 19.9 percent of the capacity of the works.[14]

Despite this contraction in operations, the operating costs continued to exceed the revenue from sales, with a resultant operating loss of $53,795. Expenses incurred at the inactive furnaces amounted to $69,063, making the total loss in manufacturing $122,858. Fortunately, revenues from other sources augmented the firm's income enough to provide a net profit of $37,901.97. Dividends were not paid; instead the net income was retained and diverted into the working capital fund.[15]

Presumably at the end of the year the company's furnaces were adequately prepared for production, that is, in all technical requirements. The furnaces were high cost plants and could only make profits

---

[14] Ibid., The Thomas Iron Company, Sixty-First Annual Report, 1915.

[15] Ibid.

for the firm when, and if, the price of pig iron should rise to some higher level. Another of the Hokendauqua furnaces had been dismantled and some of its elements had been carted to Alburtis for rebuilding No. 7 furnace. Over $100,000 was spent in refurbishing that old stone stack, but when the task was completed it was still little more than scrap.[16]

The rejuvenation of the iron trade in 1915 had falsely renewed the hopes of the stockholders, but it brought another offer to the board of directors for an option on the firm's stock. Late in 1915, Nils Kachelmacher, president of the Hocking Coal and Iron Company in Columbus, Ohio, sought the right to purchase the total stock for $3,000,000.[17] Supposedly the option was sought by the Midvale Iron and Steel Company; rumor suggested that the Lehigh and New England Railroad wanted the property. A second rumor reported that the interested parties were planning to develop a large iron manufacturing combination in the East.[18]

At that time the stockholders were quite willing to sell their

---

[16] Ibid. The Thomas Iron Co.: Papers and Doc., pp. 98 and 203. The stone foundations for these two furnaces stand to this day at their original site in Alburtis. They are symbolic of The Thomas Iron Company's failure to adapt its facilities to meet the challenge of that era, the dynamic technological innovations in the steel industry.

[17] The Thomas Iron Co.: Papers and Doc., pp. 88 and 207 ff. The offer price made by Kachelmacher of $3,000,000 was equivalent to about $45 per share, $30 less than the estimated book value of the stock. When an investment house in Philadelphia, Frazier and Company, offered $50 per share, plus a return of one-half of anything that could be secured above that price, Kachelmacher's offer was raised to $3,500,000. The latter figure would have provided each shareholder between $55 and $57 a share.

[18] Iron Age, Vol. 96 (Nov. 4, 1915), 1071. The companies to be included in the combine were The Thomas Iron Company, Wharton Steel Company, and Empire Steel and Iron Company. See The Thomas Iron Co.: Papers and Doc., pp. 209 f.

stock, but the option was not signed until the offering price was raised to $3,500,000. Though the option was open for several months, it was never put into effect, and the stockholders were left with all their old problems.

Furnace operations, while somewhat more remunerative in 1916, were hampered by difficulties in finding adequate supplies of ore and coke. The company's ore mines in Pennsylvania proved too costly to continue in operation; meanwhile, outside sources, in many cases controlled by the large integrated steel companies, could only provide limited supplies of ores for the independent companies. These conditions forced The Thomas Iron Company to place a great deal of reliance on its ore mine in New Jersey. Coke supplies also proved difficult to obtain at prices low enough to enable the firm to produce iron at remunerative costs. Complicating these conditions were continual delays in the delivery of the raw materials because of the excessive burden placed on the nation's railroad system at that particular time. The resulting delays required, on numerous occasions, the banking of furnaces, an action tending to cut down on total output. A further drawback for the firm was the shortage of mechanics, semi-skilled, and common labor at a price the company seemed to be willing to pay. Lacking the essential factors for production, the company was only able to operate an average of three furnaces throughout the year, out of a total of seven units. Yet, despite the difficulties, the firm was able to produce 171,065 tons of pig iron in 1916[19]

---

[19]The Thomas Iron Co. Fin. Rec., The Thomas Iron Company, Sixty-Second Annual Report, 1916.

That same year the firm's sales amounted to 176,273 net tons of pig iron. The total sales revenue was $2,428,777. This higher revenue was the result of both increased sales and higher prices. The average price for basic pig iron and No. 2X foundry iron in eastern Pennsylvania and Philadelphia had risen from $14.91 and $15.26 a gross ton to $21.08 and $21.18, the first sizable increases in pig iron prices in several years.[20] Unfortunately for the stockholders, as iron prices moved upward, the costs of production for the firm also increased. Wages rose about 27 percent during the year, while the cost of raw materials and supplies increased somewhat more than wages.[21] Regardless of the marked improvement in sales and production statistics, the firm incurred a loss from operations of $99,372. But once again the dividends from the railroad securities provided income enough to wipe out the operating loss and report a net income of $72,512. Dividends, however, were passed for the fourth consecutive year.[22]

During that year, 1916, another $100,000 was expended on furnace repairs and improvements in mining facilities. Inventories were increased considerably, at least in dollar terms, and the accounts payable were more than doubled. Though these changes did little to change the working capital ratio markedly, the "quick asset" ratio had dropped significantly.

---

[20]American Iron and Steel Institute, Annual Statistical Report for 1921, pp. 80 f.

[21]The Thomas Iron Co. Fin. Rec., The Thomas Iron Company, Sixty-Second Annual Report, 1916.

[22]Ibid.

That is, the ratio of cash and receivables to current liabilities had fallen below 1:1 to 0.6:1. If the firm had been forced to liquidate at that particular time, its liquidity would have been impaired unless the sales value of the inventories could have covered the difference.

While the above situation may have disturbed the stockholders, it was probably not quite as distressing as the passing of dividends for the fourth consecutive year. Casting about for a cause for the poor returns, but ignoring the firm's basic problem, the stockholders found President Sweetser their most obvious target. Under the mounting pressure of this criticism, the president submitted his resignation. Like President Fackenthal before him, in retreat Sweetser pointed out, to all who would listen, that the firm's inability to make sizable profits rested upon its technological, organizational, and supply situation.

For the second time in four years, the board of directors was advised, despite the most recent improvements made in the company's furnaces, that the works were incapable of providing economic results. In order for The Thomas Iron Company to once again reap the benefits of its situation, the firm would have to expend considerably more money to rebuild the Hokendauqua furnaces. Furthermore, Sweetser recommended that "some outlet for its [the firm's] iron through finished product" was essential, and it was also necessary for the firm to control its own supply of raw materials. From President Sweetser's statement, it is apparent that he believed that the only factor favoring the continuance of the company's iron business was the strategic location of the furnace site at Hokendaqua. It was there, he suggested, that all production facilities should be concentrated.[23]

Evidently little attention was given Sweetser's parting recommendation to integrate, and logically so, for pig iron prices, which had increased only slightly during the previous two years, suddenly shot up to their highest level in years. In 1914 the average price for No. 2X foundry iron had been $14.74, and in 1915 it had been $15.26. Another $5.00 increase in 1916 raised the price to $21.18, but from January, 1917, to July the price moved upward from $30.10 a ton to $53.13.[24] This sudden shift in demand initiated by the further expansion in war production, as the United States entered the European conflict, seemed to assure the firm higher operating profits. Thus, with their profit expectations inflated, the stockholders, interested in short run profits, did not bother to concern themselves about the long run problems of the firm.[25]

During that year Walter A. Barrows, the new president of the

---

[23] *Ibid*. In order for The Thomas Iron Company to shift from iron to steel production would probably have required a new location for the steel furnaces and any finishing mills. Presumably the site at Hokendauqua was too small for such large operations. Furthermore, there was no one in the company's management that had the requisite knowledge to set up the plant and operate it, nor did it appear that the funds required for such a task would be readily available. Interview with Oliver T. Case, November 19, 1957.

[24] American Iron and Steel Institute, *Annual Statistical Report for 1921*, p. 81.

[25] *Ibid*. Vanderblue and Crum, *The Iron Industry in Prosperity and Depression*, p. 125. Before the year had ended, the War Industries Board proceeded to exert its power to control prices, and the price of foundry iron was reduced from $53.13 to $34.25 a ton. Basic pig iron was priced at $33.75 a ton. Scrap metal, a substitute for pig iron in the production of open-hearth steel, was priced at $28 a ton.

corporation, was able to place enough of the firm's plant into operation to produce 141,055 tons of pig iron, while the sales offices sold 127,658 tons.[26] Though these statistics are not quite as impressive as those reported the previous year, the very rapid increase in iron prices enabled the president to report profits from operations of $214,805.90.[27] If development costs had not been charged to operations, and if furnace operations had not been hampered by fuel shortages arising from the continuing railroad congestion, the profit figure might have been even more striking. By the end of the year, however, the government's control over iron prices precluded the continuation of such windfall gains.

The total income for 1917 was $319,624, an amount that was equivalent to a 7 percent return on fixed capital and net worth. From this sum, dividends of $124,996 were paid to the stockholders. This payment was

---

[26]At the time the new president was selected, B. F. Fackenthal wrote to another stockholder: "Since I first learned of Mr. Sweetser's resignation (from the newspapers) I have thought a lot about a successor. The position, which is no synacure [sic], is a hard one to fill. There are doubtless good furnace managers available, and in like manner good businessmen to be had, but to get a well balanced combination of both is not so easy, and in my judgement no one should be placed at the head of this Company who is not a good businessman." Letter from B. F. Fackenthal to Edwin Fox, Easton, Pennsylvania, April 1, 1916, The Thomas Iron Co.: Papers and Doc., pp. 75 f.

W. A. Barrows, the new president, did not meet the requirements that B. F. Fackenthal would have employed as a measure. This man was a trained chemist and an experienced furnace superintendent, with twelve years of experience. For eight years he had been engaged in iron ore exploration and development and had served as a consultant on metallurgical problems. The directors believed that his experience as a consulting expert would prove to be his most valuable asset. See The Thomas Iron Co.: Papers and Doc., p. 91.

[27]The Thomas Iron Co. Fin. Rec., <u>The Thomas Iron Company, Sixty-Fourth Annual Report, 1917</u>.

tantamount to a 5 percent return on the par value of the capital stock, or approximately a 50 percent return on the original investment of $250,000.[28]

Given the favorable market conditions of the period, the firm was able to rid itself of one of its furnaces. The Island Park furnace was sold to the Northern Ore Coporation for $108,000, and the revenue from the sale was placed in the sinking fund to aid in retiring some of the firm's outstanding bonds. Furthermore, some part of the $400,000 worth of the bonds still held in the treasury was sold in order to pay short-term loans and to restore the working capital ratio to a more satisfactory level.[29] The outstanding long-term debt, at the end of the year, was equal to $669,500.

The major improvements initiated during the year included the rebuilding of No. 3 furnace at Hokendauqua, a part of the firm's program to concentrate the operations at that site. At Richard Mine more funds were buried in the mine shaft, the construction of which had been embarked upon several years earlier. The other furnaces were repaired, but only enough to permit their "safe" operation. Much of the work of repairing and rebuilding was delayed by the inability to secure materials and necessary skilled labor, a circumstance that limited the operating time of the furnaces.[30]

---

[28] *Ibid.*

[29] *Ibid.*

[30] *Ibid.*

In retrospect, the board's belated effort to rebuild the furnace at Hokendauqua and to improve Richard Mine seems rather irrational. At that late date, the more logical policy probably would have been to operate the Hokendauqua furnaces until they could not be put in blast again and to continue to work Richard Mine, without further improvements, in order to take any short run profits obtainable. The most casual reflection on the state of the merchant pig iron trade and the most recent balance sheets of the firm should have made the directors aware of the plight of the company. Quite obviously the 1917 profits were pure windfall gains consequent to the rapid price rise resulting from the swift expansion of war good production. During that year, over 85 percent of the company's sales were made to firms under government contract. The directors once again, as in the recent past, seemed to have rejected reason while clinging tenaciously to the hope that the firm could survive as a merchant furnace company despite the technological and organizational changes taking place within the iron industry. They had no plans to gain a foothold in the rising steel industry.

The last war year, 1918, proved to be less profitable than 1917, despite sales revenues of $5,306,421.88. Fuel and labor shortages were reported to have plagued the firm and pushed the costs of production upward, while prices were held relatively stable under government controls. As a consequence of this squeeze, the windfall profits of 1917 were no longer attainable. With sales of 183,043 net tons and production of 167,353 tons of pig iron, the firm only earned operating profits of $84,819. After adding other revenues from the firm's investments, the net income figure was raised to $191,361.97, a return of 4 percent on net worth and fixed assets. That year the stockholders received $150,000 in dividends, a 6 percent return on the par value of their stock.[31]

Despite the contradictions so apparent in the firm's condition, the board of directors continued to spend money for what they called "extensive repairs" on the Hokendauqua furnaces, and more money was expended on the furnaces at Alburtis and one furnace at Hellertown, the second furnace at Hellertown having been dismantled that year.

Continually maintaining the hope that the company would be able to find a market for pig iron, the board siphoned over $100,000 in cash balances into Liberty Loan Bonds for future building purposes. It was believed that such funds could be used with great benefit at some more propitious time when the costs of construction were not quite so high as they were in 1918.[32]

Post-War Operations

When the war ended, pig iron prices were cut, as inventories on hand were large and demand was halting. By the end of the summer in 1919,

---

[31] *Ibid.*, *The Thomas Iron Company, Sixty-Fifth Annual Report, 1918*. The firm's stocks were presumably selling for about $35 per share at this time. At that price the yield on the purchase price was 8.5 percent. Interview with Oliver T. Case, November 19, 1957.

[32] *Ibid.* During that year (1918) President Barrows asked B. F. Fackenthal for an estimate of the value of the Lock Ridge furnaces at Alburtis. In Fackenthal's reply he remarked: "After this boom is over I would sooner own Island Park with its improvements than Lock Ridge with its improvements. For in my opinion Lock Ridge will be worth only the price of scrap after this bubble bursts." Letter from B. F. Fackenthal to W. A. Barrows, January 10, 1918, The Thomas Iron Co.: Papers and Doc., p. 98.

the price of No. 2X foundry iron had fallen from the average price of $35.49 in 1918 to $29.60 a ton.[33] But declining prices, as well as fuel shortages and labor problems at Richard Mine, did not halt production; that year the firm proceeded to manufacture the largest tonnage of pig iron it had produced since 1911. Sales revenue, on the other hand, dropped to $5,063,379.65, while materials and labor swallowed $4,476,218.52 of the revenue. Depreciation charges absorbed another $206,927.59, and repairs cost $266,165.11. After all other expenses were deducted, the firm's operating profit amounted to a mere $709.98.

The excuses offered the stockholders for such a poor showing were no different than those offered earlier, "labor shortages, and fuel shortages." Notwithstanding the unfavorable showing, the directors continued to ask for patience until the plant could be improved. Evidently they were quite convinced that by building a new furnace, setting up a pig casting machine, and improving the railroad layout in the yard to facilitate the handling of the larger freight cars, the firm would be quite capable of maintaining "its position in the trade."[34]

Remuneration from other sources was still exceptionally high, and the company once again reported a substantial net income of $249,080.82. That year another $150,000 in dividends was paid. This evidently did not endanger the working capital ratio, for it remained at 5:1. Also the

---

[33] Vanderblue and Crum, The Iron Industry in Properity and Depression, p. 28. American Iron and Steel Institute, Annual Statistical Report for 1921, p. 81.

[34] The Thomas Iron Co. Fin. Rec., The Thomas Iron Company, Sixty-Sixth Annual Report, 1919.

cash and Liberty Bonds remained intact.[35]

Before 1919 had ended, the stimulus of both the steel and the bituminous coal miners' strikes in conjunction with sustained demand for iron tended to send pig iron prices upward once again. As these prices continued to increase in 1920, they exerted pressures for the further expansion of output. The railroad workers' strike that year interfered with the delivery of pig iron and indirectly created, as a result of the duplication of orders, an apparent growth in demand for the product.[36] By September, 1920, the price of foundry iron had reached a high of $53.51 a ton.[37] Meanwhile, increased demands for coke sent the price of fuel upward from $6.00 a ton in April to $18.00 a ton in August and September. Then, as the strikes were cleared up and the market became a little more orderly, the demand for pig iron fell, and the price of coke dropped. By December, the price of foundry iron had fallen to $35.54 a ton, while coke dropped to $5.50 a ton.[38] With these changes, the inflationary expansion had ended.

These very unusual business conditions hindered the operation of The Thomas Iron Company's furnaces during a portion of the year; yet the output for 1920 was maintained at 149,422 net tons of pig iron. Again

---

[35] Ibid.

[36] Vanderblue and Crum, The Iron Industry in Prosperity and Depression, pp. 28 f.

[37] American Iron and Steel Institute, Annual Statistical Report for 1921, p. 81.

[38] Ibid. Vanderblue and Crum, The Iron Industry in Prosperity and Depression, p. 29.

sales fell; the company reported its total revenue of only $4,719,422.74. But as revenues fell, manufacturing costs rose from $4,476,218.52 to $4,554,078.28, despite the smaller output. This condition resulted in the costs consuming the greater portion of the sales revenue. After deducting costs of extraordinary repairs and renewals, as well as writing down the loss in the market value of the inventory of materials, the operating loss amounted to $165,344.46. A further revaluation of finished goods made this loss even larger; however, the firm's railroad stocks returned enough revenue to eliminate the total operating loss and provided excess enough for a net income of $23,235.59.[39]

Regardless of this low net income, the corporation's directors paid dividends of $150,000. In order to meet these payments, the Liberty Loan Bonds, previously set aside to finance renovations, were sold and the cash account was reduced from $193,640.19 to $84,287.40.[40] This withdrawal of cash was accompanied by an expansion of the accounts and notes payable sectors of the balance sheet. The change was significant enough to reduce the working capital ratio from 5:1 to 1.9:1.[41]

The extraordinary repairs and renewal item under production costs probably included the final payments for the reconstruction of No. 3 furnace at Hokendauqua, as well as expenditures for the installation of the mine shaft at Richard Mine.

---

[39]The Thomas Iron Co. Fin. Rec., _The Thomas Iron Company, Sixty-Seventh Annual Report, 1920_.

[40]_Ibid._

[41]_Ibid._

The new blast furnace was 90 feet high and had a 16-foot bosh. The furnace top was equipped with a McKee revolving stock distributor, and the furnace was fed by an automatic skip hoist. Hot metal ladle cars were prepared to draw the molten metal to a new Uehling pig casting machine located in a new casting house near the furnaces. Also, new boilers had been set in place to operate the air pumps. In February, 1921, the furnace had not been blown in because of the depressed conditions of the iron trade.[42]

"Due to the continued depression in business and the consequent lack of demand for our product, operations at your furnaces have been much restricted."[43] It was in this manner that the president commenced his report of the firm's operations through 1921, a year of extreme depression.

The rest of the iron industry was similarly struck by the very uncertain conditions of trade in 1921. During that year blast furnace yards throughout the nation were filled with tons of ore purchased at the high prices of 1920 and inventories of pig iron produced at the high costs of the previous year. Old contracts proved unenforceable. Meanwhile, the lot of merchant furnace companies proved especially difficult, as steel companies sold their surplus iron in the open market, and iron consumers that held heavy inventories attempted to liquidate their supplies by selling in the open market in competition with the merchant

---

[42]Ibid. Iron Age, Vol. 109 (May 5, 1922), 1221 ff.

[43]The Thomas Iron Co. Fin. Rec., The Thomas Iron Company, Sixty-Eighth Annual Report, 1921.

furnace companies. The whole market became demoralized, and the price of foundry iron fell from an average of $46.92 in 1920 to an average of $25.14 in 1921.[44] The nation's pig iron production dwindled to 18,690,701 net tons, approximately one-half of the previous year's output. Production in the Lehigh Valley also declined by 50 percent.

As a marginal firm, The Thomas Iron Company suffered a tremendous loss in sales, and it was forced to reduce its production to a paltry 20,349 tons, 12 percent of the previous year's output. That figure represented the smallest output in the firm's history.[45] Sales revenue amounted to a mere $589,106.64, while manufacturing costs reached a total of $847,560.70. The consequent operating loss amounted to $343,017.36. Revenues from other sources reduced the net loss to $212,227.13. This latter figure, however, is probably an understatement for, contrary to practice in the preceding four years, no depreciation charges were recorded. In 1920 depreciation entries had amounted to $135,002.36.[46]

In 1921 dividends of $75,000 were paid. Meanwhile the firm's cash balance was reduced to $39,637.37, but $101,438.47 in United States Treasury Notes, almost the equivalent of cash, had been purchased. With

---

[44]Vanderblue and Crum, _The Iron Industry in Prosperity and Depression_, p. 29. American Iron and Steel Institute, _Annual Statistical Report for 1921_. p. 81.

[45]The Thomas Iron Co. Fin. Rec., _The Thomas Iron Company_, _Sixty-Eighth Annual Report_, _1921_. The Hokendauqua furnace remained idle throughout the year while the Hellertown and Alburtis works were operated in only two months of the year. If this report is correct, the new furnace, No. 3, was not put in blast once it had been completed.

[46]_Ibid_.

other current assets, these accounts provided total current assets of $275,991.92. These assets were slightly larger than current liabilities, then recorded at $224,212.92. Also on hand was $714,062.77 in inventories, but in opposition to these assets there still remained $585,500 in outstanding long-term debt.[47]

The difficult conditions of the trade caused the president of the firm to report:

> The general demand for pig iron has shown little, if any improvement during the past year. Prices have fallen. Collections in some instances were slow, but only small losses due to bad accounts have been incurred. Many of our customers suffer from keen competition and have failed to secure looked-for business. Contracts for iron have proven burdensome and were only with difficulty enforceable in many cases.[48]

Notwithstanding the firm's somewhat precarious position, the president, who evidently spoke for the board of directors, believed that the company had "a place in the trade," with many customers of long standing. "For this reason principally," he did not consider it essential for the firm to halt the production of iron. And, as manager of the works, he was trying to get them in shape in order to permit the firm "to successfully compete with other concerns selling in our market, when ordinary business conditions prevail."[49]

It is interesting to speculate on whether the firm could have continued operations at this juncture. During 1921 the firm's cash outlay

---

[47] *Ibid.*

[48] *Ibid.*

[49] *Ibid.*

had exceeded its cash receipts, and the firm was faced with slow payments from its customers, not to mention the possibility of defaults. The unfortunate fact that others might not pay the firm did not permit the company to reduce its payments accordingly. Creditors had to be paid or the firm would fail. That year the firm had reduced its output to an extremely low figure; yet its costs had continued at a relatively high level. Thus, even though pig iron output might have been reduced to zero quantity, there were still certain costs to be met. On the other hand, if production was continued in competition with other firms, new working capital would be required.

Assuming all production was halted, but the firm continued to maintain its offices, its fixed costs would have consisted of interest charges on long-term debt, taxes and insurance, administration and sales expenses, plus the annual payment into the sinking fund for the retirement of outstanding bonds. There were also costs of maintenance of housing provided for employees. Using the charges for these costs recorded in the 1921 business statements, the total fixed costs would have amounted to approximately $107,198.85. Revenues from sales would be an unknown factor. Revenues from securities would probably approximate $140,000, if the past could be used as an indicator of future returns. Deducting the fixed costs from this probable revenue would leave approximately $32,801.15, part of which would have to be employed to pay some of the firm's current liabilities, amounting to $224,212.92 at the close of 1921. Failure to pay those accounts would have resulted in bankruptcy, unless the sale of inventories could have returned sufficient revenues to pay the due bills, When all of these charges are taken care of, little, if any, revenue would have remained for the stockholders.

On the other hand, in order for the firm to continue operations, two barriers had to be surmounted. First, the firm's working capital fund had to be replenished, and, secondly, improvements in the plant would have required sizable capital investment. By 1921 it was quite evident that The Thomas Iron Company had to integrate its furnace works with some finishing process if it hoped to survive. But, as the directors had shown little interest in such a move in the past, it can be assumed that they did not hold any interest for such a change. By not integrating, the cost of expansion also would have been eliminated.

Assuming, however, that the firm had proceeded to continue the production of pig iron, there was still a need for working capital. As the firm was already in debt to local banks for $414,500, its borrowing capacity at that source was considerably reduced. Furthermore, to increase the firm's debt would raise its fixed costs and endanger its already unstable position. The sale of stock to obtain the necessary funds was probably impossible, too, for if the past is any indicator of the future, the firm's operations provided little hope for any sizable marginal gains through additional investments.

The firm was left with one alternative. It could sell its most salable assets, the stock it held in the Ironton and Catasauqua and Fogelsville Railroads. To sell those investments would mean the relinquishing of the firm's major source of revenue, so necessary for the payment of its fixed charges. If the firm sold these railroad stocks in order to raise working capital, the stockholders would give up assets almost sure of gaining revenue for new assets much less likely to provide returns. This was a move that would probably not have been accepted by the stockholders.

Despite the board's often repeated belief that the firm had "a place in the trade," the circumstances in which it was placed in 1921 finally forced the directors to choose between integration and liquidation. Nine years after President Fackenthal had requested the directors to make the decision, they now discovered that they really had no choice. It was probably too late for the firm to integrate and survive in the Lehigh Valley. The neighboring Bethlehem Steel Corporation, already large and growing, had firmly established itself in the steel market which, unlike the pig iron market, was divided into territories through the Pittsburgh-Plus plan.[50] Thus, freedom of entry into the steel industry at that late date seemed to have been considerably reduced for The Thomas Iron Company. Not only was entry restricted by the structure of the industry, but also by the very heavy capital requirements. Unfortunately, the iron company also faced a situation in which exit from the pig iron industry was hampered by the heavy capital investment it had in

---

[50]Frank Albert Fetter, The Masquerade of Monopoly (New York, 1931), pp. 115-91. Iron Age, Vol. 109 (Jan. 5, 1922), 55. This industrial periodical reported that the high freight rates in effect reduced the degree of competition between districts. Also, it reported that the eastern Pennsylvania pig iron market was dominated by three steel companies which were regular producers of merchant iron. The over-all situation in the industry was such that "steel company furnaces dominated the pig iron market throughout the year." The merchant furnaces remaining in production were constantly in competition with steel companies that were producing all grades of iron.

blast furnaces and other furnace facilities.

Apparently the directors' solution to their problem was to capitalize on the sale value of the railroad securities held by the firm. At the same time an attempt to recover some small portion of the value of the iron furnaces was made. To attain this end, the directors needed to sell the rilroad stocks with the iron works in a "package sale." Fortunately for the stockholders, one interested party, The Reading Company, parent company of the Reading Railroad and ally of the Lehigh Valley Railroad, was quite anxious to control those two valuable access railroads.[51]

At the end of 1921, the board of directors, evidently aware of the firm's plight and convinced that further operation of the iron works would be uneconomical, reduced the labor forces at the various plants to the requisite number to care for the property. Meanwhile, efforts apparently were made to find a buyer of the firm's stock. By June, 1922, the deal had been prepared.

On June 10 the stockholders were notified that Drexel and Company of Philadelphia had agreed to purchase all of the stock of the firm for $50 per share, the par value of the stock.[52] By July 6 the sale had been

---

[51] Iron Age, Vol. 110 (July 6, 1922), 171. Between 1907 and 1917 the value of the railroad stocks had been written up in the firm's books from $419,725 to $1,963,875. The dividends received on these holdings in 1907 amounted to 28 percent of their recorded value. The average yield on the stocks, after their revaluation, was approximately 10 percent. In 1921, a depression year, The Thomas Iron Company received $142,681.25 in dividends from these railroads, which was equivalent to a 7 percent return on the par value of the stocks. See The Thomas Iron Co. Fin. Rec., n.p.

[52] The Thomas Iron Co.: Papers and Doc., p. 59. B. F. Fackenthal left a note among the papers that indicated President Barrows had written to many of the small stockholders "offering to buy their Thomas stock at a low price, and that many of them sold their stock to him."

completed and the stockholders had received $2,500,000 for their shares in The Thomas Iron Company. The purchase agreement required that the buyer take over the firm's long-term debt as well as the railroads and the five furnaces.[53]

Drexel and Company then proceeded to transfer the properties of the iron company to The Reading Company. Later, in 1923, under a court order The Reading Company segregated its holdings and The Reading Iron Company received the iron works, while the Reading and Lehigh Valley Railroads shared the ownership of the lucrative Ironton Railroad. The Catasauqua and Fogelsville Railroad fell under the complete control of the Reading Railroad.[54]

The price paid for the Ironton Railroad, $1,500,000, was $100,000 more than The Thomas Iron Company had recorded its value in the account books. The Catasauqua and Fogelsville stock was sold to the Reading Railroad Company for $512,175, the recorded value of the stock. These sales

---

[53]Iron Age, Vol. 110 (July 6, 1922), 171; Vol. 109 (April 13, 1922), 1013. Earlier in the year the Replogle Steel Company had acquired control over the Empire Steel and Iron Company. The Replogle Company also controlled the Wharton furnaces in New Jersey. The firm's seven blast furnaces had an annual capacity of 600,000 tons.

The very favorable price paid for The Thomas Iron Company stock rests on the great value of the company's railroad holdings. Both the Catasauqua and Fogelsville and Ironton Railroads were important cement carrying roads. The former was partially owned by the Reading Railroad. Both roads had been paying to the Interstate Commerce Commission many of their profits over 6 percent; presumaably the money was to be used to support unprofitable railroads. At that time there was some speculation that the funds might be returned to the railroads. Later the Ironton Railroad received a reimbursement of $200,000 from the Interstate Commerce Commission. Inverview with Oliver T. Case, November 19, 1957.

[54]Letter to author from B. C. Clark, Financial Vice-President of The Philadelphia and Reading Corporation, December 28, 1955.

account for all but $487,825 of the sale price of the company's stock. In 1921 the iron furnaces, real estate, and Richard Mine were valued in the firm's books at $3,469,860, truly an inflated value relative to this residual figure.

With the transfer of The Thomas Iron Company's property, the number of furnaces in the Lehigh Valley was not reduced. There were still twenty-one furnaces, but only six furnaces were in active operation at the end of 1922. The other fifteen stacks were idle, including all The Thomas Iron Company furnaces. Of the total furnaces in the valley, seven were owned and operated by the expanding Bethlehem Steel Corporation; the other fourteen were owned by merchant furnace companies. Most of the merchant furnaces were old and worn out, quite ready to be abandoned. By 1922 the end of a long transitional period in the development of the valley's iron industry was drawing near. Most of the old iron companies had disappeared. Only eighteen furnaces were still available for production in 1923, and three years later only fourteen remained.[55] In 1936, after the former Thomas Company's only remaining furnace had been idle for ten years, the plant was purchased by the Bethlehem Steel Corporation and dismantled. The Lehigh Valley, which once had a furnace for every mile between Mauch Chunk and Easton, then contained but seven blast furnaces, all owned by one company.[56]

---

[55] Vanderblue and Crum, The Iron Industry in Prosperity and Depression, p. 57.

[56] The Thomas Iron Company and Ironton Railroad Company, Charters, By-Laws.

Résumé

A distinction has now been made between the operations of The Thomas Iron Company and the effects of industrial innovation of the firm, in the years of its expansion, its years of maturity and decline. The movement from one period to the next is quite difficult to designate by date, for the changes took place quite gradually; but for the purpose of interpretation it might be said that the firm's turning point, from youth to maturity, occurred sometime between 1875 and 1886. Up to 1875 the firm experienced a rapid rate of growth, both in furnace capacity and sales. Those were also years of peak profits and heavy reinvestment. From 1875 to 1886 the firm continued to show some of the characteristics of youth. The firm's fixed capital changed very little, though sales and production continued to grow but at a somewhat slower rate. From 1886 to about 1907, the firm continued to maintain its volume of sales and output, but the number of furnaces in operation declined while the rate of profit and reinvestment fell considerably. Then from 1907 to 1921 the signs of old age were clearly evident as the firm's sales, profits, and furnaces continued to diminish; only the war years permitted the company to make any sizable amount of profits, the last spasmodic burst of energy.[57]

---

[57] By 1912 and 1913 The Thomas Iron Company had reached a point when it was producing iron with average total costs above the average revenue. At that juncture, it might be said that economically the firm had failed; however, failure in this sense does not necessarily mean that the resources would be withdrawn from the industry or that production would cease. The withdrawal of capacity would depend upon the durability of the capital and the firm's ability to secure a return greater than its out-of-pocket costs. In this case, the firm had such highly specialized capital that production was maintained and the firm continued to affect

The rise and fall of The Thomas Iron Company is nothing exceptional. The business firm that maintains an extremely long life span is the exception. However, the history of this firm's corporate existence does provide an excellent example of the destructiveness of the innovation process in the capitalistic system. The very creative act of innovation upon which the capitalistic system thrives leads automatically to the destruction of the value of other real capital already in use. In this case, the technological and organizational innovations introduced in the new and rising steel industry destroyed the value of this merchant furnace company's real capital. But the organization and successful expansion of The Thomas Iron Company had also acted in much the same fashion; earlier charcoal furnace companies had been forced to withdraw from production as more anthracite iron was produced.[58]

The management of The Thomas Iron Company during all these years shows few of the characteristics of innovating entrepreneurship. From the very commencement of operations, leaders failed to experiment aggressively with new techniques as David Thomas had done earlier at the Crane works. On the other hand, if one were to measure innovation by the

---

the price and total output of the commodity for several more years.

The business concept of failure generally means that the firm has been unable to meet its financial obligations and some legal proceedings have been taken against it. In the case of The Thomas Iron Company, it did not reach that stage. Because the firm did not meet with such difficulties, it cannot be said that the firm was a "business failure." See Norman S. Buchanan, The Economics of Corporate Enterprise (New York, 1904), pp. 332 ff.

[58]The concept of the destructiveness of innovations is discussed in Schumpeter, The Theory of Economic Development, pp. 57 ff. Redlich, "The 'Daimonic' Entrepreneur," pp. 30 ff.

extent of reinvestment, the management during the first twenty years of development could be classified as innovators. The better classification, however, might be that of "imitative entrepreneurs." While the management was not aggressive in experimenting with new techniques of production, it was quite ready to adopt successful innovations already developed by other more aggressive entrepreneurs.[59]

From the early 1880's to the early 1900's the firm's management acted merely as administrators, supervising the known procedures of operation in the merchant furnace trade.[60] Evidently quite proud of the prestige that they had attained in the early years of the firm's expansion, as well as their own skill in doing the ordinary day-to-day tasks, the managment showed no inclination to meet the challenge of the era. Ignoring the great technical and organizational changes being made in the iron industry, the managers discovered too late that their firm had been left behind in the struggle for survival. Then in the early 1900's the management's ability to advance the firm with the expansion of the steel industry seems to have been blocked quite effectively by the rapid appearance of the larger iron and steel combinations controlling many of the important sources of raw materials as well as many of the firms that

---

[59]Clarence Danhof, "Observations of Entrepreneurship in Agriculture," Richard Wohl, ed., Change and the Entrepreneur, pp. 2-24. Professor Danhof conceives of four strata of entrepreneurs: (1) the innovator, (2) the imitator or adapter, (3) the cautious adapter or "Fabian" entrepreneur, and (4) the drone entrepreneur. The latter type is characterized by a refusal to adopt opportunities to make changes in production functions, even at the cost of reduced returns relative to like producers.

[60]Schumpeter, The Theory of Economic Development, p. 78.

consumed pig iron.

Not until it was too late did the management realize that its very freedom of movement, so necessary for survival, was quite effectively circumscribed by the changes that had already taken place. First, the firm lacked the necessary financial resources for the extensive expansion it would have had to undertake. Second, it lacked the skilled personnel that could provide the guidance so essential in making the shift to pig iron conversion possible. Raw materials, as already mentioned, were effectively controlled by a few firms, and the market for steel products was dominated by the the United States Steel Corporation and a few other independent firms which had been more responsive to the structural and technological changes commencing in the 1880's. However, the greatest barrier to The Thomas Iron Company's development was the directors' seeming inability to adjust their thinking to the changing times; they were always quite sure that there was a place in the trade for The Thomas Iron Company as long as there was any use for pig iron. Meanwhile, the firm's proportion of total production and sales declined, and the rate of return on its fixed assets continually diminished.

As the firm became older, its management showed, or seemed to show, signs of incompetency, although this may have been but a reflection of the changing times and not an inadequacy in the day-to-day managerial skills of the men involved. They had become trapped by the revolutionary changes in the industry. The experience of the management of the firm, after 1907, is probably not unlike that of many other management groups in a similar position. Despite the diminished flow of cash receipts from current sales, as long as there were new funds available to finance operations, even at a loss, the management postponed the decisive action to liquidate the venture.

While the directors' reaction to the change was slow, it was not necessarily irrational. Moreover, the action or inaction of the board had important economic significance. The firm's capital goods, like those of many other firms, were quite durable in nature and not immediately rendered obsolete by technological change in the industry. This very durability of the capital equipment made it rather difficult for the firm to exit from the industry. But it was inevitable that unless some change was made in the form of the firm's fixed assets the company was certain to be eliminated from the industrial scene. Because of the delay in withdrawing the firm's assets from production, as many other firms also delayed, there was a comparatively long time interval required before the needed adjustments in output within the total industry could be made. Thus, many years elapsed before the misdirected capital investment ceased to exert its influence on the condition of supply and price.

From this study of The Thomas Iron Company, it seems that there is a greater likelihood of a firm surviving in a dynamic economy if new methods of production are steadily adopted when innovations are new. At that stage of development, it is more likely that the producers are more aware of the character of the change and that the barriers to be overcome are less burdensome. But once again, as the study had indicated, adaptation and survival depend upon the attitude of the firm's administrators; survival in the capitalistic system depends largely upon management's personal characteristics and motivations.[61] For example, note the differences in the management decisions of The Thomas Iron Company's directors and those of the Bethlehem Iron Company's directors in the 1880's and later. One wonders what might have happened to The Thomas Iron Company if the managers and directors of the firm, in that period, had had more of the characteristics of the men directing the operations of the Bethlehem Iron Company. That the managements did not react in similar fashion to the changes seems to support Schumpeter's proposition that it is rare for any managers to continually hold the drive necessary to maintain a firm at the forefront of the industry. Instead, the businessman, once successful in carrying out a new innovation or combination, will settle down to running the business "as other people run their businesses."[62] Finally, the history of The Thomas Iron Company seems to

---

[61] As Arthur H. Cole has written: "The entrepreneur, whether individual or multiple, does not 'decide' in the abstract. Always such actions are taken relative to concrete living institutions, and therefore they can best be examined in concrete historical settings." Arthur H. Cole, "An Approach to the Study of Entrepreneurship," *Journal of Economic History*, Supplement VI (1946), 1-15.

It seems apparent from the study of The Thomas Iron Company that not all firms or entrepreneurs strive to maximize profits, nor does the firm know what maximum profits are, and in most instances the maximizing motive does not necessarily provide the entrepreneur with a single policy from among many, in a world of uncertainty. For a discussion of this subject, see: Stephen Enke, "On Maximizing Profits: A Distinction between Chamberlin and Robinson," *American Economic Review*, XLI (September, 1951), 566-78; Alchian, "Uncertainty, Evolution, and Economic Theory," *Journal of Political Economy*, LVII (June, 1950), 211-21; Penrose, "Biological Analogies in the Theory of the Firm," *American Economic Review*, XLII (December, 1952), 804-19; Alchian, Enke, and Penrose, "Biological Analogies in the Theory of the Firm: Comment and Rejoinder," *American Economic Review*, XLII (September, 1953), 600-609.

[62] Schumpeter, *The Theory of Economic Development*, pp. 78-80.

support Alfred Marshall's thesis that the vigor of the firm declines with the age, energy, and interest of the businessmen involved in its operation.[63] Firms, like furnaces, may wear out.[64]

---

[63]Marshall, Principles of Economics, pp. 314 ff.

[64]The following is a brief history of The Thomas Iron Company after its transfer to Drexel and Company in 1922. The material is an excerpt taken from a letter to the author from H. C. Clark, Financial Vice-President of The Philadelphia and Reading Corporation, December 28, 1955.

"The Final Decree in the segregation proceedings involving Reading Company and The Philadelphia and Reading Coal and Iron Company was handed down by the District Court of the United States for the Eastern District of Pennslvania on June 28, 1923. The Decree specifically provided that a new corporation be organized, namely, The Philadelphia and Reading Coal and Iron Corporation which company acquired from Reading Company the entire stock of The Philadelphia and Reading Coal and Iron Company. Simultaneously The Philadelphia and Reading Coal and Iron Company purchased from Reading Company the entire capital stock of Reading Iron Company. In pursuance of an agreement between The Reading Company and Reading Iron Company, entered into prior to the segregation, The Reading Iron Company purchased the stock of The Thomas Iron Company on April 21, 1924.

"The Thomas Iron Company's property at the time Reading Iron Company purchased its stock consisted of a blast furnace at Hokendauqua, Pa. and an iron ore property comprising 480 acres of land, together with full equipment of mining machinery, houses and concentrating mill at Wharton, New Jersey. The ore, at that time, was principally used in The Thomas Iron and Reading Iron blast furnaces and any excess production was sold. The pig iron produced by Thomas Iron was sold to Reading Iron.

"Because of substantial losses incurred by Reading Iron Company and its wholly owned subsidiary, the management recommended, late in 1937, that the company liquidate. The Thomas Iron Company discontinued operating the blast furnace at Hokendauqua and in 1941 sold the mining properties to E. & G. Brooks for $700,000. The company was dissolved as of June 10, 1942."

BIBLIOGRAPHY

The materials serving as the basic source of information for this study consists of financial and production statistics of The Thomas Iron Company held by the Lehigh University Library. These records also contain some correspondence between the officers of the firm as well as a complete index of the company's minute book up to 1913. This index has been carefully worked out page by page, in order to establish a chronological guide to the development and decline of the firm. These records have been supplemented with numerous references from the American Iron and Steel Association's Bulletin, as well as Iron Age. An extensive number of economic, technical, and history books have also been used in conjunction with other periodicals and journals to provide additional sources of information relating to the problems of economic and technological changes affecting the development of the iron industry.

Books and Pamphlets

[Anon.] The Empire Steel and Iron Company, Furnaces and Mines. New York, 1899.

American Iron and Steel Association. Proceedings for 1873. Philadelphia, 1873.

Ashton, Thomas S. Iron and Steel in the Industrial Revolution. New York: Longmans, Green and Company, 1924.

Bartlett, Ruhl. "The Development of Industrial Research in the United States." Economic Change in America. Edited by J. T. Lambie and R. V. Clemence. Harrisburg, Pennsylvania: The Stackpole Company, 1954.

Bauerman, Hilary. _A Treatise on the Metallurgy of Iron_. New York: D. Van Nostrand, 1868.

Bell, Sir I. Lowthian. "On the American Iron Trade and Its Progress during Sixteen Years." _The Iron and Steel Institute in America in 1890_. London: E. and F. N. Spon, 1890.

Bishop, Leander J. _A History of American Manufactures from 1608-1860_. Vol. III. Philadelphia: E. Young and Company, 1868.

Bogen, Jules I. _The Anthracite Railroads, A Study in Railroad Enterprise_. New York: The Ronald Press Company, 1927.

Boylston, Herbert Melville. _An Introduction to the Metallurgy of Iron and Steel_. 2d ed. New York: John Wiley and Sons, Inc., 1936.

Bratt, Elmer C. _Business Cycles and Forecasting_. 1st ed. Chicago: Richard D. Irwin, Inc., 1948.

Bridge, James Howard. _The Inside History of the Carnegie Steel Company: A Romance of Millions_. New York: The Aldine Book Company, 1903.

Buchanan, Norman S. _The Economics of Corporate Enterprise_. New York: Henry Holt and Company, 1940.

Burn, D. L. _The Economic History of Steelmaking, 1867-1939, A Study in Competition_. Cambridge, England: University Press, 1940.

Clapham, J. H. _An Economic History of Modern Britain_. 3 vols. Cambridge, England: University Press, 1932.

Clark, V. S. _History of Manufactures in the United States_. 3 vols. New York: McGraw-Hill Book Company, Inc., 1929.

Colquhoun, William. "Notes on the Iron and Steel Industries in the United States." _The Iron and Steel Institute in America in 1890_. London: E. and F. N. Spon, 1890.

Convention of Iron Masters. _Documents Relating to the Manufacture of Iron in Pennsylvania_. Philadelphia: General Committee, 1850.

Cotter, Arundel. _United States Steel, A Corporation with a Soul_. New York: Doubleday, Page and Company, 1921.

Daddow, Samuel H., and Bannan, Benjamin. _Coal, Iron, and Oil; or the Practical Miner_. Pottsville, Pennsylvania: J. B. Lippincott and Company, 1866.

Danhoff, Clarence. "Observations of Entrepreneurship in Agriculture." Change and the Entrepreneur. Edited by Richard Whol. Cambridge: Harvard University Press, 1949.

Dean, Joel. Managerial Economics. New York: Prentice-Hall, Inc., 1951.

Dunlap, Thomas. Statistical Report of the National Association of Iron Manufacturers for 1872. Philadelphia: J. A. Wagenseller, 1873.

________. Wiley's American Iron Trade Manual. New York: John Wiley and Sons, 1874.

Fackenthal, B. F., Jr. The Thomas Iron Company, 1854-1904. Published for Distribution to Stockholders in Commemoration of the Fiftieth Anniversary of the Organization of the Company. New York, 1904.

Fairbairn, William Iron: Its History, Properties, and Processes of Manufacture. Edinburgh: Adam and Charles Black, 1881.

Fetter, Frank Albert. The Masquerade of Monopoly. New York: Harcourt, Brace and Company, 1931.

Forbes, R. J. Man the Maker: A History of Technology and Engineering. New York: Henry Schuman, 1950.

French, B. F. History of the Rise and Progress of the Iron Trade of the United States, 1621-1857. New York: Wiley and Halstead, 1858.

Friedrich, Carl J. Alfred Weber's Theory of the Location of Industries. Chicago: University of Chicago Press, 1929.

Fritz, John. The Autobiography of John Fritz. New York: John Wiley and Sons, 1912.

Gras, N. S. B., and Larson, Henrietta M. Casebook in American Business History. New York: Appleton-Century-Crofts, Inc., 1939.

Hartz, Louis. Economic Policy and Democratic Thought: Pennsylvania 1776-1860. Cambridge: Harvard University Press, 1948.

Heller, W. J. History of Northampton County and the Grand Valley of the Lehigh. New York: The American Historical Society, 1920.

Henry, Mathew S. History of the Lehigh Valley. Easton, Pennsylvania: Bixler and Corwin, 1860.

Hewitt, Abram Stevens. "On the Statistics and Geography of the Production of Iron." Engineering Pamphlets. Vols. 5 and 9. New York, 1856.

Hidy, Ralph W., and Hidy, Muriel E. Pioneering in Big Business, 1882-1911. New York: Harper and Brothers, 1955.

Holbrook, Stewart H. Iron Brew: A Century of American Ore and Steel. New York: The Macmillan Company, 1939.

Hoover, Edgar M. The Location of Economic Activity. New York: McGraw-Hill Book Company, Inc., 1948.

Hunter, Louis C. "Heavy Industries Before 1860." Growth of the American Economy. Edited by Harold Williamson. New York: Prentice-Hall, Inc., 1951.

Jeans, James Stephen, ed. American Industrial Conditions and Competition. London: Love and Malcomson, Ltd., Offices of the British Iron Trade Association, 1902.

Jenks, Leland. "Railroads as an Economic Force in American Development." Economic Change in America. Edited by J. T. Lambie and R. V. Clemence. Harrisburg: The Stackpole Company, 1954.

Johnson, J. E., Jr. Blast Furnace Construction. 1st ed. New York: McGraw-Hill Book Company, Inc., 1918.

________. The Principles, Operation, and Products of the Blast Furnace. 1st ed. New York: McGraw-Hill Book Company, Inc., 1918.

Johnson, Walter Rogers. Notes on the Use of Anthracite in the Manufacture of Iron. Boston: Charles C. Little and James Brown, 1841.

Jones, Chester L. The Economic History of the Anthracite-Tidewater Canals, Philadelphia: University of Pennsylvania, 1903.

Jones, Eliot. The Anthracite Coal Combination in the United States. Cambridge: Harvard University Press, 1914.

Kaempffert, Waldemar, ed. A Popular History of American Invention. 2 vols. New York: Charles Scribner's Sons, 1924.

Kesler, William C. "Business Organization and Management." Growth of American Economy. Edited by Harold Williamson. New York: Prentice-Hall, Inc., 1951.

Lesley, J. Peter. The Iron Manufacturer's Guide to Furnaces, Forges and Rolling Mills. New York: John Wiley, 1859.

Marburg, Theodore F. Small Business in Brass Fabrication. New York: New York University Press, 1956.

Marshall, Alfred. Principles of Economics. 8th ed. New York: The Macmillan Company, 1949.

Mathews, Alfred, and Hungerford, Austin N., History of the Counties of Lehigh and Carbon, in the Commonwealth of Pennsylvania. Philadelphia: Evarts and Richards, 1884.

McCallum, E. D. The Iron and Steel Industry in the United States. London: P. S. King and Son, Ltd., 1931.

Nevins, Allan. Abram S. Hewitt with Some Account of Peter Cooper. New York: Harper and Brothers, 1935.

Overman, Frederick. The Manufacture of Iron in all its Various Branches. 3d ed. revised. Philadelphia: Henry C. Baird, 1854.

Pearse, John B. A Concise History of the Iron Manufacture of the American Colonies up to the Revolution and of Pennsylvania Until the Present time. Philadelphia: Allen, Lane and Scott, 1876.

Percy, John. Metallurgy: Iron and Steel. London: John Murray, 1864.

Popplewell, Frank. Iron and Steel Production in America. Manchester, England: University Press, 1906.

Redlich, Fritz. "The 'Daimonic' Entrepreneur." Change and the Entrepreneur. Edited by Richard Wohl. Cambridge: Harvard University Press, 1949.

Richardson, Richard. Memoir of Josiah White. Philadelphia: J. B. Lippincott and Company, 1873.

Roberts, Peter. The Anthracite Coal Industry. New York: The Macmillan Company, 1901.

Robinson, E. A. G. The Structure of Competitive Industry. New York: Pitman Publishing Corporation, 1932.

Rogers, Henry D. The Geology of Pennsylvania. Philadelphia: J. B. Lippincott and Company, 1858.

Sahlin, Axel. "Production of Coke and Anthracite Pig Iron in the United States." American Industrial Conditions and Competition. Edited by James Stephen Jeans. London: Love and Malcomson, Ltd., Office of the British Iron Trade Association, 1902.

Schlegel, Marvin B. Ruler of the Reading; The Life of Franklin B. Gowen, 1836-1889. Harrisburg: Archives Publishing Company of Pennsylvania, Inc., 1947.

Schumpeter, Joseph A. Capitalism, Socialism and Democracy. New York: Harper and Brothers, 1950.

________. The Theory of Economic Development. Cambridge: Harvard University Press, 1934.

Scrivenor, Harry. A Comprehensive History of the Iron Trade. London: Smith, Elder and Company, 1841.

Sisson, Charles W. The A B C of Iron. Kentucky, 1893.

Smith, Adam. An Inquiry into the Nature and Causes of the Wealth of Nations. Modern Library Edition. Edited by Edwin Cannan. New York: Random House, Inc., 1937.

Smith, Joseph Russell. The Story of Iron and Steel. New York: Appleton and Company, 1908.

Smith, W. B., and Cole, A. H. Fluctuations in American Business: 1790-1860. Cambridge: Harvard University Press, 1935.

Somers, Harold M. "The Performance of the American Economy, 1789-1865." "The Performance of the American Economy, 1866-1918." Growth of the American Economy. Edited by Harold Williamson. New York: Prentice-Hall, Inc., 1951.

Swank James M. History of the Manufacture of Iron in All Ages. Philadelphia: The American Iron and Steel Association, 1892.

________. Iron Making and Coal Mining in Pennsylvania. Philadelphia, 1878.

________. The American Iron Trade in 1876. Philadelphia: The American Iron and Steel Association, 1876.

Taussig, Frank W. Some Aspects of the Tariff Question. 3d ed. Cambridge: Harvard University Press, 1934.

________. The Tariff History of the United States. 6th ed. New York: G. P. Putnam's Sons, 1931.

Usher, Abbot Payson. The Industrial History of England. Boston: Houghton Mifflin Company, 1920.

Vanderblue, H. B., and Crum, W. L. The Iron Industry in Prosperity and Depression. Chicago: A. W. Shaw Company, 1927.

Veblen, Thorstein. The Theory of Business Enterprise. New York: Charles Scribner's Sons, 1915.

Articles

Alchian, Armen A. "Uncertainty, Evolution, and Economic Theory: Comment and Rejoinder." Journal of Political Economy, LVIII (June, 1950), 211-21.

_________, Enke, Stephen, and Penrose, E. T. "Biological Analogies in the Theory of the Firm." American Economic Review, LXIII (September, 1953), 600-609.

Bell, I. Lowthian. "Note on a Visit to Iron Works in the United States." Journal of the Iron and Steel Institute, VI (1875), 80-150.

Bining, Arthur Cecil. "The Rise of Iron Manufacture in Western Pennsylvania." Western Pennsylvania Historical Magazine, XVI (1933), 235-56.

Blackett, O. W. "Some Price-Determining Factors in the Iron Industry." Review of Economic Statistics, Vol. 7 (July , 1925), 198-207.

Campbell, R. H. "Fluctuations in Stocks: A Nineteenth Century Case Study." Oxford Economic Papers, IX (Oxford, England, 1957).

Cole, Arthur H. "An Approach to the Study of Entrepreneurship." Journal of Economic History, Supplement VI (1946), 1-15.

Enke, Stephen. "On Maximizing Profits: A Distinction between Chamberlin and Robinson." American Economic Review, XLI (September, 1951), 566-78.

Firmstone, Frank. "A Comparison Between Certain English and Certain American Blast Furnaces." Transactions of the American Institute of Mining Engineers, I (1871-73), 314-16.

Firmstone, William. "Sketches of Early Anthracite Furnaces." Transactions of the American Institute of Mining Engineers, III (1874-75), 152-56.

Forbes, D. "Quarterly Report on the Progress of the Iron and Steel Industries in Foreign Countries." Journal of the Iron and Steel Institute (London), II (1871), 103-37.

Gemmell, Alfred. "Manuscripts Shed New Light on Lehigh County's First Furnace." Proceedings (of the) Lehigh County Historical Society (1949).

Harden, J. W. "The Brown Hematite Ores of South Mountain." Transactions of the American Institute of Mining Engineers, I (1871-73), 136-44.

Hunter, Louis C. "Financial Problems of the Early Pittsburgh Iron Manufacturers." Journal of Economic and Business History, II (May, 1930), 520-44.

_________. "Influence of the Market Upon Technique in the Iron Industry in Western Pennsyvlania up to 1860." Ibid., I (February, 1929), 241-81.

Isard, Walter. "Some Locational Factors in the Iron and Steel Industry Since the Early Nineteenth Century." Journal of Political Economy, LVI (June, 1948), 203-17.

Larson, Henrietta M. "Cooke's Early Work in Transportation." Pennsylvania Magazine, LIX (July, 1935), 362-75.

Miller, William A. "A Note on the History of Business Corporations in Pennsylvania, 1800-1860." Quarterly Journal of Economics, LV (November, 1940), 150-60.

Montague, E. N. "The Pig Iron Industry in Allegheny County, 1872-1931." Pittsburgh Business Review (February 28, 1933). pp. 14-17.

Penrose, Edith T. "Biological Analogies in the Theory of the Firm." American Economic Review, XLII (December, 1952), 804-19.

Persons, Warren M. "The Iron and Steel Industry During Business Cycles." Review of Economic Statistics, Vol. 3 (December, 1921), 378-83.

Schumpeter, Joseph A. "The Creative Response in Economic History." Journal of Economic History, VII (November, 1947), 149-59.

Sweetser, Ralph H. "Blast Furnace Fuels: Their Regional Influence." Iron Age, Vol. 134 (November 29, 1934), 20-26, 74.

_________. "Anthracite Pig Iron." Ibid., Vol. 152 (December 20, 1943), 32-39.

Talcott, E. N. K. "The Manufacture of Pig Iron." American Society of Civil Engineers Transactions, I (1867-71), 1910-202.

Taussig, F. W. "The Iron Industry in the United States." Quarterly Journal of Economics, XIV (February, 1900), 149-70.

_________. "Statistics of Iron; 1830-1860." Quarterly Journal of Economics, II (April, 1888), 314-46.

Thomas, Samuel. "Reminiscences of the Early Anthracite Iron Industry." Transactions of the American Institute of Mining Engineers, XXIX (1900), 901-28.

Public Documents

Annual Report of the Secretary of Internal Affairs of the Commonwealth of Pennsylvania for 1874-5. Part III. Harrisburg, 1876.

Birkinbine, John. "American Blast Furnace Progress." *Mineral Resources of the United States, 1883-1884*. Edited by Albert Williams, Jr. Washington, D. C.: Government Printing Office, 1885.

By-Laws of The Thomas Iron Company. Chartered under the Laws of Pennsylvania. New York, 1854.

Commissioner of Corporations. *Report on the Steel Industry*, I. Washington, D. C. : Government Printing Office, 1911.

Commissioner of Patents. *Abridgment of the Specifications Relating to the Manufacture of Iron and Steel.* London: George E. Eyre and William Spottiswode, 1858.

Coxe, Tench. *A Statement of the Arts and Manufactures of the United States of America; for the Year 1810*. Philadelphia: U. S. Census Office (3d Census, 1810), 1814.

________. *Digest of the Accounts of Manufacturing Establishments in the United States*. Washington, D. C.: U. S. Census Office (4th Census, 1820), 1823.

________. *Tabular Statements of the Several Branches of American Manufactures: 1810*. Philadelphia: U. S. Census Office (3d Census, 1810), 1813.

First Annual Report of the Bureau of Statistics of Labor and Agriculture for the Years 1872-73. Harrisburg, 1874.

Hatfield & Hilles vs. The Thomas Iron Company. 154, Supreme Court of Pennsylvania (1903).

Laws of Pennsylvania of the Session of 1817-18, 1835-36, 1854, 1855, 1874.

Miller, Benjamin LeRoy. *Topographic and Geologic Atlas of Pennsylvania; Allentown Quadrangle*. Harrisburg: Commonwealth of Pennsylvania, 1924.

Swank, James. "Progress of the Iron and Steel Industries of the United States in 1892 and 1893." *Mineral Resources of the United States, 1893*. Edited by David T. Day. Washington, D. C.: Government Printing Office, 1894.

The Thomas Iron Company v. The Jackson Iron Company. Michigan Supreme Court (1901).

The Thomas Iron Company and Ironton Railroad Company. Charters, By-Laws. Held by the Lehigh University Library, Bethlehem, Pennsylvania.

Newspapers and Periodicals

American Iron and Steel Association. _Bulletin_. Vols. 1-64, 1867-1912.

_________. _Directory of the Iron and Steel Works of the United States_ (Philadelphia), 1880-1900.

_________. _Statistics of the American and Foreign Iron Trade_ (Philadelphia), 1871-1911.

American Iron and Steel Institute. _Annual Statistical Report_ (New York), 1913-22.

Easton Argus. 1854-69.

Hazard, Samuel, ed. _Register of Pennsylvania_. 1834-35.

_________. _United States Commercial and Statistical Register_. I-III (Philadelphia), 1839-41.

Hunt's Merchant Magazine and Commercial Review. XXXVIII-XLVIII, 1858-63.

Iron Age. Vols. 1-152, 1874-1922.

Journal of the Iron and Steel Institute (London), 1872-1922.

Niles, William O., ed. _National Register_. Vol. 56, 1839.

Pennsylvania _Legislative Record_. February 20, 1868.

Business Reports

American Iron and Steel Association. Minute Book of the American Iron and Steel Association. Held by the Library of the American Iron and Steel Institute, New York.

American Iron and Steel Institute. Pig Iron Statistics. Photostatic reproduction issued by the Library of the American Iron and Steel Institute.

Bethlehem Iron Company. Minute Book of Directors' Meetings. July 12, 1860-June 23, 1885.

_________. Stockholders Minutes. June 14, 1860-August 15, 1901.

Lehigh Coal and Navigation Company. _Report of the Board of Managers of the Lehigh Coal and Navigation Company_. 1831-85.

Lehigh Valley Railroad Company. Annual Report(s) of the Board of Directors of the Lehigh Valley Railroad Company.

_________. _Annual Reports of the Superintendent and Engineer, 1855- 863_. New York, 1899.

The Thomas Iron Company. Minute Book of The Thomas Iron Company. In the collection of the Lehigh University Library, Bethlehem, Pennsylvania.

_________. The Thomas Iron Company Financial Records for Fifty Years. In the collection of the Lehigh University Library, Bethlehem, Pennsylvania.

_________. The Thomas Iron Company: Papers and Documents. In the collection of the Lehigh University Library, Bethlehem, Pennsylvania.

Unpublished Material

Brzyski, Anthony J. "The Lehigh Canal and Its Effect on the Development of the Region Through Which It Passed, 1818-1873." Unpublished Ph.D. dissertation, New York University, 1957.